SO-BUC-724

COMMEMORATIVE COINS

OF THE

UNITED STATES

IDENTIFICATION AND PRICE GUIDE

FIRST EDITION

WRITTEN BY

ANTHONY SWIATEK

EDITED BY

BRAD REED

The CONFIDENT COLLECTOR™

AVON BOOKS ◆ NEW YORK

IMPORTANT NOTICE: All of the information in this book has been compiled from the most reliable sources, and every effort has been made to eliminate errors and questionable data. Nevertheless, the possibility of error always exists in a work of such scope. The publisher and the author will not be held responsible for losses which may occur in the purchase, sale, or other transaction of property because of information contained herein. Analysis and pricing information are based on historical information and market conditions. No information in this book should be construed as predictive. Past performance is not a guarantee of future performance. Readers are advised to seek independent and individualized advice before purchasing or selling any coin for purposes of financial gain.

THE CONFIDENT COLLECTOR: COMMEMORATIVE COINS OF THE UNITED STATES (1st edition) is an original publication of Avon Books.

AVON BOOKS
A division of
The Hearst Corporation
1350 Avenue of the Americas
New York, New York 10019

First Avon Books Trade Printing: September 1993

AVON TRADEMARK REG. U.S. PAT. OFF. AND IN OTHER COUNTRIES, MARCA REGISTRADA, HECHO EN U.S.A.

Printed in the U.S.A.

OPM 10 9 8 7 6 5 4 3 2 1

Dedication

Dedicated to Gloria Swiatek, Brad Reed and Bill Corsa for their assistance in making this opus a reality, as well as the many individuals who have inspired me along the numismatic trail. It is also dedicated to the advancement of knowledge of our commemorative coinage, as well as to the American Numismatic Association, the Society for U.S. Commemorative Coins and to all coin clubs who promote the series and our coin collecting hobby.

— AS

About the author

Anthony Swiatek is a nationally elected Governor of the American Numismatic Association. He is known a "Mr. Commem," highly respected by collectors, dealers and colleagues in the numismatic world, and is a recognized contemporary authority on silver and gold commemoratives. He testified in 1981 before the House of Representatives Banking, Finance and Urban Affairs Subcommittee on Consumer Affairs and Coinage regarding U.S. commemorative coinage, and his opinions are cited in the Library of Congress study, "Issuing Commemorative Coins: A Historical Overview." He again testified before Congress in 1982 in support of better Olympic Coinage designs.

Mr. Swiatek was invited by Mint Director Donna Pope to strike one of five 1982 George Washington ceremonial commemorative half dollars, as well as the 13th striking for the 1983 Olympic commemorative dollar. He was also honored by being invited to strike other ceremonial issues, including the 1986 Statue of Liberty Proof $5 gold coin; the 1-ounce 1986 American Eagle bullion specimen; and the 1987 Constitution dollar. He was later an invited guest at the White House presentation of Olympic coins to the Olympic Museum by Ronald Reagan.

He has been a Director and Judge of the Numismatic Literary Guild. He is a consultant to ANACS, and was on the Board of Governors and panel of lecturers at the Institute of Numismatic and Philatelic Studies at Adelphi University in New York. He sponsored and is part of the First Comprehensive Home Study Course, Fundamentals of Rare Coin Collecting and Investing, and has written the American Numismatic Associations Home Study Course dealing with commemorative coinage. He has lectured in many education forums at major coin shows and coin clubs throughout the United States. His goal is to help educate as many "young and senior" collectors and investors as possible about the pros and cons of coin collecting and coin investing. He conducts numismatic awareness classes for the Continuing Education Programs in Manhasset, N.Y. He is also an instructor at the ANA's Philadelphia Summer Conference held at Bryn Mawr College and currently at Colorado College.

In addition to his books, he is publisher and editor of the *Swiatek Numismatic Report*, voted Best Numismatic investment Newsletter of the year in 1983-84, 1984-85, 1987-88 and 1991-92. He also received the NLG's literary awards for Best Magazine Article and Best Book, U.S. Coins for *The Walking Liberty Half Dollar* in 1984. He also educates via radio, television and videotape.

A full-time professional numismatist since 1977, he examines $40 to $50 million worth of coins yearly for his clients' portfolios. He has been a regular columnist or contributor to *Coin World*, *COINage Magazine*, *Coins Magazine*, and *Gary North's Investment Coin Review*, among other publications.

Swiatek was appointed Honorary Lieutenant Colonel, Aide-de-Camp by Gov. George C. Wallace of Alabama for his concerns for the youth of America. He was also appointed an "Admiral in the Great Navy of the State of Nebraska" by Gov. Robert Kerry. He holds life memberships in the ANA, AINA, CSNA (CA), FUN, GENA, GSNA, ISNA, MSNA, NASC (SM), PAN and TNA. He is also a member of the 1891 Club, ANS, ESNA, NCNA, PNG, WCCC and WIN.

Among his many awards are the Heath Literary Awards, the Wayte and Olga Raymond Memorial Award for Distinguished Numismatic Achievement, the ANA Medal of Merit, the FUN A.J. Vinci Excellence in Education Award.

Contents

Introduction   1

The commemorative nature of regular coins 4

The Classic Commemoratives   9

World's Columbian Exposition 9
Isabella quarter dollar 13
Lafayette Monument 16
Louisiana Purchase Exposition 21
Lewis & Clark Exposition 24
Panama-Pacific Exposition 26
McKinley Memorial 34
Illinois Centennial 37
Maine Centennial 39
Pilgrim Tercentenary 41
Missouri Centennial 45
Alabama Centennial 48
Grant Memorial 52
Monroe Doctrine Centennial 56
Huguenot-Walloon Tercentenary 58
Lexington-Concord Sesquicentennial 61
Stone Mountain Memorial 63
California Diamond Jubilee 68
Fort Vancouver Centennial 72
Sesquicentennial of American Independence 75
Oregon Trail Memorial 80
Vermont-Bennington Sesquicentennial 87
Hawaii Sesquicentennial 90
Maryland Tercentenary 93
Texas Independence Centennial 96
Daniel Boone Bicentennial 101
Connecticut Tercentenary 107
Arkansas Centennial...110
Arkansas-Robinson 116
Hudson, N.Y., Sesquicentennial 120
California-Pacific Exposition 123
Old Spanish Trail 127
Providence, RI, Tercentenary 130
Cleveland-Centennial Great Lakes Exposition 133

Wisconsin Territorial Centennial 137
Cincinnati Music Center 139
Long Island Tercentenary 144
York County, Maine, Tercentenary 147
Bridgeport, Conn. 150
Lynchburg, VA, Sesquicentennial....................................... 153
Albany, NY, Charter 155
Elgin, Ill., Centennial 158
San Francisco-Oakland Bay Bridge 161
Columbia, S.C., Sesquicentennial 164
Delaware Tercentenary 169
Battle Of Gettysburg... 172
Norfolk, Va., Bicentennial... 174
Roanoke - Sir Walter Raleigh - Virginia Dare 176
Battle Of Antietam 179
New Rochelle, NY. 182
Iowa Statehood Centennial... 185
Booker T. Washington.. 188
Carver-Washington 193

The Modern Commemoratives   197

250th Anniversary of George Washington's Birth 197
Los Angeles Olympics.. 203
Statue Of Liberty-Ellis Island Centennial............................ 212
Constitution Bicentennial 219
Games of the XXIV Olympiad 222
Congress Bicentennial... 225
Eisenhower Centennial... 229
Mount Rushmore Golden Anniversary 231
Korean War Memorial 235
USO 50th Anniversary 237
Olympic Games.. 239
White House Bicentennial 242
Columbus Quincentenary 244
Bill of Rights-Madison 247

Norse American Medals   250

An Investor's Guide To
Commemorative Coinage   251

Appendix — Specifications   292

Index   293

Introduction

Coin writers often refer to commemoratives as "special coins." They do this to distinguish them from regular-issue coins.

I, too, like to think of "commems" as special coins. To me, though, they're special in a much broader sense of the word — not just because they're different, but because in many ways they're really better. If you stop for just a minute to think about our regular U.S. coins, and compare them to our commems, you'll soon see what I mean.

Most of our present coins have been with us since before World War II. One of them, in fact — the Lincoln cent — even pre-dates World War I. Regular U.S. coinage (in recent years, at least) has lacked variety. Commemoratives, by contrast, offer enormous diversity. We've had more than five dozen in all, and now that the series has resumed we could get dozens more in years to come. What's more, their designs are far more imaginative, in many cases, than those of our regular coins. Commemorative coins represent the work of some of the finest artists this nation has ever produced.

Commems also possess tremendous historical appeal. Uncle Sam has issued them to honor a broad cross-section of the people, places and events that have shaped our nation's history.

On top of everything else, U.S. commems have great diversity, too, from a market standpoint. In other words, they come in a wide variety of rarity levels and prices. Some of them are common and extremely inexpensive, others are rare and costly, and most of them are somewhere in between. Thus, they can be pursued and enjoyed by just about any collector or investor, regardless of his (or her) level of personal income or expertise.

Before going further, perhaps I should pause and define just what I mean by commemorative coinage. A commemorative, to me, is a coin that is produced primarily to honor a historically significant person (living or dead), place or event. Often, it is issued to mark an anniversary: the centennial, perhaps, of a person's birth or death, the sesquicentennial of a place's founding, or the 300th anniversary of a great event's occurrence. (More on what defines a commemorative a little later.)

Commems have been produced since the time of Alexander the Great, the illustrious Greek conqueror who was said to be the very first person to have his likeness placed upon a coin. Not until recently, though, did they come to be regarded as a form of special coinage outside the regular output of government mints.

A national photo album

I like to think of commems as "remembrance preservers," for they serve to remind us of elements from our heritage — to focus our attention, in the case of our own commems, on vignettes from America's past. In a sense, they might be viewed as snapshots from our national photo album. But in this case, of course, the "photos" are captured on metal, not on film.

Some of the people portrayed in America's "album" are famous historical figures whose presence on these coins is predictable. People like George Washington, Thomas Jefferson, Abraham Lincoln, Ulysses S. Grant, and Robert E. Lee. Others, however, are totally unexpected. I suspect that most Americans would be utterly amazed to learn that this country has issued special coins honoring such little-known individuals as Admiral Gaspard de Coligny of France, William the Silent of the Netherlands, Dr. John McLoughlin of Fort Vancouver, Washington, William Wyatt Bibb, first Governor of Alabama, and John Pell, Lord of Pelham Manor in 17th century New Rochelle, New York.

As it happens, each of the coins depicting these particular individuals is primarily a tribute not to the people themselves, but rather to a place or an event with which they were identified.

Admiral de Coligny and William the Silent, for instance, both appear on the same U.S. half dollar: a commemorative issued in 1924 to mark the tercentenary, or 300th anniversary, of the settlement in New Netherlands (present-day New York) by the French Huguenots and the Dutch Walloons. Each was chosen because of his close relationship with one of the two groups.

McLoughlin is depicted on a 1925 half dollar marking the centennial of Fort Vancouver, a settlement which he founded along the Columbia River in Washington State. Today, it's the site of the City of Vancouver.

Bibb is portrayed on a 1921 half dollar issued to commemorate the centennial of Alabama statehood. And Pell turns up on a 1938 half dollar marking the sesquicentennial (or 250th anniversary) of New Rochelle's founding.

Browsing through our album of commems, we also find the portraits of other historical figures whose names are more familiar: Christopher Columbus, Spain's Queen Isabella, England's Sir Walter Raleigh, and such native-born Americans as Virginia Dare, Daniel Boone, P.T. Barnum, Stephen Foster, Booker T. Washington and George Washington Carver.

By interesting coincidence, the United States Mint issued its first commemorative coin at a time when the Mint itself was exactly 100 years old. The subject of that first commem, in 1892, was an earlier happening, though, and one with far greater implications: It was issued to commemorate the 400th anniversary of Columbus' discovery of America.

Actually, the coin — the Columbian half dollar — wasn't conceived as just a historical tribute. It also was intended as a money-making device: to help raise funds for the World's Columbian Exposition, a world's fair that took place in Chicago. In this respect, it set an important precedent, for every subsequent U.S. commem also has been issued — to some extent, at least — with the goal of raising revenue for some particular agency or cause.

It's fascinating to note that the portrait of Columbus on our first U.S. commem was merely an artist's conception. Since no authentic portraits of Columbus were available, the Mint's chief sculptor-engraver, Charles E. Barber, had no choice but to use his imagination. But, while the portrait may have been inaccurate, it represents a landmark in the history of our coinage — for up until that time, no U.S. coin had depicted a real-life person.

One of the great beauties of U.S. commemorative coins is the fact that we can collect them in so many different ways.

Traditionally, regular-issue coins have been saved in two principal ways: in comprehensive date-and-mint sets, including one example from every different mint for every year of issue; and in type sets, containing just one specimen of any particular coin.

With commems, we have a great deal more flexibility.

If our budgets are big, we can save them by date and mint. A complete set from 1892 to 1954 would contain 144 different pieces, and would cost about $130,000 in Mint State 65 condition.

If we're not quite that wealthy, but decently well off, we can put together a type set of every different commem. This would consist of 50 different coins from 1892 to 1954 and would cost perhaps $75,000 in top (MS-65) condition.

These are not the only options open to us, though. We also can assemble topical sets, if we wish, bringing together commems which share a common theme or are similar in design.

One approach, for instance, would be to put together our own "Who's Zoo": a collection of all the commems on which there is a portrait of an animal or a bird. There are more than two dozen of these, by the way, and their animal-kingdom subjects range all the way from a fatted calf (on the New Rochelle half dollar) to a hippocampus (on a 1915 quarter eagle, or $2.50 gold piece, issued to commemorate the Panama-Pacific Exposition). Incidentally, you needn't feel embarrassed if the name "hippocampus" has you puzzled. In case you're ever asked on a quiz show or final exam, a hippocampus is a mythological creature with the head and forequarters of a horse and the tail of a fish.

Another approach would be to save commems with architectural portraits — in other words, designs which feature buildings or bridges. We've had about 20 of these, including such recent additions as the George Washington half dollar (which carries a portrait of Mount Vernon), the 1984 Olympic silver dollar (which shows the Los Angeles Coliseum) and the 1986 Liberty silver dollar (which depicts the reception center on Ellis Island).

An excellent way to get started collecting commemorative coins is to acquire those coins that are related to your other interests. Civil War buffs, for example, could acquire Ulysses S. Grant Memorial half dollars or gold dollars, the Stone Mountain Monument coin, the Battle of Gettysburg half dollar, or the Battle of Antietam half.

The golden age

The golden age of U.S. commems — or maybe I should say the gold and silver age — was the two-decade period of the 1920s and '30s. About three-fourths of the coins were issued during that time. Gradually, however, objections began to arise, and some of these appear to have been justified.

Critics complained, for instance, that some of the commems were issued for occasions of questionable importance, and that Congress was approving them only because of their sponsors' political clout. There was criticism, too, regarding the fact that some of the coins were issued for extended lengths of time. In one case, the same commem — the Oregon Trail half dollar — was issued on and off for nearly 15 years. Because of this, collectors who wanted complete sets were forced to buy duplicate pieces year after year.

Production of commems was suspended during World War II. After the war, they really never got rolling again — and finally, in 1954, they ground to a total halt. For nearly three decades thereafter, the series was dormant. Worse than that, it was dead. The U.S. Treasury took the position that issuing commemoratives would be counterproductive. As one Treasury official put it, such coins would "violate the principle for which our coinage system was established, introduce confusion in the system and encourage counterfeiting."

Thankfully, that attitude has changed. It's sad to realize, though, that during those "dark ages," we lost the opportunity to issue special coins for many events of truly great significance to our nation: medicine's triumph over polio, the Civil War centennial, the civil-rights achievements of the 1960s, and the first moon landing, to name just a few that come to mind.

The series was revived with the issuance of the George Washington half dollar in 1982. The renaissance was reinforced by the three Los Angeles Olympic coins. Except for 1985, U.S. commemorative coinage was continually produced.

The latest Mint offering is the 1993 Bill of Rights-James Madison program. The half dollar of the series returns to the use of silver for the half dollar, rather than copper-nickel clad planchets.

One hundred and one years of production (1892-1993) has brought us 90 different designs. Our complete set now consists of 222 pieces. And more are on the way! At the close of production for this book, the Mint was preparing to strike coins commemorating the World Cup Soccer tournament, and World War II. Other proposals come and go through Congress with some regularity.

Circulated examples (VF-EF) of the commonest pre-1955 commem — the 1892 and 1893 Columbian half dollar, with a total combined mintage of 2.5 million — can be purchased for little more than the value of the silver they contain. At the opposite extreme, the Panama-Pacific $50 gold piece — with just 483 round and 645 octagonal examples — is valued in top condition at $100,000 or more.

Compared to regular-issue coins of comparable mintage and quality, commems are really bargains at current market values. As with any coins, however, the buyer must be careful that the coins he is acquiring are accurately graded. And I can't stress enough that there isn't any substitute for knowledge: Invest your time in learning all you can before you invest a dime in any coin.

By now, I think, you should see what I mean when I say that commemoratives are "special." They have great diversity, attractive designs, unusual historical appeal, low mintages, and relatively modest price tags.

If you're looking for a specialty in coins, try the uncommon commem. You, too, will find that as specialties go, this one is really super-special.

The commemorative nature of regular coins

In coin collecting circles, the word "commemorative" has a special meaning. We generally refer to just those coins produced in limited numbers for a limited time to mark a specific event. In fact, we could say that commemoratives are the coins produced by the United States Mint that were *not* intended to be used as money.

However, that definition is a fuzzy one. For one, all commemorative coins are *legal tender*. That means that they can be used as money for their face value, if you so choose. There are many instances in our commemorative past where a special issue was minted, but did not sell as well as expected, and the unsold coins merely dumped into circulation. This accounts for the high number of some issues showing significant wear.

Our early commems were generally sold to the public at near face value. A 90 percent silver commemorative half dollar could be acquired for as little as $1.00. What a bargain that seems at today's prices! Today's commemoratives, however, have a much higher spread between purchase cost and face value: a copper-nickel clad half dollar may cost upwards of $10.00. It would be a major loss to spend it for a cup of coffee!

There is, however, one big exception. If our definition is broad enough, many coins produced for circulation may qualify as "commemoratives." While doing so may not endow them with any special financial worth, they can make for an interesting — and inexpensive — collection.

First, a little United States coinage history. When the Founding Fathers first contemplated our nation's coinage, many believed we should follow the custom of the time and portray the leader of the country on our coinage. Most European nations followed this practice, and many continue it today.

George Washington, however, and others objected. It was their intention to throw off the old ways. "No King George" was their cry, and our first lawmakers eventually agreed. It was decreed that the nation's coins bear designs "emblematic of Liberty." Now, liberty is a complex social issue, a deeply philosophical, and doesn't lend itself well to visual portrayal. A design "emblematic of Agriculture" could show corn or wheat or plowing, but what does Liberty look like?

Early American coinage artists looked to Europe for help. There, many artists were using a technique called "allegory" to visually represent abstract social concepts. It is an ancient concept, reaching back to the dawn of Western civilization, but it has served us moderns quite nicely. In 1792, in the fledgling United States of America, Liberty acquired the face of a woman.

Through the years, Liberty's features changed with the prevailing fashions, and with the engraver's abilities. Sometimes, other symbols of Liberty were used: a national shield, perhaps, or a proud Native American. But never was a design representative of a single individual.

In 1892, the half dollar created for the World's Columbian Exposition in Chicago broke the mold. A portrait, albeit a fantasy, of Christopher Columbus was placed upon legal tender coinage of the United States! This was quickly followed in 1893 with Queen Isabel of Spain's portrait on the commemorative quarter dollar for the same event.

But the nation's "real" coinage, the circulation coinage, remained allegorical or symbolic in nature. In 1900, the following designs were used to portray "Liberty": cent — young woman wearing a Native American-styled headdress; 5 cents — a somewhat stern-faced woman wearing a tiara with the word "Liberty" stamped on it, in case you miss the point; dime — Barber's Classically-styled youth wearing a laurel wreath in the Greek style; quarter dollar — ditto; half dollar — ditto; silver dollar — Morgan's now-popular woman wearing the tiara and a headdress of various vegetable matter; gold $2.50 — a woman wearing a larger coronet; gold $5 — ditto; gold $10 — ditto; and gold $20 — ditto.

Now, with the door having been cracked open in 1892 with the Columbian, followed by commemorative coin portraits of Isabel, Washington and Gen. Lafayette in 1900, Thomas Jefferson and William McKinley in 1903, and Lewis & Clark in 1904, a major shift in circulating coinage began in 1909.

    The year 1909 was the 100th anniversary of Abraham Lincoln's birthday. His profile portrait was placed onto the cent, replacing the former Indian Head design. The Lincoln head cent, with minor engraving changes, has survived longer than any other U.S. coin design — 84 years and counting (longer than Lincoln himself lived!). The cent you have in your pocket change today is doubly commemorative. In 1959, Lincoln's 150th "birthday," the Wheat design on the reverse was replaced with a depiction of the Lincoln Memorial. Therefore, it can be argued, the least expensive "commemorative" coin in the United States is the Lincoln cent, celebrating two birthdays of a great president, and picturing one of the more popular national memorials. The cost — 1 cent each!

    In 1932, Liberty was again bumped from a denomination. The 200th anniversary of George Washington's birth seemed a fitting time to honor him with a coin design of his own. His portrait was placed on the quarter of 1932, and that was that, as no quarters were made in 1933. But in 1934, nearly 32 million commemorative portraits of Washington were released into circulation, and the floodgates were opened wide! Allegorical designs quickly fell out of favor, at least with the Washington officials who decide such things.

    In 1938 (for no apparent reason) the splendid Native American portrait/ bison 5-cent design was replaced by a hollow-cheeked Thomas Jefferson, with a picture of his house on the back. In 1946, a year after his death, Franklin Roosevelt's portrait forced off the "Mercury" design from the dime, ironically

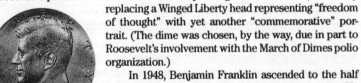

replacing a Winged Liberty head representing "freedom of thought" with yet another "commemorative" portrait. (The dime was chosen, by the way, due in part to Roosevelt's involvement with the March of Dimes polio organization.)

    In 1948, Benjamin Franklin ascended to the half dollar, but for no apparent commemorative reason. He was bumped in memory of John F. Kennedy in 1964, who followed Roosevelt's lead in attaining coinage status by dying in office.

A "real" commemorative was produced in 1921. Following World War I (the war to end all wars), it was decided to issue a silver dollar commemorating Peace. Treasury officials misunderstood the directive, however, and dusted off the dormant Morgan Liberty design. Tens of million were struck before Anthony de Francisci's beautiful (albeit allegorical) Liberty design could be implemented. (The word "Peace" appears on the rock on which the eagle stands on the reverse.

Dwight D. Eisenhower got the nod when a new dollar design was begun in 1971, and the reverse does show an eagle (representing the Apollo spacecraft "Eagle") landing on the Moon! But the designs are not generally considered to be commemorative.

The 1976 Bicentennial of the Declaration of Independence was the biggest birthday party this nation has seen! In 1975 and 1976, the usual year-of-issue dates on the quarter, half and dollar coins were replaced with the dual date 1776-1976. Also, a widely publicized design contest had yielded three special reverse designs specifically commemorating the Bicentennial of American Independence. The three coins were sold a various prices for various sets, including 40 percent silver versions. They were also struck by the hundreds of millions and placed into circulation. They can still be easily found among pocket change.

The Bicentennial coins are not generally cataloged as part of the "commemorative" coins of the United States. Nor are the others just mentioned here. So perhaps it is not merely the commemorative nature that makes the coins that are to follow special. Perhaps it is their oddity, their aloofness, the fact that they have not been handled by every man, woman and child in this great nation, that makes commemorative coins such a joy and pleasure and challenge to collect.

Some even consider the 1848 $2.50 gold quarter eagle with CAL. counterstamp to be the first U.S. commem. The letters were punched into the reverse while the coin still rested in the obverse die to commemorate the fact that the gold came from California (it was Gold Rush time, remember!). The number of pieces so marked was limited, and it was done for a particular reason, but it entailed no real design change, and to call this a commem is admittedly a stretch.

A few notes about using the book

This listing is in chronological order. Many other books list commemoratives alphabetically. However, an alphabetical listing implies a widely accepted, standardized naming system. None exists. Do you list the coin commemorating the Battle of Antietam under A for Antietam or B for Battle? Also, a chronological listing allows you, the reader, to follow the evolution of coin designs. To follow the comings and goings of key designers. To witness the disintegration of the coin boom after the excesses of the 1930s, and the long gap until — and rapid acceleration of — the so-called "modern" commems.

Each coin type is shown, with its date of issue, reason for existing, the numbers struck and sold, and a market value in several levels of preservation. Please be aware that the coin market can and does change very quickly. Certain coins are "hot" for a time, then fall out of favor as promotion ebbs. The values given here are based on "Trends of U.S. Coin Values" published in *Coin World*, a weekly publication read by many tens of thousands of coin collectors and dealers. For up to date pricing, we suggest at least an annually-published price guide, such as the *Coin World Guide to U.S. Coins, Prices & Value Trends*, and preferable a monthly or weekly source such as *Coin World.*, PO Box 150, Sidney, OH 45365, as well as the Coin Dealer Newsletter (Greysheet) or Certified Coin Dealer Newsletter (Blue Sheet), P.O. Box 11099, Torrance, CA 90510.

The author has attempted to provide a realistic assessment of the commemorative coin market. However, any statements regarding current or future value of any coin or other collectible item in this book must be considered the sole opinion of the author, and in any case is not a promise or guarantee of future value. Readers are advised to seek independent and individualized advice before purchasing or selling any coin for purposes of financial gain.

1892-1893
World's Columbian Exposition

Reason for issue: To raise funds for the World's Columbian Exposition in Chicago and commemorate the 400th anniversary of the discovery of America by Christopher Columbus.

Authorized per Act of August 5, 1892: 5,000,000

Official sale price: $1

Production figures

Date	Business Strikes	Assay Coins	Proofs	Melted	Net Mintage
1892	950,000	?	103	0	950,000
1893	4,052,105	2,105	0	2,501,700	1,548,300

Current market values

	EF-40	AU-50	MS-60	MS-63	MS-64	MS-65
1892	22.00	37.50	72.50	165.	365.	1275.
1893	20.00	35.00	65.00	145.	390.	1350.

Designs
Obverse by Charles E. Barber

Bust of Christopher Columbus facing right, a fantasy portrait based on the work by Olin Levi Warner (1844-1896). UNITED STATES OF AMERICA arcs above; COLUMBIAN HALF DOLLAR circles below. Incused on the left truncation of the collar is the letter B representing Barber's initial.

Columbus' eyebrow and cheekbone are the first locations to indicate a metal loss, as seen by a greyish-white metal texture. Do not confuse lack of metal fill marks in these areas or on the coin's devices with small nicks, cuts or scratches, as they can look similar. The latter are created during striking when metal does not flow into the recesses of the die (the high points on the coin). Also, a coin blank can be damaged before striking. Sometimes the damage cannot be eradicated by the minting process. Thus, we can have a coin "born" MS-63.

Reverse by George T. Morgan

Three-masted caravel (representing the flagship *Santa Maria* sailing to the left, in a westerly direction, above two cartographic hemispheres, representing the opening of the New World to Europeans. "14" to left; "92" to right, represents the year of Columbus' first voyage. WORLD'S COLUMBIAN EXPOSITION CHICAGO circles the design. Date at bottom. At the lower right edge of the center sail appears a small "m" in relief, Morgan's initial.

Relief is well-protected by the rim. Were we to place this issue obverse-side down and gently do a "rub test" by pushing the coin forward four inches, then examining, we would immediately notice a loss of metal on the obverse high points. However, were we to try my rub test on the ship's side, the results after five back and forth movements would only show on the coin's reverse rim. A metal loss will first be noticed on the vessel's upper point of the rear sail, center and upper sails, followed by a trace of wear on the Eastern Hemisphere. Do not confuse striking weakness on the center sail's seams or the slight loss of light cameo frost with wear.

Origins of the Columbian

It was the initial hope of the World's Columbian Exposition's Commission manager to have 40 million half dollars struck to be used as admission tokens to the Expo and souvenir keepsakes. However, only 5 million were authorized. Thus, the first United States commemorative half dollar was sold at double face value to help defray expenses. It was supposedly produced from melted-down obsolete silver coins (3-cent pieces, half dimes, etc.) as mandated by the authorizing legislation.

Struck in 1892, it was not included as part of the yearly Proof set which now flaunted the new Barber coinage. Why? A Proof Columbian half dollar would have to cost more than $1, while the Barber half would only cost the collector a few cents over face value.

For publicity purposes, Wyckoff, Seamans and Benedict, makers of the Remington Standard Typewriter (the official writing device of the fair) offered to pay the Commission $10,000 for the first specimen of the half dollar. H.N. Higinbothan was content to merely set aside the first regular strike. However, Commissioner Col. James Ellsworth, one of history's most famous coin collectors, lobbied for a Proof 1892 Columbian half dollar to be produced. Without Higinbothan's permission, Ellsworth had arranged for this creation to be produced in Proof condition. On Nov. 19, 1892, 103 pieces were struck by hand at the Phildelphia Mint.

All of the 1892 coinage, produced in November and December of 1892, was distributed. However, after the Expo closed its doors in 1894, some 3.6 million 1893-dated commemorative halves remained unsold. The Treasury Department offered the coins to the public at face value. There were few takers, though, as 2,501,700 were melted, while the rest were dumped into circulation. Remember, in the 1890s the average factory worker took home between $4.50 and $7.00 per week, and a half a dollar to be set aside as a commemorative represented quite an investment.

The Columbian Today

Both dates are readily available in grades EF-40 through AU-55. Strict MS-60 Columbians cannot be labeled scarce, but are not as abundant as many would believe. The real MS-60 or MS-60+ coin offers little eye-appeal. Surfaces can range from prooflike to blazing to pristine to dull to dipped out and gone forever on these baggy surfaces. There are too many About Uncirculated coins offered as BU-60 or MS-60, giving a false reputation of abundance to the higher grades. BU here usually means "been used."

Current MS-63 levels are over-valued, as the issue can be located with not much difficulty. If possible, collectors should concentrate on MS-63+ specimens, which offer better future value. These are the types of coins desired by some dealers in hopes of having them slabbed MS-64. Apply the same reasoning to MS-64+ specimens. However, chances are slim these coins would be slabbed MS-65, due to a detracting deep bag mark, or hairline scratch, or bag marks or hits in the primary focal area.

Strictly graded MS-64 specimens are fairly valued. Supply is certainly not abundant. More highly recommended is the MS-64+ coin. These are some of the coins once bought and sold as MS-65. For those who cannot afford MS-65 prices, the MS-64+ can be a fantastic acquisition.

Columbians strictly graded MS-65 can be elusive, especially the 1893 issue. Those grading MS-66 are extremely difficult to acquire, while the differential in the weekly trends value guides will be apparent between the somewhat higher valued 1892 and 1893 issues. While the 1893 date is rarer, lower values are reflected because its '92 twin is easier to locate, creating business activity for the sellers — as well as higher bid values.

1892 Columbian specimens grading Proof-55 and higher will enhance any collection. Past sales have ranged from $800 to $75,000! After re-examining the alleged Proof 1893 first-struck specimen housed at the Chicago Historical Society, I've come to the conclusion that it is just an exceptional presentation coin. It simply does not possess total Proof characteristics. I currently believe that no 1893 Proofs were produced. Even those few encapsulated pieces, I feel, are amazing early deep mirror prooflike strikings.

Columbian surfaces will range from deep mirror prooflike (DMPL) to semi-prooflike, to blazing brilliant, to bright satiny and to doggy dull. Due to die preparation, the business strike production 1893 issue will offer the buyer more of a DMPL surface or coin with stronger mirrored fields than the prooflike specimen of 1892. Such coins were either struck from new dies which retained their initial finish or were produced from dies repolished by the Mint to obliterate existing clash marks. Created by this polishing into the die surface are die polishing marks. They will be seen as fine raised lines, superficially resembling scratches, but they do not cut into the coin's surface as scratches do.

As observed on the Morgan silver dollar, the obverse of this coin can display a prooflike obverse, combined with a satiny reverse or vice versa. No big deal. Just be aware of the fact that the existing die surface at striking time will create an identical surface on the newly minted coin.

Variations in strike will run from full to strong to acceptable (for the issue) to weak. Areas of importance are Columbus' eyebrow, his hair detail, situated next to his forehead, his wide bottom hair curl (which normally displays little

detail) contiguous to his lower obverse jaw, the *Santa Maria's* sail seams —
especially the center sail — the vertical ribs and the horizontal planking.

 **Related material**

No official holders or mailing envelopes used by the Columbian Commission exist for this issue. However, the coin was distributed by various banks in small purse-like round or square burgundy-colored leather holders with velour interiors and the bank's gold imprint. Similar holders are known with only "Columbian Exposition" encircling "1492 — Chicago —1892" gold-stamped on the upper cover. Wells Fargo & Co. produced a lovely distributing holder for the issue. The distribution material can be quite elusive and expensive. The leather pouch can be worth $30 to $150, depending upon condition. If accompanied by a coin, value must be determined based on the state of the half dollar.

*Columbian Expo badge and
pouches*

1893
Isabella quarter dollar

Reason for issue: To commemorate the World's Columbian Exposition and Isabel, Queen of Castile, (*Isabel la primera*, Anglicized to "Isabella") who sponsored Columbus' voyage of discovery.
Authorized per Act of March 3, 1893: 40,000
Official sale price: $1

Production figures

Date	Business Strikes	Assay Coins	Proofs	Melted	Net Mintage
1893	40,023	23	103	15,809	24,191

Current market values

	EF-40	AU-50	MS-60	MS-63	MS-64	MS-65
1893	175.	250.	380.	825.	1550.	2900.

Designs

Obverse by Charles E. Barber

Crowned bust of Queen Isabel of Spain, facing left. UNITED STATES OF AMERICA circles the rim. Located in the right field parallel to the word AMERICA is the date 1893.

 A metal loss will first be observed as a dull greyish color on the crown's central oval jewel and the Queen's cheek. Beware of doctoring in the latter location. It can appear in the form of wire brushing, light polishing, or texturing or artificial toning. Wire brushing is sometimes used on Uncirculated specimens to hide facial cuts, hairline scratches, slide marks, etc. in this primary focal location.

Reverse by Charles E. Barber

A kneeling spinner facing left, holding a distaff (a staff used for holding the flax, tow, or wool in spinning) in her left hand and a spindle, which is emblematic of woman's industry, in her right hand. Encircling the inner border, aside from the beaded border which is present on both sides of the coin is the inscription BOARD OF LADY MANAGERS COLUMBIAN QUAR DOL. This commemorative is the first American coin to portray a foreign sovereign, and is the only purely commemorative quarter dollar issue.

The reverse design will display a metal loss on the strand of wool which seems to rest on the kneeling spinner's left thigh.

Origins of the Isabella

Mrs. Potter Palmer, a wealthy matron of Chicago, headed the Board of Lady Managers, which was formed at the request of Susan B. Anthony. This was a group of women designated by the promoters of the Columbian Exposition to promote the interest of women in the exposition. At Mrs. Palmer's suggestion, the Appropriations Committee of the House of Representatives assigned $10,000 to the Board of Lady Managers of the World's Columbian Exposition in the form of souvenir 25-cent pieces.

The Philadelphia Mint began production of the Isabella quarter dollar on June 13, 1893. As with the Proof Columbian '92 issue, the 400th, 1,492nd and the 1,892nd coins struck were selected and documented by the Mint, and forwarded to the Board of Lady Managers in Chicago. I believe that 100 Proof pieces of this issue were similarly struck, as were the Columbian 50-cent Proofs.

Due to a lack of publicity only small quantities were sold at the Women's Building on the Exposition grounds. Of the approximately 15,000 coins purchased by the public, most were sold via mail order to collectors and dealers during the celebration year. Scott Stamp & Coin Company procured several thousand of these commem quarters. Mrs. Palmer and her friends purchased 10,000 pieces at face value in 1893. These were apportioned through coin dealers and others for the next 34 years. Still, 15,809 coins were returned to the Mint's melting pot.

The Isabella Today

Based on present grading standards, most of the existing mintage for this issue resides between the EF-AU and low-end MS-63 category. Low-end refers to a borderline coin that just makes the grade. It can be worth somewhat less than current Trends values. However, some dealers refer to it as a questionable grade, meaning they believe, while labeled MS-63, it really is MS-62+ coin. When acquiring EF-AU specimens, make certain they are original, "undoctored" and not heavily toned brown or black. Pass on the polished or wire-brushed job, as they offer little to no future value. When acquiring MS-60 through MS-63 Isabellas, be certain the examined coin possesses eye-appeal and originality. Reject those coins with deep cuts or scratches or those that are heavily marked, unless the price is very right. Attractive specimens labeled MS-64 are not rare, but neither are they abundant. Alluring pieces grading MS-65 and better are elusive. I suggest passing on heavily toned dark brown specimens.

Proof Isabella quarters grading PF-55 and higher make an excellent addition to one's collection. For starters, they will be double struck. (Your prooflike specimen received only one blow from the coin press.) The double striking will bring out detail on both obverse and reverse designs. Beware of the lightly polished or buffed coin which at times is offered as a Proof.

As with the Columbian issues, most naturally toned specimens encountered possess colors of sea green and electric blue, as well as magenta and a combination of the colors. Beware of the vivid peacock blue accompanied by a deep purple and brilliant yellow-green. Strike seldom presents a problem for this issue to the degree where it will be responsible for a grade and/or value drop. A partial wire edge will be observed on many specimens. Luster will range from Deep Mirror Prooflike, to prooflike, to semi-prooflike, to brilliant frosty, to brilliant satiny, to dull satiny.

Related material

To date, no official mailing holders or envelopes housing the original coin have been encountered. I have seen several Board of Lady Managers envelopes in the personal correspondence files of Mrs. Palmer. Possibly, the coins were placed in smaller unmarked envelopes or simply wrapped in tissue paper and inserted in the larger printed mailer.

1900
Lafayette Monument

Reason for issue: To commemorate the erection of a monument to General
Lafayette in Paris, France, as part of the United States government's
participation in the Paris Exposition of 1900.
Authorized per Act of March 3, 1899: 50,000
Official sale price: $2

Production figures

Date	Business Strikes	Assay Coins	Proofs	Melted	Net Mintage
1900	50,000	26	10?	14,000	36,000

Current market values

	EF-40	AU-50	MS-60	MS-63	MS-64	MS-65
1900	225.	285.	600.	1775.	3600.	9500.

Designs by Charles E. Barber

Obverse

Conjoined heads of George Washington (based on Jean Antoine Houdon's
bust of Washington) and Marie Paul Jean Roch Ives Gilbert Motier Marquis de
Lafayette, possibly designed from a French medal of Cuanois which was made at
the French Mint in 1824. (However, it does appear that Barber used Peter L.
Krider's Yorktown Centennial Medal of 1881 to create his makeup.) UNITED
STATES OF AMERICA above; LAFAYETTE DOLLAR below.

 The primary focal area is bust of both figures. Wear will initially develop
on Washington's cheekbone as a difference in metal texture, looking
greyish-white. A lack of metal fill due to insufficient striking force can
resemble rub or friction and create what looks like small cuts, plus scar
marks on the portraits. If uncertain, check with the knowledgeable
when buying such a coin. This is the location that unscrupulous indi-

viduals will wire brush (whiz), or buff or lightly polish in an attempt to conceal metal loss, a deep cut, slide marks, a reed mark or a grade-lowering bag mark.

Reverse

Equestrian statue of General Lafayette riding left and holding an upraised sword pointed downward. Located at the base of the statue is the name BARTLETT which is often believed to be the name of the designer of this issue. As noted, the coin was designed by Charles E. Barber. Paul Wayland Bartlett — whose early sketch was used by Barber — was the sculptor who designed the Lafayette statue erected in Paris. Situated below and on the base of the statue is a palm branch, while located all within a beaded border is the inscription ERECTED BY THE YOUTH OF THE UNITED STATES IN HONOR OF GEN LAFAYETTE PARIS 1900.

Approximately $50,000 was raised by the school children of the United States and contributed towards the erection of the Lafayette statue in Paris.

Primary focal area is the equestrian figure of Lafayette — which is also the target but to a lesser degree of the above noted "doctoring." A metal loss will first be noticed on the horse's blinder, as the rim offers little high point protection, then on the hindquarter. Bag marks, cuts, digs, reed marks, hairline scratches and abrasions which can easily cause a lowering of the obverse grade can do likewise to this reverse design. This is especially true when we consider the damage these grade-lowering villains can inflict on those large silver dollar-sized exposed Lafayette fields. Also beware of artificially toned raw — or unencapsulated— coins which attempt to hide surface marks and "doctoring" as previously noted. Most encountered specimens display a genuine blue and/or sea green iridescent toning, or on rare occasion a rainbow play of colors.

Origins of the Lafayette Dollar

The Lafayette Commission at first requested that Congress authorize the production of 100,000 half dollars. However, the Commission later thought a silver dollar would make a better souvenir and such was approved on March 3, 1899, by Congress. The Lafayette dollar became a reality on December 14, 1899, the day of the 100th anniversary of the death of George Washington. On this single day, using an old coin press which was able to produce 80 coins per minute, the Philadelphia Mint struck 50,000 coins plus 26 pieces for assay purposes. The coin does not bear the actual production date of 1899. The commission wanted the coins to bear the date 1900, but coinage laws did not permit the predating of U.S. coins. To please the Commission, the date 1900 was included within the coin's reverse border inscription. This date, however, does not indicate the minting date, but rather the year in which the Lafayette monument was erected, as well as the year of the Paris Exposition. The coins were then sold at $2.00 each by the Lafayette Memorial Commission.

The Commission refused an offer of $5,000 for the first coin struck, the first to depict a president as well as the first American citizen. It had been previously decided that President McKinley would forward the first strike to President Loubet of France.

The first commemorative dollar was placed in a chest costing $1,000 and sent across the Atlantic via the *S.S. Champagne*. It was the government's intention that the coin be used in a special ceremony, held on Washington's birthday. However, the event occurred on March 3, 1900, in the Elysee Palace.

In 1925, George H. Clapp discovered a Lafayette dollar which differed from the piece described by Howland Wood in "The Commemorative Coinage of the United States," published in "Numismatic Notes and Monographs No. 16," by the American Numismatic Society. After a discussion with Mr. Clapp, Howland Wood examined several hundred Lafayette dollars over a period of years and discovered two more varieties. He concluded that three obverse and four reverse varieties exist. The following descriptions are based exactly on Wood's arrangement of the examined varieties and later discoveries.

OBVERSE 1: Left foot of final A in AMERICA is recut while the A in STATES is high.

OBVERSE 2: AT in STATES is recut while the final S is low. The F's in the words OF and LAFAYETTE are broken from the lower tip of the crossbar to the right base extension. The word AMERICA is spaced A ME RI CA . The period following OF is close to the A of AMERICA . The tip of Lafayette's bust falls to the right of the top of the first L in DOLLAR.

OBVERSE 3: A small point is seen on the bust of Washington while the tip of Lafayette's bust falls over the top of the L in DOLLAR. The AT in STATES is cut high.

OBVERSE 4: (Discovered by Frank DuVall). The CA in AMERICA is spaced in a different way from the above three obverses. The E in STATES is recut, as well as the U in UNITED.

REVERSE A: The palm branch has 14 leaves with a short stem bent downwards.

REVERSE B: The palm branch has 15 thin leaves on an upturned short stem. The point of the lowest leaf falls over the center of the 9 in 1900.

REVERSE C: The palm branch has 14 short leaves and a short stem. The last leaf falls between the 1 and 9 of 1900.

REVERSE D: The palm branch has 14 long leaves. The last leaf falls over the 1 of 1900.

REVERSE E: (Discovered by Frank DuVall.) The palm branch has 12 leaves. The lowest leaf points to the left of the 1 in 1900.

Rarity Scale

	(OBVERSE COMBINED WITH REVERSE DESIGN)	
OBVERSE	REVERSE	HOW RARE?
1	A	Most common
1	C	Very Rare*
2	B	Very Scarce
3	C	Rare
3	D	Rare-Very Rare
4	E	Very rare**

* Discovered by Anthony Swiatek 1980.
** Discovered by Frank DuVall 1988.

Our Obverse 1, Reverse A is the variety most often encountered. The remainder can be listed as rare to very rare. However, the rarity factor has sparked too little interest to be a value factor.

Approximately 36,000 pieces were sold. As sales came to a halt, 14 bags, each containing 1,000 Lafayettes, were returned to the Treasury Building, in Washington D.C. They were placed in the same vault which stored currency. Back in 1945, while examining government records, Aubrey Bebee of Omaha, Neb., became aware of the existence of this holding. When an inquiry was made, he was informed that the commemorative dollars were melted into silver bullion. We don't know for sure whether the Treasury Department knew the $14,000 lot was worth $140,000 or simply chose not to create problems for themselves — and melted the hoard.

The Lafayette Dollar Today

The majority of this popular issue resides in EF-AU through MS-63 condition. Many of the circulated pieces encountered over the years have been whizzed (to some degree) or buffed, in areas displaying a loss of metal or detracting marks or simply polished to dupe (in most cases) the uneducated. I strongly suggest acquiring for the joy of collecting a circulated coin possessing undoctored or natural surfaces which does not possess ugly cuts digs or scratches, nor is toned black. Pieces showing no trace of actual wear and grading MS-60 or MS-61 are underrated and can be rather difficult to locate. This is due to abuse, as well as the coin's rims which offered little protection to the high points (first areas which lose metal due to friction), because of its high relief. Lafayettes grading MS-62 and MS-63 will be easier to obtain.

Pieces grading strict MS-64 are not as abundant as is widely believed. One would be surprised especially at the number of times those identical MS-64 Lafayette dollars were re-submitted to the same and different grading service by the original or second or third possessor over the years, in hopes of attaining the upgrade — which never materialized! Unfortunately, most identification labels were destroyed and never returned for population deletion. It would certainly help to indicate the issue's true population count. It doesn't matter how flashy or mark free the coin might appear upon inspection. It's that long fine hairline scratch or two usually located on Washington's portrait or across the portraits that many fail to detect or do not want to believe will prevent the coin from grading higher making it worth $7,000 more!

Should the obverse make the grade, a bit too many reverse bag marks or a dig which is quite large and deep or the said fine hairlines located on Lafayette's horse or in the field act as the MS-65 stopper. Strictly graded MS-65 coinage must be labeled elusive. The above mentioned slabbing re-submittal scenario also has affected this category is a similar manner. Specimens grading MS-66 and better will be very difficult to locate.

I had the pleasure of seeing a genuine double struck brilliant Proof along with the Panama Pacific $50 round and octagonal struck in silver, without the "S" Mint mark, etc., in a Philadelphia collection back in 1976. The Lafayette Proof was said to be one of 10 such pieces struck. I wonder if the person who offered $5,000 for the first piece struck but was denied was offered 10 Proof pieces instead?

Luster for this issue will range from almost semi-prooflike, to very flashy brilliant frosty, to bright frosty, to dull frosty. Unfortunately, specimens displaying the noted first two desired surfaces will be infrequently encountered. Those which flaunted a mirrored surface appear to be part of the 14,000 melted specimens. Bright to dull frosty luster is usually the norm. In the attempt to create a more eye appealing brighter or better-than-new surface, for the latter two lustrous conditions, pieces were over-dipped in a tarnish removing solution or were deplorably cleaned in some manner, damaging forever their original surfaces.

Strike rarely affects the value or grade of this issue. Sharpness of detail on the saddle blanket design and/or the engraving line separating Lafayette's boot from his leg (known as the full boot specimen) and/or the folds in the General's lower coat design which rests on the blanket will typically be lacking, appearing somewhat undefined or indistinct. As noted, neither grade nor value will be affected unless the coin possesses a major weakness on the devices.

 ## Detecting counterfeits

A counterfeit specimen I encountered displayed surface roughness or graininess and roundness of lettering. Look for raised metal spikes or tooling marks above the words STATES, as well as "THE" of the inscription, on the reverse examine for same below the letter "L" of LAFAYETTE.

 ## Related material

The issue was placed in paper coin envelopes and mailed in a manila envelope imprinted: OFFICE OF COMMISSIONER-GENERAL FOR THE UNITED STATES TO THE PARIS EXPOSITION OF 1900, LAFAYETTE MEMORIAL COMMISSION, CHICAGO. The envelope with its related items are valued at $150-250.

1903
Louisiana Purchase Exposition

Reverse enlarged to show detail

Jefferson or McKinley with common reverse

Reason for issue: To commemorate the Louisiana Purchase Exposition held in St. Louis, Mo., in 1904, and the 100th anniversary of the purchase of the Louisiana Territory.

Authorized per Act of June 28, 1902: 250,000 (125,000 each variety.)

Official sale price: $3

Production figures

Date	Business Strikes	Assay Coins	Proofs	Melted	Net Mintage
1903 Jefferson	125,000	129	100	107,625*	17,375*
1903 McKinley	125,000	129	100	107,625*	17,375*

* Estimate

Current market values

	EF-40	AU-50	MS-60	MS-63	MS-64	MS-65
1903 Jefferson	240.	345.	500.	950.	1650.	2650.
1903 McKinley	230.	330.	465.	925.	2100.	2950.

Designs by Charles E. Barber, assisted by George T. Morgan

Obverse

Type I is the bust of Thomas Jefferson who made the Louisiana Purchase from France for $15 million while third president of the United States (1801-1809). Seen facing left, his portrait was designed from a Mint Indian peace medal created by John Reich, Assistant Mint Engraver, who used a Houdon bust as a model.

Type II depicts the bust of 25th president, William McKinley (1897-1901), who was responsible for signing the bill which sanctioned the Louisiana Purchase Exposition. His "life" portrait was copied by Charles E. Barber from a presidential medal. On both types, located within a beaded border almost encircling the bust, is the inscription UNITED STATES OF AMERICA.

 Metal loss will first be noticed on the cheekbone. Flatness around the ear area can be the result of die wear. Examine the areas for crisscross scratches and a difference in metal texture.

Reverse

The same for both types — depicts the anniversary dates 1803-1903 separated from ONE DOLLAR by part of an olive branch. Located around the coin's circumference within a beaded border is the inscription LOUISIANA PURCHASE EXPOSITION ST. LOUIS.

 Wear will occur on the olive branch, to the right of the digit 3 of the Purchase date 1803, then anniversary dates and denomination on this lower relief motif.

Origins of the Jefferson and McKinley Coins

Initially, this creation was only to depict Jefferson. However, after McKinley, who originally signed the Expo into law March 3, 1901, was assassinated at another Expo six month later, some behind-the-scenes negotiations made him part of this issue.

The Exposition's management requested that Congress designate part of its $5 million appropriation through commemorative gold dollars.

The Philadelphia Mint struck 75,080 gold dollars in December 1902, an apparent infraction of government procedure because these coins were dated 1903 but are supposed to bear the date of striking.

In January 1903, 175,178 additional pieces were struck, for a total production figure of 250,000 plus 258 assay coins. There were 125,000 of each type produced. Shortly thereafter, the Philadelphia Mint melted 250 specimens of the 258 assay pieces. To date, we do not know which design was first to be produced. However, all coins bear the date 1903 — the anniversary date.

Sold at $3.00 each, they were kept as souvenir gold pieces and mementoes, possibly because 16 years had passed since the United States had issued its last gold dollar. To increase sales of the coins, different types of mountings were offered, such as gold stickpins, brooches, etc. Beware of specimens which may have been mounted in such jewelry with the aid of solder. Such pieces are worth much less. Despite the gimmicks, sales were poor; approximately 35,000 coins were sold. Retail value fell to $2.00 in about a year. Famous numismatist B. Max Mehl acquired thousands of pieces from promotor and well known numismatist Farran Zerbe, which he sold into the next two decades. In 1914, the Mint received 215,000 coins which were then melted. Today, we estimate that there exist 17,500 coins of each variety.

The Jefferson and McKinley Today

Either issue can be located in circulated EF-AU with a little effort. Goal should be to locate pieces which have not been polished, display repair work, or file marks or have been doctored in some manner. Purchase only if the price is right or you simply want a low grade representative example. The Louisiana Purchase issues are not scarce in grades MS-60 through MS-64. Rarer issue is the

Jefferson design up to the MS-63 category. In the MS-64 and MS-65 states, the McKinley production is somewhat rarer. Future value resides in these gold commemoratives rated eye-appealing MS-64+ and higher. Equally as rare in the loftier grades.

There were 100 Proof coins of each design struck for the "selected." They certainly were not produced for the average numismatist. These rarities were placed into an opening of an imprinted card, covered by a wax paper window and signed by J.M. Landis, Superintendent, and R.R. Freed, Coiner, Philadelphia Mint. It was secured with heavy string, embedded in a dark red Philadelphia Mint wax seal at its end. Beware, as seals have been "doctored," and the Proof substituted. The latter then hides behind its wax paper window. When offered a raw specimen out of its holder, be certain such is double struck.

Luster will range from prooflike (not the norm) to semi-prooflike, to brilliant satiny, to dull satiny. Strike rarely affects the grade and value of this issue. Due to die wear, the Jefferson design at times will exhibit a slight flatness in hair detail over his ear and flatness in denticle design. However, the latter will keep gold coins out of the MS-66 category.

 ## Detecting counterfeits

Counterfeits of each issue exist. Examine for lack of strike sharpness, field depressions and small raised lumps of metal in the field.

 ## Related material

No official mailing holders with mailing envelopes have surfaced to date. There does exist, though not often encountered, a rectangular off-white cardboard box which housed either gold coin and gold mounting which rested on cotton. Imprinted on the top cover: LOUISIANA PURCHASE EXPOSITION, 1904 SOUVENIR GOLD DOLLAR, JEFFERSON-$3.00-MCKINLEY. This box is worth $100-300, depending upon its state of preservation

1904-1905
Lewis & Clark Exposition

Reverse enlarged to show detail

Reason for issue: To commemorate the 100th anniversary of the exploration of the Northwest (Louisiana Territory and the Oregon country) by Captain Meriwether Lewis and Captain William Clark, and the exposition which was held in their honor.

Authorized per Act of April 13, 1904: 250,000.

Official sale price: $2 (some sold at $2.50 individually and for $1.67 each if six coins were purchased).

Production figures

Date	Business Strikes	Assay Coins	Proofs	Melted	Net Mintage
1904	25,000	28	4?	15,003	9,997
1905	35,000	41	4?	25,000	10,000

Current market values

	EF-40	AU-50	MS-60	MS-63	MS-64	MS-65
1904	350.	450.	760.	2350.	3950.	6500.
1905	365.	500.	975.	3250.	5750.	16500.

Designs by Charles E. Barber

Obverse

Bust of Meriwether Lewis facing left. Located within the beaded border is the inscription LEWIS CLARK EXPOSITION PORTLAND ORE., while the date of striking (either 1904, or 1905) appears below the bust.

Reverse

William Clark facing left, encircled by UNITED STATES OF AMERICA and ONE DOLLAR. All of the aforementioned appear within a beaded border. It appears that the designer copied both portraits from Charles Wilson Peale's oil painting.

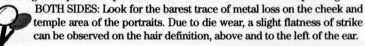

BOTH SIDES: Look for the barest trace of metal loss on the cheek and temple area of the portraits. Due to die wear, a slight flatness of strike can be observed on the hair definition, above and to the left of the ear.

Origins of the Lewis and Clark

During September 1904 the Philadelphia Mint struck 25,000 Lewis and Clark gold dollars plus 28 coins for assay purposes bearing the date of 1904. Next year, 35,000 gold dollars dated 1905 plus 41 assay pieces were produced during the months of March and June. These coins, designed by Charles E. Barber, were sold at $2.00 each. The coins were not all sold, and had to be melted by the Mint. In fact, 25,000 specimens of the '05 issue never left Philadelphia, since they were not requested.

Famous numismatist and promotor Farran Zerbe used D.M. Averill and Company of 331 Morrison St., Portland, Oregon, to deal with many orders received by the firm. To encourage public acceptance of the coin, he had them state the 1904 issue was almost sold out and raised the price to $2.50, while the newly released 1905 creation could be acquired for $2.00 or 6 pieces for $10. The majority of both issues were sold to individuals who treated these little jewels with little tender loving care. A small number of both issues were offered mounted in silver spoons and housed in brooches and stickpins. Value is especially dependent upon the condition of your coin.

The Lewis and Clark Today

Although not abundant, the Lewis and Clarks can be obtained in EF-AU condition. Object is to acquire a specimen which has not been "rim repaired," or polished or doctored in some fashion. Equally as rare in states up to MS-63. In MS-64 and higher condition, both dates offer exceptional future value. The 1905 striking is approximately two, three and four times as difficult to locate, in the respective MS-64, MS-65 and MS-66 grades.

Luster of each production will range from prooflike (not the norm), to semi-prooflike to frosty satiny, to dull satiny. Strike rarely presents a problem for the issue, nor does the surface porosity observed on a small percentage of these gold coins.

 Detecting counterfeits

Counterfeits do exist for the issue. Examine the field for depressions and small raised pieces of metal, as well as crude looking un-sharp inscription and statutory lettering.

 **Related material**

No official holders or mailing envelopes have surfaced to date.

1915
Panama-Pacific Exposition

**for photos, see individual denominations
on following pages**

Reason for issue: To commemorate the Panama Pacific International
Exposition, which was in celebration of the completion of the Panama
Canal.

Authorized per Act of January16, 1915:

Half dollars	200,000
Gold dollars	25,000
Quarter eagles	10,000
$50 Octagonal	1,500
$50 Round	1,500

Official sale price:

Half dollars	$1, 6 for $5
Gold dollars	$2.00
Quarter eagles	$4.00
$50 (both types)	$100 (as a set of all denominations)

Production figures

Date	Business Strikes	Assay Coins	Proofs	Melted	Net Mintage
1915-S 50¢	60,000	30	4?	32,866	27,134
1915-S $1	25,000	34	?	10,000	15,000
1915-S $2.50	10,000	17	?	3,251	6,749
1915-S $50					
Round	1,500	10	?	1,017	483
Octagonal	1,500	9	?	855	645

Current market values

	EF-40	AU-50	MS-60	MS-63	MS-64	MS-65
1915-S 50¢	140.	180.	340.	750.	1400.	3250.
1915-S $1	215.	315.	425.	850.	1700.	3550.
1915-S $2.50	925.	1250.	1850.	2550.	3650.	6100.
1915-S $50						
Round	15500.	20500.	26000.	32500.	48500.	120000.
Octagonal	13500.	18000.	23000.	29000.	44500.	90000.

Half Dollar Designs

Obverse by Charles E. Barber

Columbia facing left and scattering flowers. Behind her is a naked child holding a large cornucopia, symbolic of the many resources of the West. The Golden Gate and the rays of a setting sun are present in the background, while seen below the sun, separated by a wave motif is the date 1915. Located at the left of the numeral 1 of the coin's date is the San Francisco Mint mark (S). Situated around most of the coin's border is the inscription PANAMA-PACIFIC EXPOSITION.

 A metal loss will first be observed on the shoulder of Columbia and on the area between her waist and dress fold, directly above her exposed foot.

Reverse by George T. Morgan

American eagle with raised wings, standing on the national shield. Located in the right field is an olive branch, representing peace, while an oak branch symbolizing stability is situated in the left field. UNITED STATES OF AMERICA circles the rim above; HALF DOLLAR is split by the shield below. The Panama Pacific half dollar is the first commemorative to bear the motto IN GOD WE TRUST (above the eagle). It was also the first issue authorizing Act to specify a place of production.

Wear will first occur on the left side of the eagle's breast and leg as you view the coin. Look for a difference in metal texture and crisscross scratches in this location. Prime target area for the coin doctors.

Enlarged to show detail

Gold Dollar Designs by Charles Keck

Obverse

Head of a Panama Canal worker wearing a peaked cap, facing left. Some people the worker resembles a baseball player. In the lower field is the date of issue (1915). The worker faces directly into UNITED STATES OF AMERICA in two crowded lines. The sea God Poseidon and famous explorer Balboa were suggested as obverse design candidates.

Reverse

ONE DOLLAR in center almost encircled by two dolphins which indicate the meeting of two oceans. Around the border encircling the coin is the inscription PANAMA-PACIFIC EXPOSITION SAN FRANCISCO. Located below the DO of DOLLAR is the "S" Mint mark.

Gold $2.50 Designs

Obverse by Charles E. Barber

Columbia seated on a hippocampus or mythical sea monster, plunging to the left which represents the use of the new Canal. Facing right, Columbia holds in her hand a caduceus or symbolic staff of a herald, which consists of a staff with two entwined snakes and two wings at the top. Located in the upper border is the inscription PANAMA-PACIFIC EXPOSITION, while situated in the lower border is the date 1915. Placed at the extreme right of the date is the S Mint mark.

 A metal loss will first be observed on the knee and breast of Columbia. Look for a difference in metal texture and crisscross scratches in these locations.

Reverse by George T. Morgan

American eagle with raised wings facing left, standing on a classical standard. Inscribed within the standard is the motto E PLURIBUS UNUM (for the first time on a commemorative coin), while located directly below is the denomination 2½-DOL; UNITED STATES OF AMERICA arcs above.

 Wear will first be seen on the leg, breast, upper wing, then base of the classical standard.

Gold $50 Designs by Robert I. Aitken

This $50 gold piece was produced in an octagonal shape as well as the usual round coin shape because California used the aforementioned shapes following the Gold Rush. When most people refer to this particular issue, they claim that the only difference between the two coins is their shape. However, this is not the case. The obverse and reverse designs of this issue are similar, except for the fact that the design of the octagonal issue has been reduced from 44mm to 36.5mm making space for the addition of eight dolphins — which symbolize the uninterrupted water route made possible thanks to the Canal — in the angles of the coin's obverse and reverse. It is the first commemorative to bear the mottoes IN GOD WE TRUST and E PLURIBUS UNUM.

Obverse

Minerva, goddess of wisdom, skill, contemplation, spinning, weaving, agriculture and horticulture, wearing a crested helmet facing left.

Located at her left shoulder is part of a shield, bearing the date of issue in Roman numerals, MCMXV (1915). In the lower border is the coin's denomination FIFTY DOLLARS. UNITED STATES OF AMERICA arcs above; IN GOD WE TRUST appears in the upper field above and to the left of Minerva's helmet.

A metal loss will first be noticed Minerva's cheek, as well as on her crested helmet in the center of its leaf design. Examine for portrait and left field doctoring.

Reverse

Portrayed is an owl, sacred symbol of Minerva and symbolic of wisdom, who is perched on a branch of western pine, with its cones and needles. Situated between the milling and a double dot and dash border is the inscription PANAMA-PACIFIC EXPOSITION SAN FRANCISCO, while the designer's initials, RA, incused in small letters is seen below the owl's right talon, or above the letters FR in FRANCISCO, beyond the double dot and dash border. The San Francisco Mint mark S, appears in the right field directly below the bullet, after the letter M in the motto E PLURIBUS UNUM, also situated in the right field.

 Look for wear and difference in metal texture on the owl's wing, directly across from the word PLURIBUS and on the upper part of the owl's breast.

Origins of the Pan-Pac

More than $50 million dollars was spent to make the 1915 Panama-Pacific Exposition the greatest of all fairs. This Expo celebrated the opening of the Panama Canal, by the *S.S. Ancon* on Aug.15, 1914. The Expo's doors opened Feb. 20, 1915. When the sun set on this event, more than 19 million people had visited.

This issue was the first commemorative half dollar to be struck at a branch Mint, in San Francisco. Produced were 60,000 half dollars, plus 30 assay coins. All did not sell at $1 each and 32,866 pieces had to be melted. It was issued by the Official Coin and Medal Department and sold at the celebration location.

There exist extremely rare trial pieces of this issue, made at the Philadelphia Mint. These were struck without the "S" Mint mark. Two were created in gold, six in silver and four in copper for Treasury Secretary William Gibbs McAdoo — a coin collector! The San Francisco Mint struck 25,000 $1 gold coins, plus 34 assay pieces. Since not all of the pieces offered for sale at $2.00 each were sold, 10,000 coins were returned to the Mint and melted. Thus, our net mintage stands at 15,000.

There exist two extremely rare silver plain edge trial pieces, as well as nine very sought after gold $1 specimens of different thicknesses. Seven pieces have reeded edges and two possess the plain edge. Most eye appealing coin out of the gold trials — created for McAdoo — is the plain edge fourth impression specimen. It was struck on a very thick planchet, (weighing 55.6 grains), listed as E.1588 in the *Comprehensive Catalog and Encyclopedia of United States Coins* (also Judd 1793-a). None have Mint marks as all were struck at the Philadelphia Mint before the Mint mark was added.

Originally, Evelyn B. Longman, a New York City sculptor, was chosen to design the $2.50 quarter eagle. The obverse was to depict the head of an eagle, while the reverse was to portray a cluster of fruit (symbolic of the state) and a dollar sign ($) instead of the letter D. Unfortunately she became ill and could not complete her work.

The San Francisco Mint struck 10,000 Pan-Pac quarter eagles, plus 17 assay coins in June 1915. Sales were sluggish, and 3,251 pieces were returned to be reincarnated into some other coinage. During the months of June, July and August 1915, the San Francisco Mint struck 1,500 octagonal and 1,500 round $50 pieces, plus 9 and 10 assay coins respectively, with the aid of a special 14-ton hydraulic press. The press was shipped from the Philadelphia Mint, which used it to produce medals. On June 15, 1915, the first 29 out of 100 octagonal pieces were struck by guests and officials of the Mint. Included were T.W.H. Shanahan, Superintendent; Charles C. Moore, president of the Exposition; and Farran Zerbe, the well known numismatist and head of the Coin and Medal Department at the Exposition. When Superintendent Shanahan was about to strike the first $50 octagonal, he made the claim that this would be the first $50 coin issued under authority of law in this nation. He was incorrect! August Humbert (appointed U.S. Assayer) produced $50 octagonal pieces in 1851 and 1852, under the Act of September 30, 1850. (These are the very pieces, generally cataloged as "Pioneer gold," which inspired the commemorative octagonal design.)

The round design had to be reduced from 44mm to 36.5mm to have space for the addition of eight dolphins on the octagonal version. Creation of this rarer coinage had to be halted after the 62nd striking. The dies broke! The same fate hit the other pair on hand. Thus, production was postponed until additional dies were received from Philadelphia.

The octagonals were favored at the fair, due to their shape and the representation of dolphins in the border. They were sold individually, in a purple velvet lined leather case with a descriptive card, and imprinted inner top, which provided Exposition Coin Information, in gold ink, at $100. They could also be acquired along with a boxed set containing the three minor coins, at $100. (You had your choice of either $50 coin.) With gold valued at $20.67, these large and beautiful coins contained $49.99 worth of gold!

The Pan-Pac Half Dollar Today

The half dollar can be located with some effort in EF-AU condition. Most specimens encountered will display some form of abuse, such as polishing, cleaning or various degrees of whizzing — especially on Columbia's body and the reverse eagle's breast. The issue is presently undervalued in all grades. Luster, strike and marks cause many grade-value problems. I suggest a specimen grading minimum MS-64, possessing fully original attractive surfaces, should future appreciation be coveted. MS-64 material is not as plentiful as some individuals now assume. There is a definite future for strictly graded MS-65 and loftier labeled specimens. Pan-Pacs are very difficult to obtain in MS-64 and MS-65.

Luster will range from brilliant satiny (not the norm) to lifeless-dull. Beware of those toned specimens which could lack natural surface luster. Possibly they were placed in a tarnish removing solution, in the past, to brighten or improve a surface appearance that could not be bettered. Instead, the grade-value was lowered forever on a coin which has now been re-toned!

Strike can affect this issue's value by keeping it out of the MS-65 category. Columbia must not possess too much flatness of the head, cap, arm and body. Ditto for the reverse eagle's breast and neck as well as the bird's claws. A striking characteristic which should not affect coin's grade is termed a rim indentation. This is can be seen close to Columbia's Phrygian cap. Another wide indentation caused by the die and striking technique can be observed in both fields near the periphery. Primary focal areas such as Columbia and the reverse eagle are plagued by those numismatic villains named bag mark, reed mark, slide mark, hairline scratches, etc.

A matte Proof has been reported. I do not believe the coin labeled a satin finish Proof deserves the rating. It is a coin produced from new dies.

Detecting counterfeits

A newly discovered counterfeit Pan-Pac half dollar displays very sharp reeding, slightly fuzzy lettering, and has a surface that is uncharacteristically flashy for the issue.

The Pan-Pac Gold Dollar Today

The Pan-Pac gold dollar is one of the more available — though not abundant — commemorative gold dollars which can be located in EF-AU condition. Were a steady demand to develop, absorbing the thin market supply, values would naturally climb. Encountered specimens will display naturally worn as well as doctored surfaces. The coin can be obtained with little effort in grades MS-60 through MS-64. It is undervalued especially in eye appealing MS-64 and better condition, where the future potential resides.

Luster will range from blazing frosty, to dull matte-like frosty. Strike rarely presents a grade-value problem for this coin. Primary focal area portrait is usually plagued by grade lowering hairline scratches, slide marks and bag marks. Inner circle theme is your primary reverse location. Numismatic negatives usually show up on the smooth dolphins design.

 Detecting counterfeits

Counterfeits exist for this creation. On one false creation, small die scratches can be observed among the normal metal flow lines to the right of the first A in AMERICA, directly under the worker's chin. The reverse displays file marks and die scratches between the P and A of PACIFIC. Also there are several blobs of extra metal between the A and N of FRANCISCO at the 6 o'clock position.

Another counterfeit Pan-Pac dollar displays a depression in the center of the 9 in the date and another depression about midway down on DO in DOLLAR

The Pan-Pac Gold $2.50 Today

This popular low mintage issue is not abundant in EF-AU grades. Specimens usually encountered will show some form of abuse. Attempt to acquire pieces which have worn naturally. Should be purchased for the pure joy of collecting. Issue is quite undervalued and scarce in all grades! Any continuous demand will create a rapid value jump. Good future for this commemorative quarter eagle, especially in grades MS-63+ and better. Luster will range from bright satiny (not the norm), to dull grainy, satiny. Strike will vary from strong — which does not mean the designs will appear sharply struck — but strong for the issue. However, too soft a design definition on the headdress of Columbia and head and neck of the hippocampus, as well as the reverse eagle's head, neck and claw, will affect the grade-value. Obverse primary focal area is Columbia's body, plus the head and neck of the hippocampus. Reverse location is the eagle and exposed field, opposite the word UNITED. A non-detracting issue characteristic are raised metal swirls. These raised scratches were caused by steel brushing the dies at the Mint. Hairline scratches caused by abuse cut into the coin's surface and lower the grade and value.

Detecting counterfeits

Counterfeits exist, displaying a soft strike, field depressions and tooling marks within inscriptions.

The Pan-Pac Gold $50 Today

Who wouldn't like to own this rare creation? The higher the grade, the rarer the coin. More specimens residing in the EF-AU state will exhibit some form of abuse, in the form of cleaning, various degrees of whizzing and light polishing, than will not. The future looks bright for those blessed to afford the issue, in any Uncirculated grade, very undervalued in all categories. In grades MS-60 through MS-64, the round is the rarer of the strikings. In the higher states, they are equally as difficult to obtain. Luster will range from blazing frosty to frosty. Strike presents no real problem for this issue. At times, the hair by Minerva's ear and feather design on the owl's breast will display a slight weakness of strike, but not enough to lower coin's grade or value. The latter is definitely accomplished by those surface negatives, caused by some form of abuse. Needless to say, these rare $50 strikings were acquired by those who could afford them. Sold individually (as previously noted) in a leather case for $100 each. If you desired the four piece set, you received the three piece minor coinage ($7.50) at no extra charge.

 **Related material**

Each of the smaller coins — the half dollar, gold dollar and $2.50 quarter eagle — was distributed in an imprinted paper envelope (2¼" X 4⁷/₁₆"), describing the enclosed coin, listing its designer and ordering address. One version for the half dollar indicates price "$1.00 each"; another "$1 each — 6 for $5.00." The gold dollar versions indicated price of "$2.00 each" or "$2.00 — 6 for $10.00." The envelope for the quarter eagle was marked "$4 each." These envelopes for the half dollar and gold dollar are worth in the range of $20-50; envelopes intended for the quarter eagle can bring $25-75, depending upon condition.

A set of three denominations was sold in a leather case lined with purple velvet at $7.50. Inner cover is imprinted with EXPOSITION INFORMATION in gold ink. Leather cases lined with white velvet are said to be later replicas. The genuine item can bring between $400 and $800, depending on condition.

The $50 issue was offered as a complete set with the three smaller denominations and your choice of either $50 coin for $100, with both coins $50 for $200, and as a double complete set which would show obverse as well as reverse for $400. Included at no extra charge was a glass-fronted copper hammered frame or a leather presentation case. Accompanying the aforementioned were printed descriptions of each coin.

Individual $50 cases can bring between $400 and $800 at present. The five-piece case can sell in the $2,500-$5,000 range. The hammered frame housing the five-piece set can be worth $5,000 to $10,000. The double set holder which once brought $18,000 — empty — is now valued in the $8,000 to $12,000 range. Replicas of the Pan-Pac $50 round dated 1915, housed in a red lether case and gold stamped "Coca-Cola, etc., Convention 1915 USA" were produced in 1971.

1916-1917
McKinley Memorial

Enlarged to show detail

Reason for issue: To commemorate the erection of a memorial to
President William McKinley.
Authorized per Act of February 23, 1916: 100,000.
Official sale price: $3

Production figures

Date	Business Strikes	Assay Coins	Proofs	Melted	Net Mintage
1916	20,000	26	4-6?	10,023	9,977
1917	10,000	14	4-6?	0	10,000

Current market values

	EF-40	AU-50	MS-60	MS-63	MS-64	MS-65
1916	185.	290.	365.	850.	1500.	3100.
1917	190.	335.	475.	1200.	2650.	4600.

Designs

Obverse by Charles E. Barber

Head of McKinley facing left. UNITED STATES OF AMERICA appears around
the upper border; MCKINLEY DOLLAR around the lower border.

Metal loss will occur on the cheek and temple of McKinley.

Reverse by George T. Morgan

Facade of the McKinley Memorial Building with inscriptions MCKINLEY
BIRTHPLACE - NILES OHIO, located in upper border and field respectively. The date
is located above the word MEMORIAL which is in the lower border.

Wear can first be observed on the flagpole base, top section and steps of
the Memorial.

Origins of the McKinley

The Philadelphia Mint struck 20,000 coins plus 26 for assay purposes during August and October 1916, while in February of the following year, 10,014 pieces dated 1917 were minted. The dies were then destroyed, for this was a provision of the Act which also designated the Mint responsible for the coin's production. I note this because no other Act had ever specified such, with the exception of the Panama-Pacific issue, whose Act designated the San Francisco Mint as its manufacturer.

Both coins were offered for sale at $3.00 each by the McKinley Birthplace Memorial Association. According to B. Max Mehl, the great Texas Dealer, the Committee in 1917 realized that collectors could not and would not absorb any more coins at $3.00 each. Sales met with meager success and eventually came to a standstill. Mehl acquired 10,000 coins from the Commission and sold such extensively among collectors at $2.50 each. The Commission decided to return 10,023 gold dollars to the Mint. It was believed these coins were all dated 1916. Based on present day evaluation it appears that one-third to half the amount were dated 1917.

The McKinley Today

The majority of specimens in circulated condition have been cleaned or numismatically abused in some manner. Those original surface coins grading AU-55 or AU-58 will at times exhibit Uncirculated reverses! Obverse relief is much higher while the reverse's rim better protects the lower relief. The 1916 is not difficult to locate in grades MS-60 through MS-64 condition. Collectors should focus on a specimen which is appealing and grades at least MS-64+. Lower grades should be acquired for the joy of collecting. Real future exists in MS-65 and better condition. The 1917 McKinley is rarer than its 1916 brother issue in all grades, up to MS-66.

Luster will range from prooflike to semi-prooflike to brilliant satiny to dull satiny. Strike rarely presents a problem for either date. Hair detail on McKinley was designed with soft detail, thus will lack strike sharpness of the 1903 McKinley Louisiana Purchase dollar. In fact, although the same person, their respective portraits look like two different men. Howbeit, his image acts as a magnet for bag marks, hairline scratches, etc. Same in smooth fields lower coin's value.

 Detecting counterfeits

Counterfeits of each date exist. Look for lack of detail in obverse and reverse devices, as well as for field depressions and lack of lettering sharpness on the 1916 production. The fake 1917 striking will also display raised parallel striations between the rim and the letters "ERICA" of AMERICA, field depressions below the letters "IO" of OHIO and a round depression on the steps of the Memorial, directly below the statue.

Related material

Specimens were distributed in plain coin envelopes and rubber stamped on the reverse with red ink THE NILES TRUST COMPANY, NILES OHIO with a circle, as well as a paper coin envelope imprinted with THE NATIONAL MCKINLEY BIRTH-PLACE MEMORIAL ASSOCIATION, YOUNGSTOWN, OHIO plus the notation that contained is #? Souvenir McKinley Gold Dollar. Both items are rarely encountered. It was also sold in a large white coin envelope (2¼" X 2¼"), imprinted with a red berry and green holly Christmas wreath with a MERRY CHRISTMAS printed in red, glued to a printed white card (6¼" X 3¼"). Depicted is a portrait of McKinley and the words A MCKINLEY GOLD DOLLAR; TO and FROM are situated below. What a Christmas gift for some lucky person! Item makes an occasional appearance.

I have seen but two envelopes aforementioned, and would value each at $375. The Christmas item is worth $100 to $250.

1918
Illinois Centennial

Reason for issue: To commemorate the 100th anniversary of the admission of Illinois into the Union.

Authorized per Act of June 1, 1918: 100,000

Official sale price: $1

Production figures

Date	Business Strikes	Assay Coins	Proofs	Melted	Net Mintage
1918	100,000	58	4-10?	0	100,000

Current market values

	EF-40	AU-50	MS-60	MS-63	MS-64	MS-65
1918	55.00	67.50	80.00	145.	450.	950.

Designs

Obverse by George T. Morgan

Bust of Abraham Lincoln, facing right. Date below (1918). It was created from a photograph of Andrew O'Connor's statue, which presented the young beardless 16th President, that was unveiled in Springfield, Ill., in 1918. Seen around most of the coin's border is the inscription CENTENNIAL OF THE STATE OF ILLINOIS. IN GOD WE TRUST is in four lines in the left field behind Lincoln's head. LIBERTY appears in the lower right, just in front of the president's collar.

A metal loss will first be noticed on the cheekbone and hair above Lincoln's ear. Look for a difference in metal color and crisscross scratches in this area, as well as surface doctoring.

Reverse by John Ray Sinnock

American eagle with raised wings facing left, and standing partly on the shield of the United States and a rock. He holds in his beak a ribbon bearing the incused Illinois state motto STATE SOVEREIGNTY — NATIONAL UNITY, while the motto E PLURIBUS UNUM is located in the right field above the rising sun with extending rays. Above the HA in HALF DOLLAR, located in the lower border area is an olive branch, symbol of peace. UNITED STATES OF AMERICA arcs above.

The lower relief eagle will indicate wear by a loss of surface metal on the breast. Should the area display some flatness due to die wear, examine for signs of a silver loss in this location.

Origins of the Illinois (or Lincoln)

In August 1918, the Philadelphia Mint struck 100,000 coins plus 58 for assay purposes. None of these coins were returned to the Mint, since most of the issue was sold through the Springfield Chamber of Commerce, and other County Centennial outlets for $1. Famous numismatist B. Max Mehl acquired over 3,000 pieces between 55¢ and 60¢. He notes that a particular bank in Springfield housed 30,000 specimens which were handled by that city's Chamber of Commerce. During the bank holiday of 1933, that bank took a holiday and the remainder of these pieces were acquired by several dealers at less than $1 each. The market became flooded with them, but were absorbed during the commem boom which began in 1935.

This issue was the first to commemorate an occasion, event or undertaking that was confined to a single state.

The Illinois (or Lincoln) Today

This coin is not at all difficult to obtain in EF-AU condition. The majority of Lincolns are in the MS-60 through MS-64 grades. Collectors should focus on the latter classification, since there exists little value spread at present. Attempt to acquire an original eye appealing specimen. The coin's portrait and smooth obverse field should be almost free of detracting hairlines, scuff marks and scratches. It is those surface negatives, such as a reed mark or large bag mark on the portrait or a few fine hairline field scratches which downgrade many would-be MS-65 specimens. Luster can range from blazing brilliant to dull satiny. Strike rarely causes a downgrading of an issue. On the reverse the eagle can display a slight flattening of its breast feathers, due to die wear. Seldom does it reach the point where it's a detriment to a coin's value. If future gains are your game, think MS-65 and loftier, should funds be available.

Related material

Original holders for this issue are unheard of to date. The only official numismatic centennial item encountered is the wearable silvered nickel shield-shaped badges housing a Lincoln, with attached ribbon, and top hanger reading 1818 over Illinois Centennial, 1918 at bottom. Several versions of the ribbons exist. The most common is the white, blue and white striped ribbon with 21 stars. Next is the same design, but with the word OFFICIAL imprinted in gold. Another reported creation is said to exhibit a red and blue striped ribbon. Could it be that some individual simply substituted this ribbon for a damaged official version? Value is based on the condition of the enclosed coin. I would figure between the $250 and $2,500 range.

1920
Maine Centennial

Reason for issue: To commemorate the 100th anniversary of the admission
of the State of Maine into the Union.
Authorized per Act of May 10, 1920: 100,000.
Official sale price: $1

Production figures

Date	Business Strikes	Assay Coins	Proofs	Melted	Net Mintage
1920	50,000	28	4?	0	50,000

Current market values

	EF-40	AU-50	MS-60	MS-63	MS-64	MS-65
1920	47.50	70.00	90.00	185.	415.	1050.

Designs by Anthony de Francisci

The Maine was designed by Anthony de Francisci based upon specifications furnished him by the State of Maine.

Obverse

Arms of the State of Maine, which is composed of a sunken relief pine tree
and moose in a lying position, on a shield which is supported by two male figures
representing Commerce (the anchor) and Agriculture (the scythe). Above the
shield is the word DIRIGO, meaning I direct, on a scroll, while above that is a star
with five short rays. Located below the shield is another scroll bearing the word
MAINE situated between two rosettes. UNITED STATES OF AMERICA arcs above;
HALF DOLLAR below.

Metal loss will first be noticed on the hand of each male holding the
shield. The center of the countersunk pine tree will appear worn. Such is
the result of die design and striking — not wear. Determine if luster has
been disturbed and metal loss is a certainty. Fine crisscross scratches in
this area will indicate metal loss and not handling marks.

Reverse

Wreath of pine needles and cones. Within such appears the inscription MAINE CENTENNIAL 1820-1920. LIBERTY connects the tips of the wreath at the top. E PLURIBUS UNUM is squeezed between the wreath and the rim above; IN GOD WE TRUST is similarly placed at the bottom.

Examine for wear on the wreath's ribbon at the 6 o'clock position and the top section of the pine wreath extending from the 4 to almost 9 o'clock position. Raised lines appearing in the left field and above the word MAINE are the result of die polishing. They do not lower the coin's grade. However, scratches, be it hairline or heavier, cut into the surface metal and lower a coin's value.

Origins of the Maine

Originally it was the idea of Maine's delegate to the House of Representatives, John A. Peters, to have this issue placed into circulation. Its primary objective would be free advertisement for the Centennial event. The concept, however, garnered little support. The design was severely criticized by the judges at the Commission of Fine Arts.

During the late summer of 1920, the Philadelphia Mint struck 50,028 Maine half dollars, plus 28 assay coins. These coins were sold at $1.00 each from the Office of the State Treasurer. Although delivery was not made until after the Centennial Celebration at Portland was over, more than 30,000 pieces sold immediately and the remainder were offered for sale until all pieces were sold.

The Maine Today

This coin is abundant in EF-AU condition. It was used as a pocket piece by the locals, therefore many specimens will show some form of abuse. Not a difficult coin to acquire, in grades MS-60 through MS-64. Future value increase resides in specimens which are very attractive; possess a strong strike and grade at least MS-64+! Strict MS-65 eye appealing Maines are not abundant in today's marketplace. Same most definitely holds true for the higher graded coinage. Luster will range from prooflike to semi-prooflike (not the norm) to brilliant satiny, to satiny, to dull satiny. A prooflike coin is the result of heavy die polishing, after the die clashed or came together, with no planchet in between. This partial mirrored surface quickly changed to a more brilliant lustrous condition, with every blow from the press.

Strikings produced from the original die state will offer the beholder a bright to dull satiny appearance. Strike seldom affects the grade or value of the issue. Coins produced after heavy die polishing will lack the same sharpness, especially on the faces of the depicted two men. Primary focal area is the obverse shield which is usually plagued by numismatic negatives such as bag marks, slide marks, etc. Critical location for the reverse design is the wreath and area above the word MAINE. One large detracting mark in this area will downgrade your MS-65 to a MS-64. Ditto for the aforementioned shield location.

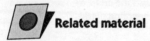

Related material

To date, I have encountered no original distribution holder or printed material.

1920-1921
Pilgrim Tercentenary

Reason for issue: To commemorate the 300th anniversary of the landing of the pilgrims at Plymouth.

Authorized per Act of May 12, 1920: 300,000

Official sale price: $1

Production figures

Date	Business Strikes	Assay Coins	Proofs	Melted	Net Mintage
1920	200,000	112	4?	48,000	152,000
1921	100,053	53	4?	80,000	20,000

Current market values

	EF-40	AU-50	MS-60	MS-63	MS-64	MS-65
1920	49.00	55.00	65.00	80.00	170.	775.
1921	60.00	72.50	105.	185.	375.	1100.

Designs by Cyrus E. Dallin

Obverse

Half-length portrait of Governor William Bradford (indicative of the Pilgrim of his time) who is wearing a conical hat and carrying a Bible under his left arm. Below his elbow appears the incused initial "D" for Dallin and not for the Denver Mint! Separated by two decorative stars are the words UNITED STATES OF AMERICA and PILGRIM HALF DOLLAR. The words are separated by dots. Behind the Governor's head is the motto, IN GOD WE TRUST. On the 1921 issue, the date will be observed in the left field opposite his upper chest. Removed from this popular Boston sculptor's initial design were the words HOLY BIBLE which appeared on the depicted book's front cover. His initials CED met the same fate.

 A metal loss will first occur on the cheekbone, then in the hair area covering the Governor's ear. Prime target for the coin doctors. Examine that portrait.

Reverse

Side view of the *Mayflower* sailing to the left, as well as the Pilgrim Tercentenary dates 1620-1920. This reverse met with some technical, historical criticism. Why? Ships of the day were equipped with a square water sail which hung under the bowsprit, or the large spar (support rigging) which projected forward from the bow or ship's nose. The *Mayflower* on the half dollar is depicted with a flying jib, a triangular sail set on a stay extending from the head of the foremast to the bowsprit, or the jibboom. This type of sail had not actually been put to use during the time of the *Mayflower* landing! PILGRIM TERCENTENARY CELEBRATION and anniversary dates 1620-1920 grace the coin's outer border.

 Examine the crow's nest, center mast and stern of the Mayflower for a metal loss or difference in metal texture.

Origins of the Pilgrim

This issue was produced by the Philadelphia Mint in October 1920. Its original mintage of 200,000 pieces was placed in the hands of the Pilgrim Tercentenary Commission for distribution in November through the National Shawmut Bank of Boston, or procured at any Boston or Plymouth Bank. They were offered at $1.00 each.

The sale of the 1920 souvenirs must have been very successful since no one at that time thought of returning any coins to the Mint. However, when sales slackened, the Pilgrim Tercentenary Commission believed they could do just as well with another issue. During the following July, the Philadelphia Mint struck an additional 100,053 half dollars (plus 53 pieces for assay purposes), of the exact design as the 1920 issue, but added the date of 1921 in relief in the left field on the obverse. This totals to three dates on the coin. We can note the anniversary dates (1620-1920) and the year of striking.

However, sales turned out to be poor. The Commission returned 48,000 pieces dated 1920 and 80,000 of the 1921 issue to the Mint for melting. This leaves us with a low mintage figure of 20,000 half dollars, dated 1921 and 152,000 dated 1920, today's commoner coin.

The Pilgrims Today

The 1920 Pilgrim is abundant in circulated EF-AU condition. It's usually encountered naturally worn to unnaturally abused. The rarer 1921 striking is not as abundant. It usually possesses some form of cleaning or doctoring. It is certainly the better buy of the dates, since value spread is little.

In grades MS-60 through MS-64, little value spread currently exists for this 1920 issue that is easily obtainable. Thus, think undervalued eye appealing MS-64, unless procuring simply for the pure joy of collecting and grade is of no concern. Potential resides here and in the loftier levels. Real value for this issue lies in the 1921 striking — the coin which introduced me to the world of U.S. commemorative coinage! It is underrated in all grades, up to MS-64 and especially in MS-65 and higher categories. Luster will range from prooflike, to semi-prooflike, to blazing satiny, to dull satiny. I have seen a few first strike examples only of the 1921 production which flaunted those prooflike obverses and blazing satiny reverses. Otherwise, both dates will display the latter satiny range. However, the lower mintage 1921 Pilgrim will exhibit a more impressive "luster look" more often than the 1920 issue.

Strike can be responsible for a grade-value lowering of this issue, especially true if the border inscription lettering — be it obverse word STATES, or HALF, or parts of the reverse word TERCENTENARY, or anniversary dates, 1621-1921 or ship's mast — appear too flat or weak. Numismatic abuse, in the form of bag marks, slide marks, reed marks, etc., usually are attracted to the primary focal locations, such as Bradford's portrait (then surrounding fields) and reverse *Mayflower*. One ugly, large bag mark observed in the obverse field or slide mark across the Governor's likeness on a blazing, eye appealing specimen can drop a coin value dramatically. These locations are often whizzed (wire brushed), polished or doctored in some fashion.

While studying this issue, I discovered several 1921 half dollars which showed evidence of die-clashing, and called it the Pilgrim 1921 Type II. My discovery concerns a lump in front of Bradford's nose, several tiny bumps behind his head above the hat brim, a raised area below the RU in TRUST and the conical hat that doesn't quite fit Bradford's head.

Through the use of film positives we can prove that the lumps were the result of clashed dies and the ill fitting hat the result of die polishing, probably an attempt at eliminating the clash marks. Clash marks occur when a blank fails to feed into the press. The dies hit each other without the blank between to absorb the blow. As a result, the outline of the design details from each die is transferred to the other die.

The faces of dies are normally slightly convex so that they impart a slight concavity to the field of the coins they strike. And because the dies are convex the centers of the dies hit first and hit hardest, with the result that the design nearest the center is more subject to the die clash transfer.

The film positives were used as overlays to show the lump in front of Bradford's nose corresponds to the area below the sail of the foremast, the tiny bumps behind the head match spaces between the waves below the center of the ship, and the raised area below RU corresponds to the curved lower edge of the sail at the *Mayflower*'s stern. The reverse has no clashmarks, indicating that possibly the reverse die had been changed after the clash and probably because of it.

I recently examined a 1920 Pilgrim which exhibited no obverse die clash marks but displayed the clash marked letters US (inverted) from the word TRUST. This too can be seen on many of the 1921 specimens, indicating this reverse die used to make the 1920 coinage was used for the '21 creation. Using 10X magnification, the Governor's index finger and collar can also be observed beneath the letters ER of TERCENTENARY and under the sail design, to the left of the rear mast, respectively.

Possibly 100 such pieces exist, but premiums asked for the offered grade have been negligible, to date. Fascination with the variety has not been over-whelming, possibly because of its infrequent appearances and lack of serious promotion.

Detecting counterfeits

1920 die trials struck in different metals were sold via a prestigious British auction house for $50,000. I informed the new owners (who had forwarded some pieces) that their coins were fakes! The dies were created by a nonprofessional!

 ## Related material

The 1920 coin was sold by the banks in a plain coin envelope or just "over the counter." The issue was also distributed in a gold colored coin box with an emerald green slit-pouch. The top cover is imprinted in black: PEOPLE SAVINGS BANK, WORCHESTER, MASS, with coat of arms.

It was also sold in a white coin box. Within, a light tan velour interior and circular coin slot, accompanying small printed insert informing about the coin, reason for striking and name of its designer. The top cover is imprinted in orange-brown ink: SOCIETY OF COLONIAL WARS, IN THE STATE OF RHODE ISLAND AND PROVIDENCE PLANTATIONS, BY ITS GOVERNOR, HENRY DEXTER SHARPE, ESQ.

These boxes are very rare and valuable today, and original specimens may be valued in the lofty $500 to $700 range!

Rare Pilgrim box

1921
Missouri Centennial

2★4 above date

Reason for issue: To commemorate the 100th anniversary of the admission of Missouri into the Union on August 10, 1821.

Authorized per Act of March 4, 1921: 250,000.

Official sale price: $1

Production figures

Date	Business Strikes	Assay Coins	Proofs	Melted	Net Mintage
1921 2★4	5,000	0	4 ?	0	5,000
1921 No 2★4	45,000	28	4 ?	29,600	15,400

Current market values

	EF-40	AU-50	MS-60	MS-63	MS-64	MS-65
1921 No 2★4	145.	210.	345.	900.	1500.	7600.
1921 2★4	175.	285.	450.	850.	1450.	7500.

Designs by Robert I. Aitken

Obverse

Portrayed is the bust of a frontiersman intended to represent Daniel Boone wearing a coonskin cap and deerskin jacket, facing left. The anniversary dates 1821-1921 appear in the coin's lower field. UNITED STATES OF AMERICA arcs above; HALF DOLLAR below. Located in the field of the low mintage variety above the '21 of the anniversary date 1821 is the incused 2★4 which indicates that Missouri was the 24th state to enter the Union.

Wear will first be observed on the cheek of the frontiersman, as well as his shoulder and on the hair behind his ear. Examine cheek area for doctoring, in the form of whizzing, surface texturing and light buffing. The rest of the coin can glow in the dark from originality. Beware.

Reverse

Depicted is the standing figure of a frontiersman wearing a powder horn and holding a rifle with his right hand, while extending his left hand. Standing beside him is a Native American, wearing a war bonnet, holding a pipe and a shield. The 24 five-pointed stars signify again that Missouri was the 24th state to be admitted into the Union. Situated around the upper border is the inscription MISSOURI CENTENNIAL, while the word SEDALIA, the site of the Exposition and State Fair which took place from August 8-20, 1921, is incused in the lower border. Robert Aitken who designed the Panama-Pacific $50 gold piece, as well as the San Diego issue, has his initials (RA) incused in the lower right field near the rifle stock. IN GOD WE TRUST, LIBERTY and E PLURIBUS UNUM simply were omitted from this issue, possibly due to the lack of space in the coin's field after the design was accepted.

A metal loss will make its appearance on the left shoulder and upper arm of the man who was supposed to represent Daniel Boone.

The Missouri Then

The Philadelphia Mint struck a total of 50,028 Missouri 50-cent pieces in July 1921. Five thousand of the 2★4 variety were struck first. To save the expense of making new dies, the 2★4 was simply polished off the first working die and 45,000 pieces plus 28 assay coins without the special symbolic mark were produced. They were first distributed at $1 each, by the Sedalia Trust Company. Several pieces were shown at the August American Numismatic Association Convention in Boston that year.

The incused symbol was the idea of James Montgomery, Chairman of the Exposition. His primary objective was to have 5,000 pieces struck, then have the special mark removed. A sufficient profit would be made enabling the payment of model and die cost at $1,750.

This issue was a very popular coin with collectors, but sales eventually started to decline. The Missouri Centennial Committee of Sedalia, Missouri, Chamber of Commerce, custodian of this issue, in one major effort to increase sales offered the new 2★4 variety of which only 5,000 pieces were minted, for sale at $1.00 each. Unfortunately not all of the large mintage issue was sold, thus 29,600 "plain" Missouri coins were returned to the Mint and melted, leaving a present net mintage figure for this issue of only 15,400 coins.

The Missouri Today

Circulated examples of either coin in EF-AU condition will display some form of abuse, such as whizzing, polishing, etc. Smart collectors attempt to locate coins whose surface is worn, but displays no nasty scratches, digs, etc., and is undoctored. Our 2★4 variety in the rarer issue in EF-AU through MS-63 condition. The allure of the incused symbol is responsible for the higher price tag. Future gains begin with eye appealing MS-63+ coinage of either production. It is a wonderful coin to possess in grades MS-64. Definitely a rare coin the loftier states! The 2★4 variety was subjected to much numismatic abuse. However, the majority of the higher mintage NO 2★4 issue was also sold to non-collectors and heavily abused making the coins virtually equally as rare, in the grades 64 through 66. In fact, the Missouri plain is a bit rarer. Luster will range from flashy, brilliant (not the norm) to satiny, to dull satiny. Creation's granular irregular surface is responsible for most of this occurrence.

A small percentage of the entire issue can be classified as sharply struck. The remainder at best can be labeled just satisfactory. The vertical leather strap extending upwards from the powder horn will show definition approximately half way up the left shoulder. Due to shallow design definition and die wear, only the earliest strikes from the new dies will display the full leather strap. Such will not affect the grade of the coin, nor the slight flat area, also created from die wear. Area can appear grainy from the original planchet or coin blank surface.

Being struck first, the incused variety displays some more definition. Detracting features such slide marks, small scratches and cuts on the primary focal area, which is the face of the frontiersman, quickly eliminates many of these coins from the MS-64 and MS-65 grades. These same negatives will do likewise to the primary focal location which is the smooth looking back of the reverse frontiersman. Thus, acquiring strictly graded and appealing MS-64+ and higher material will not be easy. Some pieces may exhibit a small planchet split on the edge. This results from a flaw in the design and manufacture of the dies. This split can lower a coin's worth.

 **Related material**

No original mailing holders or official coin envelopes have surfaced to date. There does exist a 14 karat gold badge worn by the chairman of the Centennial Commission's executive committee. The badge sold for $1,500 in May 1980. It is a very rare and desireable piece of commemorative history.

1921
Alabama Centennial

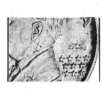  

2x2 in field

Reason for issue: To commemorate Alabama's centennial in 1919.
Authorized per Act of May 10, 1920: 100,000, both types
Official sale price: $1.

Production figures

Date	Business Strikes	Assay Coins	Proofs	Melted	Net Mintage
1921 2x2	5,000	5	4?	0	5,000
1921 Plain	65,000	39	4?	5,000	60,000

Current market values

	EF-40	AU-50	MS-60	MS-63	MS-64	MS-65
1921 2x2	105.	145.	325.	665.	1250.	5000.
1921 No 2x2	55.00	82.50	210.	590.	1200.	4800.

Designs by Laura Gardin Fraser

Obverse

William Wyatt Bibb, Alabama's first governor, and Thomas E. Kilby, the governor in 1920. Beneath their busts in small letters are their names, the date 1921 and the words HALF DOLLAR. UNITED STATES OF AMERICA arcs above; IN GOD WE TRUST in smaller letters between that and the portraits. In the field at the lower right are 10 five-pointed stars, set up in three rows. Located in the lower left field, also arranged in three rows, are 12 five-pointed stars. These 22 stars denote that Alabama was the 22nd state granted admission to the Union.

Until the issuance of the Alabama Centennial half dollars in 1921, no living person had had the honor of being portrayed on coinage of the United States. This representation was not opposed at the time, since it was not in violation of the Act of May 16, 1866. The latter forbids the portrayal of any living person on our currency. Numismatists today argue both sides — that "currency" should refer to any legal tender, including coins; or that the term refers only to paper money.

The 2X2 incused in the center of the right field of the low mintage variety additionally stresses that Alabama was the 22nd state admitted into the Union. Commonly referred to as the "two by two" the letter X does not represent the word "times" or "by." It represents the red X-shaped cross of St. Andrew, patron of Scotland, who was supposedly martyred on such a gibbet. It is also emblematic on the British Union flag, the flag of the Confederate States of America and on the state flag of Alabama.

 Wear will first be observed on Governor Kilby's forehead and earlobe. A slight flatness on his upper ear directly above the lobe is due to striking. Look for a loss of metal, and the unnatural shine where metal has been worn away. Such friction will cause a difference in the texture of the metal. I like to use no more than 10 power to look at the high points of wear. However, be certain you know what you are looking at. You could possibly interpret a flat strike as wear.

Reverse

Appearing is the seal of Alabama, composed of an eagle with raised wings, facing left (at a 9 o'clock position) set on the shield of the United States, holding arrows in its talons and a scroll in its beak bearing the state motto, incused in small letters, HERE WE REST.

STATE OF ALABAMA arcs above; 1819 CENTENNIAL 1919 below. At the 3 o'clock position appears the designer's initials, LGF.

The half dollars which received Congressional authorization in 1920 to commemorate the centennial of 1919 were not minted until 1921. Under the coinage laws at that time, a coin must bear the date of the year in which is was minted. Thus, we can also behold the date of striking (obverse) and the anniversary dates (reverse).

 When grading this issue, first examine this side of the coin. Wear will be most evident on the top of the wing diagonally below the letters ERE of the word HERE in the scroll and in the upper breast area of the eagle.

Origins of the Alabama

Initially, this issue was designated a quarter dollar, but an April 21, 1920, amendment changed the denomination to a half dollar. Mrs. Marie Bankhead Owen, Chairwoman of the Alabama Centennial Commission— appointed by Governor Kilby — informed him that the Committee judges rejected all submitted Alabama coinage designs. The subsequent selection was an obverse depicting the State Capitol, crowning Capitol Hill. The reverse portrayed Monroe and Wilson, presidents during admission and centennial time.

On June 19, 1921, Mrs. Owen submitted new sketches. The obverse depicted the state seal of Alabama, while the reverse depicted Bibb and Kilby. These designs were forwarded by Mint Director Baker to Charles Moore and then to sculptor member of the Commission, James Earl Fraser. He commissioned his wife, Laura Gardin Fraser, to create the models. She was to inform the Commission that the Alabama Committee should be aware of fact of the special 2★4 marking used on the 5,000 Missouri Centennial coins, sold at a premium. Rep. Rainey received this info and forwarded it to Mrs. Owen — who was already aware. The completed models were approved — with the reverse designated the obverse — and submitted to the Mint on Sept. 22, 1921.

According to official records, the Philadelphia Mint struck 6,006 coins in October 1921 with the St. Andrews Cross dividing the figure 2X2 at the back of Governor Kilby's head. In December 1921, an additional 10,008 pieces — presumed to be the 2X2 — plus 54,030 extra specimens of the plain variety were produced (after the 2X2 was removed from the hub).

According to John H. Morris Jr.: "The Alabama halves were sold on Oct. 26, 1921. President Harding, being a Mason, was invited to come to Birmingham to lay the cornerstone at the new Masonic Temple on Oct. 26, 1921. The Alabama halves were sold on that day. It was a holiday here and all the public schools were closed. I went down to the park to hear President Harding speak. After his speech, he walked two blocks to the Masonic Temple to lay the Corner Stone. I was at both places.

"I started collecting coins in 1915, so naturally I had to buy the Alabama half. As I had collected two of each commemorative coins issued up to this date, I had to buy two of these coins. Both coins were the plain variety, not 2X2. These Alabama halves were sold by several banks here and on the main street corners, downtown. They were sold from stalls about four feet square with a shelf on three sides, about three feet from the sidewalk. During the late 1930s when the commemoratives were very popular, I ran an ad in our local newspaper offering to buy the Alabama halves for $1.50 each. I would go to your house to pick them up. I bought 32 at this price and none were the 2X2 type. A friend of mine who worked at a bank here saw my ad and called, telling me the bank had a roll of the Alabama halves in a $10 wrapper. They had to get $20 for them, since they paid $1 each for the roll of 20. I bought the Alabama halves and they were all plain, not 2X2. Having bought two the first day and 52 about 16 years later — and none with 2X2 — they could not have been sold in Birmingham.

Since the plain issue was offered first, according to eyewitnesses who attended the celebration in Birmingham, on October 26, 1921, it would appear Mint records were incorrect and the plain variety was struck first. However, according to Mrs. Owen, Chairwoman of the Alabama Centennial Commission, "the first 5,000 of these coins received showed a St. Andrews cross between two figure '2's,' with the cross being emblematic of the state flag." (The idea of this special mark was previously conveyed to her by Rep. Lilius Rainey.)

It appears that the Commission wanted no more than 5,000 2X2 specimens and that no additional pieces would be produced by the Mint, for whatever reason. Thus, all that was offered for sale on October 26 were the 1,000 "plains" delivered along with the 2X2's!

The Alabama Today

The Alabama plain issue is not at all difficult to locate in EF-AU condition. Pieces will exhibit natural wear. Others will display forms of numismatic abuse, such as some degree of whizzing, polishing, cleaning, etc. Should you collect 2X2 EF-AU or AU specimens, they are available at present, but not in great numbers. Remember, people needed money to live during that depression of 1926-1936. These issues were spent! Many were also kept as pocket pieces, especially the plain issue. Thus, today's low price. Attempt to acquire a specimen flaunting eye appeal with only slight wear on its natural surface. Prefer the 2X2 creation.

Both Alabamas can be located with some effort in grades MS-60 through

MS-63. Values are currently underrated. Acquire for the pure joy of collecting. Pieces grading strict MS-64 are certainly undervalued and not as easily obtained as some believe! Future potential for issue which is almost equally as rare, in MS-60 through MS-64 condition — lies in the "64" state. Grading strictness and eye appeal are the key words to success. You may be offered a most eye-appealing Alabama plain issue that is not too often encountered in MS-64 and higher condition. These beautiful coins possess semi-prooflike fields and frosted devices varying in depth. They will also flaunt what appears to be a scratch or cut in the field behind Kilby's head. Don't be afraid to purchase the coin! In the early stages of striking, the dies clashed. The fields were then polished, creating a blazing new semi P/L surface. However, left behind was that small clash mark in the above mentioned location. Higher graded specimens (MS-64+) can be a most rewarding find! About Uncirculated specimens will challenge the collector to seek them out and appreciate their beauty even in this grade if undoctored.

Alabamas grading MS-64 had better be fully original, be bright or attractively toned and flaunt but a few marks, which can be spread irregularly, in the primary focal areas. Coins grading MS-65 should have no detracting marks in these areas. Primary focal locations especially prone to attack by our numismatic negatives such as slide marks, cuts, bag marks, scratches, etc., are Kilby's cheek, forehead and lower jaw. Then to a lesser degree, Bibb's cheek and forehead. The central part of the reverse eagle can also take a good hit lowering both the specimen's grade and value. For those who can afford MS-65 examples, know that they are virtually equal in rarity, possess an exceptional future an are definitely undervalued. In the loftier grades, the plain is rarer.

Fully struck examples are seldom encountered. Locating specimens with a strongly defined eagle's front and back claw holding the arrows will be almost an impossible task — especially on the plain issue. By strongly defined or struck, I mean seeing some definition on the legs of the eagle, along with slightly defined claws, and arrow shafts. Continuous die wear in this area, during the 2X2 strikings, caused these details to vanish forever. When the same dies were used to strike the Alabama plain issue (without the 2X2), the condition was not remedied. It will only be those very early struck 2X2 coins which possess the stronger strikes. Thus the coin's reverse generally possesses the poor strike — which can be grade and value lowering. On occassion, a planchet split may be seen on the coin's edge, due to a flaw in the design and manufacture of the dies. This split can lower a coin's value.

These original Mint State specimens for both creations will display a luster ranging from a bright satiny (which is usually not the norm) to medium to a dull satiny (usually the norm). Should they be toned, be certain the coin's original luster is visible beneath this veil, for it might be hiding a surface that possesses no luster because it was improperly cleaned and now had toned with time or is a toned About Uncirculated coin. Permanent destruction was caused because someone believed they could change this minted finish which accompanies most of the issue, from satiny to blazing-amazing! Needless to say, it didn't work.

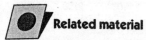 **Related material**

No original distributing holders or mailers have surfaced to date.

1922
Grant Memorial

Location of star,
both denominations

Reason for issue: The centenary of the birth of General Ulysses S. Grant,
late president of the United States.

Authorized per Act of February 2, 1922: 250,000 half dollars; 10,000 gold
dollars.

Official sale price: 1922 ★ half dollar: $1 (later $1.50)
1922 No ★ half dollar: $1 (later $0.75)
1922 ★ $1: $3.50
1922 No ★ $1: $3

Production figures

Date	Business Strikes	Assay Coins	Proofs	Melted	Net Mintage
1922 ★ 50¢	5,006	6	4?	750	4,250
1922 50¢	95,055	55	4?	27,650	67,350
1922 ★ $1	5,016	16	4?	0	5,000
1922 $1	5,000	0	4?	0	5,000

Current market values

	EF-40	AU-50	MS-60	MS-63	MS-64	MS-65
1922 ★ 50¢	325.	485.	1050.	2500.	3650.	9500.
1922 50¢	53.50	70.00	95.00	200.	385.	1350.
1922 ★ $1	850.	1075.	1400.	2200.	2800.	3250.
1922 $1	800.	1000.	1325.	2100.	2750.	3100.

Designs by Laura Gardin Fraser

Obverse

Both the gold and silver issues portray the bust of General Ulysses S. Grant, adapted from a photo by Matthew Brady, in uniform, facing right. Located in the left field and right field respectively is his name ULYSSES S. GRANT. Situated below the bust are the anniversary dates 1822-1922. UNITED STATES OF AMERICA arcs above; HALF DOLLAR or ONE DOLLAR below. A small letter G, representing the artist's maiden name, was placed between the dates by the Mint, as was previously done in other locations with the Columbian and the Pilgrim issues. Located in the right field above the N of GRANT on the variety is the incused five pointed star. The only difference in design between the issues is the word HALF and ONE indicating the denomination.

Wear first occurs on General Grant's cheekbone. Coin's rim does little to protect this area which is virtually equal in height. The slightest abuse will cause friction. Look for a difference in metal texture, in this location. Portrait is the primary focal area. Marks and negatives are detrimental to value and grade in this location. Prime target for whizzing and other forms of doctoring.

Reverse

Both the gold and silver issues depict a fenced clapboard house symbolic of the house where Grant lived as a boy in Georgetown, Ohio. Maple trees are present in the coin's field, E PLURIBUS UNUM to the left and IN GOD WE TRUST above. This issue designed by Laura Gardin Fraser (who also created the Alabama, Fort Vancouver and Oregon Trail obverse) makes no reference to a Grant memorial. She permits the design itself to tell the story. Her maiden initial (G) was most likely used by the Mint, since her husband's initial (F) was placed on the Indian Head ("Buffalo") 5-cent piece, which was also being produced that year.

Issue's rim does an excellent job of protecting the first areas to display wear. This is the central section of leaves located directly above the second and third tree trunks from the left. If this coin is to display wear, it will occur on the obverse.

Origins of the Grant Coins

These coins were struck at the Philadelphia Mint during March 1922. The first 5,000 gold coins (plus 16 for assay purposes) were struck with the "star." After the star was removed, 5,000 gold dollars were struck. With the gold production completed, 5,006 silver half dollars were produced with the star. Then with the star removed 95,055 plain Grants were coined.

Does the incused star have any significance? Had Grant been a one-star general, such would have been appropriate. However, Grant's rank in the Union Army requires three additional stars. Unfortunately, the star bears no significance, as does the incused 2X2 on the Alabama variety and the 2★4 on the Missouri variety, other than satisfying the Grant Centenary Memorial Commission.

All coins were offered for sale in April 1922, with the silver half dollars selling at $1.00 each, and the plain gold dollars selling at $3.00 each. The star variety sold for $3.50. No gold coins were returned to the Mint. When silver sales, which were previously excellent, finally came to a standstill, it was decided by the Commission to offer approximately 29,000 specimens of the plain variety at 75 cents each in lots of 10 or more coins. About 800 unsold "with star" specimens were offered for sale at $1.25 each.

There were few buyers, thus 27,650 plain specimens were returned, along with 750 "stars," to the Mint and melted. This leaves us with a present day mintage of 67,350 "Grant plains" and only 4,250 Grant "with star" specimens.

The Grant Half Dollars Today

The Grant plain or No Star half dollar is quite available in EF-AU condition. I suggest selecting naturally worn, undoctored pieces without detracting surface cuts, if acquisition is desired. Majority of this creation resides in the MS-60 through MS-63 state and to a lesser degree, in strict MS-64 condition. Surface attractiveness should be your key when buying this commem. Future potential begins at the MS-64+ level. Any grade less should be acquired for the pure joy of collecting. Eye appealing MS-65 and loftier rated specimens are not that easily located.

Luster will range from blazing frosty (not the norm), to dull frosty, displaying that powdery look. Strike rarely presents a problem for this issue. The detail in Grant's hair, beginning from the temple area and going inward above the ear about sixty percent toward the back of the head will be faintly seen. This was caused by the wearing of the obverse dies in that area as the coins were being struck, since little detail was present to begin with. (The same is not true for the small gold dollars, for all hair details is present in the aforementioned area.) The above mentioned is accepted as characteristic for the issue.

The rarer Grant star issue which is a very popular collector coin can be obtained in EF-AU condition. Unfortunately, most of the encountered pieces will display some form of surface doctoring whose objective is to hide some degree of surface wear or bag marks or slide marks, etc. It is truly a very scarce coin in grades MS-60 through MS-64 and a rare coin in the loftier classifications. This is the result of much numismatic abuse. Luster will range from semi-prooflike to blazing lustrous (both not the norm) to dull satiny. It isn't too often that one encounters blazing lustrous pieces. Strike will pose no problem for the issue. Those early specimens with no die clash marks will show fine hair detail in the center of Grant's head, while coinage displaying the clash mark will not. Approximately a few dozen were created before the dies clashed. Creation was produced from perfect, clashed, and lapped dies. Those raised lines which can be observed in the obverse field are die polishing marks. If cut into this surface, they are detracting scratches and lower the coin's value.

 ### Detecting counterfeits

In 1935, when the Grant With Star issue was selling for $65 and the Grant Plain for $3.50, a dentist decided to purchase a quantity of the less expensive issue and personally incused his own star. Since we cannot appreciate his effort in attempting to make more Grant With Star specimens — which was the highest priced commemorative of all U.S. commemorative issues in 1935 — available to collectors and investors, we must be able to distinguish between his "addition" and the Philadelphia Mint's "edition."

The following distinguishing characteristics will help you determine whether the star is genuine:

A) A most obvious clash mark will be present around Grant's chin and in the area of his necktie and by the letter G of GRANT just right of his tie. Virtually all of the genuine issue will display these characteristics.

B) Those few much rarer specimens produced before the dies clashed will not flaunt the said clash marks. They will reveal a small raised pimple or lump of metal just within the star located just below its nine o'clock location. Such can also be seen on the clashed die variety.

C) The star is located above the letter N and not the letter A of GRANT, as seen on some altered pieces.

 **Related material**

To date, original mailing holders accompanied by stamped envelopes have yet to surface.

The Grant Gold Dollars Today

Specimens of either issue residing in the EF-AU state are not abundant. Some form of numismatic abuse has caused their downfall. Based on their history, Grant golds grading from MS-60 through MS-63 (no star or star variety) should only be considered for the pure joy of collecting. The plain is a bit rarer in these grades. Future value definitely lies in these gold disks strictly grading MS-64 and better. The No Star issue will be more difficult to acquire in MS-65 and higher levels. Present value spread does not reflect this situation.

 Detecting counterfeits

Die struck counterfeits do exist. The telltale signs we should look for are file marks between UNITED and the rim, and die scratches above and between the "OF" as well as the "A" in OF AMERICA, on the reverse. Also a number of spikes will angle into the field from the P of PLURIBUS half way up to the I of IN. Cast fakes display a blurry or dull powdery appearance.

 **Related material**

To date, original mailing holders accompanied by stamped envelopes have yet to surface.

1923
Monroe Doctrine Centennial

Reason for issue: The 100th anniversary of the enunciation or announcing of the Monroe Doctrine.

Authorized per Act of January 24, 1923: 300,000.

Official sale price: $1

Production figures

Date	Business Strikes	Assay Coins	Proofs	Melted	Net Mintage
1923-S	274,000	77	4?	0	274,000

Current market values

	EF-40	AU-50	MS-60	MS-63	MS-64	MS-65
1923-S	26.50	32.50	37.50	115.	625.	3750.

Designs by Chester Beach
Obverse

Depicted are the accolated busts of James Monroe, fifth president, and John Quincy Adams, sixth president. Their names are seen directly below separated by two links. UNITED STATES OF AMERICA arcs above; HALF DOLLAR below. IN GOD WE TRUST is in the left field just below Monroe's chin. Date 1923 is to the right of Adams, with Mint mark "S" directly below the date.

 A metal loss will first occur on the cheek of John Quincy Adams. His portrait is usually a target for the whizzing specialists in their attempt to hide wear or surface negatives.

Reverse

A representation of the Western Hemisphere is depicted as two female figures. North America, holding a horn of plenty, is presenting South America what appears to be a twig. Ocean currents are represented by faint lines in the field. Centennial dates 1823-1923 are flanked by a scroll and quill pen which is symbolic of the Monroe Doctrine manuscripts. Also shown are the words MONROE DOCTRINE CENTENNIAL. At the four o'clock position is the artist's circular monogram CB. In the lower border are the words LOS ANGELES, the celebration location. The design was copied from Ralph Beck's 1901 Pan-American (Buffalo,

N.Y.) Exposition medal that he created in 1899 and copyrighted. His claim of plagiarism on July 23, 1923, fell on deaf ears from James Earle Fraser and the Mint. No lawsuit was initiated, since the design was used in different contexts during and after the Expo, by steamship and other major companies taking on the import and export trade.

 A loss of surface luster, then metal loss will first be noticed on the arm of Miss North America.

Origins of the Monroe

The motion picture industry had its share of bad press via some iniquitous events, before 1923. To help clean up the act, a public film show was organized. The American Historical Revue and Motion Picture Historical Exposition became a reality. Organization was sponsored by the Motion Picture Industry. When the mental light bulbs lit, the idea by some unknown individuals to have a commemorative coin struck as a revenue and publicity tie-in was set in motion. Political help was required. To their aid came not some movie star, but Rep. Walter F. Lineberger (R-CA). He introduced a bill which attempted to interpret how Monroe's declaration supposedly prevented England, France and Russia from striving to acquire California from Mexico. (Truthfully, we lacked the power as a nation to enforce the Doctrine.) Therefore, the event should be commemorated via commemorative coin. Despite some opposition, the bill became law. The Los Angeles clearing house, which was an association of local banks, received 274,000 commemorative halves of the 300,000-coin authorization from the San Francisco Mint. The coins were produced during the months of May and June 1923, along with 77 coins for assay purposes. Approximately 27,000 coins were sold at double face value through the banks and mail, for the most part, and at the Exposition. When sales came to a dead stop about four months later, the word "Cut!" was heard. The balance on hand was released into circulation.

The Monroe Today

This issue is quite abundant in EF-AU condition. Attempt to locate an attractive natural specimen. Readily available up to MS-63 condition. Future lies in MS-64 eye appealing coinage. Definitely in the higher grades if funds are available. Not as abundant as believed in MS-64+ condition!

Luster will range from blazing frosty, to dull frosty. Due to the reverse design, surface brightness may not be equal in flash. Issue was created in low relief. However, strike can affect grade and value. At times, reverse design be too soft or flat, lacking its limited face and head definition. Thus, should your amazing coin lack the aforementioned, expect it to grade no higher than MS-64. Detracting marks, such as fine hairline scratches, digs, cuts, etc., do a job, especially on this coin's smooth obverse surface. Primary focal areas are the portraits, especially Adams' face and the reverse continents and fields.

 **Related material**

The issue was distributed in a small imprinted white envelope (which could be easily duplicated today) as well as in unprinted white envelopes. The coin should be of first importance, as the envelopes carry little or no premium value.

1924
Huguenot-Walloon
Tercentenary

Reason for issue: 300th anniversary of the settling of New Netherland, the middle states, in 1624 by Walloon, French and Belgian Huguenots, under the Dutch West India Company.

Authorized per Act of February 26, 1923: 300,000

Official sale price: $1 ($1.50 plus 2¢ postage in 1929).

Production figures

Date	Business Strikes	Assay Coins	Proofs	Melted	Net Mintage
1924	142,000	80	4?	0	142,000

Current market values

	EF-40	AU-50	MS-60	MS-63	MS-64	MS-65
1924	55.00	70.00	77.50	105.	275.	725.

Designs by George T. Morgan (approval and modifications by James Earle Fraser)

Obverse

Portrayed are the accolated busts of two Protestant leaders of the Reformation, which occurred during the 16th century. Admiral Gaspard de Coligny of France and William the Silent of the Netherlands, whose names appear below their respective busts, are seen facing right and wearing hats of their period. The Admiral has the letter "M" incused on his shoulder, which represents the surname of the designer, George T. Morgan. Around the lower border of this issue, we can note the words HUGUENOT HALF DOLLAR. UNITED STATES OF AMERICA arcs above; IN GOD WE TRUST is in four lines in the right field, in front of William the Silent's nose.

A loss of metal will first be observed on the cheekbone, eyebrow and mustache of Admiral Coligny. Especially look for doctoring in the form of whizzing, light buffing, etc., on his image.

Reverse

Depicted is the ship *Nieuw Nederlandt* sailing to the left. Above the ship is the inscription HUGUENOT-WALLOON TERCENTENARY, while below the vessel around the bottom border is the inscription: FOUNDING OF NEW NETHERLAND. Anniversary date 1624 is in the left field, 1924 in the right.

The coin's rim does an excellent job of protecting the shallower relief of the *Nieuw Nederland*. When wear makes itself known, it will begin on the center of the main mast, crow's nest and rear supporting sail pole.

Origins of the Huguenot-Walloon

This particular half dollar was supposed to commemorate an event. It does not! Instead, it portrays two Protestant leaders of the Reformation who had really nothing to do "physically" with the founding of New Netherland, since both men departed this earthly plane several decades before any conception of the Dutch West India Company (formed in 1621) and its colony of "Nieu Nederland," became a reality. Since it is known that both men were indirectly connected with the 1624 founding, it may be safe to assume that their relationship with such was simply spiritual in nature.

This coin also has the distinction of being promoted by the Federal Council of Churches of Christ in America through the Huguenot-Walloon New Netherland Commission. American Numismatic Association President Moritz Wormser acted as its adviser of sales promotion, etc. Unfortunately, several groups became disturbed and looked upon the issue as a carrier of religious misinformation and thus un-American in nature.

The term Huguenot is a sobriquet or nickname given to the French Protestants who studied the teachings of John Calvin, while the term Walloon refers to French people who resided in southern Belgium.

During the months of February and April 1924, the Philadelphia Mint struck 142,080 pieces of the Huguenot-Walloon Tercentenary half dollars. These coins were later distributed through the Fifth National Bank of New York, which paid the Treasury fifty cents for each piece and offered them for sale at $1.00 per coin, as well as other sources. According to Rev. John Bear Stoudt, the Commission's director, 44,000 coins were sold by April 1, 1924. Of the total mintage, 87,080 coins were sold to the public, leaving a total of 55,000 unsold half dollars. They were returned to the Mint to be melted, but for some reason they were placed into circulation! Could it be that since this commemorative 50-cent piece was the only U.S. half dollar struck in 1924, someone in the Treasury Department said, "let the collectors enjoy the coin" at face value?

The Huguenot-Walloon Today

The issue is not at all difficult to find in EF-AU condition. Simply beware of those new-looking pieces whose portraits have been doctored to hide metal loss. The bulk of the production resides in MS-60 through MS-64 condition. The difference in value up to MS-63 status is minute. Collectors should zero in on at least an eye appealing, higher graded original coin, unless all that is needed is a representative example. The coin is not scarce even in MS-64 condition. Bag marks and other surface negatives keep many glamorous looking coins from attaining higher grades. Astute collectors attempt to procure flashy attractive MS-64+ coinage. Future gains lie in this and the loftier states. Primary focal areas are the obverse portraits and reverse ship. Luster will range from brilliant frosty to dull frosty. The latter will display a die polishing mark in the upper reverse field at the 11 o'clock position. A number of specimens will show what appears to be a damage or scratches on Coligny's cheek. It's actually a clash mark resembling the letter V with an additional vertical bar to the right. Strike will rarely affect the issue's value or grade. Slight die doubling can sometimes be observed on the letters HUG of HUGUENOT on the reverse.

 **Related material**

No official distribution holders with accompanying mailing envelopes have surfaced to date. I have only seen a brochure depicting a sketch of a memorial stone and photo of the first coin struck being presented to President Coolidge. The brochure has sold between $75 and $150.

1925
Lexington-Concord Sesquicentennial

Reason for issue: To commemorate the 150th anniversary of the battle of Lexington and Concord.

Authorized per Act of January 14, 1925: 300,000.

Official sale price: $1

Production figures

Date	Business Strikes	Assay Coins	Proofs	Melted	Net Mintage
1925	162,000	99	4?	86	161,914

Current market values

	EF-40	AU-50	MS-60	MS-63	MS-64	MS-65
1925	47.50	57.50	70.00	160.	300.	1100.

Designs by Chester Beach

Obverse

Depicted is the statue of the famous Minuteman, seen holding a musket. In lower right field is a plow with his coat hanging from the handles. Such was adapted from Daniel Chester French's *Grand Concord Man* statue. Inscriptions UNITED STATES OF AMERICA and PATRIOT HALF DOLLAR separated by two decorative stars are seen in the outer field. In the lower left field are the words CONCORD MINUTE-MAN, IN GOD WE TRUST in the upper right field.

Metal loss will first be visible on the thigh of the volunteer soldier, adjacent to his rifle. Examine high points for some form of doctoring.

Reverse

Portrayed is the Old Belfry at Lexington, Massachusetts, which was a hollow structure housing the bell which sounded the call to arms. It was destroyed in 1909. Beneath are the words OLD BELFRY, LEXINGTON, with two triangles at the sides. Around the outer border is the inscription LEXINGTON-CONCORD SESQUICENTENNIAL and anniversary dates 1775-1925.

 Examine lower corner of the wooden structure, directly above the R in BELFRY and parallel to the left door frame for that metal loss, flaunting its grayish white appearance. Coin's rim is virtually equal in height with the higher area of its design. At the slightest abuse, wear becomes noticeable. Be certain that beneath the "luster loss" is actually metal loss.

Origins of the Lexington

The Philadelphia Mint produced 162,000 coins of this design during the months of May and June 1925. Only 86 were returned to the Mint to be melted. Celebrations occurred between April 18th and 20th, during which 38,000+ and 20,000+ specimens were sold in Lexington and Concord respectively.

The Lexington Today

The issue is abundant in EF-AU condition, since many pieces were treated as souvenirs. Little value spread exists between the latter circulated material and specimens grading MS-63. The MS-64 category is worth double the MS-63 classification. Future of the issue resides in eye appealing specimens grading MS-64+! The Lexington is not that easy of a coin to obtain in strict MS-65 condition. No sign of wear should be present on the thigh of the Minuteman, nor on the left corner section of the Old Belfry to the left of the door. I have seen pieces showing some metal loss graded MS-65!

Primary focal areas are the soldier and hollow wooden structure. However, a dig or reed mark in the surrounding fields can easily cause a value downgrade. Same for a hairline scratch! Luster will range from semi-prooflike to brilliant frosty to dull frosty. Strike rarely causes a loss in grade or value. Due to slight die wear, this volunteer soldier from the waste up can display soft design definition.

 **Related material**

The Lexington was distributed in a small wooden box with a sliding top. The box bears a blue ink stamping of the Minuteman statue plus the anniversary dates. The Old Belfry resides on the bottom section of the most common commemorative coin holder. Often a coin possessing some degree of wear which is hidden by dark toning accompanies the pine box. Asking price is usually twice as much as the item is worth. The value should be based on grade and eye appeal of the coin, as well as the condition of the holder. Exceptions must be made if the commemorative holder for the issue is seldom encountered. Unofficial copies of the Lexington box exist, manufactured from a different type of wood! Also, one of the anniversary dates, 1775 or 1925, will be lightly stamped on, but not into, the top cover. Caveat is to know the features of pine. Several banks distributed the issue in their imprinted boxes, as well as flamboyant mailing envelopes, which are not often seen.

The wooden boxes may be valued at $20 to $50 without the coin.

1925
Stone Mountain Memorial

Reason for issue: To commemorate the commencement, on June 18, 1923, of the work of the carving on Stone Mountain in the state of Georgia, which was the inspiration of their sons and daughters and grandsons and granddaughters in the Spanish-American and World Wars, and in memory of President Warren G. Harding, in whose administration the work was begun.

Authorized per Act of March 17, 1924: 5,000,000.

Official sale price: $1

Production figures

Date	Business Strikes	Assay Coins	Proofs	Melted	Net Mintage
1925	2,310,000	4,709	4	1,000,000	1,310,000

Current market values

	EF-40	AU-50	MS-60	MS-63	MS-64	MS-65
1925	29.50	35.00	42.50	52.50	72.50	200.

Designs by Gutzon Borglum

Obverse

Depicted are the equestrian figures of Gen. Thomas J. ("Stonewall") Jackson and Gen. Robert E. Lee wearing the hat of a Confederate high ranking officer. Located in the lower left field are the words STONE MOUNTAIN and the date of issue 1925. There are 13 stars located in the upper field, each symbolizing those Southern states which had ordinances of secession. Each state, by the way, is also represented by a star on the Confederate flag. The motto IN GOD WE TRUST is seen in the upper border. Located at the extreme right border near the horse's tail are the designer's incused initials G.B. Gutzon Borglum, the famous American sculptor who created the Mount Rushmore carvings, was commissioned for the actual carving of Stone Mountain in northwest Georgia, but his plans were never fully carried out. A dispute arose between the sculptor and the Commission and Borglum was dismissed. August Lukeman was hired to complete the project.

Wear will first occur on the thigh and elbow of General Lee.

Reverse

Portrayed is an eagle with wings stretched, standing on a mountain crag. In the center left field is the inscription MEMORIAL TO THE VALOR OF THE SOLDIER OF THE SOUTH. UNITED STATES OF AMERICA arcs above; HALF DOLLAR below. E PLURIBUS UNUM in small letters is in the upper left; LIBERTY is above HALF DOLLAR. There are also present 35 dimly visible stars on the field of this coin, and not 34 stars which are supposed to represent the number of states in the Union before the Civil War.

A metal loss will first be observed on the breast of the eagle.

Origins of the Stone Mountain

The Philadelphia Mint struck 2,310,000 Stone Mountain 50-cent pieces from January through March 1925, as well as 4,709 coins for assay purposes. That's the largest number ever produced to date to determine a coin's proper metallic composition. The first 1000 pieces were produced Jan. 21, 1924, the 101st birthday of "Stonewall" Jackson. Its approved authorization was a maximum coinage figure of 5,000,000. However, this issue encountered a great deal of flak from Northerners who believed a United States coin should not honor only previous leaders of the South of an era when "brother fought against brother." To pacify the North, the phrase "and in memory of Warren G. Harding, President of the United States of America in whose administration the work was begun," was added to the bill. In fact, the bust of Mr. Harding was being debated as the main obverse design. However, there is no reference made to Harding on this issue. A total of nine changes were made to the obverse die design, one of which removed the inscription honoring Harding.

The coins were distributed through the Stone Mountain Confederate Monumental Association at $1.00 each. Several huge institutions, such as the Baltimore and Ohio Railroad, Southern Fireman's Fund Insurance Company, the Atlanta Coca-Cola Bottling Company and many banks, purchased huge quantities of these commemorative half dollars at the issue price and distributed them at face value!

Counterstamped coins

A number of Stone Mountain half dollars were counterstamped with a numeral and state name which was abbreviated. Dr. Charles R. Stearns of Lilburn, Ga., an expert in this area, has presented me with the following valuable information to use in this work.

A great distribution campaign extending from Virginia to Texas was initiated to sell the Stone Mountain issue at $1.00 each. The governors of the States of Virginia, South Carolina, Georgia, Florida, Alabama, Mississippi, Louisiana, Texas, Oklahoma, Arkansas, Kentucky and Tennessee served as campaign chairmen. (North Carolina joined the program later.) Each governor assumed a sales quota based upon population and bank deposits. The "Great Harvest Campaign," as it was called, probably would have succeeded had it not been for Borglum's abandonment of the carving project in March 1925. His subsequent arrest and ultimate departure provided bad publicity and put a heavy damper on the fund-raising project.

The Harvest Campaign administrators devised a plan to counterstamp some Stone Mountain half dollars with numbers and letters to produce unique pieces. Lettering styles indicate there was one basic source, most probably the Stone Mountain Memorial Association, for nearly all the counterstamped coins. For example all A's are square topped; periods were generally rectangular; and all 2's are square based.

The most common group are described at the "State and Number" coins. An abbreviation of the state name and a serial number have been added to the coin. There is some apparent continuity of the serial numbers within a given state, but some numbers appear more than once (Tenn. 102; Okla. 358; Va. 202). Three of this variety of coin are known to have had certificates of ownership issued when they were sold. The counterstamped pieces were meant to be sold at public auction to raise additional funds above the normal profit level. A Dec. 10, 1925, letter from J. Wilson Gibbs Jr., executive secretary in charge of South Carolina auction coins, to Mrs. R.E. Shannon of Blastock, S.C., give some insight into the plan. Mr. Gibbs reported that in South Carolina the auction prices varied from $10 to $110 with an average price of $23 realized. He recommended that a little speech be given prior to the coin being offered and thought that special mention might be made to the fact that a similar coin brought $1,300 in Bradenton, Fla. This Blastock, S.C., coin is identified with counterstamps "S.C." and "109." One specimen of this type of state and number counterstamp is known with the number "42" and no state name; it appeared in Florida a few years ago.

Close examination of "Texas 182" and "Texas 242" yielded the letters FLA under the EXA of TEXAS. This indicated that the demand in Florida was not as great as first intended and that the coins were stamped a second time to satisfy the demand in Texas.

Another type of counterstamped coin differs from this first group in that the letters "S.L." also appear. These letters are hypothesized to stand for "State Legislature." It has been suggested that these coins were presented to prominent legislatures to promote the Harvest Campaign. A Florida piece is known stamped "G.L." which might be an error or stand for "General Legislature." Unfortunately, none of these coins has been traced back to its original owner to prove the truth of this hypothesis.

A third type of counterstamped coin is exemplified by some of the Tennessee coins. The letters "U.D.C." designating the United Daughters of the Confederacy and very high serial numbers are found. These higher serial numbers have been suggested to be a membership or chapter number of the U.D.C.

The fourth and last group of counterstamp coins is the "N" series. Only three specimens are accounted for at this time. "N-6" came from the estate of a Nashville bank employee in 1925. This series differs markedly from all the other coins. The coins are much more deeply stamped. The letters are serif and much heavier in style.

A fortunate collector can sometimes acquire these counterstamped coins as mutilated coins. Unfortunately the pieces can be easily manufactured by anyone with a tool and die punch set. One would be well advised to avoid purchasing a counterstamped coin unless one knows the source as far back as the original purchaser or the coin is accompanied by an original certificate. *Caveat emptor* definitely applies here.

With several counterstamped coins recently coming on the market, there have been several articles written about them and collectors are hoping to cherrypick them.

However, most of the counterstamped coins were purchased by non-collectors who were supporting a cause. To pay the premium of the auction price for the most part, they had to be the financially comfortable citizens of their time. At this time, 45-50 years after the sales campaign, many of these individuals have passed away and their estates are coming up for settlement. For those who were non-collectors, the coins probably rattled in a dresser drawer or served as a pocket piece as a memento of the past. Most of the counterstamped coins are not Uncirculated or any grade even approaching that. For the next decade or so, they probably will continue to appear with some regularity and then slowly dry up in supply as these estates are dispersed.

Thus, we may attach no great value to it in that respect. However, when we speak of an officially documented piece with a number located between 1 and 50, we are speaking of an item with a different numismatic vein. A documented specimen of the 29th Stone Mountain struck by the Philadelphia Mint with documentation sold for $1,300 in 1937! What about the first piece struck? It was presented to President Coolidge mounted on a plate of gold. The second was presented to Andrew W. Mellon, Secretary of the Treasury. One million coins were returned to the Mint by the Association, leaving us with a total mintage figure of 1,314,000. That's still a lot of coins.

The Stone Mountain Today

This issue which Borglum referred to as the Federal Confederate or Memorial half dollar is abundant in EF-AU condition. Its availability makes a nice gift for some youngster or other individual. Who knows, it might even generate interest about our wonderful world of numismatics. Value spread is insignificant between grades MS-60 and MS-64 condition. Think MS-64, if funds allow. Our Stone Mountain half dollar will not be difficult to locate in grades up to MS-65. Attempt to procure the flashier, eye appealing coin. Acquire only for the joy of collecting. Future begins in the loftier grades.

Luster will range from blazing frosty, to frosty to dull frosty. A weakness of strike on General Lee's thigh and reverse eagle's breast can lower a coin's grade-value. However, the supply is so plentiful that a strongly struck specimen can be obtained with little challenge. Your primary focal areas are the obverse and reverse devices. Bag marks, slide marks and other elements of numismatic abuse do a good job of attacking the said locations as well as their surrounding fields. Over the last five years, I have examined more than 1,000 Stone Mountains, struck from doubled dies. I would not label them even scarce. They are fun to own for the joy of collecting. However, strictly graded MS-66, they can add more value to a specimen, because so few, if any, might be encapsulated.

 **Related material**

Some organizations sold the coins at a premium price in wooden boxes (similar to the Lexington issuing box) whose slide-off top possessed a large paste-on foil silver star (15/16") with the outline of a thin printed blue star within. Original boxes with the foil star may be valued in the $100 to $350 range, depending on the coin's condition.

Other coins were sold in a cellophane coin envelope stapled to a distributing holder which listed the name of the United Daughters of the Confederacy and depicted a Confederate flag in color.

The item was housed in the Citizens and Southern National Bank envelope. Another was distributed in a white cardboard Christmas card (57/16" X 37/16") with a coin cut-out covered on both sides by white gummed tape. Imprinted in black ink, one side notes that the coin is an emblem of peace and good will between the people of the North and the South, Complements of ___, Address_____ with Christmas Greetings. The other side depicts the gigantic Stone Mountain frieze with a circular photo of Augustus Lukeman. This was placed in an envelope with the address STONE MOUNTAIN MEMORIAL ASSOCIATION, 900 SOUTHERN BUILDING, WASHINGTON, D.C.

The Retail Credit Company distributed this creation in a cardboard holder with circular insert for one coin. Black imprinting described the issue, occasion, etc., on both sides. It was then placed inside a sheet of heavy glossy paper, folded in thirds. Within is pictured Stone Mountain before and after (superimposed). The outer section notes it was given with compliments by the above company.

Additional coins were issued by the *Atlanta Journal* in a cardboard holder insert for one coin. Black imprinting discusses the coin as a token of friendship and pledge of a united country etc. The reverse pictures Stone Mountain, the largest body of granite in the world, before the carving. Beneath is a short description of what is to come. (By the way, a chip of granite from General Lee's figure was wrapped in tissue paper, placed in a small cardboard box and sold by the association as a souvenir, today worth $20 to $30.) The issue was also distributed in a gold colored box with cardboard inner support and circular cut-out for one coin, with black imprinting on the cover. Many other unofficial distributing holders were issued by banks and various other businesses.

Holders other than the foil-star box may be valued in the $100 to $350+ range, depending on the coin's condition.

A chip off the big block

1925
California Diamond Jubilee

Reason for issue: To commemorate the 75th anniversary of the admission of the state of California into the Union.
Authorized per Act of February 24, 1925: 300,000.
Official sale price: $1

Production figures

Date	Business Strikes	Assay Coins	Proofs	Melted	Net Mintage
1925-S	150,000	200	4?	63,606	86,394

Current market values

	EF-40	AU-50	MS-60	MS-63	MS-64	MS-65
1925-S	80.00	90.00	110.	200.	400.	950.

Designs by Joseph Mora

Obverse

Portrayed is a prospector kneeling to the left, working with a gold miner's pan, in his quest for gold. This portrayal symbolizes the Gold Rush spirit, as well as California's tremendous growth which took place after the discovery of gold. Above the figure, who appears to be looking at IN GOD WE TRUST in the left field, is the word LIBERTY. Below are the words CALIFORNIA DIAMOND JUBILEE and the date of issue, 1925.

 A metal loss, indicated by a grayish-white metal texture can first be observed on the 49er's upper shirt sleeve folds. Primary focal location is a target for the "coin doctors."

Reverse

Depicted is a grizzly bear facing left, symbolic of California's independence from Mexico. Above the bear is E PLURIBUS UNUM. Below is UNITED STATES OF AMERICA. The "S" Mint mark appears at the six o'clock position, below the D in HALF DOLLAR.

Due to a slightly higher reverse design, the slightest abuse will first cause a loss of high point metal or wear on the bear's shoulder. Drop imaginary lines down from the letters "LU" of PLURIBUS. Then draw a line about three times the width of the bear's ear. Where they intersect is the location you inspect. Also a primary focal location for doctoring!

Origins of the California

One of my favorite numismatic works of art was created by Jo Mora. This local sculptor was selected by the Citizens Committee in charge of the 75th anniversary celebrations, held in San Francisco in September 1925. His initial sketches were proudly forwarded by Chairman Angelo J. Rossi to Mint Director Grant on May 4, 1925, and were eventually received by sculptor member of the Commission of Fine Arts James Earle Fraser. Unfortunately, Fraser was not impressed, labeling the presented drawings as "inexperienced and amateurish."

He did suggest some improvements, but truly believed the work should be done by a competent medalist, such as Chester Beach or Robert Aitken (creators of other commemorative coinage).

Upon arrival of the criticism, the Jubilee Committee was unawed. The recommended changes were ignored, while the recommended medalist (Aitken) was rejected because of his fee. (It appears these people had the right political pull and would obtain what they wanted.) The design was accepted by Commission members Taft and Ayres. Nevertheless, Louis Ayres did suggest "In God We Trust be placed in another position, where it does not seem as if the '49ers were frying it in oil." Thanks, but no thanks, Louis. The location remained as is!

Chairman Rossi craved bringing into being a coin commemorating the California Jubilee. Rep. John Raker (D-CA) wanted to help make this objective a reality. Nevertheless, the Bureau of the Mint was directly opposed to additional keepsake production. In fact, it prejudiced the thinking of Rep. Albert H. Vestal of the House Coinage Committee to share in its credence. On Jan. 9, 1925, Senators Dale and Green (R-VT) introduced a bill calling for the creation of a Vermont gold dollar and 50-cent piece. By Jan. 24, it was decided to eliminate the larger denomination. On February 16, Rep. Raker offered to amend their bill further, by authorizing the California souvenir coin. This bill was further amended by Rep. Albert Johnson (R-WA), attempting to authorize production of the Fort Vancouver coinage. Authorization was signed by President Coolidge, whose boyhood home is located at Plymouth Notch, Vermont! Thus, we have the first instance within the series where an authorizing Act (Public Law No. 452-68) covered more than one issue.

Between August 12 and 26, 1925, 150,200 pieces of the California Diamond Jubilee issue were produced at the San Francisco Mint. They were offered for sale at $1.00 each by the San Francisco Clearing House Association and the Los Angeles Clearing House Association.

Unfortunately, 63,606 pieces were returned to the Mint and destroyed. Chairman Rossi had requested that the San Francisco Mint produce 100 special presentation pieces. He got his wish. One pair of dies had its fields polished to what we might label a bright, chrome-like reflectivity for the special striking, which took place on August 12, 1925. (They were not brilliant or satin finish Proofs, just business strike presentation coins!)

The California Today

A large percentage of this issue resides between the EF-AU and MS-62+ category. Today's circulated specimens were used as pocket pieces, or were lightly polished or cleaned to look bright and shiny. Another circumstance which removed many coins from the Mint State category is the issue's high relief. The bear's shoulder and the miner's upper shirt sleeve folds — the high points — are virtually as high as the protective rim. Any slight abuse will cause a rub or metal loss. Such coins can be lightly whizzed in these locations to dupe the unknowledgeable.

Most MS-60 through low end MS-63 specimens observed cannot be labeled pulchritudinous wonders. Their original beauty is downgraded by numismatic negatives such as bag marks, field abrasions, slide marks, reed marks, over dipping, etc. Pay close attention to the miner's back and shoulder, as well as the bear's shoulder or actual front left leg and central portion of his body, the issue's primary focal areas. All in combination or individually darken the future of such pieces. However, to the young at heart, or to the collector with limited funds or to the young numismatist, the thrill of ownership can register an MS-68 on the enjoyment meter. Such pleasure is too precious to bear a price tag.

Coins grading MS-64, which can appear to grade MS-65 or better to the non-professional, can be located with some effort. Yet those grading MS-64+ can be labeled somewhat elusive. These (for the most part) were the disks graded MS-65 in the past. They have been downgraded due to numismatic negatives which were once acceptable but are no longer. As the spread increases, expect buyers to also set their acquisition sights on this grade, creating excellent price increases. The trick is to obtain an MS-64+ specimen at MS-64 price levels.

Strictly graded MS-65 Jubilees can be labeled elusive. MS-66 and MS-67 coins are not at all easily located. Therefore, in the MS-64+ category and higher, expect exceptional future.

Luster for the issue will range from prooflike to a deep semi-mirrored surface to chrome-like, to flashy, to dull satiny. Upon examination of the surface, one may detect a greater degree of mirroring on the 49er's side. The reverse design occupies more of the field. Thus, there exists less area to polish, which in turn offers the look of less intensity or lustrousness.

Approximately the first 75 strikings will display various degrees of frosting (or cameo effect) on the devices. The effect was created by a surface roughness on the incused parts of the design which scatters or spreads the natural reflectivity of the metal. The die was not sandblasted to create this effect, as many have noted! After the aforesaid number of strikings, a flattening or smoothing or wearing down of these incused areas takes place. This is caused by the cold metal flowing horizontally, to some extent, against the die surfaces. These areas now become polished, causing the surfaces to exhibit little field-device contrast. Created is the chrome-like looking, no-contrast silver disc.

A second pair of dies was used to strike additional coins, but was not prepared in the same manner. Born were those satin finish specimens. Its Mint mark can be observed punched at a slightly different angle, when compared to the other creation.

As far as strike is concerned, a smaller number of chrome-like specimens will display excessive flatness on the bear' snout. This condition will influence the grade, as well as the value of such a coin. Weakness of the word LIBERTY and the bear's actual front left leg can also affect a Jubilee's worth, contingent upon its degree of flatness and eye appeal. The same also applies to a weakness on the word JUBILEE, the date and reverse words HALF DOLLAR, which will at times be encountered. As noted, only a very small percentage of this issue is influenced by the weak strike.

 **Related material**

To date, no distribution holders have been encountered. On occasion, a tri-colored ribbon which was worn by members of the Coin Distribution Committee, will surface. They are usually unaccompanied by the Jubilee half dollar, which was placed into a holder and initially attached to the ribbon. Its value is based on the accompanying coin. Without the coin, the ribbon alone should be worth $50 to $75.

1925
Fort Vancouver Centennial

Reason for issue: To commemorate the 100th anniversary of the founding of Fort Vancouver by the Hudson Bay Company, State of Washington, by Dr. John McLoughlin (an employee).

Authorized per Act of February 24, 1925: 300,000.

Official sale price: $1

Production figures

Date	Business Strikes	Assay Coins	Proofs	Melted	Net Mintage
1925	50,000	28	4?	35,034	14,966

Current market values

	EF-40	AU-50	MS-60	MS-63	MS-64	MS-65
1925	165.	215.	265.	375.	625.	1350.

Designs by Laura Gardin Fraser, based on original rough sketch by John T. Urquhart and plaster models by sculptor Sydney Bell.

Obverse

Portrayed is the bust of Dr. John McLoughlin facing left with his name beneath in curved letters. UNITED STATES OF AMERICA arcs above; HALF DOLLARbelow. Split by the portrait are the anniversary dates 1825 and 1925, and IN GOD / WE TRUST.

 Look for signs of wear on the hair covering McLoughlin's temple area and on the hair which covers the top of his ear, as well as his cheekbone. Portrait is prime location for the coin doctors.

Reverse

Depicted is a standing trapper in a buckskin suit holding a musket, facing right. In the background is Fort Vancouver with its defensive enclosure. In the distance is Mount Hood.

Outer inscriptions read: VANCOUVER WASHINGTON FOUNDED 1825 BY HUDSON and FORT VANCOUVER CENTENNIAL. Below the stockade posts at the extreme right are the designer's initials LGF. The Mint mark was unintentionally omitted, but all coins were struck at the San Francisco Mint.

 Any loss of metal will be noted on the actual right knee of the pioneer or his left as you view the coin. Beware of light buffing, or polishing or whizzing in these locations.

The Vancouver Then

John McLoughlin (1784-1857) was able to convince the native tribes in the area that he and his company intended no harm. If they wronged a white man, they were punished — and vice versa. Forbidden was the evil practice of "trading firewater to the Indians." In fact, John McLoughlin dealt with such justice that he was acknowledged by these Native Americans as their "Big Chief." The San Francisco Mint struck 50,000 Vancouvers, plus 28 assay coins on August 1, 1925. On the same day, 1,378 pounds of these coins were shipped by air to Vancouver by Lt. Oakley G. Kelly, U.S.A., flight commander of the Vancouver Pearson Field Barracks. The coin was distributed by the Fort Vancouver Centennial Corporation at $1 each in August and September 1925. The Centennial's president presented Lt. Kelly (one of two pilots who made the first transcontinental non-stop flight in 1923) with the first coin from the delivered shipment. Sales quickly came to a standstill, however, and 35,034 specimens were returned for reincarnation into some other coinage.

It has recently been discovered that while on a visit to the Pacific Coast in August 1926, Governor Charles Sale of the Hudson's Bay Company purchased 1,000 of these coins! They were shipped to the Provincial Archives Building in Winnipeg, Manitoba, Canada in 1974. These coins were stolen between August 1 and September 1, 1982 by a caretaker. A civil law suit was filed by the Province of Manitoba, in connection with the theft and sale of 568 Vancouver commemorative half dollars. Over 400 coins, each with a minimum numismatic value of at least $800, were allegedly spent at face value over a short period of time by the person who stole them! According to the Canadian dealer who handled the remainder of these coins, most would not grade MS-65 by today's standards. He personally sold 522 pieces to third parties in the United States and Canada and held about 46 pieces, before the problems with the government materialized. For the record, he did check with the FBI and the Royal Canadian Mounted Police, who reported at the time that there existed no record of these coins being stolen.

The theft was not discovered by the Archives until January 28, 1983, when inventory was taken. Supposedly needing money to buy a used car, the thief took remaining 568 to a bank. There they were exchanged by a Winnipeg bank teller at face value, or $284 in Canadian paper funds. The teller then received permission from her supervisor to purchase the lot from the bank at face value! The pieces were counted via a counting machine! In turn, she sold them to a Canadian dealer for $37,500. The dealer presented a written statement of information to the police department, particularizing the transaction. Clearance was received after several weeks. Nevertheless, the Crown filed suit against all involved even though all proper procedures were followed! In the end, the dealer's 46 pieces were returned to him and settlements were made. The Crown made no effort to reclaim those pieces sold in the United States.

The Vancouver Today

Specimens residing in the EF-AU category for the most part will display some form of numismatic abuse. Depending upon one's current financial situation, I would suggest locating a specimen which flaunts most of its original surface and possesses slight wear. That is unless a representative example only is required. Specimens grading MS-60 through MS-64 are not that difficult to locate at present and are somewhat undervalued. Since value spread between MS-63 and MS-64 condition is not that great, consider a flashy eye appealing MS-64+ and higher graded specimen, if possible. Future begins here for the issue, unless simply collecting for the pride or ownership. In grade MS-65 and higher, the Vancouver is very undervalued. It is a wonderful coin to possess.

Luster will range from an almost semi-prooflike satiny, blazing satiny, to satiny, to dull satiny. Strike weakness especially on the reverse trapper's hands face, right thigh and chest will be seen on a small percentage of this issue. This weakness may cause a grade-value lowering.

Primary focal areas are the obverse portrait (then surrounding fields) and the reverse trapper, then Mt. Hood. Numismatic negatives, such as abrasions, nicks, cuts, hairlines, slide marks and bag marks plague McLoughlin and his clean fields. Reverse trapper should not appear to have been shot by some weapon, nor be flatly struck, as if you hit him lightly with a hammer. Fret not if the leather powderhorn strap is not fully visible. It's the earlier strikings which will display the most possible definition, for the issue. Don't expect to see a sharply struck, fully raised strap. However, do expect to view a series of raised die chip marks. Their irregular pattern extends from the peak of Mt. Hood, to the letter C in CENTENNIAL.

 ## Detecting counterfeits

Counterfeits were made for this issue. Present on the counterfeit's surfaces are numerous depressions. A certain "red flag" exists one nose's length in front of John McLoughlin's facial part, just above the tip of this area. Another is present directly below and to the right of the O in GOD (A little divine consumer protection here!), as well as above the 1 of the date 1825.

Tooling marks below the CEN of the word CENTENNIAL make their presence known on the reverse. A circular depression can be seen close to the foot of Mt. Hood. Making a straight line, starting at the 1 o'clock position of the O in the word FORT, go right to make your encounter. Also semi-circular striations will be seen starting at the base of the right stockade section and continuing upward over the buildings within.

 ## Related material

To date no special distribution material has surfaced.

1926
Sesquicentennial of American Independence

Enlarged to show detail

Reason for issue: To commemorate the 150th anniversary of the signing of the Declaration of Independence.

Authorized per Act of March 3, 1925: 1,000,000 half dollars; 200,000 gold quarter eagles.

Official sale price: Half dollars, $1; quarter eagles, $4

Production figures

Date	Business Strikes	Assay Coins	Proofs	Melted	Net Mintage
1926 50¢	1,000,000	528	4?	859,408	45,793
1926 $2.50	200,000	226	2?	154,207	45,793

Current market values

	EF-40	AU-50	MS-60	MS-63	MS-64	MS-65
1926 50¢	55.00	62.50	77.50	150.	650.	7000.
1926 $2.50	225.	265.	360.	1175.	2025.	8000.

Half Dollar Designs by John Ray Sinnock

Obverse

Portrayed are the accolated busts of George Washington and Calvin Coolidge, facing right. Located around the top border, between two rosettes representing a badge of office, is the word LIBERTY. UNITED STATES OF AMERICA arcs below. IN GOD WE TRUST is in two lines just below Coolidge's chin. The incused designer's initials J.R.S. appear on the truncation of Washington's bust.

 A metal loss will first be observed on the cheekbone and shoulder of President Washington. Look for a difference in metal texture. Prime target for the coin doctors.

Reverse

Depicted is the Liberty Bell, named from the Old Testament. It was this bell that proclaimed liberty "throughout all the land unto all its inhabitants thereof," rallying the Colonists to the cause of independence.

How was the Liberty Bell cracked? This famous crack occurred in 1835, as the bell tolled for Chief Justice John Marshall's funeral procession. There is a song titled "The Ballad of Davy Crockett" that claims the hero "patched up the crack in the Liberty Bell," a nice fallacy, of course. The anniversary dates 1776 and 1926 are separated by the bell, which hangs from a beam. Around the raised border is the inscription SESQUICENTENNIAL OF AMERICAN INDEPENDENCE, while the denomination HALF DOLLAR appears in the bottom border. E PLURIBUS UNUM is at the top between the beam and the border inscription. An inscription is seen in the following form upon the Bell:

EOF LEV XXV FX PROCLAIM LIBERTY

OUSE IN PHILADA BY ORDER OF THE AS

PASS AND STOW

PHILADA

MDCCLIII

The complete inscription reads - PROCLAIM LIBERTY (throughout all the land unto the inhabitants thereof, LEV(iticus, Chapter) XXV, (verse)x. By order of the AS(sembly of the Providence of Pennsylvania for the State H)OUSE IN PHILAD(elphi)A. PASS AND STOW, PHILAD(elphi)A. 1753.

 Wear will first be noticed just below the central lower inscription on the Liberty Bell, as well as the center section of the beam which supports the famous American symbol. Also a location that attracts doctoring.

Gold $2.50 Designs by John Ray Sinnock, from rough drawings by John Frederick Lewis

Obverse

Depicted is the figure of Liberty standing on a globe. She is holding the Torch of Freedom in her right hand and a scroll in her left hand, symbolic of the Declaration of Independence. Situated in the field are the commemorative dates 1776-1926. UNITED STATES OF AMERICA arcs above; LIBERTY below.

Wear will first be noticed on Miss Liberty's left thigh and breast, then bottom part of the scroll. Primary target area for the coin doctors.

Reverse

Portrayed is Independence Hall, Philadelphia, Pa., home of the Liberty Bell and the site where the Declaration of Independence was written. In the background are sun's rays — which are not clear on all pieces. The inscription SESQUICENTENNIAL OF AMERICAN INDEPENDENCE is located around the upper border, while the denomination 2½ DOLLARS appears at the lower border. Incused in small letters, above the right wing of Independence Hall are the designer's initials, JRS. IN GOD WE TRUST is split by the spire of Independence Hall. E PLURIBUS UNUM is just below the base of the building.

A metal loss will occur on the center vertical section of Independence Hall.

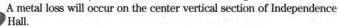

Origins of the Sesqui Coins

For a period of 150 years, the portrait of a living President of the United States had never appeared on United States coinage. While individuals such as Thomas E. Kilby, Governor of Alabama; Carter Glass, Secretary of the Treasury under President Wilson; and Senator Joseph T. Robinson of Arkansas had their portraits appear on United States commemorative coins, Calvin Coolidge, who was president at the time of the Sesquicentennial celebration in 1926, is the only president to have his portrait on a coin in his lifetime.

The Philadelphia Mint struck 1,000,000 half dollars, plus 528 assay coins, during May and June of 1926. It also produced 200,000 gold $2.50 pieces, plus 226 assay coins in this same period. Since it was believed that this Philadelphia celebration would be viewed as one of major national importance, the full numismatic authorization was produced. Unfortunately, the National Sesquicentennial Exhibition Commission, selling the half dollars at $1.00 each, saw sales come to a halt well short of the goal and returned 859,408 half dollars and 154,207 quarter eagles to the Mint to be melted. With almost 6 million people attending the Exhibition, which opened June 1, 1926, and closed Nov. 30, 1926, it makes one wonder why more coins of each issue were not sold! The possibility strongly exists that many attendees could not afford the luxury of either acquisition. The first half dollar, struck at noon by Mayor Kendrick at the May 19 striking ceremony, was presented to President Coolidge when he visited the Expo.

Aside from the half dollar and this quarter eagle, the original bill for these coins also requested the creation of a gold $1.50 coin! Unfortunately, this unusual new denomination was not approved by Secretary of the Treasury Mellon. The bill was amended and only the half dollar and quarter eagle were produced.

The Sesqui Half Dollar Today

This creation is readily available in EF-AU condition. Specimens can be obtained naturally worn or abused in some manner. MS-60 through MS-63 coinage will offer little acquisition resistance. Procure for the joy of collecting. Attempt to locate a lustrous MS-63+ coin which lacks deep cuts, scratches or detracting bag and slide marks on the primary focal areas. These are the obverse portraits, then right field and the reverse Liberty Bell, then surrounding fields. The aforesaid numismatic villains plague this issue.

Eye appealing MS-64 coinage is quite underrated. Future lies in this grade, as well as in MS-65 condition. In this state, it is an extremely rare coin, strictly graded! The only silver commemorative which is rarer is the Grant with Star. It is equal in rarity with the Missouri creations. In MS-66 condition, they are all equally as rare.

Luster will range from a prooflike gloss, to a semi-prooflike gloss, to flashy brilliant frosty (the latter three are not the norm), to frosty, to dull frosty. However, most specimens will lack that desired, original brilliant mint lustrous look.

Issue possesses a soft strike, due to its shallow relief. It also displays porous openings or minute holes located in the cheek area of presidents Washington and Coolidge. To date, I have yet to encounter a Sesqui half dollar which did not exhibit the slightest graininess or lack of metal fill in the noted locations.

The complete inscription, PASS AND STOW, PHILADA, MDCCLIII on the reverse is not often encountered. Upon inspection, its letters will be flatly struck, or partially visible, or not apparent at all. Under magnification of 10 power the inscription has the appearance of one which has been affected by the mechanical process of weathering over a long period of time. A specimen that possesses original brilliant Mint luster, a smooth clean full strike with no porosity visible in the cheek area of Washington and a completely legible inscription as previously noted on the Liberty Bell, will be a "major find."

Based on the aforementioned luster and strike problems as well as surface attacking negatives, it's easier to comprehend why strictly graded MS-64 and higher graded material is quite difficult to find.

Possibly four matte proof Sesqui half dollar exist. These are pieces which were double struck, then acid treated by the Mint (for its Chief Engraver John Ray Sinnock). One such specimen, the ex-King Farouk coin, appeared as Lot 2124 of the Stack's R.E. Cox, N.Y. Metropolitan Sale, 1962.

The Sesqui Gold $2.50 Today

While not readily available in EF-AU condition, this creation is the easiest to acquire of all commemorative gold produced from 1903 through 1926 in circulated condition. Encountered specimens will usually exhibit some form of abuse. I suggest considering pieces which display a metal loss, but possess a natural, undoctored surface — unless the price is right or you are simply acquiring the design in any condition for the joy of ownership.

The Sesqui $2.50 gold piece can also be obtained with little difficulty in MS-60 through MS-64 grades. Future lies in coinage residing in at least MS-63+ condition. These gold disks strictly grading MS-64 are undervalued. Should funds permit, attempt to locate flashy, eye appealing material with no obvious high point friction on Miss Liberty's breast or thighs. After the $50 Panama-Pacific and the 1905 Lewis and Clark gold dollar, this is the third rarest gold commemorative in MS-65 condition.

Strictly graded, it is quite undervalued. Should funds be available, consider its acquisition. In the loftier grades, this issue is a major rarity.

Numismatic negatives plague the primary focal areas which is the obverse figure and reverse building, then surrounding fields.

Luster will range from a brilliant flashy frost (not the norm), to frosty, to dull frosty. This design was executed in low relief. It will lack sharpness in the details. Varying degrees of strike do exist. What one attempts to locate is a sharp strike for the issue! Strike will affect the coin's grade-value when Miss Liberty displays weak definition on her head, cap and upper body. Same applies to the reverse, should Independence Hall display very weak window and building detail. By the way, the designer did not add hands to the clock face, therefore, no time is shown! On the 1936-S Bay Bridge, it is 12 o'clock. Closely examining the 1976 Bicentennial half dollar, the time is 3 o'clock, while on the back the current $100 bill it is 1:23.

One or possibly two extremely rare matte Proof quarter eagles exist.

 Detecting counterfeits

One of the better fakes flaunts brilliant luster, but displays some weakness in strike. It will show a small raised piece of metal on the diagonal bar of the first letter N of INDEPENDENCE on the reverse. Another will reveal depressions in the obverse field below the A of STATES, as well as between ER of AMERICA, plus a thin raised line which runs parallel to the rim, above Liberty's head, ending at the top vertical bar of the letter F of OF.

An additional example will reveal a depression on Liberty's torch and raised tooling marks above the digit 2 of the date 1926. Surfaces will be more granular than a genuine coin's.

 **Related material**

The half dollar was sold at the Exposition unprotected over the counter and distributed in an envelope (4¼" X 2⅝") through the FRANKLIN TRUST COMPANY, PHILADELPHIA, PA. imprinted blue with their name and address, the logo in a circle AT YOUR SERVICE DAY AND NIGHT, OFFICIAL SESQUICENTENNIAL SOUVENIR COINS and "AMERICA'S LARGEST EXCLUSIVELY DAY AND NIGHT BANK." Item on occasional makes an appearance, and may be valued at $25 to $75, if original.

The Sesqui $2.50 gold piece was distributed in the same envelope as described for the half dollar, as well as in a Bethlehem National Bank, Bethlehem, Pa., Christmas card imprinted with a Liberty Bell and anniversary dates and 150 Years of Independence. The latter is worth between $100 and $200.

1926-1939
Oregon Trail Memorial

Reason for issue: To commemorate the heroism of the fathers and
mothers who traversed the Oregon Trail to the Far West with great
hardship, daring, and loss of life, which not only resulted in adding new
states to the Union, but earned a well-deserved and imperishable fame
for the pioneers; to honor the 22,000 dead that lie buried in unknown
graves along 2,000 miles of the great highway of history; to rescue the
various important points along the trail from oblivion and to commemorate by suitable monuments, memorial or otherwise, the tragic events
associated with that of immigration, erecting them either along the trail
itself or elsewhere in localities appropriate for the purpose, including the
City of Washington.

Authorized per Act of May 17, 1926: 6,000,000 (for the entire issue)

Official sale price:

1926; 1926-S:	$1
1928; 1933-D; 1934-D	$2
1936; 1936-S:	$1.60
1937-D:	$1.60; $1.65 by mail
1938 PDS set:	$6.50
1939 PDS set:	$7.50

Production figures

Date	Business Strikes	Assay Coins	Proofs	Melted	Net Mintage
1926	48,000	30	4?	75	47,925
1926-S	100,000	55	4?	17,000	83,000
1928	50,000	28	4?	44,000	6,000
1933-D	5,245?	5?	4?	242	4,998
1934-D	7,000	6	4?	0	7,000
1936	10,000	6	4?	0	10,000
1936-S	5,000	6	4?	0	5,000
1937-D	12,000	8	4?	0	12,000
1938	6,000	6	4?	0	6,000
1938-D	6,000	5	4?	0	6,000
1938-S	6,000	6	4?	0	6,000

1939	3,000	4	4?	0	3,000
1939-D	3,000	4	4?	0	3,000
1939-S	3,000	5	4?	0	3,000

Current market values

	EF-40	AU-50	MS-60	MS-63	MS-64	MS-65
1926	70.00	85.00	90.00	115.	165.	290.
1926-S	77.50	90.00	95.00	120.	175.	300.
1928	90.00	110.	150.	200.	315.	440.
1933-D	140.	175.	210.	280.	325.	475.
1934-D	87.50	110.	120.	180.	235.	395.
1936	77.50	90.00	100.	135.	205.	295.
1936-S	90.00	110.	135.	180.	215.	300.
1937-D	82.50	95.00	110.	125.	210.	290.
1938 PDS set	——	——	350.	525.	750.	1050.
1939 PDS set	——	——	975.	1250.	1550.	2000.

Designs

According to Mint reports, the wagon side is the obverse. According to the designers, the Indian side is the obverse. Although I tend to side with the majority of collectors, dealers and numismatists who consider the Indian as the obverse (because it is the more eye-catching and artistic of the designs), the Mint appears to have the last word, and the official obverse is the wagon side.

Obverse by James Earle Fraser (model by Laura Gardin Fraser)

Depicted is a Conestoga wagon drawn over a hill by two oxen, guided by a figure holding a stick or branch. All are trekking westward toward the setting sun, whose rays extend across the upper field. The inscription OREGON TRAIL MEMORIAL, and five small decorative stars located below the inscription appear in the field above the date of issue. IN GOD WE TRUST is in the upper border, while the husband and wife designers' initials JE / F / LG are located at the 3 o'clock position behind the Conestoga wagon.

 Wear will first be observed on the hip of the ox and thigh of the pioneer leading the Conestoga wagon.

Reverse by Laura Gardin Fraser

Portrayed is an American Indian who appears to be signaling to an advancing person or group of individuals to stop — a gesture similar to today's traffic policeman. No particular tribe is represented. Facing to the coin's right, the Indian is wearing a long, feathered bonnet. He holds a bow in his right hand, and has a blanket draped over his left shoulder. Extending on both sides of the Indian is an outline map of the United States with a line of Conestoga wagons indicating the Oregon Trail. The inscription UNITED STATES OF AMERICA is superimposed on the map. The denomination HALF DOLLAR appears in the lower border, while the Mint mark — if the coin should possess one, is located to the right of the F in HALF.

A metal loss will first be noticed on the thigh of the American Indian opposite the word OF, then on his hand. Look for a difference in metal texture and crisscross scratches in this location, as well as doctoring in the form of whizzing, buffing or polishing.

Origins of the Oregon Trail Series

What might have prompted the Mint to make the change of obverse-reverse? Previous creations, such as the 1915 Panama-Pacific issues, displayed their "S" Mint mark next to the obverse date or displayed the year of striking on the obverse and Mint mark on the reverse.

The 1923 Monroe had its mark below the date, on the obverse, while the 1925 California Jubilee displayed an obverse date and reverse Mint mark. No problems! However, with the Oregon Trail 1926-S issue, we have the first instance where a Mint mark created a variety within an issue! No problem might have arisen had the issue been struck only at Philadelphia, which used no Mint mark. Unaccompanied by a date, a Mint mark's place is on the reverse. Examining previous creations as the Columbian, Lafayette, or Maine Centennial, we can note that these issues are dated in some fashion on the reverse. Were they to be produced at two Mints during the same year, as the 1926-P and 1926-S Oregon Trail coinage, would the Mint have called Columbus on the 1892 or 1893 Columbian half dollar the reverse side because the ship side bears the date? Thus, the correct positioning of the Mint mark would be next to the date or opposite the date side. It appears the Mint used its only option when labeling the Oregon Trail and changing the artist obverse-reverse — even though it had the look of a coin's reverse design!

The 1926 issue was to be later named the Ezra Meeker coin by the sponsors of this issue, in honor of the man who in 1907 at 76 years of age left his home in Oregon with an ox team and covered wagon. His primary objective was to travel once again the trail of his youth in order to perpetuate the memory of the Old Trail; to honor those who made it and to kindle in the breast of the new generation a flame of patriotic sentiment. After his 15-month journey, he was to rediscover and mark the trail from its beginning in St. Louis, in order that the people and nation might not forget. Meeker (1830-1928) was president of the Oregon Trail Pioneer Memorial Association, until his demise at the age of 98.

In September 1926, the Philadelphia Mint struck 48,000 coins, plus 30 pieces for assay purposes. However, during the following two months, the San Francisco Mint struck 100,000 half dollars, plus 55 assay coins. Thus, we had the first instance, as previously noted, where a Mint mark S created a variety within an issue, such as the 2X2 of the Alabama issue or the ★ of the Grant issue. These coins were distributed at $1.00 by the Oregon Trail Pioneer Memorial Association, who soon encountered a sharp decline in sales. There were 17,000 pieces of the "S" Mint coin melted, as well as 75 pieces from the Philadelphia Mint.

Although requested, no coins were struck in 1927, since the Mint had unpaid amounts of the 1926 San Francisco creation on hand. However, in June 1928, the Philadelphia Mint struck 50,000 pieces, plus 28 assay specimens, of the new 1928 Oregon Trail, later referred to as the "Jedediah Smith" coin. This production honored the man who pioneered the trails to California and the Pacific Northwest. Four years passed and this issue was not released! It was held back because the Treasury Department still had a supply of the 1926 striking and would not release the 1928 issue until the 1926 supply was purchased. Finally, the situation was resolved with the melting of 17,000 unsold pieces. The 1928 Oregon Trail was released in 1933, along with the first commemorative coinage produced by the Denver Mint!

Scott Stamp and Coin Company of New York City was to now market the issue. In an effort to increase sales of the new coins, historical names were given to each issue. These special names, which are rarely referred to today, were not designated by government approval and ended with the 1936-S issue.

The 1928 creation was offered for sale at $2.00 each. However, most collectors refused to pay the asking price for this coin with its high mintage, since they could purchase the 1933-D low mintage piece (5,245) for $1.50. Thus, sales were poor and 44,000 coins were returned to the Mint. The objective in melting them was to make the survivors rarer, leaving us with a net mintage of 6,000.

The Denver Mint produced 5,245(?) strikings plus five assay pieces in July 1933. These were referred to as the "Century of Progress Exposition" coin. With most of these pieces being purchased by collectors and speculators of the period, only 242 pieces were returned to the Mint, leaving us with a mintage figure of 5,000 coins.

In July 1934, the Denver Mint produced 7,000 half dollars, plus 6 pieces for assay, of the coin termed the "Fort Hall, Fort Laramie and Jason Lee" coin. Jason Lee (1803-45) and Marcus Whitman (1802-47) were missionaries who founded missions which were to become centers of an American settlement in the Oregon Territory. This issue sold well at $2.00 each and none were returned to the Mint.

No coins of this issue were produced in 1935. However, the Philadelphia Mint struck 10,000 coins plus 6 assay pieces in May 1936, while the San Francisco Mint produced 5,000 pieces, plus six assay coins, of an issue name the "Whitman Mission" coin. None of these coins had to be returned to the Mint since sales were excellent. Both were offered at $1.60 each. However, it was the "S" mint coin that Scott Stamp and Coin Company sold out within 10 days after the announcement that only 5,000 coins would be produced. Several months later, the distributor was willing to repurchase the 1936-S issue at $10 each! The distributor sold and promoted the 1928 through 1936 strikings. Needless to say, they also owned large quantities of these dates! The Association, which marketed the original 1926 issue, sold part of the 1936 production as well as the 1937, 1938 and 1939 issues.

The Denver Mint struck 12,000 pieces plus 8 assay coins of the 1937 issue during February 1937. They were later offered by the Commission at $1.60 each. The historical names applied to certain previous issues were finally discontinued. This was no great loss, since the entire coin's design remained the same, except for the Mint mark and date change.

In 1938, Oregon Trails from the three Mints were offered for the first time as a set, at $6.50. Each Mint produced 6,000 coins. Denver struck 5 assay coins, one fewer than the other Mints. Ditto for the 1939 set, except that it was offered at $7.50 and San Francisco minted an additional assay coin (five).

The Oregon Trail Today

The 1926-P striking can be located with little difficulty in EF-AU condition. Many of the offered pieces will bear evidence of some form of abuse. It is also available in grades MS-60 through MS-64. Price spread is insignificant between these states, thus look for an eye-appealing higher grade! Believe it or not, this issue in MS-65 condition is equal in rarity to the popular 1928, 1933-D and 1934-D strikings — underrated! Possesses a good future in MS-65 and higher graded coinage. Luster will range from brilliant frosty (not the norm) to dull frosty. The majority of this issue will lack thumb and finger definition on the Indian's hand. Only the early strikes — from a new pair of dies which were put into production — will show this detail. One might think they are examining a 1937-D striking. There exists a small die crack which extends upward from the head of the oxen team's figure on this striking. The 1926-S is the easiest of the series to locate in circulated EF-AU condition. A large percentage of the examined specimens will display some form of cleaning, polishing, whizzing, etc. Value spread between MS-60 and MS-64 is small, thus focus on the higher grade if funds permit. Available in all these grades. Equally as rare in MS-65 condition, as the not so hard to locate 1936-P, 1937-D, 1938-D and S. Future truthfully exists in the higher grades for this creation.

Luster will range from amazing prooflike (not the norm), to brilliant satiny, to dull satiny. The semi-prooflike coin flaunts amazing eye appeal, as well as die polishing marks in the field below part of the motto IN GOD WE TRUST. Great coin to possess. Striking weakness in letters of the word STATES can keep the coin out of the MS-65 category, unless the piece is amazing.

The 1928-P production is not abundant in circulated condition. Most encountered pieces were polished, cleaned or abused in some way. Little value spread exists between MS-60 and MS-63 condition, its grades of availability, at present. Thus, why not think higher grade acquisition? Good coin to own in MS-64 and MS-65 states. Great future in all higher grades. Luster will range from brilliant frosty to dull frosty. Strike seldom affects the coin's grade or value. Oregon Trails dated 1933-D are certainly not abundant in circulated condition. Those pieces usually display some form of numismatic abuse. Value spread is smallish between the EF-AU and MS-64 categories. Think the higher grade, especially MS-64, if funds are available. Real future resides in MS-65 and especially the higher, underrated states. Luster will range from brilliant satiny to dull satiny (not the norm). The date tends to a weakness of strike on the pioneer leading the Conestoga wagon. Such is a striking characteristic for the creation. Grade and value will not be affected, unless the figure and rear wagon frame canvas support are respectively extremely flat and rounded.

The 1934-D striking is not abundant in circulated condition. Such examples are usually abused in some way. Little value spread exists between the latter ratings and grade 64. Also, they can be found with little effort in these categories. Thus, think higher grade. Issue is definitely fairly valued in grade MS-64 and should be purchased for the joy of collecting. Real future lies in your MS-65 and without question, higher states. Luster will range brilliant frosty (not the norm) to dull frosty. Attractive lustrous coinage will be hard to find. However, the second T of STATES can display a weakness of strike, affecting the coin's value.

The 1936-P production can be located with little effort in circulated condition. Majority of pieces will show some from of abuse as cleaning, polishing, etc. Little value spread between EF-AU and MS-64 condition, thus think higher grade, if acquisition is planned. It is available in all grades up to MS-65 at present. Aside from the 1937-D, it is the second most common creation in the 65 state. Acquire for the joy of collecting. Future lies in the higher grades. Luster will range from Brilliant frosty (not the norm) to dull frosty. The majority of this issue will lack eye appeal, and present a stainless steel look. Strike normally presents no problem. Raised lines which are die polishing marks can be observed in the field at the sides of the Indian's head.

The 1936-S low mintage issue is not abundant, in circulated condition. It is usually the abused specimen which receives this label. Value spread between grades MS-60 and MS-64 is currently too low! Creation is not as available as some believe. Think higher grade for this underrated coin. Future lies in this Oregon grading MS-64+ and better. Luster will range from brilliant frosty (not the norm), to dull frosty. Unfortunately, much of the issue will lack eye appeal, looking as if they were struck on stainless steel planchets. Strike seldom present a grade-lowering problem.

The 1937-D Oregon Trail commemorative half dollar offers all the collector could desire in the form of strike, luster and overall beauty. It can be located will little difficulty in circulated condition, on up to MS-64. Little value spread exist between these states. The creation is the easiest to procure and most abundant of the entire series in grades MS-65 through MS-68. Should one desire an amazing example of the Oregon Trail design for the pure joy of collecting, this is the coin. Luster will range from blazing frosty to frosty to dull frosty. Strike seldom presents a problem for the date.

The 1938 P-D-S sets which fall into the circulated category do so because of polishing, cleaning, whizzing or some form of abuse. Needless to say, they are not abundant. Astute collectors attempt to acquire at type coin values. Worth twice the 1937-D EF-AU value! Little value spread exists between the MS-60 and MS-64 states. This undervalued issue that is not as abundant as is believed in these categories. However, unless steady demand causes them to rise in value, they will hopelessly be locked in, due the date's availability in MS-65 condition. Acquire for the joy of ownership. Future exists only in MS-66 for Philadelphia issue and coins graded loftier. Luster will range from brilliant frosty luster (not the norm) to dull frosty luster. Majority of creation simply lacks eye appeal. They too would make a numismatic neophyte believe stainless steel planchets were used during production. Strike seldom presents a problem for the issue.

The 1939 P-D-S set is the rarest coinage of the series. When located in circulated condition or offered at less than MS-60 values, the individual coin or set has been polished or abused in some fashion. Value spread between MS-60 and MS-64 condition is small. Coins are not that available. Definitely very underrated. Future lies in original eye appealing specimens grading MS-63+ and loftier. Luster will range from semi-brilliant frosty luster (not the norm) to dull frosty. Many encountered specimens will display an unimpressive stainless steel look. Strike will rarely present a problem, as far as grade and value lowering is concerned.

When examining the issue, we will observe what we call rim indentation on the sides of the coin's reeded edge. Such is not a form of coin damage, but rather the result of metal flow which was necessary to create the high relief on the back of the obverse Conestoga wagon.

Primary focal points such as the Conestoga wagon and ox, as well as the reverse American Indian are prime targets for those grade and value lowering, numismatic villains named bag mark, reed mark, hairline scratch, slide mark, dig, etc. They just seem to gravitate to these locations.

 **Related material**

The coins were distributed in a cardboard holder with inserts for three coins. It housed a three-piece set, two separate dates or one coin. In the case of the latter, such was cut into thirds (to be thrifty). One type is imprinted with the Association's name and address and the manufacturer, John H. Eggers, New York, while the other is plain and noted at the bottom it was patented and sold by John W. Rogers, New York. The mailing envelope is imprinted with the Association's New York City address, 1775 Broadway.

The envelope and holder together, if original, may be valued in the $75 to $150 range. Individual cards are worth $20 to $35. Material in support of the 1939 set can be worth a lofty $250 to $300.

1927
Vermont-Bennington Sesquicentennial

Reason for issue: To commemorate the 150th anniversary of the Battle of Bennington and the independence of Vermont.

Authorized per Act of February 24, 1925: 40,000

Official sale price: $1 ($1.25 by mail)

Production figures

Date	Business Strikes	Assay Coins	Proofs	Melted	Net Mintage
1927	40,000	34	4?	11,892	28,108

Current market values

	EF-40	AU-50	MS-60	MS-63	MS-64	MS-65
1927	100.	120.	140.	230.	345.	1075.

Designs by Charles Keck

Obverse

Portrayed is Ira Allen facing right. His name appears below his bust with the inscription FOUNDER OF VERMONT located in the lower border. UNITED STATES OF AMERICA arcs above. In 1777, Ira Allen helped formulate Vermont's declaration as an independent state. This Green Mountain Boy's primary objective was to free his land not only from the British soldiers, but also from those land grabbers of today's Empire State, New York.

 Wear first begins on the hair in the temple area of Ira Allen, then on his cheek. Portrait is a prime target for the coin doctors. Wire brushing will attempt to simulate the original Mint luster. Look also for an aluminum-like appearance as you slowly rotate the coin 360 degrees.

Reverse

Depicted is a catamount (short for a cat-a-mountain), or mountain lion, walking left. The original design incorporated Fay's Tavern, also known as the Catamount Tavern. Its name was derived from a stuffed member of the species exhibited atop a flagpole outside this historic meeting place. However, the design showing the tavern was regarded inartistic by the Fine Arts Commission and rejected. Preferred was the catamount. The words BATTLE OF BENNINGTON appear around the upper border, with IN GOD WE TRUST and the anniversary dates 1777-1927 in the field above the cat. AUG. 16 appears at the left, below the catamount's head. The Battle of Bennington (Aug. 16, 1777) was a positive turning point for the Colonists who were fighting the British for independence.

Around the bottom border is HALF DOLLAR, with E PLURIBUS UNUM just above it. The designer's initials CK are incused in the field located between the animal's left hind leg and tail.

Wear will first be apparent on the upper shoulder and cheek of the puma. Look for a difference in texture of the metal.

Origins of the Vermont

The Philadelphia Mint produced 40,000 Vermonts plus 34 assay coins during January and February 1927. Distributed through the Bennington Battle Monument and Historical Association of Bennington, Lock Box 432, Bennington, Vt., the coins were offered for sale by local banks at $1.00 each and $1.25 by registered mail. Approximately 75 percent of this issue was sold and the remaining 11,892 pieces were returned to the Mint.

The Vermont Today

In EF-AU condition, the issue can be obtained with some effort. A large percentage of encountered specimens will display the effects of numismatic abuse in the form of cleaning, light buffing, whizzing or overdipping. I recommend acquiring attractive pieces, exhibiting natural surfaces with little wear. That is unless all that is required is a representative example for the joy of collecting. In grades MS-60 through MS-64, the issue can be labeled available. There is little value spread between the MS-60 and MS-63 category, so think higher grade. Future of this creation rests in underrated, eye appealing Vermonts grading MS-64+ and higher. In strict MS-65 condition, this popular coin is definitely undervalued. Pieces graded loftier will be very difficult to obtain.

Luster will range from prooflike, to semi-prooflike, to brilliant frosty (these are not the norm), to frosty, to dull frosty. Strike seldom presents a problem involving a grade-value. Locating a specimen with sharp curl definition on the upper central section of Allen's periwig will not be an easy task, especially in MS-64 condition.

Primary focal obverse location is Ira Allen's portrait, especially his exposed cheek, jaw and forehead. On a small percentage of this issue, a characteristic die break which resembles a small scratch will be seen on the forehead, just above the eyebrow. Bag marks, slide marks, lack of metal, fill marks, etc., just plague the area. Smooth fields can be a target for large bag or reed marks. Reverse primary focal location is the puma which can readily display the just mentioned numismatic wounds. When looking for a nice MS-63+ or MS-64 specimen, attempt to locate a flashy eye appealing coin without major negatives in those key locations.

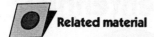 **Related material**

No official mailers from the Commission have been seen to date. However, the issue was distributed by various Bennington banks, such as the County National Bank and First National Bank, in their own cardboard folded holders (4" X 2⅞"). A cardboard insert for one coin is pasted within. Imprinted in green is VERMONT-BENNINGTON COMMEMORATIVE HALF DOLLAR FROM (bank's name), then BENNINGTON, VT. Holder may be valued at $50 to $100.

1928
Hawaii Sesquicentennial

Reason for issue: To commemorate the 150th anniversary of the discovery of the Hawaiian Islands by Captain James Cook, a British navigator, and for the purpose of aiding in the establishment of a Captain James Cook Memorial Collection in the archives of the Territory of Hawaii.

Authorized per Act of March 7, 1928: 10,000

Official sale price: $2

Production figures

Date	Business Strikes	Assay Coins	Proofs	Melted	Net Mintage
1928	10,008	8	50	0	9,950

Current market values

	EF-40	AU-50	MS-60	MS-63	MS-64	MS-65
1928	615.	750.	1200.	1750.	2500.	6000.

Designs by Juliette May Fraser (model prepared by Chester Beach)

Obverse

The bust of Captain James Cook is seen facing left. In the left field are the words CAPT. JAMES COOK DISCOVERER OF HAWAII. To the right of the word CAPT. is a compass needle. At the lower border we can note eight triangles which symbolize the eight largest islands of the chain. IN GOD WE TRUST is in the upper right field. UNITED STATES OF AMERICA arcs above; HALF DOLLAR below. Located at the right base of the bust in relief are the artist's initials C.B. Chester Beach executed the design based upon a sketch created by Miss Juliette May Fraser of Honolulu.

The rim of this coin offers its high points little protection. Therefore, at the slightest abuse Captain Cook's cheekbone and then the roll of hair over his side will display a loss of metal. This location and his face will be the primary target of the "doctoring artists." Rotate the coin slowly 360 degrees, tilting it back and forth, attempting to detect their workmanship.

Reverse

Hawaiian warrior chief in full regalia, standing at the top of a hill, extending his right arm in welcome and holding an erect spear with his left hand. In the left field is pictured a village of grass huts located at the foot of Diamond Head and Waikiki Beach. A coconut tree, representing romance, with its large leaves occupies the right and upper field. E PLURIBUS UNUM is in the lower left field, where the ocean meets the shore. The anniversary dates 1778-1928 appear in the lower border.

 Look for a metal loss in the form of a grayish white texture on the thighs, knees, sash and left hand of the warrior chief.

Origins of the Hawaiian

The Philadelphia Mint produced 10,000 Hawaiian half dollars plus 8 for assay purposes in June 1928. They were sold at $2.00 each — the highest price asked for a commemorative half dollar to that date — by the Captain Cook Sesquicentennial Commission of Honolulu via the Bank of Hawaii Ltd., in Honolulu on Oct. 8, 1928.

Of the total mintage, 50 specimens were issued in the form of sandblast Proofs and later presented to various officials and museums. Today, nine of these extremely rare pieces are located in museums. There were also 400 pieces of the regular issue kept for special presentation purposes. Supposedly, half of the remaining coins were shipped to the Territory of Hawaii and the other half was distributed on the mainland.

Low mintage, unintentional numismatic abuse and a wide distribution, especially here in the States, makes the Hawaiian one of the more valuable silver commems today. Most people who own the Hawaiian half dollar keep the coin in their possession. I personally believe that a wealthy family or group of investors in Hawaii acquired and still owns between 1,500 and 2,000 or more pieces in various Mint State grades. It is difficult for me to believe that a large number of "Islanders" so readily forked over four times face value for the half dollar. I was met with skepticism when I expressed the opinion that the Bank of Hawaii possibly possessed 500 of these coins. When inquiries were made to the bank by friends and clients in Hawaii, no one knew of their existence. However, on Jan. 23, 1986, Bowers & Merena Galleries auctioned off 137 of the coins for the bank.

The Hawaiian Today

Specimens which reside in the EF-AU category are usually encountered lightly whizzed or doctored in some fashion. Only acquire if the price is too good to pass or you just would like a representative example. Original appealing coins exhibiting some natural wear can be difficult to locate and could easily bring close to MS-60 money! Pieces grading from MS-60 through MS-65 are undervalued. Strike seldom if ever will be detrimental to the coin's grade or value. Luster will range from flashy satiny (not the norm) to dull satiny. It is those bag marks, reed marks, hairline scratches, etc., which plague this issue in the primary focal area. That's Capt. Cook's face and head, as well as the Hawaiian warrior chief's body on the reverse. One deep hit in any of these areas can lower a coin's value $1,000 to $3,500! The Hawaiian sandblast Proof — which was referred to as a token (of appreciation) when presented to Commission Chairman Col. C.P. Iaukea by Edgar Henriques, its Executive Secretary, on June 6, 1928 — is a rare item which can be owned by few people today. At times, one is offered for sale at auction or at a coin show. I suggest you examine this treasure and compare its surface and double strike to the normal business strike. Beware of a business strike which was sandblasted outside the Mint.

 ## Detecting counterfeits

All known coins produced by the Philadelphia Mint have a raised die polishing mark extending from the upper part of the warrior's cap and extending through the palm leaves. One counterfeit will exhibit a break in the border design to the right of the second "A" in AMERICA on the obverse. Its reverse will display a small circular depression above the back part of the warrior's hand. There have been attempts to hide the counterfeit diagnostics by whizzing or polishing the coin. Another counterfeit displays a glossy luster along with fuzzy details and sharp edge reeding. Examining the throat of Capt. Cook we can observe a small raised line or spike protruding from his throat, extending into the field. The reverse bears an extra piece of raised metal near the rim above the fuzzy palm leaves near the 11 o'clock position.

 ## Related material

The very rare and desirable Hawaiian sandblast Proof was distributed in an unmarked, purple, covered wooden box. Its inner top was made with a purple satiny material while a purple velour lined the lower section. A metal push button is located in the front lower section of the box. The few I have encountered possess a church-like incense aroma.

The business strike was mailed in a Bank of Hawaii Ltd. envelope (P.O. Box 2900, Honolulu, Hawaii) which contained a cardboard holder with openings for five coins. The coins were held in place by a piece of paper tape. On occasion, the enclosed coins will flaunt some degree of captivating iridescent shades of green, greenish gold, red and reddish brown. Higher graded specimens will bring greater monetary rewards.

Expect a value of $150 to $400 for the original envelope and card. However, the Proof cases may be valued at $1,000!

1934
Maryland Tercentenary

Reason for issue: The 300th anniversary of the founding of the Province of Maryland.

Authorized per Act of May 9, 1934: 25,000

Official sale price: $1

Production figures

Date	Business Strikes	Assay Coins	Proofs	Melted	Net Mintage
1934	25,000	15	4-6?	0	25,000

Current market values

	EF-40	AU-50	MS-60	MS-63	MS-64	MS-65
1934	95.00	105.	130.	150.	200.	565.

Designs by Hans Schuler

Obverse

Pictured is the three-quarter bust of Cecil Calvert, second Lord Baltimore (after whom the city is named); with name below bust. UNITED STATES OF AMERICA arcs above; HALF DOLLAR below. E PLURIBUS UNUM is in the left field; IN GOD WE TRUST in the right.

Wear first begins on the nose, jaw and left side of hair above the temple area, down to the back jaw (opposite the word UNITED). Flat nose appearance is due to striking. Portrait is a target for whizzing and other forms of doctoring. Surface negatives present in those unprotected fields can easily downgrade coin.

Reverse

Featured is the arms of the State of Maryland, adapted from the Calvert family's. The two reverse figures represent Labor (with the spade) and Fisheries (with the fish). Next to Labor's foot are the designer's initials HS. The Italian motto, FATTI MASCHII PAROLE FEMINE means "Deeds are manly, words are womanly." Anniversary dates 1634-1934 with decorative stars on each side are located in the lower field. The date 1634 represents the time of arrival at Saint Mary's by 200 plus colonists, who were the first to settle after Calvert obtained the land grant from King Charles I. MARYLAND TERCENTENARY appears in the border.

A metal loss will first be observed on the drapery folds above the heads of the male figures, then the crown. Primary focal area is the shield.

Origins of the Maryland

After the striking of the Hawaiian half dollars by the Philadelphia Mint in June 1928, Congress approved no new issues until the Texas Centennial Coinage Act of June 15, 1933. The Maryland issue was approved May 9, 1934.

The Texas issue was coined in the months of October and November 1934. However, 25,000 Maryland half dollars plus 15 assay coins were struck during July 1934 at the Philadelphia Mint. Although the Texas issue dated 1934 was authorized earlier, the Maryland issue was the first authorized souvenir coin of the Roosevelt Administration to be issued.

Beginning with this issue, the Director of the Mint was assigned the responsibility for the minting of these commemorative halves. Previously, the Acts — with several exceptions — referred only to the complete mintage which was allowed to be struck. However, in the case of the Maryland Tercentenary half dollar, a fixed production figure was given and the Director was made responsible. This Act was also the first to advert to the sale of coins selling above face value.

The Maryland issue was distributed by the Maryland Tercentenary Commission of Baltimore via banks in that state at $1.00 each. However, almost 5,000 coins remained unsold. From the remaining coins, about 2,000 coins were sold at 75 cents each, the remainder were offered for sale at 65 cents per coin.

The Maryland Today

The issue is not exactly abundant in EF-AU condition. Most encountered coins will exhibit some form of abuse in the form of polishing, whizzing (especially Calvert's portrait) or the effects of being kept as a souvenir coin. Value spread between EF and MS-64 is narrow. Thus, collectors should strive for the higher grade. The issue at this time is certainly available in the marketplace in the noted classifications and should be acquired for the joy of collecting. Luster will range from blazing satiny (not the norm), down to dull satiny.

The Maryland is difficult to locate in strict gem MS-65 and better condition because of excessive or heavy nicks, cuts, scratches and lack of metal fill marks, especially located on Calvert's portrait. Naturally, that includes the nose which always looks almost flat. Also remember that this was a "rush job," as evidenced by the poor workmanship, especially in the areas of the cheekbone, nose and lower forehead area which resembles giant eyebrows. I have not encountered an issue where the degree of strike flatness would lower the grade or value.

When purchasing this issue, look for specimens displaying natural attractive lustrous surfaces, accompanied by a minimum of marks in critical locations. Eye appeal is very important. Die abrasions are acceptable, provided they are not detracting or excessive. Reverse of the issue seldom presents a problem, although lack-of-fill marks of various sizes will make their presence known in the lower left quarter of the reverse shield. Possibly four to six matte Proofs (double-struck, acid dipped at the Mint) specimens exist. I have personally examined two such pieces:

1) Ex. J.R. Sinnock estate, 1962 ANA Convention Sale, Lot 2053.
2) Ex. J.R. Sinnock estate, 1962 ANA Convention Sale, Lot 2054.

Related material

Many of the Maryland half dollars mailed to subscribers were forwarded in a standard Dennison one-coin holder, with a green paper flap which held the coin in place. I personally would not pay more than $1 to $2 for these, simply because there is nothing special about them. In this case, be influenced by the coin, not the holder, even if accompanied by the mailing envelope. Others were mailed in tissue paper. Four line imprinting on the envelope: 1634-1934, MARYLAND TERCENTENARY COMMISSION, 902 UNION TRUST BUILDING, BALTIMORE ... MARYLAND.

Original envelope and holder together, value at $50 to $105; holder by itself, no more than $2.

1934-1938
Texas Independence Centennial

Reason for issue: The 100th anniversary in 1936 of the independence of Texas, and of the noble and heroic sacrifices of her pioneers, whose revered memory has been an inspiration to her sons and daughters during the past century.

Authorized per Act of June 15, 1933: 1,500,000 for the series.

Official sale price: 1934 $1 plus 15¢ postage
1935-1937 $1.50 per coin; $4.50 per set
1938 $2.00 per coin; $6.00 per set

Production figures

Date	Business Strikes	Assay Coins	Proofs	Melted	Net Mintage
1934	205,000	113	4?	143,650	61,350
1935	10,000	8	4?	12	9,988
1935-D	10,000	7	4?	0	10,000
1935-S	10,000	8	4?	0	10,000
1936	10,000	7	4?	1,097	8,903
1936-D	10,000	7	4?	968	9,032
1936-S	10,000	8	4?	943	9,057
1937	8,000	5	4?	1,434	6,566
1937-D	8,000	6	4?	1,401	6,599
1937-S	8,000	7	4?	1,370	6,630
1938	5,000	5	4?	1,225	3,775
1938-D	5,000	5	4?	1,230	3,770
1938-S	5,000	6	4?	1,192	3,808

Current market values

	EF-40	AU-50	MS-60	MS-63	MS-64	MS-65
1934	60.00	70.00	85.00	95.00	120.	175.
1935 PDS set	——	——	250.	275.	335.	525.
1936 PDS set	——	——	260.	290.	340.	540.

1937 PDS set	——	——	275.	300.	365.	625.
1938 PDS set	——	——	500.	650.	745.	1200.

Designs by Pompeo Coppini

Obverse

Large American eagle facing left and superimposed on a five-pointed "Lone Star," symbolic of the state of Texas. Below the oak branch held by the eagle's talons is the date of issue. UNITED STATES OF AMERICA arcs above; HALF DOLLAR below. IN GOD WE TRUST is in the upper right field; E PLURIBUS UNUM in the left field.

 A metal loss will first be observed on the breast of the eagle. Examine for whizzing in this area.

Reverse

Depicted is a winged and draped Victory holding an olive branch in her right hand, while resting her left hand on a figure of the Alamo. Appearing on a scroll situated above the figure's head is the word LIBERTY. Located in the same area are the six flags of Spain, France, Mexico, the Texas Free State, the Confederacy and the United States, which represent periods in the history of Texas.

The medallion portrait of General Sam Houston, the first president of the independent Texas Republic, appears in the coin's left field, while Stephen F. Austin, one of the founders of the state, is pictured in the coin's right field. Their names are also presented in very small letters. Located around the coin's border are the inscriptions THE TEXAS INDEPENDENCE CENTENNIAL, and REMEMBER THE ALAMO, while the designer's initials P.C. (Pompeo Coppini) are placed at the right base of the famed structure. This issue's Mint marks (D or S) are located below the left knee of Victory. Coins struck at the Philadelphia Mint bear no Mint mark.

Wear will first be observed on the head of the Winged Victory as well as her knee. Should her knee be flatly struck, examine for a difference in metal texture and fine crisscross scratches.

Origins of the Texas Coins

Texas was to celebrate its centennial in 1936, but there are issues dated 1934 and 1935! In 1933, the American Legion Texas Centennial Committee of Austin, Texas, believed that the celebration would be quite expensive. They asked for authorization to have coins produced prior to the opening of the Exposition in order to obtain the needed funds. An authorization of 1,500,000 coin was approved June 15, 1933.

On March 16, 1936, Senator Connally's Secretary R.M. Jackson gave testimony before the Senate Committee on Banking and Currency in an attempt to have five different designs created! This proposal was rejected, however. The Centennial Exposition celebration took place in Dallas between June 6 and Nov. 29, 1936.

During the months of October and November 1934, the Philadelphia Mint struck 205,000 pieces plus 113 assay coins of one of my favorite designs. Considering the mintage, which was considered large at the time, these coins sold rather well at $1.00 each. However, when sales declined, 143,650 pieces were returned to the Mint and melted, leaving a net mintage of 61,350 coins. The Treasury Department demanded the 1934 coinage on hand be paid in full before any new varieties were produced. The Committee chose to return the coins, owe nothing and obtain a new variety.

Each of the Mints struck 10,000 Texas Centennial pieces in November 1935. Only 12 Philadelphia coins were returned for melting. These coins were now distributed by the Texas Memorial Museum Centennial Coin Campaign at $1.50 each.

Sales could be labeled excellent. In fact, a letter dated April 12, 1937, from Beauford H. Jester, general chairman of the Texas Memorial Museum, notified collectors that advanced orders had reserved more than half of the 1937 Texas set which was being struck, and indicated that the 1935 set was completely sold out.

Each Mint struck 10,000 Texas commemorative half dollars in February 1936. The issue was distributed on April 3, 1936. Sales were a bit weak at $4.50 per set. Therefore, 1,097 Philadelphia, 968 Denver and 943 San Francisco coins were returned to be melted.

During the months of April and May, 1937 each Mint produced 8,000 Texas Centennial half dollars. Cost was $1.50 per coin or $4.50 per set. Sales were not up to expectations. Thus, 1,434 Philadelphia, 1,401 Denver and 1,370 San Francisco commemoratives were returned for melting.

Although the Centennial Exposition was over, in January 1938 the three Mints each struck 5,000 Texas half dollars. Collectors were notified that the coins would cost $2 each or $6 per set. They were later informed that the 1936 and 1937 sets could still be procured. But as of Nov. 1, 1938, no more orders would be accepted. Sales came to a halt and 1,225 Philadelphia, 1,230 Denver and 1,192 San Francisco half dollars were returned to be melted.

The Texas Today

The 1934 Philadelphia striking is the date within the series that will be most encountered in EF-AU condition. It was treated as a souvenir and often abused.

Other issues at times can be obtained at or near circulated values because they were over-cleaned, lightly polished, whizzed or could simply display a natural metal loss. I suggest the latter, unless all that is required is a representative example in any condition. Coins grading MS-60 through MS-64 can be located without much difficulty. Value spread is small. Think higher grade acquisition. In fact, should funds be available, focus on MS-65 coinage. It is undervalued, as an individual date, and offers greater potential. Great future in MS-66 and loftier condition for the date. Luster will range from blazing satiny to satiny to dull satiny, for this date. Striking problems, especially on the reverse, can lower the grade and value of any coin within the entire series. Should you observe too much flatness or weakness of strike on the hand and knee of the Winged Victory, your specimen possesses a weak strike. Primary focal areas are the obverse eagle, then surrounding fields, and reverse Winged Victory. Numismatic villains such as bag marks, slide marks, hairline scratches, etc., can lower a coin's grade-value by appearing in the noted locations.

Little value spread exists between grades MS-60 and MS-64 for the 1935

Texas set. At present, the trio is underrated and not as abundant as believed! The San Francisco striking is somewhat easier to locate than the coins of the other two Mints. In MS-65 condition the set can currently be located without much difficulty. Sets were "broken up" in the past to acquire the Denver Mint coin. The San Francisco Mint is the rare coin of this three-piece set in MS-65 and MS-66 condition. The other P and D productions are about equally as rare. Future lies in MS-65 and loftier categories.

Luster for the 1935 set is reflected in the following manner:

1935: Brilliant frosty (not the norm), to dull frosty. Too often the coin will lack eye appeal.

1935-D: Prooflike, to semi-prooflike, to brilliant satiny, to satiny. The most eye appealing issue within the series. Reverse will look blazing satiny on those P/L creations.

1935-S: Brilliant frosty (not the norm) to dull frosty, to dull chrome-like. Too often the coin will lack eye appeal. Original Mint struck specimens will have that over-dipped look.

Little value spread can be noted for the 1936 coins between grades MS-60 and MS-64. The set is somewhat undervalued. Think higher grade acquisition. The Denver creation will be the rarer of the three coins in the aforesaid grades. The Philadelphia issue is a bit more difficult to locate than the San Francisco striking. In MS-65 condition, the San Francisco production has a slight rarity edge. Other two are equal in difficulty of acquisition. Future exists in eye appealing MS-65+ and loftier states. In MS-66 condition, it is the San Francisco coin which is at least twice as rare as the Philadelphia issue, which is approximately twice as difficult to find as the Denver production. Luster will range from flashy, brilliant satiny, to satiny, to dull satiny. Aside from the flashy 1934-P and 1935-D strikings, flashy specimens from this issue make excellent, captivating acquisitions. Rarely will any of the remaining coins in the series equal their beauty.

In the 1937 issues, not much value spread exists between MS-60 and MS-65 categories. Should funds permit, think at least MS-64. Future of this undervalued issue resides in the loftier states. Prefer this lower mintage set over the previous issues struck, if attractive. Up to grades MS-64, the trio is about equal in rarity. In MS-65 condition, the Philadelphia and San Francisco strikings are almost equally as rare. The Denver coin is somewhat more available. Eye appealing specimens are not as abundant, as many believe! Luster will range from brilliant satiny (not the norm), to satiny, to dull satiny.

The 1938 coins grading from MS-60 through MS-62 possesses little eye appeal. It's fairly priced based on demand. Little value spread exists between MS-63 and MS-64 grades, thus think higher grade. Up to MS-63 the S Mint coin is rarer than the Denver issue, while the Philadelphia coin is the easiest to obtain. In MS-64 condition, the Denver and San Francisco strikings are equally as rare. The P Mint coin again is more available. However, Philadelphia coins residing in the undervalued MS-65 and loftier categories are rarer than the other two branch Mint strikings. The S Mint is rarer than the D Mint creation in MS-66 condition, while in the next loftier grade, the status reverses. In grades MS-64 and higher, this is the rarest set within the series.

 **Related material**

The 1934 Centennial issue was distributed through 314 banks in Texas, as well as banks outside the state. According to purchasers, some banks sold the coin at $1 each in a plain envelope, as well as without any container. Others were mailed in a plain dark green Dennison half dollar coin mailing card with one insert and gummed paper security flap.

The 1935 through 1938 issues were distributed in unprinted envelopes, as well as in unprinted cardboard coin mailers, with inserts for five coins.

Fifty gold foil presentation boxes with green velour interior, housed those early struck, prooflike 1935 Denver strikings. (Should any other Texas issue reside in this box, it was replaced!) Inner top cover is imprinted (in black): THE TEXAS INDEPENDENCE CENTENNIAL, COMPLIMENTS OF E.H.R. GREEN — he was the son of Hetty Green, known as the "Witch Of Wall Street" — famous collector of coins, railroad cars and pornography. Green also presented 50 three-piece sets in silver foil boxes with a black velour interior. Same black imprint as the gold foil box, plus the addition of the date 1935 and P Mint, D Mint, S Mint. A white folded piece of tissue paper was placed on top the coins. These presentation items are most difficult to acquire.

The envelope may be worth $25. Green's boxes are worth $150 to $300 each. A three-piece box upwards of $250 to $600!

Texas Centennial materials

1934-1938
Daniel Boone Bicentennial

Reason for issue: To commemorate the 200th anniversary of the birth of
Daniel Boone.

Authorized per Act of May 26, 1934: 600,000 for all issues.

Official sale price:

1934, 1935-D, 1935-S, 1936-D, 1936-S:	$1.60
1935, 1935 with small "1934," 1936:	$1.10
1935-D and -S, small "1934" added:	$3.70/pair
1937:	$1.60; after May 1937, only with 1937-D at $7.25 set
1937-D:	only with 1937 at $7.25 set
1937-S:	For 17 days, $5.15; afterward in 3-piece set only at $12.40
1938 PDS:	$6.50 set

Production figures

Date	Business Strikes	Assay Coins	Proofs	Melted	Net Mintage
1934	10,000	7	4?	-	10,000
1935	10,000	10	4?	-	10,000
1935-D	5,000	5	4?	-	5,000
1935-S	5,000	5	4?	-	5,000
1935 (sm '34)	10,000	8	4?	-	10,000
1935-D (sm '34)	2,000	3	4?	-	2,000
1935-S (sm '34)	2,000	4	4?	-	2,000
1936	12,000	12	4?	-	12,000
1936-D	5,000	5	4?	-	5,000
1936-S	5,000	6	4?	-	5,000
1937	15,000	10	4?	5,200	9,800
1937-D	7,500	6	4?	5,000	2,500
1937-S	5,000	6	4?	2,500	2,500
1938	5,000	5	4?	2,900	2,100
1938-D	5,000	5	4?	2,900	2,100
1938-S	5,000	6	4?	2,900	2,100

Current market values

	EF-40	AU-50	MS-60	MS-63	MS-64	MS-65
1934	60.00	65.00	80.00	92.50	105.	175.
1935 PDS set, Small '34	——	——	475.	875.	1200.	1850.
1935 PDS set	——	——	210.	250.	350.	585.
1936 PDS set	——	——	210.	250.	345.	575.
1937 PDS set	——	——	425.	650.	810.	1150.
1938 PDS set	——	——	485.	885.	1150.	2350.

Designs by Augustus Lukeman

Obverse

Portrayed is the bust of Daniel Boone facing left. It is based on the frontis-piece in *Collins' History of Kentucky* (1847 and 1848 editions) and the designer's conception of how he believed the famed Indian fighter would appear. It was accepted by the Daniel Boone Bicentennial Commission of Kentucky, when the *Lexington Herald* — a newspaper which according to Col. William Boone Douglas, president of the Boone Family Association, had more knowledge about Boone than any other publication — accepted the designs. Previous disputes between the Commission of Fine Arts and the Daniel Boone Bicentennial Commission of Kentucky finally ceased. We might say they smoked the peace pipe. UNITED STATES OF AMERICA arcs above; HALF DOLLAR below.

 A metal loss will first be observed on the cheekbone and hair above Boone's ear. Primary focal portrait is a target for the whizzing merchants.

Reverse

Depicted is Daniel Boone, in the dress of his period, holding a musket in a vertical position with his left hand while holding a peace treaty with his right hand, facing Chief Black Fish of the Shawnees, who is standing at right, holding a tomahawk. In the original design, the chief held a peace pipe. When it substituted with a tomahawk, it was also suggested by Mint Director Ross that Boone's scroll be removed and Boone armed with a knife. The designer agreed, but the change never materialized, due to lack of time.

The men are depicted discussing the treaty that put an end to the nine-day siege of Fort Boonesborough (1778), which is in the background. IN GOD WE TRUST is in large letters at the top border; E PLURIBUS UNUM is in smaller letters just below. In the left field is DANIEL BOONE BICENTENNIAL. In the right field, in the rays of the rising sun, are the words PIONEER YEAR. The issue date appears at the bottom border.

Beginning in 1935, a small "1934" was added to the design just above PIONEER YEAR, creating two 1935 varieties. The small date 1934 is supposed to represent an anniversary date. I use the word "supposed" because the compan-ion date 1734, the year of Daniel Boone's birth, is omitted entirely on this issue. Mint marks (D or S) will be found in the lower right field, to the right of the Chief's ankle.

Captaining a group of civilian soldiers during a salt-making expedition in February 1778, Boone was captured by the Shawnees. He was taken to the British command center in Detroit. Exalted as a hunter by the native Americans, his life was spared. He was adopted by the tribe, as a son of Chief Black Fish — and named Big Turtle.

During Boone's three-month captivity, he overheard a conversation between a British agent and Chief Black Fish. Their objective was to extend the campaign against the pioneers across the Alleghenies. Fort Boonesborough was scheduled for attack. Escaping, Boone allegedly ran 160 miles to warn of the impending attack. During the nine-day persistent attack, the Indians began digging a tunnel toward the citadel. Their goal was to place explosives beneath the fort's entrance to blast away a portion of the fortification. Boone ordered a tunnel dug to intercept the enemy. This too was filled with explosives. When Chief Black Fish was informed about the countermine which would destroy many of his people in their underground passageway, he withdrew his force of 500 men. Boone's James Bond-style escapades caused Chief Black Fish to claim Boone was supernatural.

Boone was the type of man who favored the rigors of field and forest over the enjoyments of home and its cozy fireplace. Nevertheless, when Boone fell fatally ill in 1825 at the age of 85, it was not the great outdoors that he loved so much which caused his demise, but an overindulgence of delightful baked sweet potatoes! He was laid to rest in Missouri alongside his wife, Rebecca.

Twenty-five years later, they were reburied in Kentucky. However, a recent investigation claims that Boone's place of burial next to Rebecca possibly holds the remains of a slave who was initially placed there! If this research is proven to be factual, it is quite conceivable that this legendary hero depicted on this coin's obverse and reverse still rests on a hilltop in Kentucky, the first state west of the Appalachian Mountains.

 A loss of metal will first be noticed on the shoulder of Chief Black Fish (diagonally above UNUM) as well as on his hand.

Origins of the Boone Series

Public Law 258-73rd Congress authorized the Director of the Mint to issue 600,000 half dollars, a fixed amount. This meant that the total authorization was to be produced at one striking. The wording of the Act was not fully understood, however, because in October 1934 the Philadelphia Mint struck just 10,000 (plus 7 for assay) coins.

The first piece struck was presented to President Franklin D. Roosevelt from the Daniel Boone Commission through Senator A.W. Barkley. The Superintendent of the Philadelphia Mint placed the coin in a specially marked envelope bearing his signature.

The Boone Today

Surfaces for the issue range widely from Deep Mirror Prooflike (DMPL) to semi-prooflike, to chrome-like, to dull satiny, to an unattractive dullish semi-matte. (The latter's grainy surface provides us with that loss of luster look.) A 1937-S creation exists with a DMPL surface, as well as with frosty luster, while a

1936-S specimen for the most part will display that attractive brilliant frosty look. Exceptions with unappealing luster or chrome-like reverses (due to die polishing) also exist.

Strike for the entire series will present no problems that will influence the coin's value or grade. Inspection will reveal a minimum or insignificant weakness of the Chief's head and hand (which appears to be covering a split in his buckskin pants). I have seen several 1936-P specimens whose reverses were produced from filled dies. In this case, some form of foreign matter clogged the incused area of the die. When the planchets were struck, a portion of Boone's hand and scroll were missing. This condition would affect the value of the coins.

Coins grading EF-AU are located with little effort. Most of the time, they will exhibit some form of numismatic abuse, such as polishing, whizzing etc. Issues usually encountered are both 1935 Philadelphia varieties, the 1936-P and to a lesser degree, the 1937-P striking. Since price spread for these dates in conditions EF-AU through MS-65 is small, it seems most logical to acquire at least an MS-64 or MS-65 specimen, funds permitting. That's unless all that matters is a representative example in any grade.

The 1934 Boone issue was sold at $1.60 through the Daniel Boone Bicentennial Commission which widely distributed this issue, and prevented their return to the Mint. Luster will range from appealing satiny bright (not the norm) to very bright with little portrait field contrast, to dull.

The 1934 Boone is not exactly an abundant issue in strict MS-64+ and MS-65 condition. Excellent future in higher grades. Majority of the existing market supply falls into the not-so-choice category (MS-60-MS-63), due to numismatic abuse. In many cases in this issue, raw MS-64+ coins are offered at MS-65 prices. These are often fully original coins which were MS-65 by past standards, but which display surface detractions in the primary focal areas.

The Philadelphia pieces, struck in March 1935 were sold at $1.10 while the Denver and San Francisco issues, produced in May, were sold at $1.60 each. Today, only 5,000 sets of this issue can be assembled, with the 5,000 remaining Philadelphia pieces offered for sale as type coins. Luster for this issue will range from brilliant frosty (the norm) to just appealing. Nevertheless, locating top quality sets of this issue will not be easily accomplished, due to past distribution and later numismatic abuse. A large number of the coins bear cuts, nicks, deep scratches, slide marks, bag marks and abrasions which were overlooked by many in the early 1960s and through the early 1970s, when the term BU was heavily applied. In the mid-'70s, they were gems because of blazing luster. Today, these coins are yesterday's gems! Grading standards have become very strict. Beware of those who offer the "bargains." If prices seem too good to be true, you can bet they are. Key date is the 1935-Denver issue in MS-65 condition and the San Francisco striking in MS-64.

In October 1935, the Philadelphia Mint produced 10,000 plus 8 assay coins with the added "small date 1934" above the words PIONEER YEAR. However, in the following month, the branch Mints struck what amounted to be the lowest commemorative mintage ever created. Denver made 2,000 plus 3 assay pieces with the added "1934," while the San Francisco Mint produced 2,000 plus 4 assay pieces. Not a single coin of this issue was returned to the Mint. The "D" and "S" specimens sold in pairs for $3.70, while the remaining "P" issue was offered at

$1.10. With mintages like these, every collector and speculator wanted a set, or whatever quantity that could be purchased. Many orders were not filled, and the Commission was heavily criticized by those who did not receive the very rare Small Date issue. Congressional hearings resulted and brought to light the abuses of commemorative coin authorizations. Afterwards, larger mintages were authorized; the number of pieces which could be secured from the Mint was fixed and each new issue would be produced at only one Mint.

Eye appealing brilliant frosty luster will be the norm for this Philadelphia creation. Some pieces will have a semibrilliant surface. However, due to a late delivery and lack of knowledge concerning the appearance of the Philadelphia coin, as well as time, no original attempt was made to alter the die surfaces of the forwarded dies. They were used as received. Thus, the rare Boones or "D" and "S" issues of 1935 display a virtual matte-like finish, especially on the obverse due to their die preparation. They will look dull or grainy instead of lustrous because the dies were not prepared in a manner similar to the Philadelphia dies.

Examining the obverse surface of this issue, we can observe die polishing marks in the field. This we can label incomplete die polishing because we are able to see these lines, referred to as a residue of wire brushing the dies. For whatever reason, the reverse of both issues were polished during a halt in production, creating a chrome-like appearance. In this case, no contrast between the coin's design and field can be observed. The Denver Mint coin will display this condition, but with much lesser chrome depth and frequency of appearance. Many of these coins were altered to increase brightness, with a resulting lowering of value. Some have been artificially toned in an attempt to hide the altered surfaces.

Make certain that your set has the small date 1934 above the words PIONEER YEAR in order to be classified the "rare date set." I have seen the 1935 set without the small date substituted in complete commemorative sets for the rare date issue. The higher mintage Philadelphia issue is not rare, and should sell at a type coin price. In other words, if an MS-65 set were to sell for $1,400 because of the low mintage "D" and "S" issues, the Philadelphia striking should be valued at $150. Should the coin be extra appealing, it would be worth more money.

I highly recommend the 1935 set with added small date in all grades, as well as the individual rare D and S specimens. The rarer pieces are not abundant. In MS-64 condition, they are about equally as hard to locate. In MS-65 and loftier ratings, the San Francisco striking is rarer.

The 1936 Boone set will flaunt a luster range between brilliant frosty (for the majority of the issue) to dull frosty (as seen on some Philadelphia creations). By current strict grading standards, we will soon find it somewhat difficult to locate or assemble an eye appealing set. It's becoming even more difficult for the higher grades. Attempt to acquire those D and S specimens, the rarer strikings within the set in MS-64 and MS-65 condition.

Another rare set was created in 1937 because specimens were returned to be remelted! In January 1937, the Philadelphia Mint produced 15,010 specimens, later offered at $1.60 each. Luster will range from deep minor prooflike to semi-prooflike (not the norm), brilliant frosty, being similar in appearance with the 1935 no small date added specimens; the 1935-P, with the addition and the 1936 creations. Where are these beautiful DMPL and prooflike coins hiding? It could be that many of those produced were bagged with the group returned for remelting, while others reside in collections. I would apply same logic to the 1937-D and -S and 1938 issues.

Five months later, the Denver Mint produced 7,506 specimens. Both issues were offered as a pair at $7.25, since the Denver issue was not being individually sold. The San Francisco Mint produced 5,006 specimens in October 1937 which were sold at $5.15. Sets were made available and the three coins sold for $12.40.

1937-D and -S surfaces will range from DMPL to semi-prooflike to brilliant frosty to dull frosty. Die polishing marks or raised surface lines resembling fine scratches but which do not scratch into the surface will be conspicuous in varying degrees.

With 2,500 available sets, consider acquisition of strict MS-64 and higher grade sets and individual D and S specimens. The rare "D" and "S" pieces make this set rare and not the common Philadelphia issue, which should sell at type coin prices.

Fifty presentation pieces were supposedly struck from a set of highly polished dies at the San Francisco Mint. Fabulous future potential exists for these issues, especially in MS-65, MS-66 and MS-67 condition. The San Francisco is the rarer of the three coins.

Possibly four 1937 Boone matte Proof sets were made for the Chief Engraver of the U.S. Mint, John R. Sinnock. The branch Mint specimens were struck in Philadelphia, before the shipment of dies to those facilities. Each coin possesses a double strike with sharp squared letters and a matte surface. Remember, anyone can dip a coin in acid to attempt to duplicate this grayish finish, but they cannot create an extra blow from the coin press.

The Daniel Boone Bicentennial Commission stated the the Boone issues would end with the 1937 set, but nevertheless went ahead and obtained 5,000 sets dated 1938. Luster for all three coins will range from DMPL (certainly not the norm) to prooflike, down to dull satiny.

Lack of sales caused 2,900 coins from each Mint to enter the melting pot. We are left with only 2,100 available sets. It is a must to own in MS-64 and better condition. Fabulous future potential for all who possess or plan to acquire the set or individual type coin. Again, the San Francisco is the rarest in grades MS-64 and MS-65. The other two coins are equally as rare.

 **Related material**

Frank Dunn, Secretary of the Daniel Boone Bicentennial Commission, was responsible for the distribution of this issue. He had the 1934 half dollar forwarded to subscribers in a Dennison half dollar coin mailer. Later, creations were mailed in a Wedge Pocket coin holder, manufactured by the Lindly Box Company of Marion, Ind. When supplies were temporarily exhausted, individual pieces and sets, were placed in tissue paper or between this cardboard, inserted into an envelope and shipped. In order to save on expenses, two coins were placed in one Wedge Pocket and one in another, if a 3-piece set was requested. If two coins were required, both were placed in this holder. The 1934 envelope and holder may be valued in the $40 to $75 range; the Dennison holder itself, $2. The Wedge Pocket coin holder has sold for between $25 and $50.

1935
Connecticut Tercentenary

Reason for issue: The 300th anniversary of the founding of the Colony of Connecticut.
Authorized per Act of June 21, 1934: 25,000
Official sale price: $1

Production figures

Date	Business Strikes	Assay Coins	Proofs	Melted	Net Mintage
1935	25,018	18	4	0	25,000

Current market values

	EF-40	AU-50	MS-60	MS-63	MS-64	MS-65
1935	155.	175.	200.	275.	400.	1350.

Designs by Henry G. Kreiss

The eagle side of the coin was referred to as the obverse in a letter discussing design revisions dated Dec. 6, 1934, sent to Henry Morgenthau, Secretary of the Treasury, by Charles Moore, Chairman of the Commission of Fine Arts. Most collectors and dealers refer to the eagle side as the reverse even today. However, Mint officials chose the Charter Oak as the official obverse side.

Obverse

The obverse of this issue depicts the Charter Oak as taken from the original painting by Charles De Wolf Brownell. Connecticut received a royal charter in 1662. In 1687, its administrator Sir Edmund Andros attempted to revoke the charter under orders from the King of England, James II. It is traditionally believed that while a discussion was in progress concerning the royal charter, the candles were extinguished and the charter was removed and later hidden in a cavity in a large oak tree, which is now known as the Charter Oak. The words THE CHARTER OAK appear in the lower right field, below the tree branches. In the lower border is the word CONNECTICUT and the anniversary dates 1635-1935. IN GOD WE TRUST is in small letters at the upper left border, while LIBERTY is in small letters at the upper right border.

Examine the base of the Charter Oak, above the letters ON and TI in the word CONNECTICUT. At times the large tree trunk sports a large hit or reed mark. A small buffing tool is used in an attempt to conceal the negative.

Reverse

A bold, standing eagle faces left. UNITED STATES OF AMERICA arcs above; HALF DOLLAR below. E PLURIBUS UNUM is in the lower left field.

 Look for wear or a difference in metal texture on the upper part of eagle's front wing, just below neck. Doctoring in the form of light whizzing is usually found in this area and can be observed by its aluminum look when the coin is rotated slowly 360 degrees.

Origins of the Connecticut

This issue was produced at the Philadelphia Mint during the months of April and May 1936. It possesses a mintage of 25,000, plus 18 coins for assay purposes. Public Law 466-73rd Congress states "the United States shall not be subject to the expense of making the models for master dies or other preparations for this coinage." However, the coins were financed through a Public Works Administration project! The Connecticut Tercentenary Commission did a fantastic job in distributing a large percentage of this issue to residents of the Constitution state. They were "circulated" in six different cardboard boxes via banks within the state, as well as through the U.S. mail system.

The Connecticut Today

As noted, the Connecticut was well distributed to many state residents. It was admired as a beautiful souvenir coin and received some degree of unintentional abuse.

Today, those not so abundant specimens residing in the EF-AU category are usually encountered cleaned, whizzed or polished to some degree. The majority of the issue which grades between MS-60 and MS-64 flaunts granular surfaces which display little to no originality, due to over-dipping in a tarnish removing solution, to a partial or complete originality. Luster, when original, ranges from almost always dull satiny, resembling a light talcum powdery white look, to semi-flashy brilliant (similar to a flashy Bay Bridge obverse). Strike rarely poses a detriment to the coin's grade or its worth. What does affect the value is the presence of numismatic negatives (in varying degrees — which give us their present grade) such as bag marks, reed marks, slide marks, hairline scratches, etc., especially located on the reverse primary focal area. Here we refer to the eagle's main body, especially that smooth wing which seems to act as a magnet for these undesirables. I suggest acquiring MS-63+ and MS-64+ coinage which is fully original and eye appealing. Connecticuts in MS-65 condition are not elusive; however, we cannot classify them abundant.

In the case of flashy MS-65 pieces, one will find them elusive. For those who can acquire higher grade material, don't hesitate to add to your collection.

Four to six double struck Matte Proofs were produced for John R. Sinnock. One appeared as Lot 2055 in the 1962 American Numismatic Association Convention auction. A Matte Proof sold for $35,000 in 1988.

Related material

Banks in the state distributed this creation in six different small cardboard boxes. They are encountered as follows:

1) Silver foil covered paper hinged box. State coat of arms in blue ink on top cover with royal blue velour interior. Plain bottom, no slit pouch to hold coin in place. The most common of the six to locate. May be valued at $50 to $100.

2) Silver gray embossed slip-out box. "Hartford National Connecticut Trust Company Old State House Square" imprinted on top. Navy blue velour interior with slit pouch to hold coins. Small silver colored ribbon at bottom to slip out section and view coin. Very difficult to locate.

3) Red circular embossed design covered box. Imprinted on inner cover "The New Haven Savings Bank, New Haven Conn." Celery green velour interior with slit pouch. Red full tab or ribbon at bottom of box was intended for a planned slip-out box. Very difficult to locate.

4) Gold fine embossed covered box. Imprinted on inner cover "Hartford National Bank and Trust Co., Hartford, Connecticut." Moss green velour interior with slit pouch. Extremely difficult to locate.

5) Gold cardboard box with green (background) and gold (depictions) adhesive label with the words "The Hartford Connecticut Trust Company." Within border on label is a street scene depicting the Trust Company building, parked cars and trees. Olive green interior with slit pouch. Extremely difficult to locate.

6) Grey and white cube design box. "Hartford National Connecticut Trust Company Old State House Square" imprinted on top. Navy blue velour interior with slit pouch. Winter-white ribbon at bottom to slip out section and view coin. Extremely difficult to locate. Boxes other than the foil may be valued at $85 to $250.

1935-1939
Arkansas Centennial

Reason for issue: To commemorate the 100th anniversary of the 1836 admission of Arkansas to the Union.

Authorized per Act of May 14, 1934: 500,000 total for issue.

Official sale price: 1935, 1936 issues: $1 per coin
                              1937, 1938 sets: $8.75
                              1939 set: $10.00

Production figures

Date	Business Strikes	Assay Coins	Proofs	Melted	Net Mintage
1935	13,000	12	4	-	13,000
1935-D	5,500	5	4	-	5,500
1935-S	5,500	6	4	-	5,500
1936	10,000	10	4	350	9,650
1936-D	10,000	10	4	350	9,650
1936-S	10,000	12	4	350	9,650
1937	5,500	5	4	-	5,500
1937-D	5,500	5	4	-	5,500
1937-S	5,500	6	4	-	5,500
1938	6,000	6	4	2,850	3,150
1938-D	6,000	5	4	2,850	3,150
1938-S	6,000	6	4	2,850	3,150
1939	2,100	4	4	-	2,100
1939-D	2,100	4	4	-	2,100
1939-S	2,100	5	4	-	2,100

Current market values

	EF-40	AU-50	MS-60	MS-63	MS-64	MS-65
Type coin	50.00	60.00	72.50	85.00	125.	475.
1935 PDS set	——	——	190.	225.	360.	1175.
1936 PDS set	——	——	190.	230.	375.	1700.
1937 PDS set	——	——	200.	250.	450.	1700.
1938 PDS set	——	——	275.	475.	725.	2400.
1939 PDS set	——	——	675.	825.	1075.	3350.

Designs by Edward Everett Burr; Models by Emily Bates

Obverse

Depicted is an eagle with outstretched wings facing right positioned atop a sun (representing enterprise) whose rays extend across the entire background of the coin. He holds in his beak a scroll bearing two mottoes. On the left, IN GOD WE TRUST; on the right E PLURIBUS UNUM. UNITED STATES OF AMERICA arcs above. The three stars located directly above the eagle are symbolic of Arkansas being the third state created from the Louisiana Purchase, and represent the flags which have flown over Arkansas, namely Spain, France and America. The single star above the word Arkansas commemorates the state's participation in the Confederacy. The eagle also showed that the flag remained under the protection of the United States. Above the eagle is a diamond shape, taken from the state flag, which was originally adopted because Arkansas was then the only state which produced diamonds. This symbol is studded with 13 stars. The lower half of the diamond shape bearing the remaining 12 stars, totalling 25 — indicative that Arkansas was the 25th state to be admitted into the Union — is not shown.

On the sun is the inscription HALF DOLLAR and date of issue. (The letter R in DOLLAR is larger than the rest of the letters, which is characteristic of the issue.) At the upper border is UNITED STATES OF AMERICA. The Mint mark is located at the 5 o'clock position or on the first right ray near the sun.

 Wear will first make its appearance on the primary focal area or neck feathers, then head and upper right wing as we view the coin.

Reverse

Portrayed are the left-facing accolated heads of an Indian Chief wearing a feathered headdress, and an allegorical Liberty wearing a Phrygian cap with a band and a wreath of cotton leaves.

The native American is most likely a Quapaw, since his tribe inhabited much of the area which became the territory of Arkansas. The word LIBERTY appears above the wreath. In the left and lower left field appear the centennial dates 1836-1936, while around the lower border are the words ARKANSAS CENTENNIAL. The second S of ARKANSAS is closely spaced to the letter A, which is a design characteristic.

 Look for wear on the primary focal area of Miss Liberty's cheek. A loss of metal will next be observed on the band of her cap, directly behind her eye. Primary target for the "whizzers."

Origins of the Arkansas Series

The original sketches created by Edward Everett Burr of Little Rock and modeled by Emily Bates were rejected because the Commission of Fine Arts thought the original reverse eagle was one of the advertising type. In fact, Mint Director Nellie Tayloe Ross was to later suggest that Miss Bates should be replaced with a medalist of successful experience. Nevertheless, the state centennial committee opposed the dismissal.

Based on sketch suggestions by Lee Lawrie, sculptor member of the Commission, the issue was modeled by Miss Bates, under the supervision of Illinois sculptor Larado Taft, an intermediary between the creators and the Commission. On December 5, 1934, the new sketch was returned to Mr. Burr with the addition of the date 1935. Models were prepared. On February 7, 1935, Mr. Lawrie informed Fine Arts Secretary H.P. Caemmerer that the finished plaster model of the original eagle reverse had an unprofessional look. Also be aware that the anniversary dates (1836-1936) were the only dates slated to appear on the original obverse in the lower field. His suggestions and criticisms were presented hurriedly in order to get the coin into production. The eagle side, which was supposed to be the original reverse, was suddenly referred to as the "United States side," while Miss Liberty and the Indian Chief were labeled the "Centennial Side." Thus, the United States side — with the eagle — side was designated the obverse with the date of issue now seen in the lower border.

Why the quick change from the artist's obverse to reverse? The obverse-reverse customs which applied to regular circulating coinage did not apply to commemoratives. The Alabama Centennial commemorative was the first to possess three dates — its year of production (1921) on the obverse and the Centennial dates (1819-1919) on the reverse. The 1934 Texas issue was the second coin to do likewise. The third coin scheduled to bear three dates was the Arkansas. The pressure was on the Mint to produce a coin as quickly as possible. With the addition of the 1935 date to the design it was decided to simply follow the Alabama-Texas three date pattern. The obverse is determined by the year in which a coin was minted, while the celebration or anniversary dates grace the reverse.

The Arkansas Centennial anniversary occurred in 1936, but the first coins struck to commemorate that event were produced in 1935. The gentlemen in charge of the Arkansas Centennial did not want to be outdone by other commemorative committees. They wanted their commemorative coins struck and issued as soon as possible. Hence, 10,000 pieces were created at Philadelphia during May 1935.

By September of that year, all the pieces were sold through the Arkansas Centennial Commission of Little Rock at $1 each. Since requests for the coin were still being received, the commission decided it might be wise to have a small additional quantity struck. They enlisted the aid of Fort Worth, Texas, coin dealer, B. Max Mehl.

I would like to bring to light some recently discovered information dealing with a special request, airmailed Mint Director Ross. After the discussion with Mr. Mehl, A.W. Parke, the Commission's Secretary, informed the Director in his typed message about the authorized purchase of the Arkansas 1935 issue, to be struck at the Mints. The correspondence requested the placement of an oversized Mint mark, so that it would be more distinguishable than the customary small D and S. In addition, he also requested half of the total branch Mint production bear the Mint mark on the obverse and half on the reverse!

His request was denied on the grounds that it would involve additional expenses which the Mint could not be reimbursed for, since there was no provision in the law permitting the latter, plus the fact that his request would involve a change in policy which the Mint did not feel justified in making.

Mehl's advice was followed and 3,000 commemorative halves were struck at Philadelphia. In November, 5,500 pieces were produced at each of the branch

Mints. Few sold at $1, since Mehl himself purchased most of these coins! In January 1936, Mehl offered the 1935-D and 1935-S issues at $2.75 each and the 1935-P at $2. If you already owned the Philadelphia coin, you could get the other two for $5. Approximately 11 years later, the lower mintage coins were offered separately from the higher production issue. A characteristic of this creation is that the digit 5 is slightly tilted to the right.

In the centennial year, 1936, 10,000 coins were struck at each Mint and were offered at $1 per coin. After Jan. 31, 1936, they were selling for $1.50 per coin. Later they sold for $6.75 per set. After year's end, the commission had no desire to direct the retail disposal of the coins. They wanted to sell out the remaining stocks to the highest bidder. Many of the coins were sold, in lots, to dealers for resale in other states. These conditions combined to make the series obtainable anywhere except in Arkansas! Accordingly, the series soon acquired the nickname of "Orphan Issue."

According to additional correspondence from A.W. Parke, we can assume the 1937 strikings were produced by the Mints in late March or early April of 1937. The 5,500 production by each facility was offered as a three-piece set for $8.75. None were returned for melting.

During January 1938, each of the three Mints produced 6,000 Arkansas commemorative half dollars for collectors and investors. They were offered at $8.75 per set.

However, the so-called commemorative bubble had burst by late 1937. Prices dropped in varying degrees, as commemoratives fell from their previous level of esteem. Due to that decline in interest in commemoratives in general, slightly more than half of the 1938 Arkansas issue was sold. The balance was returned to the Mint to be melted, leaving a very low 3,150 mintage.

It appears that in January 1939, Philadelphia and Denver each struck 2,104 coins; 2,105 were struck at San Francisco. The actual delivered quantity was 2,100 pieces from each Mint. Those 13 extra coins were used for assay purposes. One year later, the set was being advertised for $20.

The Arkansas Today

A small percentage of these Centennial halves saw actual circulation. Those that grade less than EF-AU, do so because they were truly used as "long term" pocket pieces. Those pieces which are sold below the MS-60+ price range almost always have been cleaned, whizzed, over dipped, or heavily marked or just lack eye appeal. Needless to say, they should only be purchased if the price is very right. The coin can be presented to a youngster for his or her collection. Possibly, that specimen could turn into a numismatic seed which might help the individual develop into an avid collector and preeminent numismatist! Dates most often encountered are the 1935-P and 1936 issues. Little value spread will exist between all sets produced from 1935 through 1937 in MS-60 up to MS-64 condition. Should funds be available, think higher MS-64 acquisition. Zero in on the following dates: 1937-S-P-D; 1935-S-D and 1936-P. In MS-63 status, your 1935-D and S strikings are the best. Be aware that eye appealing coins will not be easily obtained.

The 1938 and 1939 set productions are "value softened" in all grades from MS-60 through MS-67 by present market activities. Eye appealing sets or individual pieces of these creations are not plentiful. At times, the coins will encounter polishing, whizzing and other forms of abuse. Worth is based on the extent of their damage. Think a minimum of MS-63+, if debating purchase. Future lies at this level and upwards. In MS-63 condition, the 1939-S and 1938-D will be the hardest to locate. The remaining four dates are equally rare. In MS-64 condition, all 1939 coins are equal in rarity but harder to locate than the 1938 production, whose trio flaunts equality within the set. The relatively low mintage of most issues contributes to the difficulties encountered in locating pristine specimens. The physical characteristics of the dies themselves contribute even more to the difficulty. Many of the issues struck from 1935 through 1939 appear to be dull or have little lustrous life or little Mint luster.

Luster will range from brilliant frosty, to brilliant satiny (not the norm) to unattractive dull. Others are plagued by lack of metal fill marks caused by not enough striking pressure in the observed location or even planchet handling damage. Also numismatic abuse has taken its toll, especially on the reverse primary focal locations. They are the portraits of Miss Liberty and the Quapaw Chief. Pay special attention to the lady's cheek and the man's jaw. The obverse eagle's neck is the primary focal area. Silver white or pristine or naturally lustrous individual pieces, as well as sets should immediately be purchased. However, they must not possess excessive bag marks, slide marks cuts and scratches, as most often seen on the coin's reverse. Naturally, they will not grade MS-65 or MS-64+. Such is the type which can be offered unslabbed. They can grade from MS-64 down to MS-60!

Do not expect the obverse of this issue to be equal in strike with the 1936 Arkansas-Robinson coin. The A-R's die engraving was deeper and sharper, giving the finished product more relief. In many years of researching U.S. commemorative coins, I have seen but very few commems of the Arkansas Centennial with a fully struck twisted scroll across the eagle's breast. On most of them, the twist at that point will look as though it had been flattened in various degrees on different specimens. Picture a hot liquid that turned into a solid which did not fully cool. Something was placed on top of it, slightly flattening part of the design. This is true especially of the Denver and San Francisco strikes during the years 1935-1938. The Philadelphia struck coins of 1935 and 1936 have a greater percentage of creations with this worn appearance. By contrast, almost all of the 1939 issue from all Mints were well struck. Strike will thus range from sharp to very weak. When breast feathers and central ribbon begin to lose detail, you lose grade and value! Specimens which grade strict MS-65 and higher offer exceptional future value, especially all dated complete sets (1935-1939).

Be aware that few Arkansas specimens will accurately grade MS-66 or MS-67. Locating individual coins of such magnitude will be a formidable task, let alone finding a three-piece set. At times, I am asked which individual dates are the hardest and easiest to locate in MS-64 and MS-65 conditions. They are as follows: 1939 P-D; 1938-S; 1937-S; 1938-P-D; 1939-S; 1937-P; 1936-P-S; 1937-D; 1936-D; 1935-P-D-S. Simply because an issue resides in ninth place does not mean it will be easily located, especially in MS-65 condition. However, chances of acquiring one of those "Arks" occupying 12th through 15th places will be greater.

Do Proof coins exist for this issue? Yes! Before the dies destined to be sent to the Denver and San Francisco Mints were shipped, John R. Sinnock, Chief

Mint Engraver, ordered struck (each year) a few sets of the extremely rare and beautiful matte Proof (double struck, acid treated) coinage. (Their respective Mint marks were "punched in" at the Philadelphia Mint.) Coins can be acid treated or sandblasted (as the case of the Hawaiian issue) after they leave the Mint. However, what cannot be added is an additional striking! Upon side by side inspection with a business strike, the difference is readily observed. Should a possible Proof candidate cross your path, send it to me for a free evaluation. Such a set sold for $89,000 in 1988! I would personally pass on any specimen offered as a Satin Finish Proof. In my opinion they were never created at any of the Mints! If you cannot resist the offering, you must attempt to have it graded by NGC, PCGS or ANACS for your own protection.

Related material

Unprinted one-piece coin holders with inserts for five half dollars were used to distribute the 1935 and 1936 Arkansas coinage. Attempt to acquire with the 1936 stamped mailing envelope from Commission which is seldom seen. Reverse flaunts a colorful red, white and blue Centennial stamp and 1936 date. At times, individual coins of the first two issues are seen housed in B. Max Mehl's coin envelopes. No real extra value here.

Stack's, of New York City, distributed the 1937 sets at $8.75 per set of three. The coins were encased in a black velvet rectangular case. The date, 1937, appeared in the upper left corner of the outer top with "Arkansas Commemorative Half Dollars" in gold letters across the central part of the rectangular holder. Within, there appears the name of the official distributors as well as a blue Stack's advertising insert which all too often does not accompany the case when offered for sale today. Most were thrown away!

Stack's also offered the 1938 sets, again at $8.75 per set, in the same type of cases as the 1937 sets. (The '37 date was removed.)

When the existing supply of the black cases ran out, and before all of the 1938 sets were distributed, a different four by five-inch holder was substituted. The outer case and the inner top was made from a fine looking, light tan, imitation wood grained paper. A velour (either black or green) covered the inside of the bottom section which had slots for the three coins, arranged in a triangle. Same was used to distribute the 1939 issue by Stack's, at $10 per set. Orders were accepted in the fall of 1938. Demand was so great that this issue was sold out before it was struck. For the 1935 envelope with insert, value is $35 to $75. The black case for the 1937 set is valued at $75 to $150. Blue advertising insert, $15 to $50. The woodgrain, $50 to $100.

Stack's Arkansas box

1936
Arkansas-Robinson

Reason for issue: To preserve the remembrance of Arkansas' 100th anniversary of admission into the Union.

Authorized per Act of June 26, 1936: 25,000 minimum, 50,000 maximum

Official sale price: $1.85

Production figures

Date	Business Strikes	Assay Coins	Proofs	Melted	Net Mintage
1936	25,250	15	8	0	25,250

Current market values

	EF-40	AU-50	MS-60	MS-63	MS-64	MS-65
1936	55.00	60.00	70.00	92.50	195.	550.

Designs

According to Public Law No. 831-74th Congress, the reverse of this issue bears the new design, since the side bearing the date — per the Act — is referred to as the obverse. However, from a numismatic point of view, the portrait side of regular U.S. coinage is usually the obverse.

Obverse by Edward Everett Burr (models by Emily Bates)

Same as Arkansas Centennial.

A metal loss will first be observed on the neck feathers, then head and upper right wing of the eagle, which is the primary focal area.

Reverse by Enid Bell (modeled by Henry Kreiss)

The reverse of this creation depicts the bust of Senator Joseph T. Robinson, past Governor of Arkansas (1913), and Majority Leader in the Senate from 1933 to 1937, facing right. Around the upper border is the inscription ARKANSAS CENTENNIAL 1836-1936. Below the Senator's chin, in the lower right field, is his name in two lines JOSEPH T. ROBINSON. LIBERTY is at the left, just behind Robinson's neck.

Henry Kreiss, who is responsible for our Bridgeport and Connecticut commemorative coinage, prepared the model from a rough drawing made by Enid Bell. Since it is the final product that counts, his initial K appears near Robinson's shoulder, touching the coin's rim.

 Senator Robinson's cheekbone will be the first area to display any loss of metal of this official reverse. Prime target for the whizzing doctors is the portrait which is the primary focal area.

Origin of the Robinson

In 1936, the Texas Centennial Commission introduced a bill in Congress which, if successful, would allow for the creation of not one but five new reverses beautifying their beloved issue. Immediately, the Arkansas group acted, calling for three new reverse designs. The Texas bill bit the dust, but a single alteration was authorized for the Arkansas. Senator Robinson's portrait was selected and the design was quickly approved by the Commission of Fine Arts on Dec. 23, 1936.

A long-standing debate in numismatic circles is whether it was illegal for the likeness of a living human being to be placed upon United States coinage. The debate centers around a law prohibiting the portraits of living persons on United States "currency." Whether legal tender coins, particularly commemoratives, qualify as "currency" — literally "current monetary instruments" — or whether the term should be restricted to its more common reference to paper money, is the crux of the debate. At least one researcher, coin collector and attorney David L. Ganz, claims the intent of the legislators at the time of writing the law was to refer only to paper money. The pertinent statutory provision, now codified as 31 USC 5114 (b) says: "Only the portrait of a deceased individual may appear on United States currency and securities. The name of the individual shall be inscribed below the portrait." So it would seem that the statute does not apply to coinage. If it does, the Treasury Secretary must answer as to why the names of Lincoln, Jefferson, Roosevelt and Washington, et. al., are not properly inscribed below their portraits on the circulating coinage.

The supplementary Act authorizing the design change specified the minimum amount of coins which could be struck. It also had a date clause which specified that the coin must bear the date 1936, irrespective of the year in which it was minted or issued. Although a maximum of 50,000 pieces had been authorized in two allotments of 25,000 each, only 25,250 Robinsons plus 15 assay coins were minted in January 1937, in Philadelphia. Thus, for the first time, coins were produced in a year other than the indicated date, due to the Act's dating clause!

Stack's of New York City distributed the issue at $1.85 each. However, the commemorative coin bubble had burst. None of the 25,250 coins were returned to the Mint. However, Abe Kosoff, a great professional numismatist whose name is known the world over, purchased 8,000 Arkansas-Robinson pieces sometime after a major decline in sales of this issue occurred.

The Robinson Today

Nearly the entire mintage of the Arkansas-Robinson exists today in Mint State. Coins offered at EF-AU values are almost always abused in some fashion or are unattractive dipped-out Uncs. The issue is abundant in the noted grades up through MS-64. Not too much value spread between grades, so think eye appealing MS-64+, should funds permit. Future for this creation begins with attractive MS-64+ classification which is undervalued. Strictly graded MS-65 Robinsons are very underrated. Great coin to possess in the latter and loftier ratings.

Luster can vary from brilliant-frosty to dull frosty. No problem here as we select the most eye appealing brilliant or naturally toned coin. Strike presents no problem whatsoever. Just don't compare with the Arkansas Centennial obverse whose die design was not as deeply engraved. What casts this issue into the nether world of lower coin grades are some of those numismatic demons known as bag marks, slide marks, nicks, cuts, scratches and lack of fill marks. That smooth clean surface design of the Senator's cheek and jaw area are susceptible to damage. As a consequence, few coins can honestly be labeled MS-65 or higher.

The official distributor has no record of handling the Proofs. However, it is known that the Arkansas Centennial Commission did present Wayte Raymond, a leading numismatist, with four Satin Finish Proof specimens. Four others were also struck. Initially, a Satin Finish Proof does not have the mirror-like surface of a Proof coin. Its surface looks like a cross between the 1909 Lincoln cent Proof and the 1909 Roman Finish gold Proofs. This comparison I'm sure cannot be readily comprehended by the neophyte. It can be difficult for most who are not familiar with this seldom used surface because it virtually resembles the finish on your satiny surfaced coin! This is why astute numismatists of the past who examined the genuine item claimed they could not see the difference between the Proof and regular issue.

After closely examining the striking characteristics of several hundred Arkansas-Robinson commemorative half dollars, I have reached the following conclusions concerning the Satin Finish creation — that I once possessed. It was stolen! (Should you know of its whereabouts, kindly advise!)

A) The eight coins given this special finish were produced with some extra striking pressure — but not via two blows from the press.

B) Coins that were struck after the "special eight" were done so with the same striking pressure.

C) Since the identical, deeply engraved new obverse and reverse dies were used, a number of pieces (possibly 75 to 100 or more) which were produced after the Satin Proofs will be observed with a corresponding sharpness of strike. Such will be evident in the upper and middle parts of the Senator's hair and ear. In fact, the latter can look so raised, making it appear that the outer part of the ear can be peeled off the coin!

This situation will intensify, with respect to the amount of oxidation present on the surface. The heavier the tone, the greater the enhancement. Should toning be too heavy or dark, it will be extremely difficult to determine whether the coin in question is the real thing. That kind of oxidation has now become part of the surface, whose originality can never be viewed again. Lost within is that specially applied Satin Finish which was difficult to appreciate, even when fully original, since it resembles the normal satiny surfaced coin.

Unless unquestionable documentation accompanies an offered coin, I suggest passing. Having it graded by a third party is very important, since it is quite possible that the offered coin and documentation might not be related or may have never known each other.

Related material

Stack's of New York City distributed this coin in a buff colored cardboard presentation holder. On the front cover is printed in black ink the following: "SENATOR JOSEPH T. ROBINSON, COMMEMORATIVE HALF DOLLAR; A NEW DESIGN ISSUED BY THE ARKANSAS CENTENNIAL COMMISSION: AUTHORIZED BY SPECIAL ACT OF CONGRESS JUNE 26, 1936; OFFICIAL DISTRIBUTORS: STACK'S, 690 SIXTH AVE., NEW YORK, NY." The inner front cover presents a photograph of the Senator which is signed: "SINCERELY YOURS, JOSEPH T. ROBINSON." Beneath this photograph is the following inscription: THIS COIN IS ISSUED IN RECOGNITION OF THE REMARKABLE SERVICES THAT THE HONORABLE JOS. T. ROBINSON HAS RENDERED TO THE STATE OF ARKANSAS. Page three, or the back inner cover, has slots for five coins; while on the back cover is printed the official distributor's advertisement. While not rare, this holder cannot be labeled abundant. Value the original envelope with holder at $75 to $150; the holder alone at $35 to $75.

1935
Hudson, NY,
Sesquicentennial

Reason for issue: To commemorate the 150th anniversary of the founding of the city of Hudson, N.Y.

Authorized per Act of May 2, 1935: 10,000

Official sale price: $1

Production figures

Date	Business Strikes	Assay Coins	Proofs	Melted	Net Mintage
1935	10,008	8	4?	0	10,000

Current market values

	EF-40	AU-50	MS-60	MS-63	MS-64	MS-65
1935	265.	360.	425.	540.	1000.	2200.

Designs by Chester Beach

Obverse

Depicted is Hendrik (Henry) Hudson's flagship, the famous *Half Moon*, a small but sturdy merchant ship, sailing to right. Located in the field is a fancifully-stylized quarter moon. UNITED STATES OF AMERICA arcs above; HALF DOLLAR below. IN GOD WE TRUST is in smaller letters above the ship. Below the ship, located on the wave and field is the word HUDSON. The designer's monogram C.B. is located at the lower border.

 A metal loss will make its ugly appearance just below the center of the mainsail. If present, a difference in metal texture, grayish white color and fine crisscross scratches will be seen. In an attempt to conceal the wear, the coin can be polished or whizzed or have this small area surface textured.

Reverse

Portrayed is an adaptation of the seal of the City of Hudson composed of Neptune, who is riding backwards on a spouting whale while holding a trident in his right hand. In the left background is a mermaid blowing a conch shell. The inscription CITY OF HUSDON N.Y. appears in the upper border, while the city's motto ED DECUS ET PRETIUM RECTI ("Both the honor and the reward of the righteous") appears on a scroll below the border inscription. Located in the lower border are the anniversary dates 1785-1935, with the motto E PLURIBUS UNUM directly above.

 The first location to show the negative effects of friction will be the city's motto ED DECUS ET PRETIUM RECTI — which usually appears softly struck. Add to this location Neptune's thigh and shoulder directly above the thigh.

Origins of the Hudson

In June 1935, the Philadelphia Mint struck 10,000 pieces, plus 8 coins for assay purposes, for an issue which honored the city founded by Henry Hudson in 1785. The Mint delivered the souvenir issue on June 28, 1935, to the First National Bank and Trust Company of Hudson. This financial institution was selected by the mayor, as required in the authorizing legislation, for delivery to the Hudson Sesquicentennial Committee. Orders were received by John R. Evans at the bank. Required for delivery was $1 per coin, plus 18¢ for registry fee and 3¢ for each two coins mailed. Thus, one Hudson would have cost $1.21. A great deal of criticism developed shortly thereafter, because only a small number of collectors were able to obtain this issue which was claimed to be "sold out" five days after delivery!

Evans advised the infuriated collectors that the situation developed because people pre-ordered the issue in early May. Demand was so great that the authorization was sold out. One month later, a retail high of $12.50 was asked for the commemorative half dollar! Who bought all the coins? It is believed that Julius Guttag of Guttag Brothers, New York City, acquired approximately 7,500 pieces at 95¢, while Hubert W. Carcabla of St. Augustine, Fla., purchased 1,000 Hudsons at the same price. The coins were abundant in the marketplace several months after Evans's announcement — at between $4.50 and $7.00 each! However, large numbers were purchased by many individuals at these new levels, thus, becoming truly well distributed and valuable. The Spanish Trail with a similar mintage is not as rare in MS-65 condition as the Hudson because it did not receive as much numismatic abuse. It is rarer, however, in MS-60 through MS-64 condition.

The Hudson Today

This issue is not readily available in EF-AU condition. When spotted, it will usually display some form of cleaning or doctoring. Popular single issue is not that difficult to obtain in MS-60 through MS-63 condition. Numismatic abuse in the form of bag marks, reed marks, hairline scratches, over dipping, etc., places much of the issue in this category. For the joy of collecting, look for specimens in these grades that possess eye appeal. Pass on the lackluster, dipped out coin, as well as one which looks as if the whale survived a harpooning attack or the *Half*

Moon displays the scars of a sea battle. Those are your primary focal points. Attractive MS-64 specimens are the specimens which offer the collector the chance to own a more valuable coin in the future. Specimens grading strict MS-65 and higher are not abundant and should be added to one's collection, if possible.

Surface luster will range from brilliant frosty (not the norm) to dull frosty. On a very rare occasion, strike will be a detriment pertaining to grade or value. Design definition was not meant to be crisp or sharp. As an example, the ship's main sail definition (ribbing) will rarely display completeness. What minute definition was present on the die, quickly was lost after a small number were struck.

 Detecting counterfeits

A counterfeit specimen will flaunt raised obverse tool marks resembling spikes or spears by the letter "F" of HALF and "AR" of DOLLAR protruding into the field, as well as a depression in the second "A" of AMERICA. The reverse will exhibit a re-tooling of Neptune's face — by an unknown numismatic plastic surgeon — plus two depressions above the "P" of PRETIUM.

 **Related material**

Orders were mailed to lucky subscribers by the First National Bank and Trust Company, Box 148, Hudson, N.Y. in their kraft envelope housed in an unmarked cardboard holder with a plain blue backing. A red wax seal was used by the bank on the back of these very hard to locate items. The holder itself may be valued at $75 to $150; with original envelope, $100 to $200.

Mailing envelope, holder with coins

1935-1936
California-Pacific Exposition

Reason for issue: To commemorate the ideals and purpose of the California-Pacific International Exposition, held at San Diego.

Authorized per Act of May 3, 1935:
1935 issue: 250,000
1936 issue: 180,000

Official sale price:
1935-S $1
1936-D $1.50

Production figures

Date	Business Strikes	Assay Coins	Proofs	Melted	Net Mintage
1935-S	250,000	132	4?	180,000	70,000
1936-D	180,000	92	4?	150,000	30,000

Current market values

	EF-40	AU-50	MS-60	MS-63	MS-64	MS-65
1935-S	45.00	52.50	57.50	65.00	85.00	140.
1936-D	42.50	50.00	65.00	80.00	100.	165.

Designs by Robert I. Aitken

Obverse

Depicted is Minerva, goddess of wisdom, seated and looking to her right. This, by the way, was adopted from the arms of the State of California. She is wearing a crested helmet, while holding a spear with her right hand. Her left hand has a firm grip on a shield which bears the head of Medusa, who could turn a beholder into stone with her glance. Above the head is the word EUREKA, a word shouted by Archimedes when he discovered a method for determining the purity of gold, and an exclamation used to express triumph on a discovery by us today. It is also the state motto. Resting against the shield is an overflowing cornucopia, (a carved goat's horn overflowing with fruit and ears of grain) symbolizing the state's abundance.

A bear facing left who appears to be looking at a "lightly struck" miner with pickaxe is at Minerva's side. Also appearing lightly struck in the field is a three-masted sailing ship, while mountains are outlines in the coin's upper background. The artist's initials, RA, are located at the extreme left border. UNITED STATES OF AMERICA arcs above; HALF DOLLAR below. LIBERTY appears just below Minerva's throne.

 A metal loss will first be detected on the breast and knees of Minerva, as well as the back of the bear's head.

Reverse

Portrayed are the two structures located on the Exposition grounds. They are the California Tower (right) and the Chapel of Saint Francisco (left) of the State of California Buildings. At the base of the two structures is the motto IN GOD WE TRUST. Located below the first T in TRUST is the Mint mark. Above the chapel in the left field is the name of the city, SAN DIEGO, while the date of issue appears in the right field. A simple design exists mostly in the upper field. Encircling the coin is the inscription CALIFORNIA PACIFIC INTERNATIONAL EXPOSITION.

 Examine for a difference of metal texture on the right edge of the California Tower crisscross scratches, if present, will indicate a metal loss, if accompanied by a grayish-white metal color.

Origins of the San Diego Coins

The San Francisco Mint produced 250,000 plus 132 assay coins, in August 1935. These coins bearing the date 1935 and the "S" Mint mark were sold in San Diego during the years 1935 and 1936 by the California-Pacific International Exposition Commission, at $1 each. Tremendous efforts to sell this issue were made and supposedly 68,132 specimens were sold in 1935. It was during this time that the interest in the commemorative series was just beginning to gain momentum, as well as a time when the collector, the dealer and the foresighted-investor viewed such an issue — with its large mintage — with little enthusiasm. Their reasoning was that this coin would take a decade to be sold, since a large quantity would be available for too long a period of time, preventing the occurrence of any significant monetary gains in a reasonable span. Being conscious of the collector, the dealer and the speculator's rationale concerning large mintage figures, plus the fact that the sales of 1935-S San Diego's were coming to a standstill, the Commission was able to have Congress pass a bill (May 6, 1936) which gave birth to the 1936-D San Diego issue. Public Law No. 566 74th Congress stated that "the coins shall be of the same design, bear the 1936 date irrespective of the year in which they are minted or issued and shall be coined at one of the Mints of the United States." This issue's maximum authorization was not to exceed 180,000, and no coins were permitted to be issued after the expiration of one year after the date of enactment of this particular Act.

A whopping 180,000 1935-S specimens were returned to the Mint to be melted. "Reincarnation" occurred and 180,000 new San Diegos, plus 92 assay coins were reborn at the Denver Mint, bearing the date 1936 and the "D" Mint mark. They were sold at $1.50 each. Thus, a total of 430,224 souvenir half dollars were produced at two Mints, via two authorizations. The following year, the Commission decided to sell either issue at $3.00 per coin to create the facade of demand and future rarity. It didn't work.

You might ask: "Where did they obtain the additional '35-S pieces if they were reincarnated?" All were not destroyed! The members of this Commission envisioned a later demand for the '35 issue, after the appearance of the '36 coin and thus vaulted 2,000 pieces for this purpose, rather than returning them to the Mint.

In 1938, Emil Klicka, Treasurer of the Exposition, endeavored to sell the 1936-D issue at $1 each, placing a limit of 10 coins per order. How many orders under a brother, sister, or friend's name do you think would have been accepted, especially when sales for both issues virtually ceased? Large hoards of both dates remained in San Diego!

The San Diego Now

The 1935-S issue is definitely available in EF-AU condition. Pieces will display abuse, while others, natural wear. Ditto the 1936-D striking, except it will be not as abundant. With little value spread between the just noted condition and the loftier MS-65 grade, for each year, who really cares? Think flashy or lustrous MS-65, should funds permit, unless any grade is fine. Only acquire for the pure joy of collecting! Thousands of coins from each date have recently surfaced, while thousands which were acquired at face value, reside in the bank vaults of their wealthy owners! Your 1936-D creation is underrated, when compared to the 1935-S issue. Problem is that too many of each issue exist and few care. A promotion will bring about a quick value increase. However, when such ceases, its back to those previous low realistic levels. Future exists only in your MS-66 category, especially for the Denver creation, which is more than three times as rare as the San Francisco striking. Luster will range from blazing frosty, to frosty, to dull frosty.

Strike at times can affect the grade-value especially for the 1936 issue. Locating 1936-D specimens that are fully struck or equal in strike with a sharply struck 1935-S piece must be considered the impossible dream, at present! After 25 years, I'm still searching!

The California Tower is flatly struck on the upper right corner of the building, beginning with the section opposite the 1 in the date 1936 (center right field) and working up two sections, appearing to be marked off by the inverted right angle (below the letters IA in CALIFORNIA) that appears to be part of the building at first glance. It is possible that virtually all the coins which displayed a sharp strike were melted. What remains are those pieces produced with a worn reverse die or struck with less pressure to save die wear from an over polished die, eliminating design definition or in the existing hoard. Grade-value is lowered when this location displays too much strike softness or lack of detail. There have been instances where the "S" Mint mark on the '35 issue appears as a blob of metal. If you look carefully, part of the "S" will be visible. Locating specimens of this issue with a fully defined "S," or fully struck Mint mark will be a "find," since many pieces have this "blob-like" characteristic. No grade-value lowering based on the aforesaid.

Those numismatic villains named bag mark, reed mark, lack of metal fill marks, slide marks, etc., make their presence felt on the obverse portrait or primary focal area. They especially attack the sensitive smooth surfaces of

Minerva's knee and long dress. Reverse primary focal location, being the California Tower and surrounding smooth fields are not immune to these numismatic negatives.

So-called Satin Finish Proofs are no more than lustrous sharply struck — *not double struck* — specimens which received angelic protection. In other words, true Satin Finish Proofs do not exist!

 **Related material**

This issue was distributed in a plain white coin envelope and in two types of a heavy unprinted holders, with an insert for one and three coins. They were contained by a gummed paper cover. Superior mailing vehicles were three different types of folder holders (3⁷/₁₆" X 2³/₈"), with cut out for one coin, glued to a piece of thin cardboard backing 4¹/₂" X 3³/₈". At times, celophane tape was added to contain the commemorative. Front cover on one portrays the issue's two reverse buildings in silver and blue ink. Another features Merry Christmas in blue lettering and silver background. Both have thin royal blue velour interiors. The third is an additional distributing Christmas card with green and red lettering, red poinsettia and green velour interior. It's the nicest of the above mentioned. All orders were accompanied by a golden-yellow Exposition paper advertising insert (5¹¹/₁₆" X 3³/₈"), printed in blue ink. Most were folded in some manner.

Value regular holders with mailing envelope at $35-$75; the deco holder, $75-$150, $150 to $200 with mailing envelope.

1935
Old Spanish Trail

Reason for issue: To commemorate the 400th anniversary of the expedition of Cabeza de Vaca and the opening of the Old Spanish Trail.
Authorized per Act of June 5, 1935: 10,000
Official sale price: $2.00 plus 10¢ postage

Production figures

Date	Business Strikes	Assay Coins	Proofs	Melted	Net Mintage
1935	10,000	8	4?	0	10,000

Current market values

	EF-40	AU-50	MS-60	MS-63	MS-64	MS-65
1935	450.	525.	665.	700.	900.	1150.

Designs by L.W. Hoffecker (models prepared by Edmund J. Senn)

Obverse

Depicted is the head of a cow, but not the head of the explorer, Cabeza de Vaca. Since there exists no known portrait of this individual and because Cabeza de Vaca means "head of a cow," the cow's head was selected for the obverse. Below the animal is located the name of the 16th century explorer ALVAR NUÑEZ CABEZA DE VACA. UNITED STATES OF AMERICA ARCS above; HALF DOLLAR below. E PLURIBUS UNUM and LIBERTY are above and between the cow's horns.

 Wear will first develop on the top of the cow's head opposite the horns, then in the center of its face. Location is a prime target for the coin doctors.

Reverse

Portrayed is a yucca tree in full bloom which is superimposed upon a map of the Old Spanish Trail, the route the explorer took through the present states of Florida, Alabama, Mississippi, Louisiana and Texas. Those cities though which the expedition passed — St. Augustine, Jacksonville, Tallahasse, Mobile, New Orleans, Galveston, San Antonio and El Paso — are represented by dots. Since the trail ended at El Paso, the city's name appears in left field. In the upper border is the inscription OLD SPANISH TRAIL. IN GOD WE TRUST appears in the lower right field, while the anniversary dates 1535-1935 are located in the lower border. The designer's initials LWH (L.W. Loffecker) are faintly visible at the lower right border, near the edge.

 A metal loss will first be observed on the central lower section of the yucca tree.

Origins of the Spanish Trail Coins

The Philadelphia Mint struck 10,000 pieces, plus 8 assay coins of this issue, in September 1935. These commemoratives were distributed by the El Paso Museum Committee at $2.00 each plus 10¢ postage and the profits applied to furthering the work of the museum. The chairman of this committee was L.W. Hoffecker, a famous numismatist. He was later elected president of the American Numismatic Association. Mr. Hoffecker's goal was to keep this issue out of the hands of speculators, which was accomplished through a fair and wide distribution.

The Old Spanish Trail Today

Those coins which fall into the circulated category will usually exhibit some maltreatment, in the form of light polishing or whizzing to hide natural wear on those used as pocket pieces. Specimens naturally grading EF-AU will seldom be seen. It is the second most expensive single issue silver design after the Hawaiian creation in these grades. What makes an example worth less than current values is the type and amount of incurred numismatic abuse. In other words, how heavily is it polished or whizzed? Thus, the coinage in question might only have a worth of half the trend value! Think original surfaces, and a disk which lacks deep cuts, scratches and large bag marks unless required is simply a representative example of the design with condition being unimportant.

It will be difficult to obtain Spanish Trails encapsulated by the major third-party grading services (ANACS, NGC and PCGS) in grades MS-60 up to MS-62, since few are submitted. Value spread is not significant in grades MS-60 through MS-64 at present. All categories are undervalued. If funds are available, think higher grade. Popular creation is available in MS-64 and MS-65 status, but is undervalued right now. Future lies in the latter and loftier levels. It is not as rare as the 10,000 mintage Hawaiian or Hudson, since the latter two received more numismatic abuse from non-collectors. Luster will range from very brilliant satiny (not the norm), to brilliant satiny, to dull satiny. Strike seldom causes a problem for the issue. What does however, are those bag marks, slide marks, etc., which attack the primary focal location of the cow's head, then surrounding fields, as well as the reverse unprotected field design and field.

Detecting counterfeits

Counterfeits do exist. One example displays a field depression, just above the cow's right horn, directly below the m of unum on the obverse, as well as in the field opposite the d of GOD (just off Florida's west coast). Coin will look grayish and can display sharp reeding if undoctored. Another fake will show small raised pimples on the right side of the cow's head, where this part of the design and field meet. On its reverse, look for field irregularity, or unevenness, especially below the words SPANISH TRAIL. It resembles an area of soil which has recently been raked. Do not confuse the latter with fine field die polishing marks. These raised lines are the result of the dies being steel brushed at the Mint. Genuine strikings do not have prooflike fields.

 **Related material**

The issue was distributed in an unprinted cardboard holder, having inserts for five, as well as six coins. L.W. HOFFECKER, 1514 MONTANA ST., EL PASO, TEXAS, on the plain front cover. These were the same coin mailing vehicles he used to deliver the Elgin half dollar. The holders are valued at $20 to $25; with original envelope, $50 to $125.

1936
Providence, RI, Tercentenary

Reason for issue: To commemorate the 300th anniversary of the founding of Providence, the first settlement in Rhode Island.

Authorized per Act of May 2, 1935: 50,000

Official sale price: $1 per coin, $1.50 by mail

Production figures

Date	Business Strikes	Assay Coins	Proofs	Melted	Net Mintage
1936	20,000	13	4?	0	20,000
1936-D	15,000	10	4?	0	15,000
1936-S	15,000	11	4?	0	15,000

Current market values

	EF-40	AU-50	MS-60	MS-63	MS-64	MS-65
1936	65.00	67.50	72.50	80.00	110.	400.
1936 PDS set	——	——	235.	255.	400.	1400.

Designs by John H. Benson and Arthur G. Carey

Obverse

Depicted is Roger Williams, often called the father of Rhode Island, kneeling in a canoe, with his right hand raised in welcome, holding the Holy Bible with his left hand, and being welcomed in friendship by an Indian at State Rock. In the left background is a stalk of maize symbolic of the many contributions given to us by the Indians. Beneath the stalk will appear the D or S Mint mark. Located in the center background is the sun, with extending rays, symbolic of religious liberty, for "Little Rhody" was the first colony to have such. The word LIBERTY appears within these rays. IN GOD WE TRUST, the anniversary dates 1636 and 1936, plus the words RHODE ISLAND appear between the thin inner and outer border. LIBERTY appears in small letters just inside the inner border.

Wear will first be observed on the tip of the canoe and upper shoulder of the Indian.

Reverse

Pictured is the shield of Rhode Island which consists of the anchor of Hope, and mantling located in the background. Above the shield is a ribbon bearing the word HOPE. UNITED STATES OF AMERICA ARCS above; HALF DOLLAR below. The denomination is located in the lower field with the motto E PLURIBUS UNUM appearing on the mantling above.

A metal loss will first occur on the lower vertical section of the Anchor of Hope, the coin's highest area of relief. Prime target for the coin doctors.

Origins of the Rhode Island Coins

The act which authorized this issue was combined with the act authorizing the Hudson Sesquicentennial half dollar. Three mints produced the Rhode Island, whose maximum authorization was 50,000 pieces.

The Philadelphia Mint produced 20,000 coins plus 13 assay pieces, during January 1936. In the following month, the Denver and San Francisco Mints each struck 15,000 coins, plus 10 and 11 assay coins, respectively.

This issue was distributed by the Rhode Island and Providence Plantations Tercentenary Commission, Inc. at $1.00 each and Grant's Hobby Shop of Providence, Rhode Island, at $1.50 each. The Rhode Island Hospital National Bank acting as depository and banking distributor of the coins had exhausted its supply by noon March 5, 1936, and was unable to fill repeat orders. Arthur L. Philbrick, Treasurer of the Commission, thereafter claimed that approximately 45,000 pieces of the maximum authorization (50,000) was disposed of in 30 banks throughout the state, with most being sold before noon, on March 5, 1936. He also noted that the residents received their coins before the mail orders were filled. Horace M. Grant of Grant's Hobby Shop originally received 6,750 pieces and had to request an additional 5,000 coins to fill the 11,500 orders he had received from almost all 48 states, Canada and the other foreign areas, as well as all additional orders he would receive by March 6, 1936.

With the available supply rapidly decreasing, orders were scaled down by the banks. By 11:00 a.m. people who desired six to 10 coins were given a smaller number. Depending upon your location, you received from one to three coins. Did this situation develop because of a tremendous advertising campaign? The Commission wanted to create a wider distribution. However, there are those individuals who did not believe most of the aforementioned statements. Some claimed that an influential banker owned more than 1,000 sets of this issue and was selling such in lots of five or 10 to the highest market price. Others claimed that for a small premium they had access to 450, and so on. Their claims of deceiving disposal appears valid. The Commission had the first 100 coins produced at the Mints placed in numbered envelopes in order of striking and accompanied by Mint documentation. According to this June 24, 1936, notice, the three-piece numbered sets would be sold to the highest bidders before the close of business on July 13, 1936. Handling the orders would be a special three-man sub-committee, consisting of Ira L. Letts, (Committee Chairman), A.P. Monroe and A.L. Philbrick. All three enclosed coins should display original captivating prooflike surfaces. To date, I have never seen such coinage!

The Rhode Island Today

Our three-Mint issue is available in EF-AU condition. It can be located displaying lightly circulated natural surfaces, as well as in abused condition. The Philadelphia creation which bears no Mint mark will be the more abundant of the trio. In grades MS-60 through MS-64, value spread is currently small for individual type coin or three piece set. Based on its design, this coin is not the most popular. Value wise, it is underrated in MS-64 condition and above. Up to grades MS-63, the Denver striking is somewhat rarer than the other two issues. In MS-64 condition, the San Francisco creation is a bit rarer than the Denver production. The Philadelphia coinage is the most common. In MS-65 and higher condition, this San Francisco commemorative is the key to the set. It is twice as rare as the others, a great underrated coins to possess. I also like the Philadelphia and Denver coins in MS-66 condition.

Luster will range from prooflike, to semi-prooflike (not the norm), to brilliant frosty to dull frosty. Strike will rarely present a problem.

Numismatic negatives in the form of bag marks, slide marks, etc., gravitate toward the primary focal locations. They are the canoe and two men, as well as the reverse anchor and surrounding fields. The aforesaid are responsible for lowering the grade-value of many coins within the issue.

Beware of polished or slightly buffed pieces which are offered as prooflike pieces. If the genuine article makes its appearance, especially in grades MS-63+ and higher, acquire it! A small number of pieces were produced from rusty dies, which should have been rejected by quality control.

 **Related material**

The issue was distributed unprotected by the banks or placed in a white plain paper coin envelope. Other orders were wrapped in plain tissue paper or placed in an unprinted five-coin insert cardboard holder, then mailed in a light tan envelope (6" X 3⁵/₁₆"), imprinted: RHODE ISLAND HOSPITAL NATIONAL BANK, 15 WESTMINSTER ST., PROVIDENCE, R.I. and its logo. Others were mailed in the same manner, but in an envelope imprinted: GRANT'S HOBBY SHOP, HORACE M. GRANT, PROP. 109 EMPIRE ST., PROVIDENCE, R.I.

Original mailing envelopes may be valued at $50 to $75.

1936
Cleveland Centennial &
Great Lakes Exposition

Reason for issue: The 100th anniversary of Cleveland, Ohio, which was to be known as the Great Lakes Exposition, and to also commemorate Cleveland's contribution to the industrial progress of the United States for the past 100 years.

Authorized per Act of May 5, 1936: Minimum 25,000, maximum 50,000
Official sale price: $1.50

Production figures

Date	Business Strikes	Assay Coins	Proofs	Melted	Net Mintage
1936	50,000	30	4?	0	50,000

Current market values

	EF-40	AU-50	MS-60	MS-63	MS-64	MS-65
1936	42.50	50.00	62.50	87.50	140.	420.

Designs by Brenda Putnam

Obverse

Portrayed is the bust of Moses Cleaveland (1754-1806) a lawyer, Revolutionary War General, and later state congressman from Canterbury, Ct., seen facing left and wearing a wig of his period. He became one of the directors and surveyors for the Connecticut Land Co., which bought 3,267,000 acres of the "Western Reserve" area in what is now Northeastern Ohio. UNITED STATES OF AMERICA arcs above; HALF DOLLAR below. Paralleled within is the name MOSES CLEAVELAND. We also note the word LIBERTY in the left field. In the field below the bust of Cleaveland are the incused initials of the coin's artist, Brenda Putnam of New York City.

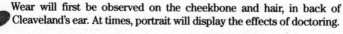

Wear will first be observed on the cheekbone and hair, in back of Cleaveland's ear. At times, portrait will display the effects of doctoring.

Reverse

Map of the Great Lakes region with a compass pointing to the city of Cleveland and the other end encircling the Great Lakes. We can note nine five-pointed stars, of which the largest represents Cleveland. The other eight also represent the cities on the Great Lakes. Reading from right to left we have: Duluth, Milwaukee, Chicago, Toledo, Detroit, Cleveland, Buffalo, Toronto and Rochester. Also present on the reverse is IN GOD WE TRUST in the upper field, E PLURIBUS UNUM in the upper left and the inscription 1836 GREAT LAKES EXPOSITION 1936 CLEVELAND CENTENNIAL. The city was incorporated in 1836, thus we have the choice of this date for the centennial celebrations.

A metal loss will first occur on the compass top. Examine for a difference in metal texture.

Origins of the Cleveland

The Cleveland Centennial and Great Lakes Exposition was held in Cleveland from June 27 to October 4, 1936, on a 125-acre lakefront site, "A Glamorous Spectacle of Supreme Significance, ...Presenting Outstanding Attractions Worthy of a World's Fair ...presenting achievements of the Arts and Science in understandable ways(!) ...portraying the drama of Industry and Commerce in fascinating and colorful manners ...unfolding the romance of Iron and Coal (!!) in impressive methods..." to quote puffery for the $25 million event. This provided Thomas G. Melish, a coin collector, with another chance to request that Congress strike a commemorative coin. Such was duly approved, "to commemorate Cleveland's contribution to the industrial progress of the United States for a century," in the orotund phrases of the Act of May 5, 1936.

The Cleveland issue was minted in connection with a legitimate celebration, and as 25,000 to 50,000 were authorized, Melish's sales strategy was very different: The coins would have to be aimed at the Exposition visitors and the general public at $1.50 apiece. As soon as the Commission of Fine Arts approved the design, June 2, 1936, Medallic Art Company of New York reduced Ms. Putnam's models to half dollar size and shipped them to the Philadelphia Mint, where 25,000 were struck in July 1936 (with an extra 15 reserved for assay). Sales were excellent. Thus, in February 1937, the Philadelphia Mint struck 25,015 more "Clevelands." Under the coinage laws of the United States of America, these coins must bear the date of the year in which they were manufactured. However, the act which created this commemorative required the entire issue to be dated 1936. The result is one date and one type of issue, and a total mintage of 50,030 coins.

As with the special 200 Cincinnati sets, Mr. Melish arranged with the Philadelphia Mint to have the first 201 coins struck and placed in specially marked envelopes in the order of the coins' striking. Thus, the first coin struck was placed in a separate envelope so marked until the 201st striking was reached. From that point on it was business as usual for the Mint operator.

In comparing the 6th, 14th, 32nd and 33rd pieces struck of the Cleveland with other gem or original pieces, it was noted that the dies used for this issue were not highly polished, thus the early presentation pieces are not prooflike in appearance. However, these coins possess a much sharper strike and their fields have a shiny smooth aluminum-looking finish, as compared to the satiny finish of the regular issue. Early numbered holders, possessing one coin, have sold for $750! Just be certain that the coin you are examining wasn't switched!

After receiving the first 201 coins from the Mint, Mr. Melish had these selected specimens taken from their numbered envelopes and placed in specially numbered black cardboard holders which had a slot for one coin, or in some cases, two coins, which were protected by a celluloid strip that covered the slot. On the back of these rare holders, there is pasted on that much-sought official documentation which states the numbered coin which is enclosed, the signature of a Notary Public, his notarial seal and the signature of Treasurer Thomas G. Melish.

These holders, along with an accompanying letter were mailed to prominent individuals and some close friends.

At the Exposition, the commemorative was issued in the same cardboard holder minus any documentation, as well as in a small paper envelope, with an ink stamped inventory number. Ohio banks also sold the commemorative half dollar.

Counterstamped coins

The Western Reserve Numismatic Club of Cleveland celebrated its 20th anniversary in 1941. It was during this event that 100 Cleveland half dollars were counterstamped with an obverse die having a portrait of Moses Cleaveland, the club's name, the date 1921 and the words Cleveland, Ohio below the portrait. The reverse die bears the inscription "10th Anniversary and the dates 1921-41." After, the 100th counterstamp the dies were destroyed. The club later requested, via a letter, that these coins be returned by their owners. Why? The Secret Service at the time felt this should not have been done. Most owners obliged. Would estimate that 25 pieces are extant. No problem today.

To celebrate their 50th anniversary, the Western Reserve Numismatic Club of Cleveland had counterstamped only 13 Cleveland half dollars when the die was allegedly destroyed. (I say allegedly, because a few too many pieces have entered the marketplace in the last two years. However, anything is possible.) The obverse die shows a portrait of Moses Cleaveland, facing the words FIFTY YEARS 1971. Below the bust of the Brigadier-General is an error! His name is spelled incorrectly! We can note the following: MOSES CLEVELAND! The letter "a" is missing from his name. Around the border is the inscription Western Reverse Numismatic Club and the date 1921. No reverse die was used. No problem with the government here.

As previously noted, back in 1796, Moses Cleaveland surveyed the territory and laid out the present area of today's Cleveland, Ohio. This location was originally named Cleaveland, honoring the man. However, when the area's first newspaper, the "Cleveland Advertiser" came into existence about 1830, the headline was too long for the form and the letter "a" was taken out of Cleaveland. This revision was readily approved by the people of the area and thus, we have today's spelling.

The Cleveland Today

The issue is quite available in circulated EF-AU condition. Encountered pieces will display original surfaces with some metal loss, as well as numismatic abuse. Value spread between the noted rating and MS-64 is quite small. Think MS-64, since the common Cleveland is readily attainable! Eye appealing, strictly graded MS-65 specimens are undervalued. Future resides in the latter classification and your loftier states.

Luster will range from brilliant frosty, to dull frosty. Strike will rarely be responsible for a grade-value lowering! Bag marks and other surface negatives can plague obverse portrait and reverse compass, plus its surrounding fields, removing many coins from the MS-65 category.

 **Related material**

As previously mentioned, 201 coins were distributed in Wynne leatherette single and double coin holders, with notarization on back. Others sold to collectors, etc., were housed in the said holders without notarization ($10), as well as a cardboard holder (4"x3") with an inverted triangular pocket (4³/₈" base; 3¹/₁₆" sides), in which one or two Clevelands were inserted unprotected! Such was imprinted with Melish's mailing address ($25 to $50). This commem was also sold at the Exposition in a 3¹/₂"x2" coin envelope, imprinted GREAT LAKES EXPOSITION, CLEVELAND CENTENNIAL, COMMEMORATIVE HALF DOLLAR and accompanied by a blue stamped inventory number.

Notarized empty holders may be valued in the $100 to $300 range. Remember that an MS-64 Cleveland is currently worth around $100, and can be substituted for the genuine item.

Documentation certifying the 6th Philadelphia coin struck

1936
Wisconsin Centennial

Reason for issue: The 100th anniversary of the establishment of the Territory of Wisconsin.
Authorized per Act of May 15, 1936: 25,000
Official sale price: $1.50. Lots of 10 or more, $1.25 each

Production figures

Date	Business Strikes	Assay Coins	Proofs	Melted	Net Mintage
1936	25,000	15	4?	0	25,000

Current market values

	EF-40	AU-50	MS-60	MS-63	MS-64	MS-65
1936	145.	155.	175.	205.	225.	350.

Designs by Benjamin Hawkins, originated by David Parsons

Obverse

Depicted is a badger, the state animal, facing left, standing on a log. Below this log in relief is the designer's initial H. Located behind the badger are three arrows which represent the war between the settlers and the Black Hawk Indians, while on the right side of the animal is an olive branch, representing the peace which paved the way for the creation of the Territory of Wisconsin. UNITED STATES OF AMERICA arcs above; HALF DOLLAR below. E PLURIBUS UNUM and LIBERTY are in smaller letters inside the other legends, and IN GOD WE TRUST is wedged between the arrows and the olive branch.

 A metal loss will first occur on the badger's ribs, then shoulder. Primary target for the coin doctors.

Reverse

Portrayed is the Wisconsin Territorial seal, (which is not reproduced "line for line") and depicts a miner's right forearm with his sleeve rolled up to the elbow, holding a pickaxe. In the background at a distance appears a pile of lead ore and soil. Situated below this is the inscription 4TH DAY OF JULY ANNO DOMINI

1836, indicating a day when Henry Dodge, the first Governor of the Wisconsin Territory, took office. Around the border is the inscription WISCONSIN TERRITORIAL CENTENNIAL. The date 1936 appears at the six o'clock position, between two five-pointed stars.

Wear will first be noticed on the hand holding a pickaxe.

Origins of the Wisconsin

The original models of the Wisconsin were prepared by David Parsons, an art student of the University of Wisconsin. However, Benjamin Hawkins, a New York artist, made extensive changes in the designs and inscriptions in order to meet various Mint specifications. Thus he is credited with the finished creation. His initial appears on the coin which was produced at the Philadelphia Mint during July 1936. The additional 15 pieces were struck for assay purposes.

The Act for this issue did not limit the number of coins that could have been manufactured by the Mint upon receiving an order. However, Fred W. Harris, a coin collector who was Director of the Coinage Committee of the Wisconsin Centennial which distributed the coins at $1.50 each (plus 7¢ postage for the first piece and 2¢ for additional half dollars), believed the 25,000 pieces received from the Mint was sufficient. As noted in a letter from L.M. Hanks, Treasurer of the State Historical Society, he was correct, since one could still purchase this issue in lots of 10 or more for $1.25 per coin as late as March 7, 1945. In fact, one could acquire the coin for $3.00 plus 7¢ postage seven years later.

The Wisconsin Today

The Wisconsin is not abundant in EF-AU condition. Encountered specimens will usually be cleaned, or possess a slight metal loss from mishandling or show some doctoring. Value is dependent upon the type and extent of abuse. It can be worth as much as a MS-60 coin or less than EF-AU values. There is a small value spread between pieces rated MS-60 and MS-64. The Wisconsin can be acquired with little effort in MS-60 through MS-65 condition. Flashy, attractive "badgers" are what should be acquired, possessing no ugly digs, hits, slide marks or too many hairline scratches. Acquire for the pure joy of collecting. (This issue, as well as the York, Elgin, Roanoke, Stone Mountain, Iowa, Rhode Island, P-Mint, and San Diego [1935-S and 1936-D] entered the marketplace in large numbers, over the last two years.) Future resides in the loftier grades. Luster will range from blazing satiny, to satiny, to dull satiny. Strike rarely presents a problem for the issue. Surface negatives, such as slide marks and bag marks are attracted to that obverse badger, and the reverse forearm and surrounding fields.

 ## Related material

The issue was distributed in a plain five-piece cardboard holder with inserts for five coins. One to two coin orders were wrapped in tissue paper and mailed in an envelope imprinted L.M. HANKS, FIRST NATIONAL BANK BUILDING, MADISON, WISC. or rubber stamped: AFTER 10 DAYS RETURN TO STATE SUPERINTENDENT, STATE CAPITOL, MADISON, WISC. These stamped envelopes can be valued at $25 to $50.

1936
Cincinnati Music Center

Reason for issue: To commemorate the 50th anniversary of Cincinnati, Ohio, as a center of music and its contribution to the art of music.

Authorized per Act of March 31, 1936: 15,000

Official sale price: $7.75 per set

Production figures

Date	Business Strikes	Assay Coins	Proofs	Melted	Net Mintage
1936	5,000	5	4?	-	5,000
1936-D	5,000	5	4?	-	5,000
1936-S	5,000	6	4?	-	5,000

Current market values

	EF-40	AU-50	MS-60	MS-63	MS-64	MS-65
1936 PDS set	——	——	760.	950.	1400.	2400.
1936 single	165.	190.	240.	315.	365.	760.

Designs by Constance Ortmayer

Obverse

This issue depicts an idealized, almost unrecognizable bust of Stephen Foster. This popular composer and songwriter was born on July 4, 1826, in now part of Pittsburgh, Pa. He wrote such songs as "Oh Susannah," "Old Kentucky Home," "Old Black Joe." STEPHEN FOSTER AMERICA'S TROUBADOUR appears below the bust. The origin of this expression cannot be traced. UNITED STATES OF AMERICA arcs above; HALF DOLLAR below. Located in the left field in a direct line with the U in UNITED and the nape of the neck in faint relief are the designer's initials, C.O., in monogram. At times, the initials are virtually nonexistent!

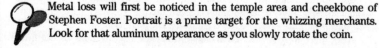
Metal loss will first be noticed in the temple area and cheekbone of Stephen Foster. Portrait is a prime target for the whizzing merchants. Look for that aluminum appearance as you slowly rotate the coin.

Reverse

Depicted is a female, which represents music, on one knee, playing a lyre that she is holding with both hands. In the lower right field is the anniversary date 1936, while in the upper left field is the other. 1886 was chosen on the basis of no historical event whatever, in order to obtain a suitable year for convincing Congress to authorize the coin, "to commemorate the 50th anniversary of Cincinnati, Ohio, as a center of music, and to commemorate Cincinnati's contribution to the art of music in the United States for the past 50 years," to quote the authorizing act. The Denver (D) or San Francisco (S) Mint mark is located below the date 1936 on the respective issues. The Philadelphia Mint uses no identifying mark on this issue. Below the kneeling figure are the inscriptions IN GOD WE TRUST, E PLURIBUS UNUM and LIBERTY. Around the coin's border is the inscription CINCINNATI A MUSIC CENTER OF AMERICA. The word OF appears somewhat weakly struck. This is a design characteristic.

Examine the female's breast for a difference in metal texture and crisscross scratches, as well as her thigh opposite the date 1936. Also a prime target area for the coin doctors.

Origins of the Cincinnati Coins

False claims were at once used as grounds for rejection by the Federal Commission of Fine Arts, whose Chairman Charles Moore wrote on May 13, 1936, complaining about them to Mint Director Nellie Tayloe Ross. First of all, Stephen Foster had no association with the musical life of Cincinnati; his only relevance to the city was that he worked there as a bookkeeper in his brother's firm for three years in the 1840s. He lived in Pittsburgh and New York. In addition, as Moore pointed out, Cincinnati had become the locale for musical festivals going back to the year 1873 with the May Festival Association, organized by George Ward Nichols, and conducted by the illustrious Theodore Thomas, using a chorus of over 1,000 voices assembled from 35 midwestern musical societies. He became director (1878-81) of the newly founded Cincinnati College of Music, and in later years acquired the title of "Musical Missionary" by taking the Cincinnati Symphony Orchestra (itself and outgrowth of the biennial festivals) on nationwide tours, gradually creating an appetite in audiences from Massachusetts to California for symphonic music, at a time when most people's musical experience consisted of village band concerts, singing around the parlor piano, or watching song-and-dance routines done in "Uncle Tom" shows or blackface minstrel shows. Possibly, the word troubadour was mentally created from the above mentioned. Thus, a commemorative coin struck to preserve the remembrance of Cincinnati's immense contribution to American's cultural life should have possessed the dates 1873-1923 and it should have portrayed Theodore Thomas.

Unfortunately for rationality and historical accuracy, the "Cincinnati Musical Center Commemorative Coin Association" (unknown to any of the Cincinnati musical groups then or later) put pressure on the Treasury to overrule the Commission of Fine Arts, and the design was adopted as is.

Also, there were neither local celebrations nor any attempts to coordinate publicity for the coin with any musical event in Cincinnati. In fact, as it was an even numbered year, there was not even a Festival to tie in with publicity for the coins, let alone to justify the act's wording. The aforementioned complaints and rationale proved ineffective.

The Mints each produced 5,000 specimens of this issue. San Francisco struck one additional coin for assay purposes. Thomas G. Melish, Treasurer of the Cincinnati Musical Center Commemorative Coin Association, as well as Treasurer of the Cleveland Centennial Commemorative Coin Association, was a coin collector, as well as a businessman. He originally attempted to have the Philadelphia Mint strike 10,000, Denver 2,000 and San Francisco 3,000 of these commemorative pieces. Wow! Imagine if that was pulled off! However, this promotor had the "pull" to have the first 200 pieces struck of each issue caught by an operator wearing a soft glove (to avoid any nicks or scratches). Each piece was then placed in a specially marked envelope (at each Mint) in the order of each coin's striking.

After the specially marked envelopes were received by the Association, the specimens were taken from their containers and placed in black cardboard holders which had slots, for each Mint's issue. A celluloid strip covered the exposed set of coins. On the back of these holders there is pasted that much desired official documentation which states the numbered set of coins enclosed. If you had a numbered holder which states that the enclosed coins are the sixth piece struck at each Mint, this is what should be contained, unless the coin was substituted. The signature of a notary public, his seal and the signature of the Treasurer, Thomas G. Melish, is also present on the document. An accompanying letter was mailed with each numbered set of coins — sealed in cellophane — to prominent individuals as the president, senators, etc., and close friends. These specimens exhibit no special surfaces.

Ordered sets were forwarded by the Association to those "most fortunate" individuals in the same type of holders, — but without official documentation — at $7.75 each. I say most fortunate, because the issue was oversubscribed before these sets were released!

This Cincinnati set was mailed during the height of the commemorative speculation bug, or mania, a time when many people wanted commemorative half dollars; a time when many were attempting to invest as much as possible in an issue, thereby decreasing its availability to bona fide collectors who would be forced to pay a prohibitive price for them. Cartoons of the time depicted this scene whereby speculators buying commemorative coins for $5.00 would sell these pieces to the rushing collector for $10.00.

In August 1936, when this low mintage set was released, the asking price to the "late bids," or those who were fortunate to be classified "an oversubscriber," was $45.00. This was due to both a great demand and a good distribution, plus the fact that few owners wanted to part with their sets at any price! In fact, the set was later offered for sale at $75.00 or about $625 in today's dollars! The Association attempted to have a '37 issue minted, but the "bill got killed!"

When reading the Acts during this period which authorized the various issues, they specify that the issues will be coined by the Director of the Mint. Thomas G. Melish was able to "pull a few political strings" and had the phrase "at the Mints" inserted which permitted this small authorization (15,000) to be divided among "the Mints." However, this was the last time this phrase "at the Mints" was to be inserted during the 1930s.

The Cincinnati Today

Virtually all coins which are offered at circulated values are of the polished, whizzed or doctored variety. Since value spread between the EF-AU and MS-64 categories is presently insignificant, focus on the highest grade of coin. Bag marks and numismatic abuse place a large number of this issue in the MS-60 - MS-63 category. In the latter condition, the Denver striking is harder to locate, at present than the Philadelphia and San Francisco coinage. However, in the MS-64 state, it is the easier of the three coins to locate, the other two being equal in rarity. In strict MS-65 condition, our San Francisco striking is difficult to obtain. It's definitely more than three times as rare as the Philadelphia piece, which is certainly more than twice as hard to locate than the Denver issue, the coin that reflects your type coin value! MS-66 coinage offers great potential.

It is an outright score for a collector or dealer to acquire a strictly graded 1936-S slabbed MS-65 Cincinnati for a type coin value. Each mint striking has its own value, especially in grades MS-64+ and higher. Luster will range from brilliant frosty, to dull frosty, as well as chrome-like (not the norm) for Philadelphia coinage. It's brilliant frosty to dull frosty for the Denver production and brilliant satiny (not the norm) to dull satiny for the "coast" creation. This issue was designed to exhibit soft detail. On occasion, too soft of a strike can lower a coin's grade and value, if the hair detail above Stephen Foster's ear displays too much flatness or the head of the reverse female does likewise.

True MS-65 sets are difficult to find. Ditto the MS-66 coinage which is not easily obtained, especially the 1936-S and 1936 Philadelphia strikings. This would be a set that possesses full original mint luster, no detrimental, ugly bagmarks and is fully struck (for the issue). A specimen can possess almost all these qualities — and a fair number do — but what might spoil the piece is a large bagmark or slide marks on Stephen Foster's portrait, or similar marks located somewhere on the reverse female — your primary focal points — or field. On occasion, should a coin be so spectacular or eye appealing, the surface negative is overlooked and the coin is graded MS-65. However, just know how to grade!

Set No. 134 is still housed in its holder and sealed in the original cellophane. Upon inspection, the San Francisco Mint coin sports a large bag mark on the female's arm! However, for some strange reason, the Denver Mint specimens received a little more care. It is usually found in better "shape," followed by the Philadelphia Mint and San Francisco Mint issues, when comparing the depth of strike, surface luster and surface negatives.

Should you observe scratches behind Stephen Foster's head near the letters TED in the word UNITED, do not panic. These raised lines are die scratches. Remember, it is the scratches that scratch into the surface that one should be concerned about. Also be alert for those fine hairline scratches resulting from improper drying with a cloth or towel. Tilt that coin back and forth, to observe if these are present. Long or large hairline scratches can quickly lower a coin's grade from MS-65 to MS-64, if present in primary focal areas.

Detecting counterfeits

Cast counterfeits are high quality coins made from a genuine specimen. Aside from the strange surface (which is unlike ordinary mint bloom), these show raised granular defects especially on cheek and in field near TROUBADOR. On the reverse, there are raised die file marks at CINCINN, and more of the same kind of granular raised "bubbles" around dates and mottoes.

A more recent counterfeit will reveal what resembles minute pinholes above the ear and temple area of Stephen Foster and metal spike under the "A" of the word HALF. Reverse design will reveal thin file marks between the letters "AMER" of AMERICA, "ATI" of CINCINNATI and "NT" of CENTENNIAL. The coin's rim is rounded.

 Related material

This issue was distributed to 200 lucky people in a holder previously described with its notarization notice pasted on the back. Also included were three manila coin envelopes. The paper container which housed the Denver coin had the following typed: THE ENCLOSED COIN IS NO. 134 OF THE FIRST 200 HALF DOLLARS STRUCK AT THE DENVER MINT FOR THE CINCINNATI MUSIC CENTER COMMEMORATIVE COIN ASSOCIATION. MARK A. SKINNER, SUPERINTENDENT, BY ACTING SUPERINTENDENT and signed by the latter. The number (134) is also stamped on the envelope. The accompanying two envelopes are blank except for the stamped number. One was pencil marked "P" and the other "S," most likely by Melish. The same Wynne black leatherette holder without back notarization and imprinted CINCINNATI, MUSICAL CENTER GOLDEN ANNIVERSARY, COMMEMORATIVE HALF DOLLARS, P, D, S (both small and large) housed the coin set, mailed from Thomas G. Melish, 105 East, Third Street, Cincinnati, Ohio.

Original numbered holders can be valued in the range of $150 to $400. As the described #134 above, $200 to $600.

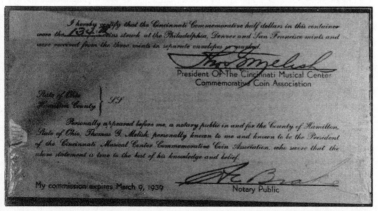

Documentation attesting that the enclosed coins are the 134th from each Mint

1936
Long Island Tercentenary

Reason for issue: The 300th anniversary of the first white settlement on Long Island, New York.

Authorized per Act of April 13, 1936: 100,000

Official sale price: $1

Production figures

Date	Business Strikes	Assay Coins	Proofs	Melted	Net Mintage
1936	100,000	53	4?	18,227	81,773

Current market values

	EF-40	AU-50	MS-60	MS-63	MS-64	MS-65
1936	53.50	60.00	67.50	80.00	125.	635.

Designs by Howard Kenneth Weinman

Obverse

Depicted are the accolated heads of a Dutch settler and an Algonquin Indian facing right. This Dutch settler symbolizes the Dutch settlement at Jamaica Bay in 1636 which was named *Breuckelin*, after a town in their former country. This name was later changed to one that almost everyone has heard of: Brooklyn, home of the famous "bums" or Brooklyn Dodgers baseball team. The Indian symbolizes the 13 tribes of Algonquin Indians that lived on the island when Henry Hudson discovered it in 1609. LIBERTY is located at the upper border, while E PLURIBUS UNUM appears in the lower border. Below the Indian's chin is the designer's monogram which appears in relief, H.W

Howard Kenneth Weinman is the son of A.A. Weinman, creator of the famous Walking Liberty half dollar and Mercury dime.

 Wear will first be noticed on the Dutch settler's cheekbone. Examine for a difference in metal texture and fine crisscross scratches in this location. Also be aware of doctoring on the portraits.

Reverse

Portrayed is a Dutch three-masted ship sailing to right. Motto IN GOD WE TRUST is incused on the waves below the ship. Date 1936 appears below motto with the inscription LONG ISLAND TERCENTENARY placed below date in the lower border. Around the upper border appears UNITED STATES OF AMERICA and HALF DOLLAR.

 Metal loss first occurs in the center of the ship mainsail. Lack of metal flow marks which resemble small scratches and digs can be present. They could detract from the specimen's eye appeal — and value — depending on their location as well as size on these sails. Prime target for whizzing and doctoring of some form to make coin appear better than it actually grades.

Origins of the Long Island

Section 2 of the Act which approved this issue on April 13, 1936, stated the following: "The coins herein authorized shall bear the date 1936 irrespective of the year in which they are minted or issued; not less than 5,000 coins shall be issued to him at any one time and no such coins shall be issued after the expiration of one year after the date of enactment of this Act." A previous section also states that "there shall be coined at a mint of the United States and not the mints," thus doing away with any hope of having the branch Mints create "mint varieties" of the same issue.

In the case of this issue, with a maximum authorization of 100,000 pieces, a required single date prevented this coin from being minted in 1936, 1937, 1938, etc. The minimum number of coins also stated in the Act prevents the possibility of small mintage issues.

The Philadelphia Mint produced 100,053 coins in August 1936 for the tercentenary celebrations which unfortunately had taken place several months earlier! This issue was sold by the Long Island Tercentenary Commission and distributed through banks on Long Island at $1.00 each. It was originally delivered by armored truck to the National City Bank, 181 Montague St., Brooklyn, N.Y. They were called for by its vice president and Long Island Tercentenary Committee Treasurer Dewitt A. Forward and received by Louis C. Wills, Chairman, and John W. Smith, Secretary of the Committee.

Advanced sales amounted to almost 19,000 pieces. Approximately 50,000 of these creations were designated for sale near my birthplace in Brooklyn via an office at the *Brooklyn Eagle* newspaper. One half that figure would be aimed at potential sales in the Borough of Queens, 15,000 at Nassau County and 10,000 at Suffolk County. When sales came to a standstill, 18,227 pieces were returned to the Mint and melted, leaving us with a total mintage of 81,826.

The Long Island Today

Quite available in EF-AU condition. Attempt to acquire an undoctored, appealing specimen, even if funds are limited. No problem in locating creation graded MS-60 through MS-64. Current value spread between these grades is small. Thus, collectors should target an attractive MS-64. Surface negatives, on the primary focal areas of the issue (obverse portraits and reverse ship) keep many coins out of the MS-65 category. Real future of issue resides in the latter and higher grades. Luster will range from brilliant flashy to dull satiny. Strike rarely, if ever, affects grade and value.

 **Related material**

The issue was distributed in a Dennison unprinted, cardboard holder with inserts for five pieces. Mailing envelope is imprinted with the Commission's name, in care of the National City Bank and noted address within chapter. Teal blue rectangular hinged presentation cases with gold peripheral trim design and embossed LONG ISLAND TERCENTENARY COMMITTEE [PRESENTED] TO and the individual's name seldom surface.

Original holders may be valued at $35 to $75; with envelope, and at times the actual invoice, $50 to $125. The presentation case — if genuine — $100 to $250.

1936
York County, Maine, Tercentenary

Reason for issue: The 300th anniversary of the founding of York County, Maine.

Authorized per Act of June 26, 1936: 30,000

Official sale price: $1.50 local, $1.65 out of state

Production figures

Date	Business Strikes	Assay Coins	Proofs	Melted	Net Mintage
1936	25,000	15	4?	0	25,000

Current market values

	EF-40	AU-50	MS-60	MS-63	MS-64	MS-65
1936	135.	145.	155.	170.	225.	275.

Designs by Walter H. Rich

Obverse

Depicted is a stockade which is supposed to represent Brown's Garrison which was situated on the Saco River and is approximately the site of the present city of Saco, Maine. Situated in the foreground are four sentries, one mounted. Seen above the stockade is the rising sun, with the word LIBERTY resting on the serene orb's rays, E PLURIBUS UNUM is below the stockade, while UNITED STATES OF AMERICA and HALF DOLLAR form the border. Located below the IBUS in PLURIBUS are the designer's initials WHR.

 Wear will first develop on the mounted sentry and right section of the stockade.

Reverse

Portrayed is the seal of York County, Maine, which is composed of a cross on a shield. Located in its upper quarter is a pine tree which symbolizes the state of Maine. Anniversary dates are present at sides of the shield, with motto IN GOD WE TRUST in curved letters located at the lower inner border. Around the outer border is the inscription with decorative stars YORK COUNTY FIRST COUNTY IN MAINE.

  A metal loss will first occur on the pine tree located in the upper left quarter of the symbolic design. This seal is a target area for the coin doctors.

Origins of the York

The Philadelphia Mint produced 25,000 coins plus 15 assay pieces during August 1936. This issue was distributed by the York County Tercentenary Commemorative Coin Commission, Saco, Maine.

By not requesting the maximum 30,000 silver 50¢ pieces permitted by the Act, they were unable to obtain the additional 5,000 Yorks. It was explained to the Commission that it had to secure the full authorization at one time — but not less than 25,000 coins. Any difference would be their loss. Two fifths of this issue were put aside for the residents of York County and their state at $1.50 per coin. However, this amount had to be increased, since the demand was greater than the allotted supply. All out of state orders required an extra 15¢ to cover handling and shipping charges. When sales came to a halt, approximately 18,500 of this issue were sold. Instead of returning the remaining coins to the Mint, the Association vaulted and later offered them for sale, in the late 1950s, in half roll minimum (10 coins) for $15.50.

The York Today

This creation is not plentiful in EF-AU condition. Located pieces will be cleaned, lightly mishandled or display some form of doctoring. It can be equal in value to a MS-60 coin or an EF-AU specimen. All is determined upon the kind and extent of mistreatment. There currently exists a small value spread between coins grading MS-60 through MS-64. If funds are available and the issue desired, it would be illogical not to think highest grade procurement. Our York can be obtained with little difficulty, in grades MS-60 through MS-66. Acquire for the joy of collecting.

Luster will range from blazing satiny, to satiny, to dull satiny. Strike will not offer the issue any problems. Numismatic negatives such as slide marks and bag marks will especially attack the reverse seal of York County (primary focal point) and surrounding fields. Obverse stockade and field below is the reverse focus.

 **Related material**

The issue was distributed in a paper holder which depicts on the front cover black and white sketches of Brown's Garrison, and the York National Bank of Saco, Maine.

Page two, or the inner front cover states the following:

"In the early days of York County probably most transactions were carried on by barter and it was not until 1803 that the business of the county had become complex enough to require a bank. It was then, one hundred and thirty three years ago that our bank was

chartered and as York County is the 'First County of Maine' so The York National Bank is the 'First Bank in Maine.' On the day of its opening and until 1831, all the entries were made by a stocky gentleman with a serene and self confidence countenance wearing long black silk stockings, short trousers, shoes with large silver buckles, and a stock, predecessor of the collar. He took great pride in the fact that he served for a brief period for General Washington as his clerk. There are many other interesting historical facts in the records of the bank and we take particular pride in the fact that we have stood the test of time and are an active, strong bank today servicing the entirely changed requirements of the public.
"YORK NATIONAL BANK"

Page three has slots for five coins, while the back page, or cover is blank. Within the accompanying mailer was placed a ssue paper insert. ited on it was the following:
"We thank you for your interest in our commemorative half dollar, and extend to you the hospitality of York County, Maine.
"York County Commemorative Coin Commission."

Envelopes were imprinted YORK COUNTY TERCENTENARY, COMMEMORATIVE COIN COMMISSION, YORK NATIONAL BANK, SACO, MAINE and AFTER 5 DAYS, RETURN TO CLERK OF COURTS, ALFRED, MAINE. On back of some envelopes was a red-orange paper seal. Envelope and mailer are worth between $50 and $125, depending on condition. With tissue insert, $50 to $150.

The first 100 Yorks minted were mounted in the lower right corner cutout of an attractive map of "Olde York County Maine." Below the coin and outside the map border was printed: THIS COIN IS NO.___ OF THE ISSUE. Framed under glass, these rare strikings, which possess no prooflike or special Mint-produced surface, were presented for cooperation showed in making the Tercentenary celebration a success in the recipient's community. It was referred to as a token (of appreciation) by Ralph W. Hawkes, Secretary and Treasurer of the York County Tercentenary Commemorative Coin Commission. In the early 1980s, a Massachusetts dealer acquired the above item with its beautifully colored toned York, in a frame, at a flea market for $75! He turned down my $2,500 offer. These have sold in the past in the $2,500 to $4,000 range.

1936
Bridgeport, Conn.,
Centennial

Reason for issue: To commemorate the 100th anniversary of the incorporation of Bridgeport, Conn.

Authorized per Act of May 15, 1936: 25,000 minimum, unlimited maximum

Official sale price: $2

Production figures

Date	Business Strikes	Assay Coins	Proofs	Melted	Net Mintage
1936	25,000	15	4?		25,000

Current market values

	EF-40	AU-50	MS-60	MS-63	MS-64	MS-65
1936	82.50	90.00	100.	140.	190.	480.

Designs by Henry G. Kreiss

Obverse

Portrayed is the head of the one-time Mayor and best known showman of Bridgeport, Conn., Phineas Taylor Barnum, facing left. Around the coin's border is the inscription BRIDGEPORT CONNECTICUT CENTENNIAL 1836-1936. Above the centennial dates is the name P.T. BARNUM.

 The coin's rims offer this issue's lower relief designs excellent protection. Therefore, a loss of metal or rubbing will first be seen on the rims and does not at all affect the grade! When a difference in metal texture does make its presence known, it will do so on Barnum's cheekbone and on his hair, diagonally above the ear, directly below the vertical bar of the second letter "T" of CONNECTICUT.

Reverse

Depicted is a modernistic, thrusting metallic stylized eagle with upraised wings, standing atop a ledge, facing right. (A new configuration of our national bird?) Inverted, it resembles a shark! Below the ledge is the denomination, while appearing in the lower right field are IN GOD WE TRUST and E PLURIBUS UNUM, and the word LIBERTY. Around the upper border appears the inscription UNITED STATES OF AMERICA. Slight die doubling can be noted in this location on some specimens. The letters AM of AMERICA are partly covered by the eagle's right wing. Located in the lower right field near the border is the incused initial K. We can also note that the eagle's beak, as well as some of the reverse lettering outstretch into the raised rim.

 A loss of metal molecules will be evident on the central part of the eagle's wing tip, inwards, between the "AM" of the word AMERICA and beak. The modernistic eagle is a prime target for the "whizzing doctors."

Origins of the Bridgeport

According to the Bridgeport Centennial, Inc., P.T. Barnum's portrait appears on this half dollar because of his character as a showman, citizen, mayor and philanthropist of the city of Bridgeport. He laid the streets and lined them with trees. He also reserved a grove of eight acres which is now known as Washington Park. The organization believed that in 1936 this was the beginning of an industrial development in their city which has grown to great proportions.

Barnum, possibly the most innovative and celebrated showman ever to thrive in this country, began his career as a showman in 1835. One of his first ventures was the purchase and exploitation of a Black woman, Joice Heth, alleged to have been the nurse of the infant George Washington. Phineas claimed she was 161 years of age! After a short, successful exhibition period, Miss Heth died. However, it was later proven on her death that this woman was near 80. Remember some of his other ventures? There was the famous 25-inch midget, Charles S. Stratton, ballyhooed as General Tom Thumb, who helped the promoter sell 20 million tickets to his museum. What about the Feejee Mermaid? She had a human head and the finned body of a fish! Yes, the legendary sea creature was proven to be a fake. Recall Jenny Lind, the soprano dubbed a "Swedish Nightingale," or Barnum, Bailey and Hutchinson's, "The Greatest Show on Earth" or Jumbo the huge elephant purchased for $10,000?

The Philadelphia Mint struck the minimum allowance of 25,015 coins during September 1936. The Act which approved this issue on May 15, 1936, stated that there would be no limit to the number of pieces which could be minted! In fact, this issue could be struck indefinitely provided each coin would possess the date 1936. Why? This Act listed no expiration date! Have you seen the 1915 Austrian Corona or the 1947 Mexican 50 peso gold bullion restrike pieces? Imagine a 1936 Bridgeport commemorative half dollar struck in 1993! Fortunately, an Act was passed on August 5, 1938, which prohibited the further coinage or issuance of commemorative coins which were authorized before March 1, 1939.

An attempt was made to widely distribute this coin and limit the sale to five coins per buyer. Unfortunately, almost 1,000 pieces remained unsold. During the late 1950s most of this supply came on the numismatic market and was purchased by Allen Johnson, son of Toivo Johnson, a well known East Holden, Maine, dealer. Allen sold most of this hoard to Joe Flynn Sr., a Kansas City dealer, and the balance to First Coinvestors, Inc. of Long Island, New York.

The Bridgeport Today

The majority of the lightly circulated specimens offered for sale are either lightly cleaned, polished, whizzed, dipped-out bright (which can look better than new to the neophyte) or even an extremely unattractive unc coin. On occasion, a pocket piece or good-luck piece will make its appearance.

The Barnum creation is easily obtainable in grades MS-60 through MS-64. Due to their easy accessibility in this range, collectors should only consider procuring for the pride of ownership. The just-mentioned states are at times targeted by promoters who buy low and sell high. When the promotion ceases, so does the price increase! Thus, acquire, if the price is very right in your favor.

What places the multiplicity of existing P.T.B. commemorative half dollars in these lower levels? Due to the nature of its design, all that exposed smooth area on Barnum's portrait and large modernistic reverse wing, simply act as huge magnets attracting all forms of numismatic abuse. Bag marks, reed marks, slide marks, hits, cuts, scratches, etc., just have an affinity for the cheek, lower jaw and bald reverse forelimb. Those are your primary focal areas!

Low end or "just made it" MS-64 or MS-64.5 coinage is what one should receive when paying between $150 and $175. However, MS-64+ pieces can be interpreted as the eye appealing coin which just misses the MS-65 category. Due to current grading standards, it's that bag mark or several small marks or hairline scratch that are viewed as a bit too large, keeping the coin out of the MS-65 category, especially if located in the primary focal areas. These are excellent additions to one's collection depending upon its makeup. Eye appealing strictly graded MS-65 specimens — and not those optimistically labeled MS-65 pieces — will not be easy to locate. MS-66 and MS-67 Bridgeports will be exceptionally hard to find. All are recommended for purchase. Excellent future potential.

Surfaces for this commemorative half dollar will vary from semi-prooflike, to flashy satiny, to semi-dull satiny (the norm) and to dull satiny. That grainy appearance observed on this issue is the result of a turbulent metal flow which causes the grainy wear of the dies. The coin surface will resemble the die surface! Raised lines seen in the fields were originally created when a steel wire brush was used to polish the dies. Fine scratches which cut into this metal become fine raised lines on the coin's surface. In most cases, they will not influence the price or grade. However, lack of metal fill, which can resemble small cuts or scratches, can lower a specimen's worth, depending on size, location and number.

 **Related material**

Local residents could purchase up to five coins from their bank. Out-of-state requests were handled by the First National Bank and Trust Company. The item was distributed in a dark blue and gold cardboard presentation box, housing either one or three pieces. Depicted in gold ink on the cover is the city arms and two gold diagonal bands. The inner covers present an inscription about the man who went from promoter to impresario. I've seen both holders marketed in the $20-$85 range, depending on condition and demand. Possibly 500 single and 200 3-piece boxes exist today. It's the second most available coin mailer or holder after the genuine Lexington wooden box. However, if accompanied by its stamped mailing box, it becomes worth at least $50 more.

1936
Lynchburg, Va.,
Sesquicentennial

Reason for issue: To commemorate the 150th anniversary of the issuance
of the charter to the city of Lynchburg, Virginia.
Authorized per Act of May 29, 1936: 20,000
Official sale price: $1 (plus 25¢ per order)

Production figures

Date	Business Strikes	Assay Coins	Proofs	Melted	Net Mintage
1936	20,000	13	4?	0	20,000

Current market values

	EF-40	AU-50	MS-60	MS-63	MS-64	MS-65
1936	110.	130.	175.	220.	325.	575.

Designs by Charles Keck

Obverse

Portrait is Sen. Carter Glass of Virginia, facing left. His name is below, in the
lower border. UNITED STATES OF AMERICA arcs above; LIBERTY is at the lower left,
beneath Glass' chin, and IN GOD WE TRUST is at the right, behind his neck.

 Wear will first be noticed on the cheekbone and area above the ear of
Carter Glass. A softness of strike can also be seen here but should not
affect grade, unless upper ear details look flattened.

Reverse

Portrayed is the standing figure of Liberty, with hands outstretched symbol-
izing "You are welcome here." Located in the right background is part of the
Monument Terrace and the old Lynchburg Courthouse. Placed in front of the
Courthouse is the Confederate Monument. Around the upper border are located
the words LYNCHBURG VIRGINIA SESQUICENTENNIAL. The letter I of SESQUICEN-
TENNIAL is covered by Liberty's hand, thus no Mint error here. Our motto E
PLURIBUS UNUM — with the S of PLURIBUS located partly behind the standing

Liberty — appears in the left field with the anniversary date 1786 below it. The other half of the commemorative date appears in the right field, while the denomination appears below the standing figure. Charles Keck also designed the Vermont and the Panama-Pacific gold dollar.

Wear begins on knee and head, then breast of Liberty. Should the high points be flat due to die wear or low striking pressure, look for difference in metal color and fine crisscross scratches to determine wear.

Origins of the Lynchburg

Senator Carter Glass, Secretary of the Treasury in the Wilson administration, vigorously protested having his portrait appear on the Lynchburg commemorative 50-cent piece which was honoring his home city. In fact, he called the Philadelphia Mint to determine if it were permissible for the profile of a living person to appear on the coin. He was informed that "There was no law against it" and replied, "I had hoped there would be an avenue of escape." Such only applied to paper currency. Glass was chosen because no likeness of the city's founder, John Lynch, could be located.

Glass was elected honorary president of the Lynchburg Sesquicentennial Association, which sold the coins Sept. 21 — three weeks before the celebration — at $1.00 each plus 25¢ postage per order. There were 20,000 pieces plus 13 assay coins produced at the Philadelphia Mint in September 1936. Fred W. McWane, Secretary of the Association, which was headquartered at the Virginian hotel, informed potential buyers by Sept. 2 that the issue was sold out — including the balance of 5,000 pieces allotted to them.

The Lynchburg Today

This issue is not abundant in EF-AU condition. Specimens usually encountered have been cleaned or doctored in some fashion. Issue is available in all grades from MS-60 through MS-65. Not much of a price spread exists from EF-AU up to MS-63. Thus, think MS-63. Should funds be available, go for the higher MS-64 coin which possesses appeal and a strong strike. Luster will range from semi-prooflike, to brilliant satiny, to dull satiny. Strike at times can be responsible for lowering a coin's value and preventing it from grading MS-65 or even MS-64! In this case, an obvious flatness will be noticed on Liberty's head and thigh next to motto E PLURIBUS UNUM. Any future possibility lies in eye appealing MS-65 and higher graded material.

Related material

The Lynchburg was distributed in a buff-colored cardboard holder with inserts to hold five coins, manufactured by J.N. Spies Mfg. Co. of Watertown, N.Y. The front page is imprinted with the following: LYNCHBURG IN OLD VIRGINIA IS CELEBRATING ITS 150TH BIRTHDAY WITH THE ISSUANCE OF THIS COMMEMORATIVE HALF DOLLAR AND PAGEANTS, PARADES, BOOKLETS, MUSEUM, ART EXHIBIT AND EXHIBITION and the dates October 12-16, 1936. Page two and four are blank, while page 3 contains slots for the placement of five coins. The holder may be valued at $35 to $75; with original mailing envelope, $40 to $120.

1936
Albany, NY, Charter
250th Anniversary

Reason for issue: To commemorate the 250th anniversary of the founding of the city of Albany, New York.

Authorized per Act of June 16, 1936: 25,000

Official sale price: $2

Production figures

Date	Business Strikes	Assay Coins	Proofs	Melted	Net Mintage
1936	25,000	13	4?	7,342	17,658

Current market values

	EF-40	AU-50	MS-60	MS-63	MS-64	MS-65
1936	160.	180.	200.	225.	350.	700.

Designs by Gertrude K. Lathrop

Obverse

Appearing is an American beaver (present on the seal of the city), facing right, gnawing on a branch of maple, the New York state tree. (Like Canada we too have a beaver depicted on our coinage!) UNITED STATES OF AMERICA and HALF DOLLAR encircles the obverse separated by two maple keys, which represent growth and fertility, at about the four and seven o'clock positions. E PLURIBUS UNUM is to the left of the beaver; IN GOD WE TRUST to the right.

Wear will first be observed on the hip of the beaver. If present, the metal texture will appear grayish-white. Any slight abuse will bring about this condition due to the area's high relief. Examine beaver closely for some form of doctoring, especially whizzing performed to hide a slight metal loss or, at times, slide marks.

Reverse

The scene depicts Governor Dongan bidding farewell to Robert Livingston and his secretary and Peter Schuyler, the first Mayor of Albany, holding the newly acquired Albany City charter of July 22, 1686, (currently housed in the Manuscript Room of the State Library in Albany). Located over the group of men is an eagle with outstretched wings. The word LIBERTY can be noted in minute letters above the eagle. Encircling the coin is the inscription SETTLED 1614 CHARTERED 1686 ALBANY NY, separated by two pine cones in the same position as the maple keys on the obverse. Incused in very small letters beside Dongan's foot are the designer's initials GKL.

 The reverse design is better protected from wear than its obverse mate. However, a metal loss will first be observed on the sleeve of Governor Dongan.

Origins of the Albany

The Albany Dongan Charter Coin Committee, which was responsible for distribution, sold approximately 72 percent of the entire issue (25,000 pieces; there were 13 coins struck for assay purposes) that was produced in October 1936 by the Philadelphia Mint. Only 17,658 specimens were purchased. When the commem boom of 1937 passed, the Committee got tired of holding meetings, etc. to account for sales of a dozen pieces. The decision was made in 1943 to return all 7,342 coins being held to the Mint for melting.

According to Lee F. Hewitt of Florida, his "brother accumulated 638 of these low mintage souvenirs over the years. (That equates to nearly 32 rolls!) In February 1979, the safe deposit boxes where these estate coins were housed was burglarized. Those coins were in rolls in a box marked 'half dollars.' At the same time they were taken, these thieves threw a complete type set of commems contained in their lucite holders on the floor, not knowing what they were! Silver at the time was on the road to higher and higher prices. Is it possible that the 638 Albanys were melted?" Based on $350 per coin, I derive a total market value of $223,300. WOW! What a loss, if the coins actually were melted!

The Albany Today

The issue is not abundant in EF-AU condition. Most encountered pieces will flaunt some form of abuse, especially polishing or some degree of whizzing on the obverse beaver or natural metal loss of the hip. Little value spread exists between specimens graded MS-60 through MS-64. Since the creation is available in the grades, it seems most logical for collectors to think higher grade, if funds permit. Albany's rated MS-65 are not hard to locate. Key is to acquire flashy eye appealing specimens. Acquire for the joy of ownership. Such should not flaunt hip rub or slide marks. These are not MS-65 coins! Real future lies in the loftier graded coin.

Luster will range from blazing, brilliant frosty to dull frosty. At times, when comparing both sides of the coin, we can observe the obverse will flaunt more intensity. The uninformed or unscrupulous will "dip" (in a tarnish removing solution) the reverse side, in an attempt to duplicate the luster intensity. Due to die preparation and surface, this cannot be accomplished. Thus, the surface is "hurt" and the coin's grade-value lowered. Strike rarely cause the Albany any problems.

In the past six years, when a very eye appealing, blazing lustrous coin was purchased by dealer or collector, a bag mark or two on the primary focal area of the obverse beaver or the reverse coat of the Governor or on what appears to be one large coat housing both Robert Livingston and Peter Schuyler, fazed virtually no one, unless it really was detracting. Why? These coins — as with every other issue — were continuously bought and sold at gem or MS-65 levels.

Today, as most of us are now aware, to solidify the grade it takes — in most cases — more than flash or eye appeal. Those detracting marks in the primary focal areas are no longer accepted. Consequently, fewer Albanys make the grade. Therefore, we have higher prices brought about by demand and low mintage. The aforesaid applies to all of American numismatics.

Detecting counterfeits

Counterfeit Albanys display a washed-out luster. Surface color is dull gray. Lettering is not sharp. Look for a depression near the center of the D in DOLLAR at the obverse 6 o'clock position, as well as raised lumps of metal in the field adjacent to the top of Peter Schulyer's head, down to his coat's cuff on the coin's reverse.

Related material

Many of coins were offered for sale at $2.00 each in an official original holder, which pictures the obverse and reverse of the coin, plus the word Albany centered above the photographs. Page two of the holder presents us with a short history about Albany, while page three contains five slots in which one to five coins were placed when filling an order. Page four or the back of the holder was blank.

Official mailing envelope is imprinted: ALBANY DONGAN CHARTER COMMITTEE, 60 STATE STREET, ALBANY, N.Y. The rarer vehicle are cardboard boxes which housed a single coin. Such was distributed by THE NATIONAL COMMERICAL BANK AND TRUST COMPANY OF ALBANY in a red box with a red velour interior and slit pouch for the coin. Bank's coat of arms imprinted in gold ink graces the top cover, as well as a white box with blue velour interior, but with blue ink. When encountering the above mentioned holders, simply remember that it is the coin which determines the worth of a coin-holder offering. Holders can be valued at $25 to $50; with original official mailing envelope, $50 to $125. The rarer boxes have brought between $350 and $600.

Rare Albany box

1936
Elgin, Ill., Centennial

Reason for issue: To commemorate the 100th anniversary of the (1835) founding of the city of Elgin, Illinois, and the erection of the heroic Pioneer Memorial.
Authorized per Act of June 16, 1936: 25,000
Official sale price: $1.50

Production figures

Date	Business Strikes	Assay Coins	Proofs	Melted	Net Mintage
1936	25,015	15	4?	5,000	25,000

Current market values

	EF-40	AU-50	MS-60	MS-63	MS-64	MS-65
1936	145.	155.	175.	215.	265.	465.

Designs by Trygve Andor Rovelstad

Obverse

The obverse of this issue depicts the head of a bearded pioneer wearing a fur cap, facing left. Widely spaced in the upper border is the word PIONEER. Trygve Rovelstad, the designer of this issue has his monogrammed initials (TAR) placed in the field below the beard, while in the lower field is the motto IN GOD WE TRUST.

Below the pioneer is located the commemorative dates 1673 1936 separated by a star. Elgin, a city located on the Fox River approximately 29 miles northwest of Chicago, celebrated its 100th anniversary in 1935. Therefore, the dates which appear on this issue (1673-1936) have no connection with Elgin, Ill. These dates refer to the year in which the French explorers Joliet and Marquette first entered the territory, a section of which today is Illinois. The date 1936 refers to the date of striking, since the centennial of the city was 1935!

Wear or a difference in metal texture will first be noticed on the cheek-bone of the pioneer. I suggest looking for surface doctoring such as whizzing in this area, since a limited number of Elgins will exhibit real wear. Primary focal location is the face of this early settler. A detracting mark here will hurt the coin's grade and value.

Reverse

The reverse of this issue depicts a group of five pioneers. Can you count the five? At the left we note a pioneer holding a rifle in a horizontal position. It is his head, by the way, which is depicted on the coin's obverse just described and was designed from the Pioneer Memorial Statue. We also observe a standing boy who is holding a stick and another male in the background. The baby being held in the mother's arms is the fifth pioneer..

Around the upper border is UNITED STATES OF AMERICA. Directly below is the legend LIBERTY (barely visible). In the lower field appears E PLURIBUS UNUM and the coin's denomination. Located in the left field is the inscription PIONEER MEMORIAL while in the right field we note the inscription ELGIN ILLINOIS.

Metal loss will make its appearance on the actual left shoulder (or right body part as you view the coin) of the pioneer holding the rifle with both hands. Primary focal point is the smooth surface of the pioneer woman's dress. The presence of a reed mark or large bag mark or large lack of fill mark will quickly remove this coin from the MS-65 category!

Origins of the Elgin

The Philadelphia Mint struck 25,000 coins plus 13 pieces for assay purposes during October 1936. This issue was well distributed by the Elgin Centennial Monumental Committee through M.L. Hoffecker — the anti-speculator — of El Paso, Texas, who designed the Spanish Trail issue.

By mid-November 16, 1936, 170 coins were sold at $1.50 each! During the month of July 1937, it appears that all in numismatic circles who desired the issue had made their purchase. The general public had little interest. W. A. Schneider, an Illinois numismatist whose name appears in Mr. Rovelstad's record book as desiring 6,000 pieces and who only purchased five coins, was not excited about the possibility of acquisition at a lower rate. Rovelstad and the Committee decided to return 5,000 coins to the Mint to be melted. Hoffecker requested that he be sold 500 to 1,000 of these coins at face value, based on the fantastic job performed in distributing the coins. His expectations never materialized. I knew Trygve personally, and everything in his character indicates that he didn't think much of Hoffecker's idea.

The Elgin Today

A small amount of Elgins reside in the EF-AU state. Those encountered over the years have been cleaned or abused in some manner. The retail worth is close to Uncirculated values. Think Mint State, unless the price is far below Trends. Virtually all of the issue resides in the MS-60 through MS-64 category. Bag marks, reed marks, lack of fill marks, slide marks, etc., and lack of surface allure are responsible for this situation. Little value spread currently exists between these grades. Thus, collectors should think eye appealing MS-64 acquisition, when possible or even MS-65 — but only for the joy of ownership at this time. Past value history for this issue will never repeat itself in grades MS-64 and MS-65, due to availability. Luster will range from a flashy brilliant satiny (not the norm) to unattractive matte-like dull. Typical examples in-between this spectrum will offer little device-field contrast. Examining the reverse with its granular field, we can observe a die polishing mark located below the first "A" in AMERICA (which is present on most of the found pieces). This characteristic does not take away from the coin's value or grade. Issue was not designed to offer sharpness of detail — especially on the reverse. Many specimens will display a varying degree of weakness, when examining the facial detail of the Pioneer mother, as well as or the child (later named "Gloria" by Tryvge) that she holds. I have found that strike will seldom affect the value and grade for specimens labeled up to MS-65. However, it can when the grade of MS-66 or higher is to be considered, unless there is something special about the coin, such as amazing natural color or iridescent toning. Real future potential for this issue lies in MS-66 and higher graded coins.

Those early 10 strikings received by the designer from the Mint will lack that die polishing mark. Today some of those pieces are toned, while some are brilliant. They do not blaze with flash, since the dies were not polished to any great extent. In fact, one of these creations flaunts a matte surface! However, Chief Mint Engraver John Ray Sinnock had the coin acid treated — but the coin received by Mr. Rovelstad was given only one strike from the press! (A Proof coin must be given two or even three strikings to show all the required details.) This specimen was sent to the three major grading services. The coin was returned by each with the notation "altered surfaces." I personally would not grant the coin a Matte Proof status. Unfortunately, it resembles a regular issue which was properly acid dipped outside the Mint. It is possible Mr. Sinnock had a few other pieces double struck and acid treated. Only time will tell.

Elgins housed in a promoted hard plastic holder — exactly as the Bay Bridge issue — are worth the coin's grade plus $20 for the holder.

 **Related material**

The Elgin Centennial half dollar was mailed to subscribers in a plain off-white colored coin holder with inserts for five as well as six coins. The front cover was rubber stamped once or twice with the name L.W. Hoffecker, 1514 Montana St., El Paso, Texas or in other instances simply forwarded unstamped, (as received from the supplier). The latter should be accompanied by postal mailing envelope and canceled stamps. The envelope will note his name, distributor, Elgin Centennial Coin, P.O. Box 75, El Paso, Texas. Value these holders at $20 to $25; with original stamped envelope, $50 to $125.

1936
San Francisco-Oakland Bay Bridge

Reason for issue: To commemorate the opening of the San Francisco-Oakland Bay Bridge.

Authorized per Act of June 26, 1936: 200,000

Official sale price: $1.50; $1.65 by mail

Production figures

Date	Business Strikes	Assay Coins	Proofs	Melted	Net Mintage
1936-S	100,000	55	4?	28,631	71,369

Current market values

	EF-40	AU-50	MS-60	MS-63	MS-64	MS-65
1936-S	77.50	85.00	97.50	125.	175.	440.

Designs by Jacques Schnier

Obverse

Portrayed is a large California grizzly bear, which is the emblem of the State of California. However, his presence on this issue was highly criticized by numismatists, since Monarch II the "model bear" was confined for 26 years of his life in a cage in Golden Gate Park. Is this symbolic of freedom and liberty? Figuratively speaking "on the other side of the coin" the grizzly bear also symbolizes California's freedom from Mexico. Do you remember that famous bear flag of the Republic of California? That bear represented the state's arms.

Located near the animal's paw is the Mint mark "S." The monograms JS in the upper right field represents the designer's initials (Jacques Schnier). Below Monarch II is LIBERTY and denomination. In the left field is the motto IN GOD WE TRUST. Around the upper border is UNITED STATES OF AMERICA, while four decorative stars appear around the lower border.

A metal loss will first occur on Monarch's left shoulder (actually right one as you examine the coin). This area is a prime target for the "coin doctors!"

Reverse

Seen is an emblematic — rather than documentary — creation, which depicts the Bay Bridge stretching from a point over the Embarcadero with that celebrated ferry tower seen in the foreground. Its opening sadly antiquated ferry traffic heading towards Yerba Buena Island. SAN FRANCISCO-OAKLAND BAY BRIDGE circles above.

As a note of interest, the present Treasure Island is not shown because it is an artificial island which had not yet been completed. The next section of this structure leads towards the Emeryville, Oakland and Berkeley area. Passing the ferry tower are two steamships.

At celebration time, the cost of the bridge proper and its interurban car installation plus approaches was estimated at $77,200,000. It was financed entirely without taxation via the sale of 4³/4% bonds, issued against protective revenues. There were 15,000 men and women who labored for its completion, and 24 men died in its construction. It requires 200,000 gallons of paint to beautify the bridge. When finished, it's time to begin once again!

On this lower relief design, wear will be observed on the vertical steel bridge support (directly between the "AN" of the word OAKLAND and on the cloud mass below the "O" of OAKLAND.

Origins of the Bay Bridge

Jacques Schnier, local artist, sculptor and designer, is the reason collectors can today enjoy this lovely coin. At the suggestion of Lee Lawrie, sculptor member of the Commission of Fine Arts, the major design change recommendations were simply the remodeling of the bear's snout and replacing the legend "E Pluribus Unum" with IN GOD WE TRUST.

Though the authorizing act of June 26, 1936, had specified a maximum of 200,000 to be coined, only 100,000 (plus 55 assay coins) were produced in November by the San Francisco Mint. This amount was struck to discourage speculation, for such was considered large for speculative undertakings. The San Francisco-Oakland Bay Bridge Celebration and the San Francisco celebration committee offered them for $1.50 apiece, with some being offered via the Clearing House Association. Others could be acquired at kiosks near the Bay Bridge entrances with motorists not having to leave their vehicles. According to clients who had this experience on and from November 20, these small booths resembled a newspaper stand. A large number of coins sold after the Nov. 12-14, 1936, celebrations had ended.

When sales came to a standstill in 1937, some 28,631 pieces of the minting were returned to the Mint for remelting, leaving a total of 71,369 as the net mintage.

Committee Chairman Frank R. Havenner requested the Mint place the first 200 strikings in numbered envelopes, accompanied by official documentation. Twenty-two of these specimens numbering from the mid-50s — which were never officially presented — became available. It was offered for sale with documentation in attractive Capital holders. These specimens were not struck from highly polished dies, nor is there anything special about their surface features. However, these fully original coins will grade at least MS-65 today. To assist with a dealer promotion, Schnier in 1980 autographed approximately 500 cards — for $5 each — that pictured him holding his creation. It also has a cutout for the half dollar. These were placed in sealed hard plastic holders, accompanied by pieces grading AU-55 through MS-63. I would base acquisition on the coin's grade plus $20 for the holder. Ditto the promoted Elgin coin housed in the exact same sealed plastic holder.

The Bay Bridge Today

The issue can be located without much difficulty in EF-AU condition. Specimens usually flaunt numismatic abuse. Little price spread between EF-AU and MS-64 categories. Thus, concentrate on very attractive MS-64 pieces, if possible, unless purely buying for the pride of ownership. Creation is available in these grades. Bay Bridges grading MS-65 can now be located without much effort. However, those flaunting enticing surfaces can be elusive. Real future for issue lies here and in the loftier grades. The greater the eye appeal or coin's appearance, the greater the specimen's future price performance. Long hairline scratches, or slide marks or deep nicks, or ugly bag marks hurt the coin's grade and value. In other words, Monarch II should not appear as if he were being chased through the forest and wounded by several hunters. One major detracting mark on this primary focal area will place this issue in the MS-64 category.

The obverse of this issue with its granular die surface is most vulnerable to the noted problems. This is where I begin my visual inspection when attempting to purchase quality specimens for myself. The reverse is seldom affected because of its surface design, which can hide negatives, unless severe or without question detracting! However, a bad hit on the ferry tower can lower your grade.

Luster will range from intense satiny (not the norm) down to dull satiny. At times, the reverse will appear less lustrous than the obverse, due to die preparation and wear. However, it will not be as obvious as with the Albany issue.

Strike rarely presents a problem. I have at times encountered specimens with poor snout detail or steamship detail, but this is the exception. Monarch's right eye, as you observe the coin (or the bear's actual left) will appear not strongly struck. Such is characteristic for the issue. The strongest definition will appear only on those earlier strikings.

 **Related material**

Coins were distributed in a thick cardboard holder with openings for six coins, accompanied originally by an unattached folder cover. Individual coins were wrapped in tissue paper and also enclosed in a mailing envelope. Imprinted on the envelope is SAN FRANCISCO-OAKLAND BAY BRIDGE CELEBRATION, ROOM 615 - 625 MARKET STREET, SAN FRANCISCO. Holder has no real value without that mailing envelope; with it, put it in the $35 to $125 range. It's the grade of an offered coin which accompanies the holder that your value should be based on.

1936
Columbia, SC,
Sesquicentennial

Reason for issue: To commemorate the sesquicentennial of the founding of Columbia, South Carolina.

Authorized per Act of March 18, 1936: 25,000

Official sale price: $6.45 per set; $2.15 each

Production figures

Date	Business Strikes	Assay Coins	Proofs	Melted	Net Mintage
1936-P	9,000	7	4?	–	9,000
1936-D	8,000	9	4?	–	8,000
1936-S	8,000	7	4?	–	8,000

Current market values

	EF-40	AU-50	MS-60	MS-63	MS-64	MS-65
1936 PDS set	——	——	500.	600.	950.	1375.
1936 single	135.	150.	165.	205.	235.	305.

Designs by Abraham Wolfe Davidson

Obverse

Pictured is Justice, standing and holding a sword in her right hand, pointed downward with "scales" in her left hand. (Where is the blindfold?) In the right background is located the new State Capitol building, with the anniversary date 1936. The Old State House (with the anniversary date 1786 appearing below it), is situated in the left background. Above this structure in the upper left field is the word LIBERTY. The inscription SESQUICENTENNIAL CELEBRATION OF THE CAPITAL OF SOUTH CAROLINA appears between an outer and inner border encircling the obverse.

Since three Mints produced this issue, the Mint mark for the Denver coin (D) or the San Francisco coin (S) is located at the base of Justice. The Philadelphia Mint used no Mint mark during this period.

Wear or a loss of metal will make its presence known as a difference in metal texture, on the breasts of Justice. (It actually begins on her left breast, as you view in the coin, which is slightly higher.) Wear can also be observed on the central fold of her dress, which is not equal in height to the aforementioned location. How is that possible? Coins were housed in albums with moveable celluloid strips. At times, the strip was stuck and became very difficult to move. Some individuals would push down and sideways with a thumb or a finger against the celluloid window, pushing it into contact with the coin's surface, in an attempt to free the coin. The area abused could have been the central fold or her breasts. If the breasts only display the loss of metal, the cause if in the album would be too much back and forth movement of the strip in order to examine the coins. We have a coin with slight wear that can be new and very lustrous or toned. It will grade almost uncirculated (AU) or slider AU+, depending on surface marks, eye appeal, etc., because of its actual condition. The above mentioned AU coin can be lightly wirebrushed by the unscrupulous to hide the loss of metal, in order to deceive the unknowledgeable and be offered as Mint State.

Reverse

Depicted is a palmetto tree, the state emblem of South Carolina, with oak branches at its base. Barricades this soft tree were constructed to offer protection to the Union batteries on Sullivan's Island, in Charleston Harbor against shells fired by the ships of the British Navy in an attempt to capture Charleston. Most British missiles just buried themselves into the soft trees and caused little damage after a 12-hour bombardment! When all was said and done, 12 Colonists and 200+ British lost their lives. The latter also incurred extreme damage to their oaken ships from Ft. Moultrie's shells. Charleston was not captured. Thus the association of the crossed arrows tied to the palmetto tree. By the way, in December 1936 some people referred to the palmetto side of the coin as the obverse. Why? Just local pride, based on state symbolism. The broken oak branches at the base of the tree symbolize the defeat of the British Navy's ships. A semicircle of 13 five-pointed stars symbolizes South Carolina's being one of the original 13 states. UNITED STATES OF AMERICA arcs above; HALF DOLLAR below. E PLURIBUS UNUM is just above the palmetto, while IN GOD WE TRUST is in the right central field. Davidson's initials do not appear on his creation.

When a metal loss does occur, it will be observed at the top of the palmetto tree. However, before this happens, the obverse Justice would lose one-fifth of her breast design. Her relief is much higher than the reverse high point.

Origins of the Columbia

This issue was produced at the three United States Mints for the most part in September 1936. When the final tally was taken, the Philadelphia Mint struck 9,000 specimens; Denver and San Francisco 8,000 each. The wording of the Act made the use of three Mints possible. This issue was distributed by the Sesquicentennial Commission, Columbia, S.C., who were appointed by the city's mayor. They pledged that these coins would receive the widest distribution possible, thereby keeping them out of the hands of speculators and placing them into the hands of true collectors, who would not be required to pay a large premium for their acquisition.

John Flitter, Coin and Wooden Money Historian of the Columbia Bicentennial Committee, had discovered on March 22, 1986, extensive documentation in respect to this issue, as well as six sets recovered from a 1936 time capsule, sealed since the celebration! Flitter writes:

"As my investigation into the history of the Columbia, S.C., commemorative half dollar proceeds, the amount of material uncovered continues to grow. Extensive numbers of original documents and materials continue to be found which give a detailed documentation to the complete history of the coin. The latest find being the original eight-inch plaster cast of the obverse and reverse from which the master dies were made. As the amount of materials is too extensive to cover in only one article, I have developed a short chronology about the distribution of the coins in the latter months of 1936.

"Friday, September 11th, 1936

"Dies for the Columbia coin completed and a check for three hundred dollars sent to the mint in payment for the making of the master die.

"Wednesday, September 16th, 1936

"Commission sets price of coin at $2 plus 15 cents for postage and insurance. Sales to be restricted to no more than ten sets (three coins per set — PDS) to any individual, company or organization. Sale of coins will not begin until all three issues have been received. Columbia residents will be given first chance to purchase coins, sale starting locally 24 hours before mail order sale.

"Monday, September 21st, 1936

"Nine thousand coins from Philadelphia Mint received in Columbia today. Coins are stored at the South Carolina National Bank which has loaned the commission the money to pay the Mint face value of $4,500. James H. Hammond, Chairman of the Commission, expects to receive coins from the other two mints within ten days. All coins will remain in the vault at the South Carolina National Bank until the day they are placed on sale.

"Wednesday, October 7th, 1936

"15,300 coins arrive in Columbia today from Denver and San Francisco Mints. Denver Mint shipment contains only 7,300 of the 8,000 pieces expected. Sale of coins held up until whereabouts of remaining 700 coins resolved.

"Monday, October 10th, 1936

"Orders received for 16,000 coins to date. Expect orders to exceed 20,000 by end of week. Columbians urged to place orders so as not to be left out. Denver says 700 coins have been shipped, but they have not arrived in Columbia as yet.

"Thursday, October 15th, 1936

"Largest number of orders received at Columbia today. Approximately 23,000 pieces of money have been ordered. Tomorrow's mail expected to bring enough orders to exhaust authorized mintage of 25,000 coins. U.S. Senator James F. (Jimmy) Burns of South Carolina notified by Mary M. O'Reilly, Acting Director of the Mint, that the 700 missing coins will be shipped in a few days. She explains that the Denver Mint shipped the 7,300 pieces in order to assist the Commission in early sale of the coins and planned to furnish remainder as soon as they are minted!

"Monday, October 19th, 1936

"Orders considerably exceed mintage. Commission continues to be flooded with orders. No coins have been issued. Extra care in reviewing orders is taken in order to prevent speculation.

"Thursday, October 29th, 1936

"Due to oversubscription, it will be necessary to reduce maximum number of sets available to subscribers. Orders will be limited to three sets per order instead of ten sets as specified in order form. Columbians may place orders in person at Chamber of Commerce offices all day Friday through Saturday noon. Preference for orders will be given to Columbians. Orders for 35,000 coins received thus far.

"Saturday, October 31, 1936

"9,000 coins will go to Columbians unless many orders are rejected or reduced. Total orders received exceeded mintage by 15,000.

"Friday, November 6th, 1936

"Wire sent to the numismatic editor of *New York Herald Tribune* declaring no Columbia coins have been issued. Seems circulars have been sent by someone to some coin collectors saying that Columbia coins have already been distributed. Coins have been 100% oversubscribed. Orders received being reviewed to prevent speculation. Date for delivery of coins not yet set.

"Wednesday, November 18th, 1936

"Members of the Commission, Anderson, Haltiwanger, and Henning given final authority to check all order received to prevent duplication and speculation. Will exercise every possible care to prevent anyone receiving a large amount of coins for resale at inflated prices.

"Friday, December 11th, 1936

"Mail orders for single coins and single sets are mailed out this afternoon. Following delivery of small orders will be orders for two and three sets.

"Friday, December 18th, 1936

"Distribution to Columbia residents began at 11:00 a.m. and will continue through 12 noon Saturday at the Chamber of Commerce offices. Nearly all out-of-town orders have been mailed.

"Friday, January 5th, 1937

"Commission authorizes Hammond (Commission Chairman) and Columbia Mayor Owens to present President Roosevelt, Senators Burns and Smith, and Congressman Fulmer with sets of commemorative coins.

"Monday, February 15th, 1937

"Hammond and Mayor Owens, accompanied by Senator Burns, presented President Roosevelt with a set of Columbia coins and set of wooden nickels at the White House."

Since the Columbia 50-cent pieces were not delivered to the Commission in one complete shipment by the Mint, it was decided that the mailings would begin only when possession of all three varieties by the Commission materialized.

The Columbia Today

Circulated specimens are not plentiful. Those usually encountered have been polished or wire brushed (whizzed) to some degree, hurting their numismatic value. Little value spread between MS-60 and MS-65 graded coinage at present. Think at least MS-64, when considering acquisition. Same reasoning should be applied to the three-piece set. In MS-63 condition, the Denver creation has the slight edge in rarity. The other two strikings are equal in standings. At the MS-64 level, Denver is the rarest Columbia, followed by the San Francisco and more abundant Philadelphia coin. In MS-65 condition, the S Mint coin is somewhat more difficult to locate that the other two issues which are about equally as rare. At the lofty MS-66 level, the Philadelphia coin is harder to acquire than the Denver striking, which is rarer than the San Francisco piece. Future lies in eye appealing MS-64+ and higher graded material.

Concerning this issue's luster, obverse coin surfaces will range from semi-prooflike (early strikes), to brilliant, to satiny, to dull-satiny. On the coin's "other side," surfaces will display a reflecting quality which can appear satiny, or dull satiny or just unappealing dull. Die polishing marks can be observed at times in the obverse fields, especially on the sides and above the head of Justice. What appears to be a depression behind her head may be the result of minor hub damage, and is characteristic for the issue. Where the reverse die has been steel brushed, expect to see small, *raised* hairline swirls.

Strike seldom presents a problem, thus the majority of this issue can be obtained possessing a strong strike. However, due to slight die wear, later strikings from all mints can exhibit some trivial weakness on the rim of the inner circle opposite the letters PITA in the word CAPITAL. A slight loss of detail can also be detected by the knowledgeable on the palmetto trunk, leaves, etc.

Based on current grading standards, MS-65 specimens cannot posses any detracting marks on the main devices or coin's fields. That is unless the coin posesses amazing eye appeal. If anything minute is present, if should be hidden in the coin's design. Same for the reverse palmetto or field. MS-64 coins must be fully original. It can have a mark or two in critical locations. A pinhead sized dig hurts. Primary focal areas are Justice, the palmetto tree and surrounding fields.

 **Related material**

The issue was distributed in a cardboard holder with inserts for three coins, manufactured by John H. Eggers. Imprinted with: 1786-1936 HALF DOLLAR COMMEMORATING THE SESQUICENTENNIAL OF THE FOUNDING OF COLUMBIA AS THE CAPITAL OF SOUTH CAROLINA. It was mailed in Karolton Klasp 3⅜"X6" envelope imprinted with a similar representation of the coin's obverse in dark ink. The holder may be valued at $35 to $75; with original mailing envelope, $50 to $150.

1936
Delaware Tercentenary

Reason for issue: To commemorate the 300th anniversary of the landing of the Swedes in Delaware.

Authorized per Act of May 15, 1936: 20,978

Official sale price: $1.75

Production figures

Date	Business Strikes	Assay Coins	Proofs	Melted	Net Mintage
1936	25,015	15	?	4,022	20,993

Current market values

	EF-40	AU-50	MS-60	MS-63	MS-64	MS-65
1936	155.	175.	200.	225.	315.	725.

Designs by Carl L. Schmitz

According to Mint records, the obverse is the Old Swedes church. Some collectors and dealers refer to the ship side as the obverse.

Obverse

The obverse of this issue shows the Old Swedes Church at Wilmington which was dedicated in 1699 and is still standing near "The Rocks" in Wilmington. It is claimed to be the oldest Protestant Church building in our country still used for worship. It was also near this location that the *Key of Kalmar (Kalmar Nyckel)* finally anchored. Above the church appears the sun's rays piercing the clouds. Below the church is the motto IN GOD WE TRUST. The authorization date 1936 is located below the motto with the denomination appearing in the lower border. UNITED STATES OF AMERICA is around the upper border.

 The design is well protected by the coin's rim. Wear will first begin to occur in the central section of the church roof directly above the triangular section of the door.

Reverse

On the reverse of this commemorative half dollar appears the *Kalmar Nyckel*, the ship which carried the first Swedish colonists who left Gothenburg in

1637 and arrived in Delaware Bay in March 1638. Others left on the *Fogel Grip*, which is not depicted. The ship design was made from a model made in Sweden, which is a copy of the authentic model of the actual ship now in the Swedish Naval Museum. "Kalmar Nyckel" means the Key of Kalmar. A skeleton key — symbolic of the ship — was positioned on the rim of a rejected plaster model reverse design by Adam Pietz. Kalmar is a port city in southeast Sweden.

Incused in small letters at the right of the ship are the designer's initials CLS. Around the upper border appears the inscription DELAWARE TERCENTENARY, while E PLURIBUS UNUM and LIBERTY appear below the waves in the lower field. At the lower border is located the anniversary dates 1638-1938 with three diamond-shaped figures appearing on the sides and in between the dates symbolizing the state's size, its fertile soil and its three counties of Kent, New Castle and Sussex. This is why Delaware is at times called the Diamond State.

 The design will first display a loss of metal on the central or lower middle sail. Look for a difference in metal texture and fine crisscross scratches in this area.

Origins of the Delaware

This issue along with the Bridgeport and Wisconsin issues were all approved May 15, 1936. They could be produced indefinitely, since they possessed the minimum coinage clause which allowed these issues to be produced in any quantity desired, until the expiration date was reached. During March 1937 the Philadelphia Mint struck 25,000 pieces, plus 15 assay. This issue had to bear the 1936 date of authorization according to the Act, although the anniversary celebration took place in 1938. Thus we have an issue which was authorized in and dated 1936 and struck in 1937 for a commemoration in 1938! In 1938 Sweden struck a 2-kronor coin depicting King Gustaf V and the *Kalmar Nyckel* on its reverse.

The Delaware was distributed by the Delaware Swedish Tercentenary Commission at $1.75 through the Equitable Trust Company of Wilmington, Delaware. Unfortunately, 4,022 coins remained unsold and were returned to the Mint to be reincarnated into some other coinage.

The Delaware Today

Luster for the issue will range from prooflike, to semi-prooflike, to brilliant frosty, to dull frosty. Prooflike pieces will be most difficult to locate. Semi-prooflike strikings displaying such surface on both sides of the coin will also be hard to find. Most available regular specimens encountered in the EF-AU category usually display the effects of cleaning, polishing or some degree of whizzing. Most of the issue resides in the MS-60 through MS-64 category. Currently, there exists little value spread between these grades. Thus collectors should take advantage of this situation. Why buy an MS-60 coin when an MS-64 specimen can be had for $70-$110 more? This is an issue which should only be purchased for the joy of collecting in the just noted categories.

Numismatic abuse in the form of nicks, cuts, hits, bag marks, reed marks and especially lack of the metal fill marks keep many coins out of the MS-65 category. Strictly graded MS-65 coinage possessing true eye appeal are not easily obtained. I personally believe a large percentage of Delawares rated as MS-65 in certain slabs are too liberally graded. Also very underrated in higher grades.

If Proofs exist, and I believe they do, they reside in Matte Proof condition — not in Satin Finish! Satin Finish specimens are simply those early struck coins produced from a new die which were struck with one blow of the press, with possible extra striking pressure. They are certainly seldom encountered and are worth as much as potential owners want to pay. Beware of the polished coin being offered as prooflike or semi-prooflike.

Strike rarely affects the grade or value for this issue. Locating specimens with a clean-surfaced center sail or the sail located in the exact center of the coin's reverse, plus an obverse with a fully struck triangular top section above the door's entrance that resembles a wide arrowhead which appears to be pointing to the clouds above the church will be a "real find." Most issues possess a flatness due to striking in this area on the reverse, while the sail previously referred to usually possesses slide marks or fine scratches or lack of fill marks — created by the striking process — on its surface. At times these locations can have the appearance of being battle scarred.

 **Related material**

The Equitable Trust Company distributed these coins at $1.75 each in a thick paper holder which had inserts for five coins. This holder's outer cover pictures the coin's obverse and reverse, gives the name of the issue and states the event commemorated. The inner cover offers a small history of Delaware plus a description of the coin. The back cover is blank. Holders may be valued at $25 to $50; with original mailing envelope, $50 to $125.

Delaware holder and mailing envelope

1936
Battle Of Gettysburg

Reason for issue: To commemorate the 75th anniversary of the Battle of Gettysburg.

Authorized per Act of June 16, 1936: 50,000

Official sale price: $1.65 (later raised to $2.65)

Production figures

Date	Business Strikes	Assay Coins	Proofs	Melted	Net Mintage
1936	50,028	28	4?	23,100	26,900

Current market values

	EF-40	AU-50	MS-60	MS-63	MS-64	MS-65
1936	150.	165.	190.	235.	335.	950.

Designs by Frank Vittor

Obverse

The obverse depicts the accolated busts of a Confederate and a Union soldier in uniform facing right. UNITED STATES OF AMERICA and BLUE AND GRAY REUNION form the outer border. LIBERTY is widely spaced above the soldiers. E PLURIBUS UNUM appears in the top field.

 Wear can be first noticed of the cheekbones of the soldiers, your primary focal area or location of most concern. Coin doctoring usually is performed here.

Reverse

The coin's reverse bears the shields of the Union and Confederate armies, divided by a double-bladed fasces. Below and at the side of the shields is located an oak and olive branch, which symbolize war and peace. IN GOD WE TRUST appears divided above each shield, while the coin's date 1936 and denomination appear in the lower field. Located on the outer border on a raised rim is the inscription 1863 75TH ANNIVERSARY 1938 BATTLE OF GETTYSBURG.

Crisscross scratches and a difference in metal color or texture (all signs of wear) if present will be discerned on the three ribbons which bind the fasces.

Origins of the Gettysburg

In June 1937 the Philadelphia Mint struck 50,000 half dollars, plus 28 coins for assay purposes. Here is an issue like the Delaware authorized in and dated 1936 and minted in 1937 for the Blue and Grey Reunion celebration which took place July 1, 1938.

The Gettysburg was distributed by the Pennsylvania State Commission in Gettysburg at $1.65 each. Paul L. Roy, executive secretary of the Commission, was a not-so-truthful promoter of the issue. He counted on three Mints striking the issue. When it was obvious this would not occur, his fable was still directed toward potential buyers. Purchasers were hesitantly informed that three coins from the Philadelphia Mint would be delivered, unless a refund was desired. By mid-May of 1937 he informed all on his mailing list that the maximum authorization of 50,000 pieces was oversubscribed — another fabrication which may have worked were it not for the declining interest in this market. Thirteen months later, the coins in inventory were delivered to the American Legion, Department of Pennsylvania, with the hope that they could distribute the issue at $2.65. The "rarity lure" did not work as the commemorative mania bubble had already burst.

The Gettysburg Today

In the non-abundant grade of EF-AU specimens usually encountered will be cleaned or abused in some manner. Retail worth is close to Mint State coinage. Only acquire when price is very right or if the About Uncirculated coin possesses more eye appeal than an MS-60-62 specimen. The majority of this remembrance preserver resides in the MS-60 through MS-64 grades. Value spread between these states is small. Thus, collectors should attempt to concentrate on higher graded MS-64 coin for the joy of collecting. Luster will range from brilliant frosty to unappealing dull. Strike offers no problems when the Gettysburg is involved. However, the same cannot be said about those surfaces negatives such as bag marks, reed marks, scratches, etc., which are drawn to those reverse smooth shields as if they were magnetized. Future potential lies in specimens grading MS-65 and higher.

 **Related material**

The issue was mailed in an unprinted coin mailer with inserts for three coins. Accompanying mailing envelope is attractive. When offered as a pair, along with accompanying documentation, such has sold between $75 and $200.

1936
Norfolk, Va., Bicentennial

Reason for issue: To commemorate the 300th anniversary of the original
Norfolk land grant (1636) and the 200th anniversary of the establishment
of the city of Norfolk as a borough (1736).

Authorized per Act of June 28, 1937: 25,000

Official sale price: $1.50 locally; $1.65 by mail for first coin; $1.55 for
additional coins

Production figures

Date	Business Strikes	Assay Coins	Proofs	Melted	Net Mintage
1936	25,000	13	4?	8,077	16,923

Current market values

	EF-40	AU-50	MS-60	MS-63	MS-64	MS-65
1936	330.	345.	360.	380.	400.	525.

Designs by William Marks Simpson and Marjorie Emory Simpson

Obverse

Portrayed is the official seal of the City of Norfolk, Virginia. A three-masted
ship in stylized waves sails to the right. Below is a plow and three sheaves of
wheat. Underneath is the word CRESCAS, meaning "may you prosper." Above the
ship is another motto, ET TERRA ET MARE DIVITIAE, meaning "both land and sea
are your riches." Within the cable border is TOWN 1682 BOROUGH 1736 CITY 1845
CITY OF NORFOLK VIRGINIA. The outer border displays the anniversary date 1936
(coin was actually struck in 1937) between two scallop shells. BOROUGH OF
NORFOLK BICENTENNIAL is placed within this border.

 A metal loss will first be observed on the first and second lower rear sails
of the ship. At times the area is doctored to hide wear in this area. Look
for that buffed or aluminum appearance, telling you that doctoring has
occurred.

Reverse

Depicted is The Royal Mace, with the British crown on its top, the only one
presented to an American city during Colonial times. Date of the original land

grant 1636 has sprigs of dogwood on each side. IN GOD WE TRUST and E PLURIBUS UNUM appear on either side of the mace handle, with denomination and designers' monograms above the LL in DOLLAR. LIBERTY is in the lower left field; UNITED STATES OF AMERICA forms the upper border. NORFOLK VIRGINIA LAND GRANT is spaced to either side of the mace head.

 Wear will first be noticed on the central upper section, just below the base of the British crown. Look for a difference in metal texture.

Origins of the Norfolk

This creation was authorized in 1937 for a 1936 celebration. Reason given the numismatic world for this occurrence was the unsuccessful passage of a 1936 bill which created purported confusion as to whether a medal or coin should be produced. The Philadelphia Mint in September 1937 struck 25,000 Norfolks plus 13 assay coins dated 1936, per the Act.

These commemorative disks were distributed locally by the Norfolk Advertising Board at $1.50 per coin. Limit was set at 20 coins per order. The limit was later rescinded to allow bulk sales to dealers at a slightly lower price.

Mail orders cost $1.65 for the first coin, and $1.55 for each additional specimen. Sales came to a halt, thus 5,000 pieces were returned to Philadelphia. Later on, another 3,077 were sent back for reincarnation into other coinage. This coin flaunts five dates — 1636 (original land grant); 1682 (town) ; 1736 (borough); 1845 (city); 1936 (anniversary year) — but not the date of actual striking (1937)!

The Norfolk Today

Certainly not abundant in circulated condition. Specimens encountered will flaunt some sort of abuse, such as cleaning and at times whizzing of the obverse ship, to hide a dig or slight wear on the sail. At present there exists little value spread between EF-AU and MS-66 condition! WOW! Thus, it is most logical to think eye-appealing higher grade. It appears that this creation received angelic protection. Actually, its cluttered design plays an important role by protecting the design and fields from bag marks, etc. Luster will range from blazing satiny, to dull satiny. I have yet to examine a specimen where strike would affect the value or grade.

Related material

The coins were mailed by the Norfolk Advertising Affiliated with the Norfolk Association of Commerce Board, Inc., 107 W. Main St., Norfolk, Va., in a light lime green imprinted paper mailer with cardboard inserts for five coins.

Within a rectangular black border on the front cover is the name of the issue, reason for commemoration, sponsor and affiliated groups. For whatever reason, it lists William Marks Simpson as the designer but omits mention of his wife, Marjorie. Back cover presents a poem by Charles Day. Holder cannot be labeled abundant, but it certainly isn't rare. Value the holder at $35 to $50; $50 to $125 with original mailing envelope. However, the golden-orange original application for the issue is very difficult to locate. A few have sold for between $100 and $300.

1937
Roanoke Colonization
350th Anniversary

Reason for issue: To commemorate the 350th anniversary of the founding of the "lost colony" on Roanoke Island, North Carolina, and the birth of the first child of English parents on the American continent, Virginia Dare.

Authorized per Act of June 24, 1936: 25,000 minimum; unlimited maximum

Official sale price: $1.65

Production figures

Date	Business Strikes	Assay Coins	Proofs	Melted	Net Mintage
1937	50,000	30	4?	21,000	29,000

Current market values

	EF-40	AU-50	MS-60	MS-63	MS-64	MS-65
1937	125.	145.	160.	185.	250.	315.

Designs by William Marks Simpson

Obverse

Facing left on this coin is the bust of Sir Walter Raleigh, the explorer, poet and historian, wearing a ruffled collar, an earring and a hat with a showy feather. Below his shoulder is his name, while in relief is the artist's monogram, WMS. UNITED STATES OF AMERICA arcs above; HALF DOLLAR below. E PLURIBUS UNUM and LIBERTY form an inner border with SIR WALTER RALEIGH. The date 1937 is located in the lower left field.

Sir Walter resembles Errol Flynn. Flynn specialized in Elizabethan dramatics at the time Mr. Simpson was composing this work. Thus, the movie actor's portrait may have been adopted!

Wear will first occur on the brim of Raleigh's hat, as well as his cheekbone. Prime target area for the coin doctors.

Reverse

Depicted is Eleanor Dare, dressed in a costume of her time, holding infant Virginia Dare in her arms. Located in the right and left center fields are two English sailing ships. Around the outer border are the words THE COLONIZATION OF ROANOKE ISLAND NORTH CAROLINA. At the six o'clock position appear the commemorative dates 1587-1937. Virginia Dare was born the first Christian in America August 18, 1587.

The motto IN GOD WE TRUST appears in the lower left field. The inscription THE BIRTH OF VIRGINA DARE is located at the sides of her mother.

A metal loss will first be noticed on the head and upper left arm of Mrs. Dare, as well as on the length of her skirt covering her left hip down to her knee. That's directly above the 9 in the date 1937. Prime doctoring area.

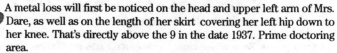

Origins of the Roanoke

The Philadelphia Mint produced 25,000 Roanoke half dollars plus 15 assay pieces in January 1937. Since the Act stated that "not less than twenty-five thousand silver 50 cent pieces shall be coined," an additional 25,015 plus 15 assay coins were struck in June, just days before the coinage rights expired on July 1, 1937. This, by the way, was the first time that a specific date was stated in an Act irrespective of the year in which coined. Also this was the only issue which was authorized in 1936 that was minted in 1937 and possesses the actual year of minting.

This coin started out as one of those postdated "cousins," like the Delaware and New Rochelle issues, authorized in 1936, coined in 1937. However, they carried the date 1938, in anticipation of an anniversary to occur in that year. Fortunately, these were the only two issues which fell into this chronological mess.

However, would you believe that the man commemorated on this issue had his name spelled incorrectly? Such is the case! Despite the documentary evidence cited by Mr. Simpson that "Sir Walter" used one spelling from June 9, 1584, until his death in 1618, that being "Ralegh," the Comission was simply unwilling to yield. The models were approved only after the artist inserted the "i" in the name Raleigh.

The Roanoke Colony Memorial Association sold these coins for $1.65 each ($1.50 each plus 15¢ handling). Only 29,000 coins were sold. Thus with a total halt in interest, it was decided to return the balance of 21,000 coins to the Mint to be reincarnated into other coinage.

The Roanoke Today

The limited number of specimens which reside in the EF-AU category for the most part have received some form of numismatic abuse. Value spread between the noted category and MS-65 at present is insignificant! Therefore, think a higher grade coin like MS-64, should funds permit. Today, the Roanoke is a common coin and is readily available in MS-65 condition. Procure only for the joy of collecting. Future promotions will make values rise to some degree. Little effort is required at present for an MS-66 acquisition. Future lies in the loftier grades. Concerning this issue's luster, both obverse and reverse surfaces will range from prooflike (early presentation strikings) to semi-prooflike, to brilliant, to satiny and to dull satiny. Needless to say (for this issue), the flashier the better. Purchase should also be based on the number of bag marks, cuts, nicks, scratches, abrasions and any other numismatic negatives present.

Strike seldom presents a problem. On occasion, weakness can be observed on the hat's brim and ear of Raleigh, as well as the head of Mrs. Dare. Numismatic negatives in the form of bag marks, slide marks, etc. are attracted to the primary focal areas such as the obverse portrait and reverse mid- to lower section of Eleanor Dare's long skirt.

In my opinion, brilliant Proofs or Satin Finish Proofs of this issue do not exist! The first example is nothing more than a bewitching early-struck Roanoke with prooflike surfaces! It possesses a very sharp strike without any field die polishing marks. Somewhere along the way, a die was repolished. Its fields will display prooflike surfaces, accompanied by die polishing marks. However, it will not be equal in strike when compared with these early struck pieces.

The so-called Satin Finish Proof is nothing more than a captivating, early struck specimen, of high grade, flaunting a strong strike and angelically protected surfaces. Both are worth much more than an average MS-65 or higher graded specimen, based on their appearance and numismatic charm.

 **Related material**

The Roanoke was distributed in a thick paper holder, which pictures the coin's obverse and reverse and the dates 1587-1937 on the front cover, plus a short history about the first English settlements in America and description of the coin, on the inner cover, as well as inserts for the placement of five coins, on the back inner cover.

Light tan mailing envelopes were imprinted with: ROANOKE COLONY MEMORIAL ASSOCIATION OF MANTEO, MANTEO, N.C. The words VALUE ____ and NO.____ are located in the lower left corner. A dab of dark red sealing wax was applied to the back flap. Holder can be valued at $35 to $75; with original mailing envelope, $40 to $120.

1937
Battle Of Antietam

Reason for issue: To commemorate the 75th anniversary of the Sept. 17, 1862, Battle of Antietam, the bloodiest one-day battle of the Civil War, where 25,000 soldiers lost their lives near Sharpsburg, Md.

Authorized per Act of June 24, 1937: 50,000

Official sale price: $1.65

Production figures

Date	Business Strikes	Assay Coins	Proofs	Melted	Net Mintage
1937	50,000	28	4?	32,000	18,000

Current market values

	EF-40	AU-50	MS-60	MS-63	MS-64	MS-65
1937	205.	265.	375.	400.	445.	750.

Designs by William Marks Simpson

Obverse

Depicted are the profiles of General George B. McClellan, the Union Army's exceptional organizer and trainer of troops, and the distinguished Confederate General Robert E. Lee, in uniform, facing left. Below their busts are their ranks and names. UNITED STATES OF AMERICA arcs above; HALF DOLLAR below. IN GOD WE TRUST is under McClellan's chin, while LIBERTY is behind Lee's neck. To the right of the words HALF DOLLAR are three stars representing Lee's rank as General in the Confederate Army, while to the left are two stars representing McClellan's rank as Major General in the Union Army. Near Lee's shoulder and partly in the field appear the designer's initials WMS, in monogram, in relief.

 Issue will show a trace of wear on the cheekbone of General Lee. Look for possible crisscross scratches in this area. The portraits of Lee and McClellan are a primary target for the whizzing specialists. Beware of the "aluminish" appearance in this location.

Reverse

Portrayed is designer Simpson's perspective of Burnside Bridge over the Antietam Creek. It was constructed in 1836 by John Weaver at a cost of $2,300.

We can note that the fury of the Battle of Antietam was centered about the possession of the bridge, later named after General Burnside of the Union Army. Militarily speaking, this bridge was the central point for the troops' flanking attack on the southern edge of Sharpsburg. When Burnside's men finally crossed this structure (with its 12-foot wide road bed) that important high ground looking down on the city was eventually won. Below the bridge in small letters are the words: THE BURNSIDE BRIDGE, SEPTEMBER 17, 1862. At the left of the bridge appears a group of trees, while a single tree is located to the right of the bridge. Above the trees is E PLURIBUS UNUM.

Encircling the border in large letters interspersed by small triangles is the inscription SEVENTY FIFTH ANNIVERSARY BATTLE OF ANTIETAM. At the six o'clock position, we find the date 1937.

 Wear will first be observed on the leaves in the upper central area of the tree in front of the bridge. Simply draw a mental line across from the dot located to the right of the letter M in UNUM to the aforementioned area described.

Origins of the Antietam

A leaflet which contained a description of the Antietam commemorative half dollar plus a short history of the battle, as well as an application for purchasing the coin at $1.65 each, was distributed by the Washington County Historical Society of Hagerstown, Maryland. Park W. T. Loy, Chairman of the Society and Secretary of the United States Antietam Celebration Commission, believed that because of this issue, the worldwide fame of General Lee and the honored place of General McClellan would always be held in out national history.

It was the objective of the sponsoring agency to have the Antietam commemorative pass directly into the hands of interested citizens and private collectors, thereby avoiding the possibility of much speculation. Anticipating that the half dollar would be ready for distribution on or before August 1, 1937, the Society was disappointed when the 50,028 half dollars were not produced at the Philadelphia Mint until some 10 days later. The first piece struck was given to President Roosevelt on August 12, according to the *Washington Post*.

The Washington County Historical Society wanted to avoid the possibility of speculation, as previously noted. Paradoxically, any individual could purchase whatever quantity of the Antietam desired, as long as the proper amount for each half was enclosed! Unfortunately, it was during this time that a sharp decline in interest for commemoratives started to take hold. Thus, the Antietam issue was not sold out; 32,000 pieces were returned to the Mint for melting, leaving us with a total mintage of only 18,000 coins!

The Congressional Act of June 24, 1937, which authorized the Antietam striking has the distinction of being the only Act approved in 1937 for which there is an issue dated 1937 and produced in that year. (The Roanoke commemorative is also dated 1937. However, it was authorized on June 24, 1936.)

The Antietam Today

Since few Antietams were used as pocket pieces, collectors of such circulated coins will have a difficult time obtaining them. Such accounts for its bid price in EF-AU condition. Those issues which are fully lustrous, but have slight friction on the high points are usually offered as MS-65 (if mark free). Known as FLS on teletype or fully lustrous sliders (AU-58). Good profit to be made, and at bargain prices. Whizzed coins are worth less. Especially examine portraits for the latter. Pass on such material, unless the price is very right. Large percentage of issue resides in the MS-60 through MS-65 state. Personally, I would recommend buying MS-60 through average-looking MS-65 pieces only for the joy of collecting. Value spread between these grades is small. Thus, think higher grade if financial situation permits. Any real future potential resides in strict eye appealing MS-65 and loftier graded specimens.

Luster will range from flashy or intense satiny (which is significantly desirable), to the dull satiny. Pass on the latter "DS," unless the price is very right. There is no way to make this kind of surface naturally alive or eye-appealing. Dipping, etc., will not create the desired result, but rather an unnatural shiny metal disk. Nevertheless, there are those who prefer this condition to a dull objectionable Antietam.

Strike seldom, if ever, will affect the grade-value. Remember that the Antietam's primary focal areas or critical locations where our eyes first make visual impact should flaunt no severe imperfections. This refers to the faces of Lee and McClellan. Only a few barely noticeable marks can be present if the coin is to be labeled MS-65. Also required are original luster, a strong strike and no fine hairlines. Bullet wounds to the face, forehead and cheekbone must be absent. The bridge should not show its battle scars! Be concerned with the location and size of these numismatic negatives on both sides of the coin and their influence on the coin's seductiveness.

 ## Detecting counterfeits

Counterfeit creations of this issue do exist. Such pieces will possess that dull greyish look or color. Surfaces will appear as if they were submersed in a tarnish removing solution for an extended length of time or just too many times, creating that washed out lustrous look.

When I examine a questionable Antietam commemorative half dollar, the first area targeted is the word ANNIVERSARY, on its reverse. Should there be present a raised metal line extending through the letters ERSAR, I know immediately that the coin is counterfeit. A similar raised metal line will be seen piercing the letters TES of STATES, diagonally to the 8 o'clock position of Lee's cheek and on the lower shaft of the letter D in UNITED on the obverse. Small depressions can also be noted above the E of THE and the R of BURNSIDE above the creek, as well as near the center, on the right arch of the bridge.

 ## Related material

Issue was distributed in a coin mailer manufactured by J. N. Spies, Watertown, N.Y. Front page is imprinted with: 75TH ANNIVERSARY OF THE BATTLE OF ANTIETAM COMMEMORATIVE HALF DOLLAR, as well as the sponsor and the names of its coin committee. Pages 2 and 4 are blank; page 3 displays the five coin insert. Value the holder alone at $35 to $75; with mailing envelope, $75 to $150.

1938
New Rochelle, NY
250th Anniversary

Reason for issue: To commemorate the 250th anniversary of the founding and settlement of New Rochelle, N.Y.

Authorized per Act of May 5, 1936: 25,000

Official sale price: $2; $2:18 by mail; 5 pcs. for $10.27

Production figures

Date	Business Strikes	Assay Coins	Proofs	Melted	Net Mintage
1938	25,000	15	4-10?	9,749	15,251

Current market values

	EF-40	AU-50	MS-60	MS-63	MS-64	MS-65
1938	210.	225.	250.	285.	375.	650.

Designs by Gertrude K. Lathrop

Obverse

Depicted is John Pell, Lord of Pelham Manor, dressed in the style of his period, receiving and holding a protesting "fatt calfe" on a rope with both hands.

When the French Huguenots purchased 6,000 acres of land in 1688 from John Pell, various provisions concerning the transfer of title were agreed upon. One such consideration required that the new inhabitants deliver to the lord, his heirs and assigns one fatted calf yearly every June 24, the Festival of St. John the Baptist of Pell, forever, if demanded. Thus, appears the calf.

Around the coin's upper border is the inscription SETTLED 1688 INCORPORATED 1899, while around the lower border we read NEW ROCHELLE NEW YORK. Located in the lower right field, opposite the Y in YORK in relief is the designer's initials, GKL. Gertrude K. Lathrop also designed the Albany commemorative half dollar.

Wear will first be seen on the hip of the fatt calfe. Areas of graininess, coarseness or light striking can be seen on the hip and should not be mistaken for wear. Examine for crisscross scratches and a difference in metal texture.

Reverse

Portrayed is a fleur-de-lis, symbolic of France and the coat-of-arms of La Rochelle, France, an area from whence the French Huguenots came. It is also a quarter part of the shield of the city of New Rochelle, N.Y. Above the denomination in the lower field is the date 1938. E PLURIBUS UNUM, LIBERTY and IN GOD WE TRUST surround the fleur-de-lis. UNITED STATES OF AMERICA arcs above; HALF DOLLAR below.

 Metal loss will begin on the main vein of the central petal and left edge of the flower. Due to die wear, light strike, or surface graininess or coarseness, area can look worn. Examine for wear. Location is prime target for the whizzing merchants.

Origins of the New Rochelle

On March 12, 1937, the Treasury Department received $300 to make dies for the issue. Three weeks later, $12,500 was forwarded to pay for the 25,000 coins to be minted.

In April 1937, the Philadelphia Mint struck 25,000 New Rochelle commemorative 50-cent pieces, the maximum amount permitted by the Act which was authorized on May 5, 1936, plus 15 coins for assay purposes. The Act further stated that the date 1938 must appear on this issue, regardless of in what year the coin was minted. Thus, we have an issue which was authorized in 1936, produced in 1937 and dated 1938, for the 250th anniversary celebration of a local event which began June 10, 1938, and lasted 10 days. This issue was sold at $2.00 each through the mail by the New Rochelle Commemorative Coin Committee. The six people in charge of packaging were instructed by its chairman on the proper way to handle coins and to cull heavily scratched or marred pieces. Only two out of 4,859 mail orders were returned for exchange! They were also sold through banks and other distribution locations. When sales came to a standstill, some members of the Westchester County Coin Club — of which I'm a member — purchased hundreds of coins at face value, according to Committee Chairman Pitt M. Skipton.

Unfortunately, this issue was not completely sold out, thus 9,749 pieces were returned to the Mint and destroyed, leaving us with a total mintage of 15,251 pieces. We can note the original request was for an authorization of 20,000 coins. Pitt Skipton's wife, Amy, Executive Secretary wrote a book *One Fatt Calfe* published by the Committee which presents the story about the coin.

The New Rochelle Today

Most coins offered at circulated prices — and there are not many — have received some form of abuse, such as light cleaning, polishing or having its devices whizzed, especially the reverse fleur-de-lis. Value spread between circulated condition and MS-64 is small. Therefore think MS-64, not less, if funds permit. Creation is available in grades up to MS-65. Should be acquired for the pure joy of collecting. Unfortunately, real future now resides in the higher grades.

Luster will range from prooflike to semi-prooflike to brilliant frosty. Strike will rarely present a problem. Surface negatives such as slide marks, hairline scratches, bag marks and reed marks gravitate toward the fatt calfe and fleur de lis, the primary focal areas, lowering a coin's grade, while field abrasions can do likewise.

Fifty pieces were struck on Proof planchets, receiving one blow from the press. They possess deep prooflike surfaces and a strong strike. Not all such New Rochelle strikings are presentation coins. These will display a lack of contrast between the main designs. One genuine Matte Proof came from the estate of John Ray Sinnock, by way of lot 2056, 1962 American Numismatic Association Convention auction.

 **Related material**

The special 50 prooflike coins were presented to various dignitaries, members of the Committee and selected members of the Westchester County Coin Club, in small dark red boxes with an inner red velvet coin slot for the specimen. It was accompanied by a popular sterling medal which depicted the city seal; the words 250TH ANNIVERSARY, plus dates 1688-1938 and the incorporated date 1899. Reverse informs the beholder that it was presented to the WCCC, by the 250th Anniversary Committee and the date June 1938. The Tiffany medal, when found, can be valued at $300 to $450.

This coin was mailed in a distribution holder with inserts for one, two, five or 10 coins. Page one presents a picture of the seal of the City of New Rochelle, an inscription and the names of the following individuals: Mayor Harry Scott, Honorary Chairman; Pitt M. Skipton, Chairman; Ernest H. Watson, Treasurer; and Jere Milleman, Secretary.

The inner front page offers a short history of the city, as well as some information about the coin and its designer, while the inner back page has the coin inserts. Value these inserts at $35 to $50; $50 to $125 with mailing envelope.

Sterling silver Tiffany medal

1946
Iowa Statehood
Centennial

Reason for issue: To commemorate the 100th anniversary of Iowa's admission into the Union on December 28, 1846.

Authorized per Act of August 7, 1946: 100,000

Official sale price: $2.50 for Iowa residents, $3.00 to others; after 1/16/47, $3 to all

Production figures

Date	Business Strikes	Assay Coins	Proofs	Melted	Net Mintage
1946	100,000	57	?	0	100,000

Current market values

	EF-40	AU-50	MS-60	MS-63	MS-64	MS-65
1946	47.50	50.00	55.00	65.00	75.00	125.

Designs by Adam Pietz

Obverse

Depicted is the Old Stone Capitol in Iowa City with a cloud formation in the background. Below this structure is the inscription THE OLD STONE CAPITOL IOWA CITY. Looking in the area of the building's lower right corner, we locate the artist's initials. In the upper field is located the motto IN GOD WE TRUST, while LIBERTY and denomination appear in the lower field and the lower border area. The words UNITED STATES OF AMERICA appear at the upper border of the coin.

A metal loss will first be observed on the cloud mass, directly below the words IN GOD of the motto, as well as on the shafts of the Old Stone Capitol building.

Reverse

Portrayed is an eagle holding a ribbon in his beak, bearing the inscription: OUR LIBERTIES WE PRIZE AND OUR RIGHTS WE WILL MAINTAIN. Below this inscription is the motto E PLURIBUS UNUM. Situated between the upper portion of the eagle's wings are 29 stars which indicate that Iowa was the 29th state to be granted admission into the Union. The inscription outside of the beaded circle reads IOWA STATEHOOD CENTENNIAL 1846-1946.

 Wear will occur on the head and neck of the eagle. Since this area at times will display a weak strike, examine for the barest trace of metal loss.

Origins of the Iowa

President Franklin Roosevelt wanted to put an end to the minting of commemorative coins because of the abuse which resulted from them. He had corresponded on several occasions with the Committee of Banking and Currency in order to express his disdain. On August 5, 1939, an Act was passed which prohibited any further commemorative minting and prohibited the issuance of any commemorative coins which were authorized prior to March 1, 1939. Thus, this Act put an end to those issues with large authorizations, such as the Oregon Trail (6,000,000); the Texas (1,500,000); the Boone (600,000) and the Arkansas (500,000). Note the total quantity minted for each issue — the Oregon Trail (264,419), the Texas (304,193) the Boone (108,603) and the Arkansas (94,901). Also, the final mintage figures for each issue was becoming smaller and smaller as the years progressed, due to lack of interest in the series. We can use as an example the Arkansas 1938 creation with its 3,155 sets available, and the 1939 striking with 2,104 sets, to illustrate the further continuation of annual small issues for a possible period of 30 years due to large authorizations, were it not for the above mentioned Act!

In 1945, Iowa led the vanguard for a centennial commemorative coin, which was passed by the House on July 15, 1946. Three weeks later, on August 7, 1946, Harry S. Truman gave his approval for the issuance of the Iowa Statehood Centennial half dollar, as well as the Booker T. Washington issue.

On November 20, 1946, beginning at 10:12 AM, the Philadelphia Mint struck 100,000 Iowa commems plus 57 assay coins in approximately 24 hours. Die manufacturing cost was $545! These pieces were handled through the Iowa Centennial Committee, State House, Des Moines, Iowa, which made excessive attempts to insure a proper distribution to the general public. By accomplishing such, the Committee was able to surmount the dominant abuse against the previous souvenir half dollars — that of an unjust distribution — which would lead to the usual speculative market.

Local residents were first given the opportunity to purchase their state's coin, a memento of the state's first century of progress and a sharing in creating a Centennial Memorial Fund, at $2.50 each. The coins were apportioned by county and population and sold through the banks via a lottery system. If you wanted to purchase this issue you would select a numbered ticket. After a drawing, you would present the ticket to the distributing bank, giving you the right to make a purchase if you had the selected number. Unfortunately, this did not guarantee one the right of obtaining a coin. If that particular bank's allotment was exhausted before you received your coin, you were possibly out of luck until more commemorative half dollars were shipped from another bank which could not sell its allotment. It was reported by Committee Executive Secretary Edith W.

McElroy on March 12, 1947, that 85,000 of the 90,000 Iowas were sold under their distribution plan during a 30-day campaign! Wow!

Five percent, or 5,000 specimens were reserved, plus the total amount of unsold pieces for out-of-state sales at $3.00 per coin. No great speculative market developed for this issue due to excellent sales, fair distribution practices plus the fact that 100,000 coins were supposed to be considered a large amount for speculation. By the end of March 1947, all available pieces were sold out.

For the state's sesquicentennial in 1996, and for its bicentennial in 2046, 1,000 coins were set aside. Half this amount is to be presented individuals during the celebration dates via an order of the Governor and the Centennial Commission. However, the State began sales of the 1996 allotment in 1992 (see Investment Section). The commemorative half dollars reside at the Norwest Bank, 666 Walnut Street, Des Moines, Iowa.

Adam Pietz, the coin's designer, had personally spent $25 on associated work photographs. He suggested he be paid in commemorative coins. His proposition was favored, as the Treasurer of State John M. Grimes mailed him 25 Iowas in appreciation for services performed — aside from the reimbursed $25 expenses — in compliance with a request from Governor Robert D. Blue and Ralph Evans, Sub-Committee Chairman on Stamp and Coin.

The Iowa Today

Specimens which can be placed in the circulated category were abused in some manner or cleaned. Issue is abundant in grades ranging from MS-60 through MS-66! Over the last two years, they came out of the "numismatic woodwork." Little value differential exists between the MS-60 and MS-65 category. Thus, collectors should zero in on the higher graded piece. Even your lofty MS-66 grade is attainable. Unless you are contemplating a MS-67 disk, acquisition should be made for the pure joy of collecting! Luster will run the gamut from brilliant satiny to dull satiny. The reverse eagle's head and part of its neck can display a weakness of strike. If pronounced, weak strike will affect the coin's grade and value. MS-66 coinage should flaunt a strong strike! Obverse primary focal area is the upper section of the Capitol building and field above. A die clash mark can be seen in the left cloud mass on part of the issue and will not affect the grade. Our reverse eagle is the main target for bag marks, etc. Presentation coins which have a "chrome look" or appear as if they were overdipped in a tarnish removing solution were provided gratuitously to select individuals.

One such creation was given to John M. Grimes, Treasurer of the State, for his assistance in distributing the Centennial half dollar, by State Governor Robert D. Blue, on January 4, 1949. These early strikes were given one blow from the striking press. Proof coinage must display the results from that second strike. All so-called Satin Finish Proofs that I have examined to date were lovely coins, but were not double struck! They are worth more than the regular issue. Just don't go overboard. Seek the advice of the knowledgeable.

 **Related material**

The regular issue was distributed in paper coin envelopes by the distributing bank such as the Farmers State Bank, Jesup, Iowa.

1946-1951
Booker T. Washington

Reason for issue: To perpetuate the ideals and teachings of Booker T. Washington, and to raise funds to purchase, construct and maintain memorials to his memory.

Authorized per Act of August 7, 1946: 5,000,000

Official sale price: 1946: $1 plus 10¢ postage per coin
                 1946-D, -S: $1.50 each
                 1947 PDS: $6.00 set, plus 30¢ postage
                 1948 PDS: $7.50 set, plus 30¢ postage
                 1949 PDS: $8.50 set, plus 30¢ postage
                 1950 PDS: $8.50 set, plus 30¢ postage; $1 for S-Mint coin
                 1951 PDS: $8.50 set, plus 30¢ postage; $3 each

Production figures

Date	Business Strikes	Assay Coins	Proofs	Melted	Net Mintage
1946	1,000,000	546	4?	500,000*	500,000*
1946-D	200,000	113	4?	100,000*	100,000*
1946-S	500,000	279	4?	180,000*	320,000*
1947	100,000	17	0	90,000*	10,000*
1947-D	100,000	17	0	90,000*	10,000*
1947-S	100,000	17	0	90,000*	10,000*
1948	20,000	5	0	12,000	8,000
1948-D	20,000	5	0	12,000	8,000
1948-S	20,000	5	0	12,000	8,000
1949	12,000	4	0	6,000	6,000
1949-D	12,000	4	0	6,000	6,000
1949-S	12,000	4	0	6,000	6,000
1950	12,000	4	0	6,000	6,000
1950-D	12,000	4	0	6,000	6,000
1950-S	512,000	91	0	235,000*	277,000*
1951	510,000	82	0	230,631*	279,369*
1951-D	12,000	4	0	5,000	7,000
1951-S	12,000	4	0	5,000	7,000

* Estimate

Current market values

	EF-40	AU-50	MS-60	MS-63	MS-64	MS-65
1946 single	10.50	11.50	13.00	18.00	22.50	47.50
1946 PDS set	——	——	37.50	50.00	70.00	150.
1947 PDS set	——	——	40.00	52.50	72.50	240.
1948 PDS set	——	——	72.50	105.	140.	215.
1949 PDS set	——	——	175.	200.	225.	300.
1950 PDS set	——	——	70.00	110.	140.	220.
1951 PDS set	——	——	60.00	115.	150.	285.

Designs by Isaac Scott Hathaway

Obverse

Portrayed is the bust of leading American educator Booker Taliaferro Washington (1858-1915). He is facing three quarters to the right. His name is placed in the lower border, while the words UNITED STATES OF AMERICA are located around the upper border. Washington appears to be looking at the inscription E PLURIBUS UNUM, in two lines in the right field. Situated in the left field are the words HALF DOLLAR. Appearing above the denomination is the date of issue. This can be from 1946 through 1951.

 Wear will first develop on the cheekbone of Booker T. Washington. Should his portrait look exceptional, examine your raw or unslabbed coin for possible doctoring.

Reverse

Depicted is the Hall of Fame, a structure which is composed of a series of columns that are set at regular intervals, which support the base of observed roof structure. This colonnade, located at New York University, houses many busts and tablets which honor famous Americans. Located above the legend LIBERTY in the lower border is the unfortunate residence of Booker T. Washington — a slave cabin. Mint mark (D or S) appears below. In the left field are the words FRANKLIN COUNTY, VA. (in three lines) which indicate his birthplace. Situated between the two structures is the inscription FROM SLAVE CABIN TO HALL OF FAME, while encircling almost 80 percent of this reverse in the border area is the inscription BOOKER T. WASHINGTON MEMORIAL. The motto IN GOD WE TRUST is located in the lower left field. This issue was created by Isaac Scott Hathaway, who also created the George Washington Carver-Booker T. Washington commemorative half dollars.

 Wear will be observed on coin's central inscription from SLAVE CABIN, etc. and on length of lower, horizontal section of the Hall of Fame.

Origins of the B.T.W.

The Coinage Weight and Measure Committee met on July 2, 1946, to consider several House resolutions. They dealt with the possible creation of the Iowa, B.T.W. and Will Rogers commemorative half dollars. For whatever reason, the latter bill (HR 98 and HR 1281) was never reported out of committee. However, the other two half dollar bills (HR 6528 and HR 2377) were unanimously passed July 15, 1946, after just 31 minutes of discussion. Congressman McCormack (MA) commented that he'd never seen a bill acted on so quickly (except for emergency legislation) after it was reported out of committee! Less than one month later, on August 7, 1946, President Truman authorized their minting. The B.T.W. Act stated the issue could be produced by the Mints, but for not more than a five-year period.

Well-known artist Charles Keck previously designed the Lynchburg, Vermont and Panama-Pacific ($1) commemorative coinage. He was solicited to create an appropriate representation for this issue. His models were accepted by the Commission of Fine Arts and Dr. Phillips. Suddenly an obscure Black designer by the name of Isaac Scott Hathaway entered the scene. This individual possessed the only existing life mask of Washington — and offered to prepare models free of charge. The Commission recommended his work. Keck was offended. However, Keck was paid for his work and bid farewell. Reverse drawing was provided by a nameless Commission member.

The issue was marketed under the direction of Dr. S.J. Phillips, who was quite influential among the Baptists and black Elks. He exclaimed that a sell-out of the entire mintage would be a reality within three months. Great expectations! Production begin at the Mints in December 1946. On the 14th of that month, the B.T.W. Birthplace Memorial Commission began taking orders. However, sales were disappointing. In February 1947, Stack's of New York City was appointed authorized agent. In November, the Philadelphia Mint produced 100,000 coins; the following month, the branch Mints did likewise. Sales for this issue were not up to expectations, because the mintage figure was high and the issue was not of a new design. It sold as a set for $6, plus 30¢ postage.

In May 1948, each of the three Mints produced 20,000 coins. The set was distributed by Stack's, Bebee's of Omaha and the Commission. However, the famous Nebraska dealer advertised as its exclusive distributor for $7.50 per set. To help protect the design from bag marks, etc., Bebee's had the Mints place each coin in a cellophane envelope. The charge per coin was 50¢. Be aware that the pieces were made using high speed presses. After they bounced off each other and resided in a bin, they were then put in the envelope! Also be aware that special handling cannot prevent lack of fill marks on BTW's portrait. They resemble small cuts and scratches and are a characteristic of striking. Sales were not up to expectations.

During January 1949, the Mint facilities each produced 12,000 of these commemorative half dollars. They were sold at $8.50 per three-piece set. Ditto 1948 sales expectancies for this issue.

In January 1950, Philadelphia and Denver struck 12,000 coins each. However, the San Francisco Mint created 512,000 of these B.T.W. half dollars, supposedly designated for building additional schools and hospitals. (To date no evidence can be located to prove any were built through this promotion of the 1950 and 1951 issue.) Set also sold for $8.50.

In January 1951, the Philadelphia Mint struck 60,000 BTW coins, while the branch Mints produced 12,000 each. In August, a needless 450,000 pieces were struck at Philadelphia. Three-piece set was sold for $10. (Examine the tabulation at the beginning of the chapter for all issues returned for melting and used for assay purposes.)

The hopes and aspirations of Dr. Phillips selling out the entire authorization never materialized.

The B.T.W. Today

In circulated condition, the higher mintage dates, especially the 1946 coinage plus 1950-S and 1951-P pieces, are the easiest to locate. They also are the least expensive of all the commemorative coinage produced from 1892 through 1954, except for the common date Washington-Carver issues which are equally priced.

Value spread for the common dates grading EF-AU up to MS-64 is so little that one cannot afford to think anything but MS-64! Our 1946 set is so abundant that it should only be acquired for the joy of collecting in grades up to MS-64. Future lies in MS-65 condition, where if strictly graded is quite undervalued. The Denver coin is rarer than the other two Mint strikings which are equally as rare. Situation exists that the issue is not popular with most collectors and there are better dates within the series to choose from. Excellent future in very underrated MS-66 grade and higher states. The 1947 set is the rarest set within the series! At present, it is not that difficult to locate up to MS-63 condition. In strict MS-64+ status, it is quite undervalued. Such is definitely the case in our MS-65 category and extremely difficult to acquire in the loftier states. Grading strict MS-64+, the Denver coin will be the hardest to locate, followed by the San Francisco and Philadelphia coins. When thinking B.T.W., think 1947.

The 1948 issue is not difficult to locate in grades up to MS-64. Undervalued in strict MS-64+ and loftier states. Labeled strict MS-65, it is underrated. Situation is such that there are a number of dates from which to select. Thus, a lack of interest here. In MS-64 condition the San Francisco coin is slightly more difficult to locate than the other issues which are equally as rare. In MS-65, it's more abundant than the other creations, which are equal in status. Really undervalued in the loftier grades.

Our 1949 set was once labeled the "King of Series," due to its low mintage. That's now changed, based on current grading standards and slabbing population awareness. It is underrated, but not that difficult to locate, based on present demand, up to your MS-64 level.

In the latter grade, the San Francisco coin is the more difficult to locate. The P and D Mints are equal in rarity. Grading MS-65, it is just the opposite. The S Mint is more abundant. Real future lies at the loftier levels.

The 1950 trio can be located with little difficulty, at present, up to MS-63+ condition. In grades MS-64 and higher, it is underrated. It's the P and D Mints which are the rarer, undervalued coins that make the set in our MS-64 and MS-65 categories. They are wonderful acquisitions in the 65 state. Future definitely lies in the loftier grades.

Our final three-coin production is dated 1951. It's underrated in grades MS-64 and higher. In the MS-64 category, the S Mint will be the hardest to locate followed by the Denver and more abundant Philadelphia striking. Grading MS-65, P and D coinage, which make great acquisitions, are about equally as rare, while the S striking is the more abundant. Future lies in the higher status coinage.

Luster will range for the entire issue from prooflike (repolished dies), to semi-prooflike, to brilliant satiny, to satiny, to dull satiny. Strike will seldom present a grade-value lowering problem. However, those numismatic villains, in the form of bag marks, lack of metal fill marks (resembling small scratches or cuts), reed marks, abrasions, slide marks and hairline scratches, plague the obverse portrait, which is your primary focal area. The surrounding field also takes its share of hits. Design offers the reverse more protection. Primary focal area is the log cabin and surrounding field. When acquiring this issue, attempt to locate a flashy looking coin with a portrait as free of negatives as possible.

 **Related material**

The 1946 issue was distributed in plain paper envelopes and several types of black leatherette cardboard holders. These have openings for three coins, contained by a movable celluloid strip. Value these holders at $50 to $75. Stack's holders (6" X 3⅛") is imprinted in silver with their name and New York City at the bottom. The Memorial's New York Headquarters (261 W. 125th St., N.Y. 27, N.Y.) distributed the three coin set in a similar holder (6" X 3") with their 12 line blue imprinted advertisement glued to the reverse. Imprinted in gold ink on the upper front part is the BOOKER T. WASHINGTON MEMORIAL HALF DOLLAR. Beneath the coin openings are the Mint marks P, D, S and below bottom, STRUCK AT THREE UNITED STATES MINTS ($25-$50). It was also forwarded in the same holder, but without the reverse promotion ($5-$10).

Christmas cards with two different scenes housed one coin, while a mailing card entitled the GEMS OF WISDOM had a coin taped to its inner right centerspread. Others were sold as prizes in a colorful, 10-coin punch board. Christmas holders can be worth $300 to $400. Another rare item is the BTW Memorial contest certificate which is a facsimile of a $3,500 check. If your name was selected first — and $12 were donated — you were the winner. These items have sold for between $150 and $300 when available.

Sets dated 1947 through 1951 were housed in cellophane envelopes, then placed inside a paper envelope. Bebee's also offered a single piece in a brown coin envelope (2X2) as an official souvenir of the 1947 New Orleans Mardi Gras. It was imprinted with black ink on back flip, his address and $1.25. As they are quite easily duplicated, they are worth only $1 to $3.

1951-1954
George Washington Carver
— Booker T. Washington

Reason for issue: To commemorate the lives of Booker T. Washington and George Washington Carver.

Authorized per Act of September 21, 1951: Supplemental Act allowed the unissued Booker T. Washington authorization to be used for the Carver-Washingtons. Therefore, authorization was 3,415,631, consisting of 1,834,000 uncoined, 1,581,631 melted BTWs.

Official sale price: $10 per set of 3 coins. (However, many 1952 Phildelphia coins were sold at or near face value by banks; ditto the 1953-S and to a lesser degree, the 1954-S issue.)

Production figures

Date	Business Strikes	Assay Coins	Proofs	Melted	Net Mintage
1951	110,000	118	0	70,000*	40,000*
1951-D	10,000	4	0	0	10,000
1951-S	10,000	4	0	0	10,000
1952	2,006,000	292	0	883,000	1123,000*
1952-D	8,000	6	0	0	8,000
1952-S	8,000	6	0	0	8,000
1953	8,000	3	0	0	8,000
1953-D	8,000	3	0	0	8,000
1953-S	108,000	20	0	60,000*	48,000*
1954	12,000	6	0	40,000	8,000
1954-D	12,006	6	0	4,000	8,000
1954-S	122,000	24	0	80,198*	41,802*

* Estimate

Current market values

	EF-40	AU-50	MS-60	MS-63	MS-64	MS-65
Type coin	11.00	12.00	13.50	19.00	27.50	60.00
1951 PDS set	——	——	38.50	75.00	125.	400.

1952 PDS set	——	——	40.00	80.00	145.	485.
1953 PDS set	——	——	41.00	87.50	170.	530.
1954 PDS set	——	——	42.00	90.00	115.	500.

Designs by Isaac Scott Hathaway

Obverse

Depicted are the accolated busts of George Washington Carver and Booker Taliaferro Washington, facing right. UNITED STATES OF AMERICA, IN GOD WE TRUST and E PLURIBUS UNUM form an outer border with three decorative stars. An inner border is formed by their names and denomination. Date of issue is located at the nape of G.W.C.

A metal loss will first be noticed on the cheekbone of Dr. Carver. Look for a difference in texture and fine crisscross scratches in this area, which usually flaunts a poor strike and lack of fill marks, resembling small cuts and scratches. Prime target for the coin doctors.

Reverse

Portrayed is map of the United States superimposed with the initials U.S.A. The inscription FREEDOM AND OPPORTUNITY FOR ALL and the word AMERICANISM separated by two decorative stars on each side are located around the outer border. The Mint mark, when present, is located above the letter IC of AMERICANISM.

Examine the letters U.S.A. for first loss of metal. Period after the S of U.S.A. is usually seen weakly struck or not as pronounced as the other periods. At times, it is almost nonexistent.

Origins of the Carver-Washington

Dr. S.J. Phillips had to sell the balance of the original Booker T. Washington authorization by the August 7, 1951, deadline. Such became an impossibility. In order to raise more funds, he helped engineer the passage of a bill which became the supplementary Act of September 21, 1951. Inserted was a clause which cited that profits would be used "to oppose the spread of Communism among Negroes, in the interest of the national defense." Remember that this occurrence was taking place during the McCarthy anti-communist hysteria years! The magic words were successful, as the bill was passed and quickly signed by President Truman. To Dr. Phillips, this victory meant the usage of the remaining 1,834,000 B.T.W. authorization, plus the melting and reincarnating into new coinage the balance held by his Commission and Treasury Department. Now 3,415,631 Carver-Washingtons would become a reality!

Original anti-communist designs created by Hathaway were rejected by Dean Acheson, Secretary of State. Virtually all of the accepted composition had to be altered by Chief Mint Engraver Gilroy Roberts. This was especially true of the reverse, since the map of America was higher than the border of its design. This meant the coin would not stack. The lettering was poor. With the aforesaid and those high relief portraits, this coin would be impossible to strike, due to metal flow problems. In fact, careful examination of the map will reveal that Delaware and part of Maryland were omitted.

In December 1951, the Philadelphia Mint struck 110,000 Carver-Washington, while the branch Mints each produced 10,000 such coins. Official distributors were Bebee's, Stack's and R. Green of Chicago. Sets were sold at $10 each, while individual coins were offered at $5.50. During March 1952, the Philadelphia Mint struck 2,006,000 coins. It was hoped that various banks could distribute quantities of individual pieces at premium prices. Thus, the larger mintages. The idea was a bust as large numbers were sold at or close to face value. Both Denver and San Francisco produced 8,000 pieces. They were distributed by the same firms, at the same set price.

In January 1953, Philadelphia and Denver each struck 8,000 Carver-Washingtons while the San Francisco facility produced 108,000 pieces. Stack's did not care to offer its services. Distributorships now were opened to almost any firm. The sets were sold at $10.00 each. During January 1954, the Mints each produced 6,000 half dollars. Ditto the following month. However, between August 1-6, the San Francisco Mint struck 110,000 additional halves. No more commemorative coinage would be minted until July 1, 1982! The three-piece set sold for $10. By the end of the year, sales came to a standstill. Few cared about the issue. The writing was on the wall, thus 1,091,198 were returned for melting.

The Carver-Washington Today

As with the BTW issue, the larger 1952, 1954-S, 1953-S and 1951 strikings will be located with no trouble in grades EF-AU through MS-64 condition. Value spread is almost nonexistent, so think MS-64. In fact, the entire 1951-1954 coinage can be located with little effort in grades MS-60 through MS-64. Current values are somewhat low, but few seem to care. When promoted, the sets rise in worth to some degree. However, when the promotion is over, prices return to past levels. Set rarity order in MS-64 condition: 1951, 1953, 1952, 1954. Best bet singles within the series are the 1951, 1951-D, 1952-D and 1953-D. Acquire for the joy of collecting. Future lies in the MS-65 category. Best MS-65 singles within the series are the 1951, 1953-D, 1954-D, 1952-D and 1953.

Set rarity order in MS-65 condition: 1953, 1954, 1951, 1952.

In MS-66 condition, we are talking about a rare coin, if accurately graded! The only date that one might have a chance of acquiring slabbed by the three major services (ANACS, NGC, PCGS) is the 1952 Philadelphia striking. Luster will range from semi-prooflike, to very brilliant satiny, to satiny, to dull satiny for the series. I have seen some semi-prooflike 1952 Philadelphia pieces. Strike will cause a grade-value lowering. Weakness will be observed on the heads of these two Black educators, as well as on the superimposed letters (U.S.A.), especially the period after the S, and map. What really downgrades this coin are those numismatic negatives such as bag marks, lack of metal fill marks, slide marks, hairline scratches, and abrasions on your primary focal portraits and reverse map, then surrounding fields. Attempt to locate eye appealing Carver-Washingtons which are virtually free of detracting marks and are well struck. If acquiring just for the joy of collecting, look for a coin or set that is fully original and is attractive. It shouldn't display ugly deep bag marks or cuts or deep scratches which really take away from the coin's beauty. Some pieces display clash mark within the outer border inscriptions. These may prove more valuable in the future. However, base value on the coin's condition. Many collectors assemble the three-piece or complete 12-piece set via individual purchases over a period of time. Of all the commemorative coinage produced from 1892 through 1954, this design has been voted the least popular, followed the Monroe and Rhode Island (obverse) creations.

 **Related material**

This issue was distributed in a cellophane coin envelope, which was placed in a paper envelope. The larger mintage issues were sent out on approval by the B.T.W. Birthplace Memorial Foundation in a small envelope, housing one coin. If you liked the souvenir after inspection, you were to send $2 to the Peoples National Bank of Rocky Mount, VA. It was also noted in 15 lines of dark red imprint that a $1.50 is deductible for tax purposes and a supply of these coins could be obtained from your Federal Reserve Bank. Small quantities were also mailed out in two types of Christmas cards with a cutout for one coin. The aforesaid envelopes can be valued $25 to $50. The Christmas cards, between $150 and $400.

1982
250th Anniversary of
George Washington's Birth

Reason for issue: To commemorate the 250th anniversary of George
    Washington's birth.

Authorized per Act of December 23, 1981: 10,000,000

Official sale price: Denver Uncirculated: $ 8.50; later $10

                       San Francisco Proof: $10.50; later $12

Production figures

Date	Business Strikes	Assay Coins	Proofs	Melted	Net Mintage
1982-D	2,689,204	?	-	478,716	2,210,458
1982-S	-	?	5,762,370	868,326	4,894,044

Current market values

	MS-60	MS-63	MS-64	MS-65	PF-65
1982-D	5.15	5.25	5.35	5.50	*
1982-S	*	*	*	*	5.50

Designs

Obverse by Elizabeth Jones

Depicted is George Washington on horseback at approximately 50 years of
age. GEORGE WASHINGTON and 250TH ANNIVERSARY OF BIRTH 1982 appear in the
upper and lower fields, respectively. The word LIBERTY is located in the central
left field; the designer's initials, EJ adjacent to the lower forearm. The Mint mark
either D or S is located to the left of the horse's lower mane.

Reverse by Elizabeth Jones and Matthew Peloso.

Portrayed is the eastern facade of Mount Vernon, Washington's home on the
Potomac. UNITED STATES OF AMERICA arcs above; HALF DOLLAR below. IN GOD
WE TRUST is in smaller letters in the upper field. Below the building rests the
heraldic eagle, bearing the banner E PLURIBUS UNUM. The designer's initials EJ
appear below the columns in the right field while the two letters of Matthew

Peloso's name are cleverly placed and hardly noticeable in the first section of foliage opposite the left rim.

Origins of the Washington Half Dollars

Eleven years have passed since the first 1982 George Washington half dollar made its debut, so this might be a good time to pause and take a look at how U.S. commemoratives came to be reborn.

The 1920s and 1930s were the golden age of our nation's commemorative coinage — or, more precisely, the silver age. That was when the preponderance of U.S. commems came into being.

The 1960s and 1970s were, by sharp contrast, the dark ages. The lights went out on the series in 1954, when the U.S. Mint completed production of the Washington-Carver half dollar — and, for nearly 30 years thereafter, commems were a dead issue at the Treasury.

There seemed to be no reason to look for new life in the series as the the Eighties got under way. Ronald Reagan's victory in the 1980 presidential election did serve notice that changes would be made in the nation's capital, but only cock-eyed optimists held any serious hope that the changes would trickle down to commems.

Thus, most observers of the numismatic scene took only casual note, in the early days of the 97th Congress in 1981, when a Georgia congressman named Doug Barnard Jr. announced his intention to introduce a new coinage bill: a bill to authorize production of a commemorative half dollar honoring George Washington on the 250th anniversary of his birth. Nor was there any perceptible gasp of excitement on March 16th of that year, when Barnard actually did introduce the legislation.

The bill picked up important support when Rep. Frank Annunzio of Illinois, chairman of the House Subcommittee on Consumer Affairs and Coinage, joined Barnard in co-sponsoring it. Still, even then, few gave it very much chance of success. Numerous other bills proposing special coins had come up for discussion through the years, but — with the exception of the Bicentennial coinage legislation — anything that sounded remotely like a new commemorative had crashed on the rocks of Treasury opposition.

This time, however, something totally unexpected took place. Instead of opposing the bill, the new Treasury leadership — made up of Reagan appointees — went along with it.

U.S. Treasurer Angela M. Buchanan disclosed this astounding new attitude on May 7, 1981, when she testified before Annunzio's panel:

"While the Department of the Treasury has a history of objecting to the issuance of commemorative coins for the benefit of private sponsors and organizations," Miss Buchanan said, "it has not objected to special coinage authorized by Congress for the government's own account (such as the proposal we are discussing today). The Treasury Department, thus, did not object to the Eisenhower 40-percent silver dollar program, enacted in 1970, or the American Revolution Bicentennial 40-percent silver set program, enacted in 1973.

"The Treasury Department believes that the 250th anniversary of the 'Father of Our Country' is an occasion which justified the issuance of a special non-circulating commemorative coin."

It was my privilege and pleasure to be in attendance at that hearing — for I, too, had been invited by Chairman Annunzio to present my views on the bill as an expert witness. I was, of course, delighted by the Treasurer's remarks — and it's interesting to note that in my prepared testimony, I had called upon the Treasury and the Mint for just such a change of heart — for what I described as "a simple softening of their stance."

"Let us put an end to this continuous neglect of inadequately honoring those exceptionally important events in our nation's great history," I declared. "Remember the U.S. moon landing? On whose coinage is it commemorated? Isn't it time that we begin remembering our heroes. Let us revive the custom of striking commemoratives — the most colorful coinage of the United States of America."

Annunzio's subcommittee gave the bill its immediate — and unanimous — approval. Less than two weeks later, on May 19, 1981, the full House did likewise in a voice vote.

Progress was slower in the Senate. Sen. James McClure of Idaho introduced a companion bill on May 18 — the day before the final House approval — but the Senate didn't act for more than six months. Finally, on Dec. 9, the Senate passed the bill and sent it to President Reagan, who signed it into law on Dec. 23.

Clearly, the Treasury's willingness to accept the Washington coin was a key to its eventual approval. And, by taking the position it did, the department not only cleared the way of this specific coin but also reopened the books on commemorative coinage as a whole.

Treasurer Buchanan insisted, however, that there really hadn't been a fundamental change in department policy.

"We appreciate the reasons why past administrations have opposed commemorative coins and believe there was a lot of solid reasoning involved," Miss Buchanan said. "But we also feel that each proposal deserves to be reviewed on its own merits, rather than being rejected with a flat, across-the-board statement."

Whatever the official thinking may have been, hobbyists naturally hailed what was taking place as a welcome sign of new cooperation — and new consideration — by the Treasury.

I think it's especially fitting that his first new commemorative honored George Washington, a man who was himself a first in many important respects. "First in war, first in peace, first in the hearts of his countrymen" — that's an epigram often used to describe our nation's first president.

Under the legislation authorizing the Washington half dollar, the coin was to be 90 percent silver, like all previous U.S. commemorative halves. Up to 10 million examples could be struck, with production continuing through 1983 if necessary, even though all the coins would be dated 1982. And the coins would be sold a premium reflecting the actual costs of production and distribution plus a surcharge of not more than 20 percent.

An unusual amendment inserted by Annunzio specified that all profits from sale of the Washington coin would be used to help reduce the national debt.

"When George Washington was president," the congressman pointed out, "our country had almost no debts."

A similar provision was inserted in the legislation authorizing the Constitution coins. Surcharges have been added to the issue prices of both new coins and earmarked for reducing the national debt. These amount to $35 for each half eagle and $7 for each silver dollar.

By interesting coincidence, the Washington half dollar gained final approval in Congress only a few weeks after the swearing-in of Elizabeth Jones as new chief sculptor-engraver of the Mint. Thus, it was only natural that Jones — the first woman ever to hold that post — should get the pleasant assignment of being its designer.

She set out at once to give it a distinctive appearance: Instead of simply using a traditional bust of George Washington, she got the idea of showing him on horseback.

"I knew right away that I wanted to put Washington on a horse," she later revealed. "He was so famous as a horseman and a general, and there are so many equestrian statues and paintings of him, that I thought it would be appropriate to show him in that part of his life, rather than just in his older years when he was president.

"I wanted to make a break with tradition," she said. "I have seen so many collections of medals and coins of Washington where everything is either a head or a profile view. They're all variations on the same basic theme. Bu this is something different — something we haven't seen much in the U.S. coinage tradition."

Equestrian designs hadn't been totally foreign to U.S. coinage. One earlier commem, the 1925 Stone Mountain half dollar, shows two Confederate generals — Robert E. Lee and Thomas "Stonewall" Jackson — on horseback. Another, the 1900 Lafayette dollar, depicts an equestrian statue of the Marquis de Lafayette. Still, as Jones pointed out, U.S. coinage had tended to be conservative and repetitive, especially in its treatment of George Washington. Thus, her design was an interesting departure from the norm. In creating her design, she had drawn on an 1824 Rembrandt Peale portrait which hangs in the portrait gallery of Philadelphia's Second Bank of the United States.

The Washington quarter is the only regular-issue U.S. coin ever produced in honor of the nation's first president — and, of course, it shows him in a standard profile portrait. Two other commems had carried his likeness; but, there, too, the portraits were standard.

Curiously, both of those previous commems had depicted Washington along with somebody else. He appeared with Lafayette on the 1900 dollar and with Calvin Coolidge on the 1926 half dollar marking the sesquicentennial of U.S. independence.

In authorizing the 1982 commem, Congress stipulated that both sides of the coin should bear designs "emblematic" of the Washington anniversary. At first, Elizabeth Jones intended to show the house where Washington was born — a little-known dwelling in Wakefield, Va. — on the reverse. She later reconsidered, though, and showed his famous homestead at Mount Vernon. The reason, she explained to me, was that after completing her original design, she learned that the present-day "Washington birthplace" at Wakefield is a total reconstruction of the original.

Jones got a helping hand in fashioning the reverse: Using her artwork, Matthew Peloso, an assistant staff engraver at the Mint, prepared the plaster model. Numismatic sleuths will find Peloso's initials hidden in the shrubbery to the left of Mount Vernon — and this, by the way, is a helpful point of reference in determining the sharpness of a strike. Miss Jones has her initials on both sides of the coin.

Business-strike "G.W. halves" were produced at the Denver Mint and Proofs at San Francisco. July 1, 1982, marked the start of production, and special ceremonies took place on that day at both locations.

It was, of course, a truly historic occasion: the dawn of a new age in U.S. commemorative coinage. For that reason, I consider myself extremely fortunately to have been a participant in the program — even though I had to do some fancy cross-country flying to be on hand for both sets of ceremonies.

At Denver, I was privileged to strike the fifth ceremonial piece, after the first four had been struck by Mint Director Donna Pope, Denver Mint Superintendent Nora W. Hussey, Denver Mayor William H. McNichols Jr. and ANA President Adna G. Wilde Jr.

The whole thing seemed like a dream. I was almost walking on air as I stepped up and selected one of the 16 remaining silver planchets. Then I placed it on the press, and within a few seconds a remembrance-preserver emerged. I examined it at once, and found to my delight that its fields were semi-Prooflike.

Following the program in Denver, I left at once and headed for the airport — along with some of the others — for a quick flight to San Francisco, where similar ceremonies were scheduled just a few hours later. I found the second part of the day's "double-header" an equally exhilarating experience. All in all, it was one of the most memorable days of my life.

Initially, I suspect, there were doubting Thomases — at the Treasury and also in the hobby — who didn't expect the Washington coin to make very much of a splash. Even those who liked it, myself included, had no real way of gauging its sales potential, since three decades had passed since the last new commem and the market had changed dramatically.

As things turned out, there wasn't any cause for concern. Orders poured in, and the Mint had to work full blast to keep up with demand. There were 3,084 dies produced by the Philadelphia Mint for this issue during the fiscal year of 1983! By the time production ended, on Dec. 31, 1983, some 8 million pieces — all bearing the original 1982 date — had been struck. The overwhelming majority of these were sold. By Dec. 31, 1985, when sales officially ended, the Mint has sold a total of nearly 4.9 million Proof San Francisco examples and more than 2.2 million Denver Uncirculated pieces — not meant for circulation — at issue prices of $10.50 and $8.50, respectively — and grand total of more than 7.1 million coins. That made this the most successful commem, from the standpoint of sales, in U.S. history. A profit of over $36 million was made which was deposited in the Treasury's general fund to help reduce the national debt! It's interesting to note that Proofs outsold business strikes by a 2-to-1 margin. This was a numismatic first: Never before had this happened with any U.S. coin that was offered for public sale in both versions.

The Washington half dollar has proven to be popular not only with the public but also with coinage critics. In 1984, Krause Publications chose it as the winner of the first annual "Coin of the Year" contest, in head-to-head competition with new coin issues from all over the world. The entries were judged on the basis of their beauty and historical significance.

I, too, give the Washington coin high marks — especially from the standpoint of historical significance. After a full generation with no new commems, the Washington half dollar got the U.S. back on the track.

Now that the series is moving again, I look for it to keep going full steam ahead. And I strongly suspect that hobbyists of the future will view two dates as particularly special in the history of U.S. commemorative coinage: 1892, when the series was born — and 1982, when it was born again.

The George Washington Half Dollars Today

One of my favorite late date designs happens to be our G.W. half dollar. However, it's the most abundant and easily located of all the post-1982 commemorative creations. It currently sells for half its original issue price. However, don't get too excited. Based on their mintage, handling and given protection, they are not worth really much more than current value levels. Many of the high mintage Proof pieces will grade between PF 65 and PF 68, while a large percentage of the Uncirculated specimens will grade between MS-64 and MS-67. Locate a specimen you believe will grade PF 67 or higher or MS-66 or higher and submit for slabbing, instead of paying an outrageous amount for one already graded. Early 1982 Denver Mint Uncirculated coinage flaunted a small field scratch or two, or nick which naturally lowered their grade. Complaints were received by the Mint. It was told to me that planchets which were delivered from the San Francisco Mint lacked in quality. The coast mint responded by saying the planchets were not properly handled by the Denver Mint after they were delivered. Whatever the cause, this situation was remedied with later production receiving better care, thus higher grades. Only acquire creation for the pure joy of collecting.

There exist two very rare Proof G.W.'s which were struck 10% off center! One sold for $5,000. When examining the date 1982, one may notice its digit 8 will resemble the open letter S. We observe "19S2." This common polishing variety was created when the die surface was cut below the level of part of the digit, eliminating sections of the 8.

This issue's Proof coin is encapsulated in a plastic coin holder, housed within a burgundy colored cardboard box. The encapsulation is located in an opening of a velour-lined coin holder with rear picture frame stand, should display be desired. A descriptive insert is contained. Top of box cover is imprinted with a silver outline of G.W.'s bust and autograph reproduction. Inner top lid is covered with silver paper. The Uncirculated version is sealed in mylar or polyester film wrap, housed within a descriptive insert with opening to view the coin, and placed within a bluish green colored box. This container is exactly the same as the burgundy box, except the inner bottom is elevated by a piece of cardboard covered by a bluish-green paper. Ceremonial Press kits containing galvano photos of the issue and information about the issue are rare, as are the official Mint invitations to the ceremony. Since 99.9% of these coins will rarely be removed from their mint encapsulations or vary little in grade and did not receive the abuse of past commemorative issues (1892-1954) grading information is irrelevant.

1983-1984
Los Angeles Olympics

Reason for issue: To commemorate and support the 1984 Los Angeles
Olympic Games.

Authorized per Act of July 22, 1982: 50,000,000 silver dollars (combined
1983 and 1984 authorization); 2,000,000 gold $5

Official sale price:

Silver dollars:

Philadelphia single, $28

P-D-S Uncirculated set, $89; later $100

Denver and San Francisco Unc. sold in sets only. All three coins included
in other Mint packaging options.

1983-S Proof, $24.95; later $29, then $32

1984-S Proof, $32; later, $35

1984 gold $5: all Proofs, $352
W-Uncirculated, $339

Production figures

Date	Business Strikes	Assay Coins	Proofs	Melted	Net Mintage
1983-P $1	*	?	-	?**	294,543
1983-D $1	*	?	-	?**	174,014
1983-S $1	*	?	-	?**	174,014
1983-S $1 Proof	-	?	*	?**	1,577,025
1984-P $1	*	?	-	? **	217,954
1984-D $1	*	?	-	? **	116,675
1984-S $1	*	?	_	? **	116,675
1984-S $1 Proof	-	?	*	? **	1,801,210
1984-P $5	-	?	?	?	33,304*
1984-D $5	-	?	?	?	34,533*
1984-S $5	-	?	?	?	48,551*
1984-W $5	-	?	?	?	381,085*
1984-W $5 Proof	?	?	-	?	75,886*

*The actual number of coins struck by the Mint was not released.
**According to the *1985 Annual Report of the Director of the Mint*, the actual number of 1983 and 1984 dollars melted was not declared. It is estimated that 1,170,511 pieces were destroyed.

Current market values

	MS-60	MS-63	MS-64	MS-65	PF-65
1983-P dollar	20.00	20.25	20.50	21.00	*
1983-D dollar	27.00	28.00	29.00	30.00	*
1983-S dollar	20.50	20.75	21.00	21.50	15.00
1984-P dollar	21.00	21.50	22.00	22.50	*
1984-D dollar	37.50	40.00	42.50	45.00	*
1984-S dollar	40.00	42.50	45.00	47.50	15.50
1984-P eagle	*	*	*	*	250.
1984-D eagle	*	*	*	*	225.
1984-S eagle	*	*	*	*	220.
1984-W eagle	200.	205.	210.	215.	215.

1983 Dollar Designs

Obverse by Elizabeth Jones

Depicted is a figure of the Discus Thrower inspired by the ancient work of the Greek sculptor Myron. Around coin's border is the inscription LOS ANGELES XXIII OLYMPIAD and the word LIBERTY. The date 1983 appears beneath the Thrower's thighs while the designer's initials EJ are below his foot. In the right field appears the motto IN GOD WE TRUST and the Olympic "Star in Motion" symbol. The horizontal bars express the speed of the competitors while the repeated star shape represents the spirit of competition between equally outstanding physical forms. Below is the graphic rings logo.

Reverse by Elizabeth Jones and John Mercanti

Portrayed is the head and shoulders of an American eagle. In the outer border is UNITED STATES OF AMERICA and ONE DOLLAR separated by olive branches. Located in the left central field is the motto E PLURIBUS UNUM. The designers' initials EJ-JM are located behind the eagle's neck.

1984 Dollar Designs by Robert Graham

Obverse

Depicted is the artist's "Olympic Gateway" sculpture of two headless figures separated by an Olympic flame on a lintel, supported by two columns. In the background is an outline of the Los Angeles Memorial Coliseum (where Robert Graham's actual bronze creation was placed). The word LIBERTY, date and LOS ANGELES 1984 XXIII OLYMPIAD appears in the outer border. The motto IN GOD WE TRUST is located in the central field. The Mint mark is situated above the second E of ANGELES.

Reverse

Portrayed is a full figure of a perched American eagle looking right, holding an olive branch. Beneath this bird of prey is the motto E PLURIBUS UNUM. In the field under the oliver branch are the designer's initials RG. Located in the upper field is UNITED STATES OF AMERICA and ONE DOLLAR.

1984 $5 Designs

Obverse by John Mercanti, from a sketch by James M. Peed

Depicted are the Olympic torch runners. To their left (as you view the coin) are the words LOS ANGELES; below the Olympic rings. To the right is the motto IN GOD WE TRUST. Directly below is the date and Mint mark. In the upper field is LIBERTY and in the lower field (the exergue) is OLYMPIAD XXIII. The engraver JM and designer's JP initials appear below the actual right foot of the male torch runner.

Reverse by John Mercanti

Portrayed is the Great Seal of the United States which is slightly modified. In the outer border is UNITED STATES OF AMERICA. Lower part of the border displays the coin's denomination, TEN DOLLARS. Below the eagle's tail feathers are the designer's initials JM.

Origins of the Los Angeles Olympics Coins

Rich in history and controversial from the day they were first proposed. That is how one might describe the Olympic commemorative silver dollars and gold eagles.

To fully understand the turmoil that surrounded the birth of the United States Olympic coin program, it is important to put it in some historical context. In 1981, the United States had been without commemorative coin production for almost three decades. The commemorative coin program had ceased to be an active part of the Mint's yearly activities because of a checkered past which included programs with too many coins, others where the private marketing of the coins was suspect, and others where even the reason for the commemorative was suspect. While the coins may have been beautiful and exciting, the programs which had spawned them were often marginal if not simply embarrassing. Under this cloud, the commemorative program had been stopped.

In 1981, there was reason to believe that there was a thaw in the frosty attitude of the Congress toward commemorative programs. A proposal for a George Washington commemorative half dollar which was viewed as a non-controversial way of making a modest venture into a potentially new era of commemoratives had received strong support in the House of Representatives. While admittedly a modest beginning, it must be remembered that there were many at the time who did not trust the notion of commemorative coins because of the past problems.

In this atmosphere, where even talk of a single commemorative was enough to send sparks of excitement through collector ranks, came a bolt of lightning. A peculiar threesome composed of Occidental Petroleum and its colorful chairman Dr. Armand Hammer, the Paris banking house Lazard Freres, and the Franklin Mint stunned everyone by calling for an Olympic commemorative coin program involving 26 basic coin designs and denominations to be produced in gold, silver, and copper-nickel in both Proof and Uncirculated to total some 53 coins for a complete set.

The basic outline for the huge program appeared in legislation introduced on May 20, 1981, by Senator Alan Cranston (D-California). The Cranston bill (S. 1230) called for four different $100 gold pieces, four different $50 gold pieces, sixteen different $10 silver pieces and five different copper-nickel dollars. The silver and gold coins were to be produced in both Proof and Uncirculated, with the dollars only produced as business strikes for a total of 53 different coins.

Senator Cranston was hardly alone in supporting a large Olympic commemorative program. In the House of Representatives a similar bill (H.R. 3958) was introduced by Rep. Patterson on June 17, 1981. The proposals had the backing of groups such as the United States Olympic Committee which stood to gain from the sale of the coins. The USOC supplied noted athletes to testify in support of the proposals. While amended in committee, a 25 coin proposal passed the U.S. Senate. The bill among other things called for the private marketing of the Olympic coins.

When the Cranston bill moved over to the House of Representatives it ran into a hailstorm of opposition headed by the powerful chairman of the House Subcommittee on Consumer Affairs and Coinage, Rep. Frank Annunzio (D-Ill.) and a wide range of hobby leaders. As the proposed legislation would have to pass the subcommittee which Annunzio chaired, its fate was sealed early as Annunzio would have no part of 53 coins or private marketing.

Understanding the problems, Rep. Patterson introduced a new measure (H.R. 5933) which called for 17 coins including four gold coins, 12 silver coins and one copper-nickel. The Senate passed this measure, but again Frank Annunzio stood firm in his opposition.

Sensing the time had come for a final struggle, the proponents rallied behind H.R. 6058, a 17-coin proposal introduced by House Banking Committee Chairman Fernand St. Germain and supported by Deputy Secretary of the Treasury Tim McNamar, a host of lobbyists, President Reagan, the Los Angeles Olympic Organization Committee and the U.S. Olympic Committee.

The 17-design or 33-coin (with Proof and Uncirculated versions of all but the one copper-nickel coin) proposal had carried the day in committee by a 32 to 7 margin. Still carrying the private marketing provision and complete with a $30 million guarantee to the Los Angeles Olympic Organizing Committee, the 33-coin proposal was all but signed according to most.

For his part, Annunzio stuck by his guns. He countered the proposal with a three-coin bill (H.R. 6158) which followed other unsuccessful efforts to gain approval for a limited coin bill. The three-coin proposal called for 1983 and 1984 silver dollars with an authorization limit of 50 million coins. It also called for a 1984 $10 gold piece with an authorization of 2 million pieces. The coins were to be sold in the U.S. by the Treasury and overseas by a private corporation. Prices were to be sufficient to cover production costs plus a surcharge of at least $10 on the silver dollars and at least $50 on the gold coin. The money collected through the surcharges was to be split evenly between the Los Angeles Olympic Organizing Committee and the U.S. Olympic Committee.

The final showdown took place on May 20, 1982, on the floor of the House of Representatives. Debate was over the 33-coin proposal, and it lasted for hours. When it came time for a vote, all were stunned as by a margin of 302-84 the House of Representatives voted NO on 33-coins, approving instead the Annunzio plan for three Olympic coins.

Faced with three coins or none, the Senate agreed to go along with the House on July 1, 1982. On July 22, 1982, President Reagan signed P.L. 97-220 making the three-coin (actually six if you count separate Proofs and Uncirculateds) bill into law.

The troubles with the Olympic coins hardly ended with the final House showdown. In fact, the ink had barely dried on the bill before the next round of difficulties surfaced. The next problem was over the designs. Working under severe time constraints, the Treasury unveiled preliminary sketches for the three coins. The response was well short of enthusiastic. In fact, there were howls of protest.

Although probably the least criticized of the Olympic coin designs, the 1983 dollar obverse was considered too similar to a platinum 150 rouble coin by many. It was the first commemorative coin to bear the P Mint mark.

The 1984 Olympic silver dollar was the work of Robert Graham, an American sculptor. The Coliseum in particular drew reviews which were well short of raves, and was likened to an automobile hood ornament by at least one critic.

Although the two dollars were not exactly popular, it was the $10 gold eagle, the first commemorative coin of that denomination and the first U.S. gold coin since 1933, which particularly upset the critics. With an obverse of two runners, one male and one female bearing an Olympic torch and a reverse modeled after the Great Seal of the United States, the $10 gold design was greeted with howls of outrage. The most quoted comment came from none other than Rep. Frank Annunzio, who suggested that the two figures on the obverse looked like "Dick and Jane." Even the person responsible for the design was in dispute as the sketches were prepared by James Peed, an exceptional graphic artist with the Mint, while the later modification fell to John Mercanti.

The whole design controversy ultimately found its way to the House Subcommittee on Consumer Affairs and Coinage where chairman Frank Annunzio and others vented their anger, while Treasurer Angela "Bay" Buchanan and few others supported them. Finally, with some modifications, the designs were used.

The Treasury Department began taking orders for the Olympic coins on October 14, 1982. At the time, Proof dollars were offered from San Francisco along with a Proof $10 gold coin which was to be produced at West Point and carry the first "W" Mint mark in the history of American coins. Had the eventual coins produced been limited to those three, it is likely that there would have never been a strong possibility for buyers to profit from the Olympic commemorative coins.

What happened, was that the Treasury decided there were ways to create more coins, thus increasing sales and revenue. Ultimately, $10 gold coins were issued at West Point, Denver, San Francisco and Philadelphia. An Uncirculated version was also produced at West Point. The silver dollars were issued as Uncirculateds from Philadelphia, Denver and San Francisco while Proofs were produced at San Francisco. In total, 13 different coins, safely beyond anything that had been imagined when Annunzio won his victory in the House of Representatives.

As might be expected, all the different coins prevented most from obtaining a complete set. The large majority of the silver dollar orders were for the San Francisco Proofs of 1983 and 1984. The 1983 Proof dollar finished with a total production of 1,577,025. In 1984 the total was 1,801,210. The Uncirculateds are a completely different story with 294,543 Philadelphia Uncirculated 1983 dollars and 174,014 Uncirculated 1983 dollars from both Denver and San Francisco. In 1984, Uncirculated Philadelphia dollar sales were 217,954 while sales at Denver and San Francisco were 116,675. Clearly the Olympic silver dollars are not equal in rarity.

While the Olympic coin program had more than its share of troubles, it has to be viewed as a program of major importance. It gave birth to our first commemorative silver dollars since the Lafayette dollar in 1900. It provided us with our first gold commemorative since 1926, and our first gold $10 commemorative. In addition, it provided us with the first "W" Mint mark and our first gold coin of any description since 1933. That is an impressive list of achievements for any program. Considering the troubles, a remarkable commemorative program.

The official ceremonial striking for the 1984 $10 Proof issue occurred at the West Point Bullion Depository on September 13, 1983. Present were Cliff Barber, its Superintendent; Donald T. Regan, Secretary of the Treasury; Donna Pope, Director of the U.S. Mint; Col. F. Don Miller, Executive Director of the U.S. Olympic Committee; amd Edwin W. Steidle, Senior V.P. of the Los Angeles Olympic Organizing Committee. Olympic medalists present were Floyd Patterson, Donna De Varona and Melissa Belote Hamlin. I personally enjoyed the music of the U.S. Military Academy Band. For the first time in numismatic history the W Mint mark was placed upon our coinage, joining the family of seven other continental facilities which served or still serve our government. (Let us not forget that there was a branch Mint in Manilla, the Philippines, under U.S. sovereignty in 1920 and after. The M Mint mark was used.) There was no special law passed for the new identifying letter. It was a decision made by Donna Pope which was contained in an interim memo she signed in January 1983! Sales of the Proof W issue (381,085) and Uncirculated version (75,886) came to a standstill. A

South Korean entrepreneurial group was happy, since they previously purchased a very large number of Uncirculated specimens. Their primary objective was to sell this modern low mintage striking at much higher prices to collectors in the very near future, when Seoul would hold the Olympic games. In an effort to revive sales, it was announced that Proof coinage would be produced at Philadelphia, Denver and San Francisco, flaunting their respective Mint marks. The Act called for one design — but it did not specify that only one facility would be permitted to produce the issue! Not only were the Koreans ticked off, collectors became angry. They would have preferred to choose the lowest mintage issue and/or the mint of their choice. Also, if they wanted all five creations $1,747 would be required for acquisition.

This was the first gold commemorative struck since the $2¹/₂ 1926 Sesquicentennial issue. It was the only commemorative design to be struck by four different mints of this nation and it was the first Proof only issue of any denomination to be created by the Denver facility. Numismatically speaking, it's the first gold coin to be produced by this Mint since its 1931 $20 Saint Gaudens rarity. It is Philadelphia's first gold coin since the rare 1933 $10 Indian and illegal to own 1933 $20 Saint-Gaudens, as well as San Francisco's 1930 rare $10 eagle and $20 double eagle!

Via the sale of 4.7 million 1983 and 1984 silver and gold coins struck for this issue, the Treasury received $307 million. Approximately $67.7 million was collected to help support the Olympic program! An audit by the U.S. Government's Accounting Office showed plainly that only $6.4 million of the $49.2 million given to the United States Olympic Organizing Committee was used to train athletes. Only $338,000 went overseas for royalties and coin sales. The balance was placed in interest bearing investments. Irrefutably, this was not the design of the original legislation!

The 1983 U.S. Olympic Dollar Today

Since virtually all the coinage produced for this program in 1983 had received the best of care and Mint encapsulation, I suggest acquiring only for the pure joy of collecting. All of the issues are now selling for less than half their original issue price. The only coin I would recommend adding to one's collection from the four produced at the mints in this year would be the Denver creation. The majority of all the Mint encapsulations will grade between MS-65 to MS-68 and PF-65 to PF-68. Send in your own gems for grading submission to a recognized service instead of buying one already slabbed at some outrageous price because PF-68 is seen on the insert. Do the same for all similar modern coinage!

By the way, there were 12 ceremonial 1983-S Olympic dollars produced on Press 19 at the San Francisco Assay Office, on February 10, 1983. I had the honor of striking the last Proof coin. Unfortunately, even with three blows from the press, a section of the eagle's feathers and neck area did not strike up well. All were destroyed. Design modifications were made. According to a personal friend working at this facility, there were a small number of these coins accidentally produced with a 180-degree reverse die misalignment. This means the obverse discus thrower and reverse eagle will both be in an upright position as you rotate it to see the reverse. The normal die orientation would show the eagle inverted. If flipped from the obverse to reverse, the error coin would show the eagle upside-down, while the correct die alignment would show the bird of prey right side up. He believes that "all were destroyed, but it's possible some may have escaped." Therefore, it is suggested one examine their 1983-S Proof Olympic dollars to see if a such a rare error coin exists in your collection.

Offered individually, the 1983-P Uncirculated dollar was housed in a blue box, while the Proof creation was presented in a burgundy velvet case. The latter was also included with the standard 1983 Proof coinage (1 cent through half dollar), creating the Prestige Set. All three P, D and S Uncirculated strikings were offered as a set and housed in a blue box.

The 1984 Olympic Dollars Today

Out of the four coins struck for this issue, as well as the four dollars produced in 1983, the only real dark horse possessing a numismatic future is the 1984-D creation. One might say the S.F. Uncirculated has the same mintage. This is true and it is somewhat underrated. Howbeit, those looking for a representative 1984-S example can also choose the more impressive looking Proof coin. The same cannot be said for the Denver Mint creation — which is well distributed and greatly undervalued. To acquire the Denver Uncirculated coin - which was not sold individually by the Mint — one had to purchase the three piece Uncirculated set! Specimens displaying what appears to be two different varieties of obverse machine doubling are rather common and offer no extra value. Also for the record, the 1984 Philadelphia and San Francisco Uncirculated coinage may exhibit near and far rims (small or large inside diameter) depending on the hub which was used to produce the die. All Denver productions should have far rims (large inside diameter). The latter two dollars (along with the USO and White House issues) appear to be the only modern commemorative coinage (1982-present) which is selling for more than its original issue price! The Philadelphia uncs and S.F. Proofs of this 1984 production should only be acquired for the joy of collecting. As with the 1983 strikings, many of these mint encapsulated pieces will range from the 65 through 68 grade. Don't be too impressed with the loftier grades, since they exist in large numbers due to the care received.

Offered individually, the 1984-P Uncirculated dollar was housed in a blue box, while the Proof creation was presented in a burgundy velvet case. The latter was also included with the standard 1984 Proof coinage (1 cent through half dollar), referred to as the Prestige Set. All three P, D and S Uncirculated strikings were sold as a set and housed in a blue box.

The Olympic $10 Coinage Today

At present, the West Point Proof and Uncirculated coins, as well as the San Francisco production, are selling for slightly over bullion value. Any future for the design lies in the Philadelphia striking which once sold for $850+ and the Denver creation, a $750 item in the past. Both are now bid at just over bullion value! Howbeit, what does bid values mean when the coins are difficult to locate in quantity? Small hoards of these well distributed low mintage eagles exists. Several investment companies are attempting — as of this writing — to acquire and place the underrated P, D and S creations into their clients' portfolios, in anticipation of gold rising and a hot coin market. Since these pieces can be removed from their coin capsules, a small percentage have been abused. Pass on those which display fingerprints or hairline scratches. Full frosted pieces are very desirable.

All $10 Proof coinage was offered individually in dark blue velvet cases, while the Uncirculated version was housed in a blue box. The three piece Uncirculated set included the $10 W striking, plus the 1983 and 1984 silver dollars, housed in a burgundy velvet case. There were 29,975 sets sold at $395. A three Proof set, offered before the creation of the San Francisco Proof $10 coin was envisioned, consisted of the 1983-S and 1984-S dollars, plus the W Proof coin. At $352, there were 260,083 sets sold. When the San Francisco eagle was struck, another three-piece set was conceived. It was made up of the 1983-S and 1984-S dollars, plus the new S Proof. There were 4,000 of the latter sold, at $352, then $416. All these coins were housed in a burgundy velvet case. Descriptive literature accompanied. Each coin was encapsulated. A six-piece set contained in a cherry wood box consisted of the following coins: 1983 and 1984 Philadelphia and San Francisco Uncirculated dollars, the low mintage $10 P Mint Proof and the $10 W Uncirculated coin. There were 8,926 of these sets sold. I have examined some of these original $850 sets where the rarer $10 P Eagle was replaced with the common $10 West Point Proof and the descriptive literature missing. Be alert!

The 13 coins of the 1983-84 Los Angeles Olympics

1986
Statue Of Liberty-Ellis Island Centennial

Reason for issue: To commemorate the centennial of the Statue of Liberty.
Authorized per Act of July 9, 1985: 25,000,000 half dollars
   10,000,000 dollars
   500,000 gold $5
Official sale price:
   Uncirculated Denver clad half dollar: $5, later $6
   Proof San Francisco clad half dollar: $6.50, later $7.50
   Uncirculated Philadelphia dollar: $20.50, later $22.00
   Proof San Francisco dollar: $22.50, later $24.00
   Uncirculated West Point gold $5: $160, later $165
   Proof West POint gold $5: $170, later $175

Production figures

Date	Business Strikes	Assay Coins	Proofs	Melted	Net Mintage
1986-D 50¢	?	?	-	?	928,008*
1986-S 50¢	-	?	?	?	6,925,627*
1986-P $1	?	?	-	?	723,635*
1986-S $1	-	?	?	?	6,414,638*
1986 W $5	?	?	-	?	95,248**
1986 W $5	-	?	?	?	404,013**

*Actual minting and melting figures were not released by the Mint. Net mintage figures shown represent the net quantity distributed by the Mint.

**The complete authorization was struck. Total net mintage or distribution reflects 499,261 pieces. The missing 739 pieces were presumably used to replace damaged or lost shipments.

Current market values

	MS-60	MS-63	MS-64	MS-65	PF-65
1986-D clad 50¢	5.00	5.25	5.50	6.00	*
1986-S clad 50¢	*	*	*	*	6.00
1986-P dollar	17.00	17.25	17.50	18.00	*
1986-S dollar	*	*	*	*	14.00
1986-W $5	130.	132.	135.	150.	145.

Half Dollar Designs

Obverse by Edgar Z. Steever IV

Depicted is the growing New York City skyline, circa 1913, with the Statue's uplifting gesture, welcoming an in-bound liner seen against the sun rising in the east, conveying the start of a new or different life in the New World. The word LIBERTY and the motto IN GOD WE TRUST are located in the outer field, with the date situated in the lower field. Its Mint mark appears to the left of the second T of TRUST.

Reverse by Sheri Joseph Winter

Depicted is an immigrant family of four people with luggage behind them, standing on a pier or wharf at Ellis Island, observing the New York City skyline and New York harbor. UNITED STATES OF AMERICA appears in the upper border. Below this are the words A NATION OF IMMIGRANTS. In the lower field is the denomination; above it, the motto E PLURIBUS UNUM.

Dollar Designs

Obverse by John Mercanti

Portrayed is the Statue of Liberty with the main building at Ellis Island seen in the background. Above this edifice are the words ELLIS ISLAND. In smaller letters underneath, GATEWAY TO AMERICA. To the right of this famous statue (officially known as *Liberty Enlightening the World*) is the motto IN GOD WE TRUST. Underneath the first T of TRUST are the designer's initials JM, while below the letter U is the Mint mark location. Above the Lady is the word LIBERTY.

Reverse by John Mercanti, assisted by Matthew Peloso

Depicted is Miss Liberty's hand, holding her torch, which emits flaming light. Below are four lines taken from Emma Lazarus' poem, *The New Colossus* (November 2, 1883): GIVE ME YOUR TIRED, YOUR POOR, YOUR HUDDLED MASSES YEARNING TO BREATHE FREE (Part of line 10 and line 11). Underneath is E PLURIBUS UNUM and the denomination. To the latter's right are the designers' initials MP, JM. In the upper border is UNITED STATES OF AMERICA.

$5 Half Eagle Designs

Obverse by Elizabeth Jones

Depicted is the bold head of the Statue of Liberty as seen from below, as she gazes toward the future of freedom and opportunity. In the right upper field is the date 1986. Along the right outer border is the word LIBERTY with its letters E and Y incused in order to keep the lettering below the coin's rim. Mint mark is located in lower right field beneath her hair. The designer's initials EJ are located above the fourth window of the crown, in the field.

Reverse by Elizabeth Jones and Philip Fowler

This design pays homage to gold coinage of the 19th century by combining the traditional layout and lettering with a contemporary treatment of the usual eagle symbol. UNITED STATES OF AMERICA appears in the outer field. Beneath , separated by the eagle, are E PLURIBUS UNUM and IN GOD WE TRUST. in the lower field is the denomination. To the left of the word FIVE are six five-pointed stars, while to the right of the word dollars are seven stars. Mr. Fowler executed only a part of the initial modeling. Thus no EJ-PF lettering.

Origins of the Statue Of Liberty Coins

The 100th anniversary of the Statue of Liberty and its need for restoration were rather well known before there was even a suggestion of a commemorative coin program.

The hints of a possible Statue of Liberty coin stretched back to the Republican national convention in 1984, when in her keynote address Treasurer of the United States Katherine Davalos Ortega states, "My fellow Americans, on the minted dollar of the United States is the face of Liberty, the profile of the woman of that great statue whose centennial we celebrate in 1986, the midterm year of the second Reagan Administration."

Treasurer Ortega continued, "There is on the face of Liberty on that coin ... the words 'In God We Trust' and the words 'E Pluribus Unum' — `Out of many, one."

Treasurer Ortega was hardly alone, or even the first in suggesting that something might be done in conjunction with the anniversary of the Statue of Liberty. Thelma Marcus Beckerman, a Brooklyn, N.Y., artist, had written the Statue of Liberty-Ellis Island Centennial Commission in 1983 about a coin. In fact, Beckerman had prepared a design called "Miss Liberty" which had been part of an exhibit organized by the American Medallic Sculpture Association in late 1983.

A final public force for a Statue of Liberty commemorative coin program was Chrysler Chairman Lee Iacocca. Iacocca was also chairman of the Statue of

Liberty-Ellis Island Centennial Foundation, and it was a position he took very seriously. Iacocca wanted a commemorative coin program, and he was willing to use his considerable influence to get one.

There was really very little question that a Statue of Liberty commemorative proposal would have its day in the 99th Congress. The only real question was the type of program which would be proposed. That question was answered on January 3, 1985, when Frank Annunzio (D-Il) the chairman of the House Subcommittee on Consumer Affairs and Coinage and the man who had beaten back proponents of a large Olympic commemorative program, introduced legislation for Statue of Liberty commemoratives.

The Annunzio legislation (H.R. 47) was matched in the Senate by a bill introduced by Senator Al D'Amato (R-N.Y.). Both bills showed that lessons from previous programs had been learned, and that none seemed to want the Statue of Liberty commemorative program to endure the sort of legislative fighting which had accompanied the effort for Olympic commemoratives.

The Statue of Liberty proposals called for a $5 gold coin weighing 8.359 grams of .90 fine gold, identical measurements to the traditional half eagle. The legislation also called for a silver dollar of .900 fine silver weighing 26.730 grams. The final coin authorized in the legislation was a copper-nickel half dollar.

Taking a page from the Olympic program, surcharges were called for, but they were reduced to $35 for the gold coin, $7 for the silver dollar and $2 for the half dollar.

While the legislation allowed for both Uncirculated and Proof versions of the coins, it did stipulate that all coins of a denomination and condition had to be struck at the same facility, thus eliminating the possibility of what happened in the Olympic commemorative program where Mint mark varieties were created by having coins struck at various facilities.

The coins were to be marketed and distributed by the Mint with maximum mintage figures set at 500,000 for the gold coin, 10 million for the silver dollar and 25 million for the half dollars, all more realistic than the enormous allocations which accompanied the Olympic commemoratives.

The legislation also had features which were clearly a consequence of the Olympic coins program and the problems experienced in its designing process. As many including Frank Annunzio had been very unhappy with the initial designs for the Olympic coins, some guidance for the Statue of Liberty designs was included. The gold coin was to symbolize the Statue of Liberty. The silver dollar was supposed to depict Ellis Island as the major entry point for new immigrants, while the half dollar was to depict the contributions of immigrants to the nation.

In addition, the legislation required that the Treasury Secretary consult with chairman of the Fine Arts Commission as well as the chairman of the Statue of Liberty-Ellis Island Foundation which was in charge of the restoration project. Clearly Annunzio wanted no repetition of the Olympic coin problems.

Along with his other efforts, Annunzio had sought in the legislation to avoid potential problems. The bill contained a provision exempting the program from Federal procurement procedures, thus avoiding a time-consuming competitive bidding process.

Another provision was that the silver dollars could be struck from any federally owned stock of silver, a clause designed to gain support of senators from silver producing states.

To the surprise of no one, the Statue of Liberty coinage bill virtually sailed through the House of Representatives. On March 5, 1985, the bill was passed by the House on a voice note and sent to the Senate where backers hoped that a quick passage would follow.

In the Senate, however, the Statue of Liberty coinage proposal sat, and sat, and sat some more. The problem was really that the Statue of Liberty proposal was too popular. It had become an inviting vehicle for those with less popular ideas. Attached to the Statue of Liberty bill, a more marginal proposal might get the added votes it needed.

As the days turned into months, leaders became concerned. Finally steps were taken to break the logjam. Senate leaders helped to strip away some of the various riders, and on June 21, 1985, the Senate passed its version of the Statue of Liberty coinage program. The version still had one rider attached, an authorization for a silver bullion coin.

As Senate and House versions were not identical, the measure returned to the House where Annunzio once again took over. There he faced a last stand by those who wanted not just a silver bullion coin, but also a gold. Rep. Jerry Lewis (R-Calif.) was the prime force behind a gold bullion provision. Before dropping his objection to passing the bill without a gold bullion coin provision, Lewis was given assurances from Annunzio that the gold bullion coin would receive his attention once the Statue of Liberty legislation had passed. With this Lewis went along and the legislation was adopted and sent to the White House for the President's signature.

Designing the Statue of Liberty coins was necessarily a rapid project. Chief Engraver Elizabeth Jones did the $5 gold coin with its Liberty's crowned head obverse and American Eagle reverse. The silver dollar, with the Statue and Ellis Island on the obverse and torch on the reverse was the work of John Mercanti, assisted by Matthew Peloso. The half dollar featured the statue and New York skyline behind an inbound liner on the obverse while the reverse depicted immigrants on Ellis Island. It was the work of Edgar Z. Steever IV and Sherl J. Winter. The designs were actually not released until the coins were ready to be struck. By that time the designs had been approved by Fine Arts Commission chairman J. Carter Brown.

While the designs were moving along on one front, the Mint was engaged in a range of activities including the designing of friction-fitted plastic capsules for the coins and a marketing plan that held forth the potential for sales in excess of anything enjoyed before in other programs.

A marketing program was not needed in the case of the $5 gold coin. With a 500,000 mintage limit, many suspected it might well sell out. Those suspicions were correct. Orders before January 1, 1986, received discounts, and collectors used that opportunity wisely. By the time the pre-issue discount period had ended enough orders were on hand to enable officials to announce that the gold coin was sold out a couple of weeks later.

With the sell out, the only question remaining on the gold coins were how high their price would rise. With four out of every five orders for gold coins being for Proofs, it was the Uncirculated version which would enjoy the greatest price increase. Before the peak was reached, a three-coin Uncirculated set had climbed from a $165 price from the government to around $750 retail. A three-coin Proof set rose from $175 to about $550 retail.

In the months following the gold coin sellout, the government continued with their marketing plans and educational programs designed to help interest Americans in the dollar and half dollar. By the time the program ended on December 31, 1986, the sales of the six Statue of Liberty coins had already reached record levels. Surcharges alone reached more than $78 million while gross sales stood at $292.8 million. Clearly the program had been a success beyond anyone's expectations.

The revenue raised by the Statue of Liberty coin sales played an important role in the restoration and celebration of the statue's centennial. Similarly, collectors had benefitted with the investment success of the gold coin. All had benefitted through the educational programs launched in the nation's schools, as a whole new generation was being exposed to coins. Coupled with extensive television advertising, it is safe to suggest that the Statue of Liberty commemorative program helped increase public awareness of coins and thus probably planted many new seeds which will later develop into the new collectors the hobby needs.

In sum, the Statue of Liberty commemorative program was a success in every way. It showed the true potential for moderately priced commemoratives both in terms of popularity and in terms of the revenue their sale might raise for worthy projects. If the lessons from the program are learned, it will prove to be an excellent springboard for future successful programs.

The Statue of Liberty $5 eagle striking ceremony took place at the West Point Mint on October 18, 1985. Secretary of the Treasury James A. Baker III struck the first two Proof gold coins, the first at 12:47 p.m., the second at 12:49 p.m. Others to strike this popular issue were Lee A. Iacocca, Rep. Frank Annunzio, Donna Pope, Katherine D. Ortega, U.S. Treasurer, and Florence Schook, American Numismatic Association president. After having the honor of striking one of these ceremonial pieces, I examined the coin closely and said to both the Mint Director and Treasurer: "This coin will sell out in three months." It did just that in 2½ months! In fact, it was the only issue struck from 1982 through 1991 which sold out the maximum authorization. The first coin struck by Secretary Baker will not be seen until October 28, 2086! This half eagle was placed in a time capsule at the Statue of Liberty Museum in the "Big Apple," where it is scheduled to rest for 100 years.

A special striking ceremony was held for the dollar creation on October 18, 1986, at the San Francisco Mint. The first piece was struck by Deputy Mint Director Eugene Essner upon authorization (via telephone) from Secretary Baker, at 12:20 p.m. Baker was attending the West Point $5 gold striking ceremony.

After the ceremonial Liberty dollars were struck by telephone order from Secretary of the Treasury Baker, it was time for the striking of our first clad Proof coinage. The first piece was created by Thomas H. Miller, officer in charge of the San Francisco Assay Office. (This facility regained its Mint status on March 31, 1988! Coinage was officially discontinued in March, 1955). Nora Hussey, Superintendent of the Denver Mint, struck the first commemorative clad half dollar

December 9, 1985, at the Denver facility during a small ceremony.

The Statue Of Liberty Half Dollar Today

This issue has the honor of being the first clad commemorative coinage produced in Uncirculated, as well as in Proof condition. Its two outer layers consist of a copper-nickel alloy (.750 copper and .250 nickel) bonded to an inner core of pure copper.

Combined, it also flaunts the highest production or distribution figure of all commemorative coinage produced from 1892 through 1992!

With mintages figures like these — 928,008 Denver Uncs., 6,936,627 San Francisco Proofs — this issue should be purchased only for the pure joy of collecting.

The creation was sold individually in blue felt lined boxes and offered for sale with the other denominations within the issue. Its Proof version (along with the dollar) was included with the regular Proof coinage for the year and offered as the Prestige Set.

The Statue Of Liberty Centennial Dollar Today

With a huge 6,414,638 Proof mintage, plus an Uncirculated total of 723,635 existing dollars, I strongly suggest acquisition only for the pure joy of collecting.

The Proof San Francisco dollar was distributed in a blue velvet case, while the Philadelphia Uncirculated version was sold in a blue cardboard box. Proof cartwheel was sold along with the Proof Liberty half dollar. The unc dollar and unc half were also combined to create two-coin sets. All coinage was encapsulated. Many will grade between MS-65 and PF 65 through MS-68. The Proof dollar (as well as the half dollar) was combined with the regular Proof coinage for the year (1 cent - half dollar) and offered as the Prestige Set.

The Statue Of Liberty $5 Gold Now

Both strikings were well distributed. While the Proof is more impressive looking, the underrated creation is the Uncirculated version. Any real future resides with this gold disk. Proof half eagles were offered individually or along with the half dollar and $1 Proof strikings. They were housed in a blue velvet box, accompanied by a descriptive insert. The Uncirculated coinage was sold the same way, but placed in a blue box. Each coin was encapsulated. All six disks struck were offered in a cherry wood box, accompanied by a descriptive insert. Advance sale price was $375 and later increased to $439.50! There were 39,102 sets sold.

1987
Constitution Bicentennial

Reason for issue: To commemorate the 200th anniversary of the United States Constitution.

Authorized per Act of October 29, 1986: 10,000,000 dollars
1,000,000 gold $5

Official sale price: Uncirculated Philadelphia dollar: $22.50, later $26
Proof San Francisco dollar: $24, later $28
Uncirculated West Point gold $5: $195, later $215
Proof West Point gold $5: $200, later $225

Production figures

Date	Business Strikes	Assay Coins	Proofs	Melted	Net Mintage
1987-P $1	?	?	-	?	451,629*
1987-S $1	-	?	?	?	2,747,116*
1987-W $5	?	?	-	?	214,225*
1987-W $5	-	?	?	?	651,659*

*Minting and melting figures were not released by the Mint. Net mintage figures shown represent the net quantity distributed by the Mint.

Current market values

	MS-60	MS-63	MS-64	MS-65	PF-65
1987-P $1	11.75	12.00	12.25	12.50	*
1987-S $1	*	*	*	*	12.50
1987-W $5	92.50	95.00	97.50	110.	110.

Dollar Designs by Patricia Lewis Verani

Obverse

Depicted is a quill pen lain across a sheaf of parchments and reads WE THE PEOPLE. Originally, these first three words of the Constitution were part of the reverse design, but that was changed by the Treasury. To the right of the second E of PEOPLE in the field is the Mint mark. The anniversary inscription THE U.S. CONSTITUTION 200TH ANNIVERSARY occupies the outer border. At the bottom border is 1787 LIBERTY 1987. Above the parchments is the motto IN GOD WE TRUST, while below are 13 five-pointed stars.

Reverse

Portrayed are 13 human figures in diverse dress, representing the wide cultural and social spectrum this nation has embraced and represented for over 200 years. Below the group is the word DOLLAR. Directly above the second S of state is the digit 1. Thus "Dollar 1." UNITED STATES OF AMERICA and E PLURIBUS UNUM separated by three circular links appear in the outer border. The designer's initials PV are located in the field below the back right figure.

Half Eagle Designs by Marcel Jovine

Obverse

Depicted is a highly stylized flying eagle with quill pen in its talons. The word LIBERTY appears in the left border. Below upper wing is the motto IN GOD WE TRUST. In lower field, the date. Designer's logo appears on second lower feather to the right of date digit 7.

Reverse

Portrayed is a quill pen in a vertical position. The Constitutional slogan WE THE PEOPLE appears calligraphically across the pen's lower section. Below is the denomination. To the left of the writing instrument we have the date SEPT. 17, 1787; to the right, E PLURIBUS UNUM. The upper border consists of UNITED STATES OF AMERICA with an arc of 13 stars split by the top of the quill. The bottom border is BICENTENNIAL OF THE CONSTITUTION. The West Point Mint mark is located opposite the letter U of the word CONSTITUTION.

Origins of the Constitution Coins

The first strike ceremony for the dollar took place at the Philadelphia Mint on July 1, 1987. It officially began at 11:15 a.m. with a welcome by Anthony H. Murray, Jr., Superintendent of the facility. After Secretary Baker struck and flaunted the first Uncirculated Constitution dollar, he then pressed a palm button marked West Point located alongside the stage area. Upon depression, an electronic impulse was transmitted over telephone lines through modems to West Point. The signal activated the press and the first Constitution gold specimen was created within a fraction of a second! His nine year old daughter, Mary Bonner Baker, struck the second dollar and $5 gold piece. Members of the Society for U.S. Commemorative Coins such as Helen Carmody and I had the honor of striking one of those ceremonial dollars.

The Constitution Dollar Now

With a 451,629 Uncirculated and 2,747,116 Proof mintage, I suggest this issue be acquired only for the pure joy of collecting! Due to care given these creations — and all commemorative coinage since 1982 — many coins will grade between MS and PF 65 through 68. These strikings were sold individually, in navy blue velvet cases, or in a two-coin Uncirculated or Proof set, accompanied by the respective $5 gold piece. Also placed in navy blue velvet cases. The Proof dollar was included along with the standard 1987 Proof coinage (1 cent - half dollar) and offered as the Prestige Set.

The Constitution Bicentennial $5 Gold Now

With 214,225 Uncirculated and 651,659 Proof creations sold, only acquire for the pure joy of collecting. Both coins are currently selling at slightly above bullion value! This coin was sold individually. They were housed in a blue velvet case which was placed in a blue cardboard box. Also sold along with the respective Proof or Uncirculated dollar coin. These two-piece sets accompanied by a descriptive insert were packaged similarly to the individual offerings. All four strikings were presented in a mahogany case which included a certificate of authenticity. Originally offered at $465, then $525. In total, 89,258 sets were sold. Every coin was encapsulated by the Mint.

1988

Games of the
XXIV Olympiad

Reason for issue: To support the training of American athletes participating in the 1988 Olympic Games.

Authorized per Act of October 28, 1987: 10,000,000 dollars
1,000,000 gold $5

Official sale price: Uncirculated Denver dollar: $22, later $27
Proof San Francisco dollar: $23, later $29
Uncirculated West Point gold $5: $200, later $225
Proof West Point gold $5: $205, later $235

Production figures

Date	Business Strikes	Assay Coins	Proofs	Melted	Net Mintage
1988-D $1	?	?	-	?	191,368*
1988-S $1	-	?	?	?	1,359,366*
1988-W $5	?	?	-	?	62,913*
1988-W $5	-	?	?	?	281,465*

*Minting and melting figures not released by the Mint. Net mintage figures shown represent the net quantity distributed by the Mint.

Current market values

	MS-60	MS-63	MS-64	MS-65	PF-65
1988-D $1	25.00	26.00	26.50	27.00	*
1988-S $1	*	*	*	*	14.50
1988-W $5	110.	115.	120.	130.	115.

Dollar Designs

Obverse by Patricia Lewis Verani

Depicted is Lady Liberty's torch and the Olympic torch merging into a single symbolic flame. Olive branches which are emblems of peace encircle the torches. Upper and lower fields show the words OLYMPIAD (originally "Olympiad XXIV") and LIBERTY, respectively in large letters. The motto IN GOD WE TRUST is situated in center left field, while date and Mint mark are located in center right field. Patricia Verani's initials PV are positioned between the hand and lower section of Olympic torch.

Reverse by Sheri Joseph Winter

Featured is the five-ring logo of the U.S. Olympic Committee, framed by a pair of olive branches. Above this symbol and the letters USA is the digit 1, the word DOLLAR below it in smaller letters. In the lower field is motto E PLURIBUS UNUM, while UNITED STATES OF AMERICA encircles most of outer border. Between the C and A of AMERICA, adjacent to the branch stem, are the designer's initials, SJW.

Half Eagle Designs

Obverse by Elizabeth Jones

Depicted is Nike, goddess of Victory in a crown of olive leaves. The word LIBERTY in large letters is placed partially in field and across her neck. IN GOD WE TRUST is situated in the ribbon of wreath. Date of issue is located in the left center field, while its designer's initials are incused in the lower neck, below the letter E of LIBERTY.

Reverse by Marcel Jovine

Featured is a stylized Olympic flame which evokes the spectacle of the Games and the renewal of its spirit every four years. Situated above is that Olympic logo. Beneath is the motto E PLURIBUS UNUM, denomination and UNITED STATES OF AMERICA. W Mint mark is located to the left of letter E of AMERICA. To the left of W, within lowest flame, is the designer's logo.

Origins of the 1988 Olympic Coins

It didn't matter that the games of the XXIV Olympiad were not to take place in this country. What it presented was the chance to produce commemorative coinage, whose primary objective was to raise funds for the American athletes participating in the 1988 Olympic Games, held in Calgary, Alberta, and Seoul, South Korea. During creation of the dollar design, the United States Olympic Committee exclaimed it would not authorize use of their logo — unless the letters USA were situated above the rings in a specific manner. The Mint at first objected to the addition of these letters, because the inscription UNITED STATES

OF AMERICA was already incorporated within the design. However, allowances were made and this nation is twice acknowledged.

First strike ceremony took place at the Denver Mint on May 2, 1988. Secretary of the Treasury James A. Baker III struck the first two pieces.

When Secretary of the Treasury James A. Baker III struck the first 1988 Olympic dollar at the Denver Mint ceremony, he gave the OK — through audio hook-ups — for 1984 Olympic gold-medal swimmer Theresa Andrews to proceed with the initial coining of our Olympic $5 gold piece at the West Point Mint. This marked the first time that a Secretary of the Treasury, Mint Director or Mint Superintendent did not strike the very first ceremonial coin! Initially, there were those in the numismatic community who exclaimed that the classical obverse and modernistic reverse designs should not be combined. The creators felt likewise.

The 1988 Olympic Dollars Today

With 191,368 Uncirculated and 1,359,366 Proof pieces produced for this attractive issue, it is strongly suggested they be acquired only for the joy of collecting. Both versions were sold individually in burgundy velvet cases. The Proof was included in the Prestige Set which consists of the commemoratives and the yearly 1988 Proof coinage.

The Olympic $5 Gold Pieces Today

Most collectors believe it's the Elizabeth Jones obverse which makes this coin so popular. Such is especially true of the 281,465 Proof mintage issue. It should be acquired for the pure joy of collecting. If there is to be a future for this design, it resides with the 62,913 Uncirculated production. Both versions are currently valued slightly above bullion. They were sold individually in a burgundy velvet case, or offered as a two-coin ($1, $5) Uncirculated or Proof set in a similar case. Those four specimens produced were made available in a mahogany box, at $550, but later reduced to $510! 13,313 such sets were sold. All coins were encapsulated. Due to the care given these coins, may grade between MS and PF 65 through 68.

1989
Congress Bicentennial

Reason for issue: To commemorate the Bicentennial of the United States
Congress.

Authorized per Act of November 17, 1988: 4,000,000 half dollars;
3,000,000 dollars; 1,000,000 gold $5

Official sale price: Uncirculated Denver clad half dollar: $5, later $6
Proof San Francisco clad half dollar: $7, later $8
Uncirculated Denver dollar: $23, later $26
Proof San Francisco dollar: $25, later $29
Uncirculated West Point gold $5: $185, later $200
Proof West Point gold $5: $195, later $225

Production figures

Date	Business Strikes	Assay Coins	Proofs	Melted	Net Mintage
1989-D 50¢	?	?	-	?	163,753*
1989-S 50¢	-	?	?	?	767,897*

1989-D $1	?	?	-	?	135,203*
1989-S $1	-	?	?	?	762,198*
1989-W $5	?	?	-	?	46,899*
1989-W $5	-	?	?	?	164,690*

*Minting and melting figures not released by the Mint. Net mintage figures shown represent the net quantity distributed by the Mint.

Current market values

	MS-60	MS-63	MS-64	MS-65	PF-65
1989-D clad 50¢	15.00	16.00	16.25	17.00	*
1989-S clad 50¢	*	*	*	*	12.00
1989-D $1	31.00	32.00	33.00	34.00	*
1989-S $1	*	*	*	*	33.00
1989-W $5	135.	140.	145.	150.	150.

Half Dollar Designs

Obverse by Patricia Lewis Verani, adapted from Thomas Crawford's Statue of Freedom atop the Capitol dome

Depicted is the bust of the Statue of Freedom. Situated in outer border is THE BICENTENNIAL OF CONGRESS and word LIBERTY in large letters. Above the latter, we see the motto IN GOD WE TRUST. Located in central left field is the date 1789 while diagonally below its digit 9, we observe the designer's initials, PV. In central right field is the date 1989. Below latter two digits is the Mint mark.

Reverse by William Woodward, modeled from the line drawing by Edgar Z. Steever IV

Portrayed is a full view of the Capitol Building, surrounded by a wreath of 13 stars. Located in the upper border is UNITED STATES OF AMERICA. Below this Capitol is the motto E PLURIBUS UNUM. Directly above its letter E are the designer's initials WW, while situated above M of UNUM is the other creator's letters, EZS. Its denomination is in the lower field.

Dollar Designs by William Woodward, assisted by Chester Young Martin (adapted from Thomas Crawford's Statue of Freedom)

Obverse

Depicted is the bronze *Statue of Freedom* which sits atop the dome of the United States Capitol. In the background, sun's rays emanate from the clouds. LIBERTY appears in large letters in the coin's upper border, while the motto IN GOD WE TRUST is located in the lower border. Situated on each side of Freedom are the anniversary dates, 1789 and 1989, with Mint mark below the latter.

Reverse

Featured is the mace of the House of Representatives, highlighting the staff topped by an eagle astride a world globe. UNITED STATES OF AMERICA and ONE DOLLAR encircle the outer border. Located to the left of the mace is the motto E PLURIBUS UNUM and to the right the words BICENTENNIAL OF THE CONGRESS. The designers' initials WW and CYM appear at either side of the bottom of the mace.

Half Eagle Designs by John Mercanti

Obverse

Featured is a rendition of the Capitol Dome. Above in large letters is the word LIBERTY, while below are the anniversary dates, 1789-1989. At Dome's right base is the Mint mark. The motto IN GOD WE TRUST is situated in the central left field.

Reverse

Depicted is the majestic American eagle overlooking the canopy of the Old Senate Chamber. Above is BICENTENNIAL OF CONGRESS. Beneath the eagle is the motto E PLURIBUS UNUM. UNITED STATES OF AMERICA is separated by the eagle. At the canopy's right base is the designer's initials, JM. Located in lower field is the denomination FIVE DOLLARS.

Origins of the Congress Bicentennial Coins

The original legislation provided that this half dollar as well as the dollar design could be struck in Uncirculated and Proof quality — but not more than one Mint would be permitted to produce any combination of denomination or quality. It also stated that the $5 gold coin be struck at West Point. Creations were minted in 1989 and 1990.

Not since 1792 were official U.S. coins struck outside any Mint facilities. Four coin presses painted light blue were set up for the first-strike ceremony, which took place on the Capitol grounds. At 11:11 a.m. on June 14, 1989, Secretary of the Treasury Nicholas F. Brady struck the first ceremonial $5 Proof gold piece — which bore the West Point W Mint mark. It received two blows from the press. After flaunting the coin to the media, he went to the opposite end of the podium to strike the first ceremonial dollar coin. Would you believe the press jammed! Using the back-up press which was also set up with San Francisco Proof dollar dies, the design was created using three blows from the press. Several members of the House of Representatives then struck the dollar commemorative which depicts the House mace, while a number of Senators did likewise with the $5 gold Proof. This portrays the eagle design adapted from one such creation in the Old Senate Chamber. Mint Director Donna Pope coined the last ceremonial half eagle. Shortly thereafter, she ordered the Associate Director of the Mint to telephone the West Point and San Francisco facilities to begin production for their respective issues. At this point, Deputy Mint Director Eugene Essner then requested the invited guests to strike their ceremonial remembrance preservers.

The Congress Bicentennial Half Dollar Today

The Uncirculated (163,753) and Proof (767,897) production for these copper-nickel clad half dollars is rather large. I suggest acquiring only for the pure joy of collecting. The issue was individually offered for sale in a brown velvet lined box (Unc.) and brown velvet case. The first clad copper commemorative coinage produced was the Statue of Liberty half dollar produced at the Denver and San Francisco Mints

The 1989 Congress Dollar Today

With large Uncirculated (135,203) and Proof (762,198) mintages, I suggest that these coins be acquired only for the joy of collecting. The good news for some fortunate owners of the Uncirculated Denver Mint creation is that approximately 50 to 100 pieces were produced with "medal" alignment instead of the normal coin alignment. In other words, when the coin is flipped left to right — and not top to bottom — to see the other side, medal orientation will show the reverse design upright. Proper coin obverse-reverse relationship upon rotation will show the reverse motif upside down. I strongly recommend your Congress Bicentennial dollars be examined! It is a rare item which has sold for between $1,000 and $2,000.

Both strikings were sold individually. They were housed in a dark brown box (Unc.) and brown velvet case (Proof). They were also offered as a two piece Uncirculated set (placed in a dark brown box) or a two piece Proof set (housed in a brown velvet case), accompanied by the respective half dollar. The latter two commemorative coins were combined with regular 1989 Proof coinage and sold as the Prestige Set.

The Congressional Half Eagle Today

While Uncirculated (46,899) and Proof (164,690) mintages are rather low, it appears that those who wanted the issue made their purchases. Currently, demand is almost non-existent for the issue, whose future, if any, appears to only exist in the Uncirculated state. Acquire the Proof coin for the joy of ownership.

Both coins were sold individually, or in three piece Uncirculated or Proof sets (half dollar, $1, $5), as well as in cherry wood boxes, housing all six coins produced. Every specimen was encapsulated. There were 24,967 of the latter sets sold at $435, then $480.

1990
Eisenhower Centennial

Reason for issue: To commemorate the 100th anniversary of the birth of
Dwight D. Eisenhower.
Authorized per Act of October 3, 1988: 4,000,000
Official sale price: Uncirculated W: $23, later $26
   Proof P: $25, later $29

Production figures

Date	Business Strikes	Assay Coins	Proofs	Melted	Net Mintage
1990-W	?	?	-	?	241,669*
1990-P	-	?	?	?	1,144,461*

*Minting and melting figures not released by the Mint. Net mintage figures shown
represent the net quantity distributed by the Mint.

Current market values

	MS-60	MS-63	MS-64	MS-65	PF-65
1990-W	27.00	27.50	28.00	28.50	*
1990-P	*	*	*	*	23.00

Designs

Obverse by John Mercanti

   Portrayed is a right-facing profile of the Dwight D. Eisenhower, the 34th
President of the United States, superimposed on a left-facing profile of Five Star
General Eisenhower. They symbolize his military service and peacetime leader-
ship. The words EISENHOWER CENTENNIAL appear in the coin's outer border,
while the anniversary dates 1890-1990 are situated beneath the President's bust.
In the lower left field is the word LIBERTY, with Mint mark underneath. The motto
IN GOD WE TRUST is located in its right field. The designer's initials JM can be seen
adjacent to the bottom bar of the letter Y of LIBERTY on "Ike's" jacket.

Reverse by Marcel Jovine (modeled by Chester Young Martin)

Featured is the Gettysburg National Historical Site, the retirement home of Dwight and Mamie and not his birthplace, which was Dennison, Texas. Below the left section of the structure are the words EISENHOWER HOME. Above the first E of his name, in the shrubbery is the designer's logo. In the lower right field is the motto E PLURIBUS UNUM and denomination. UNITED STATES OF AMERICA is seen over the home.

Origins of the Eisenhower Centennial Dollars

On January 16, 1990, a special coin — not striking — ceremony was held in Gettysburg, Pa. There, the Proof Eisenhower dollar was flaunted by Mint Director Donna Pope for all invited guests to view. It had been previously struck without any formal ceremony. Two additional pieces were presented to U.S. Treasurer Catalina Villalpando and Pennsylvania Congressman Bill Gooding, sponsor of the legislation authorizing the issue. The Philadelphia facility struck the Proof issue; It's located in the same state where our 34th President resided. West Point produced the Uncirculated version. As most of us are aware, he graduated from the Military Academy, on June 12, 1915. This creation marked the first time the W cachet would be placed on a silver dollar coin. Gold $5 and $10 modern commemoratives were previously produced at this facility. Less than three months after production began, over 1 million coins were sold. However, sales began to slow down soon afterwards.

The 1990 Eisenhower Silver Dollars Today

This is the only U.S. commemorative coin struck which portrays more than one portrait of the same person on the same side of a coin! It is also an issue which should be acquired for the pure joy of collecting. Both coins were offered individually, encapsulated in dark green velvet presentation cases. The Proof version was also included with the standard 1991 yearly Proof coinage, to create the Prestige Set.

1991
Mount Rushmore
Golden Anniversary

Reason for issue: To commemorate the Golden Anniversary of the Mount
Rushmore National Memorial.

Authorized per Act of July 6, 1990: 2,500,000 half dollars;
2,500,000 dollars; 500,000 half eagles

Official sale price: Uncirculated Denver clad half dollar: $6, later $7
Proof San Francisco clad half dollar: $8.50 later $9.50
Uncirculated Philadelphia dollar: $23, later $26
Proof San Francisco dollar: $28, later $31
Uncirculated West Point gold $5: $185, later $210
Proof West Point gold $5: $195, later $225

Production figures

Date	Business Strikes	Assay Coins	Proofs	Melted	Net Mintage
1991-D 50¢	?	?	-	?	172,754*
1991-S 50¢	-	?	?	?	753,257*
1991-P $1	?	?	-	?	133,139*
1991-S $1	-	?	?	?	738,419*
1991-W $5	?	?	-	?	31,959*
1991-W $5 Proof	-	?	?	?	111,991*

* Minting and melting figures not released by the Mint. Net mintage figures shown represent the net quantity distributed by the Mint.

Current market values

	MS-60	MS-63	MS-64	MS-65	PF-65
1991-D clad 50¢	11.50	12.00	12.50	13.00	*
1991-S clad 50¢	*	*	*	*	15.50
1991-P $1	26.00	27.00	28.00	29.00	*
1991-S $1	*	*	*	*	31.50
1991-W $5	130.	140.	150.	190.	235.

Half Dollar Designs

Obverse by Marcel Jovine

Featured is the world's largest carved stone sculpture, the Mount Rushmore Memorial by Gutzon Borglum, and a sunburst. Above is the word LIBERTY in large letters, while in the lower field is the memorial's name. Below the carving in the field is the motto IN GOD WE TRUST and the date 1991. Located diagonally below Lincoln's beard is the designer's logo (which resembles hieroglyphic symbols).

Reverse by T. James Ferrell

Depicted is the classic design of the great North Western American bison, native to the Black Hills. (The buffalo is native to Europe, Eurasia and Africa. Because the bison is similar, it is commonly referred to as the buffalo.) Above this mammal are the words GOLDEN ANNIVERSARY (which replaced the original inscription, "50th year anniversary"). Beneath, by the observed right front hoof are the designer's initials TJF. Behind the bison is the Mint mark. UNITED STATES OF AMERICA and HALF DOLLAR circle the design, and a circle of stars surrounds all.

Dollar Designs

Obverse by Marika H. Somogyi (modeled by Chester Young Martin)

Featured is the famous mountainside carving portraying the busts of George Washington, Thomas Jefferson, Theodore Roosevelt and Abraham Lincoln. Below in small letters are the inscriptions GOLDEN ANNIVERSARY and MOUNT RUSHMORE NATIONAL MEMORIAL. at the lower border are two crossed laurel wreaths, with the motto IN GOD WE TRUST incused in the ribbon. Underneath the right evergreen stem are the designers' initials, MHS and CYM.

Reverse by Frank Gasparo

The former U.S. Mint Chief Engraver depicts the well known eagle crest or Great Seal of our nation, with background sunburst. This covers most of the northern part of North America. The five pointed star on the map marks the location of Mount Rushmore. Beneath is the inscription SHRINE OF DEMOCRACY. UNITED STATES OF AMERICA arcs above; E PLURIBUS UNUM and ONE DOLLAR below. To their left in the field is the designer's initials FG. The Mint mark is located in the field off the Virginia coast. Add to Mr. Gasparo's credits the 1959 Lincoln Memorial cent and 1964 Kennedy half dollar reverse designs, as well as the creation of the 1971-1978 Eisenhower dollar: (except Bicentennial reverse) and the 1979-1981 Susan B. Anthony dollar.

Gold $5 Designs

Obverse by John Mercanti

Featured is an American eagle in flight over Mount Rushmore. The large bird of prey holds sculptural tools, a chisel and mallet in its claws. Ribbon in beak displays the incused motto IN GOD WE TRUST. Inscription LIBERTY and large date 1991 are located in the central field, opposite five decorative stars. The famous carving is situated mostly in the lower right quarter of the creation. Designer's initials were placed at the left mountain base diagonally below the mallet.

Reverse by Robert Lamb, modeled by William Charles Cousins

Displayed is the calligraphic inscription MOUNT RUSHMORE NATIONAL ME-MORIAL. Encircling the outer border is UNITED STATES OF AMERICA, FIVE DOLLARS and motto E PLURIBUS UNUM. Beneath the word MEMORIAL are the designers' initials RL and WC and Mint mark.

Origins of the Mount Rushmore Coins

On February 15, 1991, U.S. Treasurer Catalina Villalpando announced the official launch of Mount Rushmore commemorative coinage. The primary objective was to raise funds to preserve and restore the South Dakota landmark and its surrounding National Park, which receives more than 2 million visitors each year. All three coins — which were struck without any first strike ceremony — were unveiled at a ceremony held in Ford's Theatre in Washington, D.C. It was officiated by Deputy Secretary of the Treasury John Robson. Present were the Treasurer, Mint Director Donna Pope, South Dakota Congressman Tom Johnson, prime sponsor of the legislation, members of the Mount Rushmore National Committee, Mary Ellis Borglum Powers, Gutzon Borglum's daughter, and invited guests. The same coins were later displayed at the U.S. Mint's booth during the 1991 American Numismatic Association's Dallas, Texas, Mid-Winter Convention. These creations were distributed to subscribers in Spring 1991.

I personally believe a commemorative design similar to the reverse of the $5 gold coin, if submitted between 1892 and 1954 to the Commission of Fine Arts, might have been rejected. Why, you ask? It resembles more of a medal reverse than a coin's reverse! With all due respect, lacking is a decorative composition. There is no figures or symbols included, but is solely made up of lettering. Such is definitely a first in commemorative history!

Sales for this program totaled just 35 percent of the authorized maximums.

Surcharges raised $12 million, half of which was paid to the Mount Rushmore National Memorial Society to improve, enlarge and renovate the memorial. The other half of the surcharges were placed in the Treasury general fund to reduce the national debt.

The Mount Rushmore Half Dollar Today

These beautiful commemoratives should be acquired for the pure joy of collecting. The Uncirculated version was sealed in a Mylar envelope, while the Proof coin was encapsulated in plastic. Both were housed in a gray cardboard box. This creation's Proof clad disk was included (along with the Proof dollar) in the Prestige Set, accompanied by the standard Proof coinage of 1991.

The Mount Rushmore Dollar Today

These beautiful coins should only be acquired for the pure joy of collecting. Both pieces were sold individually, or in two-piece Proof or Uncirculated sets, housed in gray cardboard boxes. Added to the standard 1991 Proof coinage was this issue's dollar and half dollar. Such is called the Prestige Set.

The Mount Rushmore $5 Gold Pieces Today

Acquire for the pure joy of ownership. Both pieces were offered individually or in a three-piece Uncirculated or Proof set, accompanied by the clad half dollar and silver dollar. They were housed in a gray cardboard box. All six coins produced for the issue were sold in a cherry wood box at $445, then $490.

1991
Korean War Memorial

Reason for issue: To commemorate the 38th anniversary of the ending of the Korean War and in honor of those who served.
Authorized per Act of October 31, 1990: 1,000,000
Official sale price: Uncirculated Denver: $23, later $26
    Proof Philadelphia : $28, later $31

Production figures

Date	Business Strikes	Assay Coins	Proofs	Melted	Net Mintage
1991-D	?	?	-	?	213,049*
1991-P	-	?	?	?	618,488*

*Minting and melting figures not released by the Mint. Net mintage figures shown represent the net quantity distributed by the Mint.

Current market values

	MS-60	MS-63	MS-64	MS-65	PF-65
1991-D	22.00	22.50	23.00	23.50	*
1991-P	*	*	*	*	27.00

Designs

Obverse by John Mercanti

Depicted is a military figure charging up a hill. Naval ships are situated in the foreground, F-86 Sabre jets are overhead with eight decorative stars placed in the upper border. Anniversary inscription THIRTY EIGHTH ANNIVERSARY COMMEMO-RATIVE KOREA is located in four lines in the left field. Below is the motto IN GOD WE TRUST. Anniversary dates 1953-1991 are seen on the hill. In the lower border is the word LIBERTY while designer's initials JM are located in front of central ship's bow.

Reverse by T. James Ferrell

Depicted is a map of Korea with the yin-yang symbol located below the 38 degree N parallel, in South Korea. To its right is the earnest looking head of our American bald eagle. Below its neck is the Mint mark. Denomination and UNITED STATES OF AMERICA are situated in the upper and lower border, with motto E PLURIBUS UNUM in left central field. Designer's initials TJF appear above the second S of STATES. The words "38th Parallel" and the United Nations seal on the original sketch were excluded.

Origins of the Korean War Memorial Dollar

On May 6, 1991, a first strike ceremony was held at the Philadelphia Mint. Treasurer of the United States Catalina Vasquez Villalpando, Mint Director Donna Pope, General Richard G. Stilwell, Counsel General of the Embassy of the Republic of Korea, National Commanders of 16 leading veterans organizations, Mr. Myongbai Kim, Chairman of the Korean War Veterans Memorial Advisory Board and other invited guests were present at the event.

The 1991 Korean War Memorial Dollar Today

These remembrance preservers should only be acquired for pride of ownership. Both were sold individually in a turquoise velvet lined case. A total of $5.8 million in surcharges was raised toward the construction of the first national memorial honoring all who served in Korea, from 1950 to 1953.

1991
USO 50th Anniversary

Reason for issue: To commemorate the 50th anniversary of the United Service Organizations, founded at the beginning of war in 1941.

Authorized per Act of October 2, 1990: 1,000,000

Official sale price: Uncirculated Denver: $23, later $26
     Proof San Francisco: $28, later $31

Production figures

Date	Business Strikes	Assay Coins	Proofs	Melted	Net Mintage
1991-D	?	?	-	?	124,958*
1991-S	-	?	?	?	321,275*

*Minting and melting figures not released by the Mint. Net mintage figures shown represent the net quantity distributed by the Mint.

Current market values

	MS-60	MS-63	MS-64	MS-65	PF-65
1991-D	75.00	76.00	77.00	78.00	*
1991-S	*	*	*	*	55.00

Designs

Obverse by Robert Lamb (Modeled by William Charles Cousins)

Featured is a pennant based directly on the design of the USO flag. Above is the calligraphic inscription 50TH ANNIVERSARY and the motto IN GOD WE TRUST. Designers' initials AL and WC appear above letter L or LIBERTY which is located in the lower field, adjacent to coin's date, 1991. The modeling was done by William Charles Cousins for this issue (as well as for the 1991 Mount Rushmore Golden Anniversary $5 gold commemorative issue) because Robert Lamb was extremely busy with other planned undertakings.

Reverse by John Mercanti

Beneath UNITED STATES OF AMERICA is depicted an American bald eagle perching on top of the world, holding in its beak a ribbon, incused with letters USO. The USO's anniversary theme is split into the left and right fields. At left, FIFTY YEARS SERVICE. Underneath letters SE of SERVICE are the designer's initials JM. Situated in right field is the remainder of the theme, TO SERVICE PEOPLE. Under second E of PEOPLE is the Mint mark. The motto E PLURIBUS UNUM is seen across the southern hemisphere. Below the globe is an arc of 11 decorative stars and the denomination.

Origins of the USO Dollars

There was no official first strike coin ceremony for this issue. It made its formal entrance into the numismatic world on June 8, 1991, as part of a Desert Storm Victory Parade. Onlookers were treated to a 10-foot reproduction of the obverse which was part of one float that presented a lifelike representation of a classic USO performance.

A $7 surcharge on each coin raised $3.1 million, half of which was paid to the USO to fund its programs. The national debt was reduced by the other half of the funds.

The USO Dollars Today

At the time of this writing, dealer promotion has pushed the Uncirculated version to three times its issue price, while the larger mintage Proof creation has almost doubled in value. When promotion ends, expect values to decline, and the preferred low mintage Uncirculated can be acquired at lower values. Were the market to get hot in the near future and this issue promoted again, this creation could be a moneymaker for its owners. The issue was offered individually in Uncirculated and Proof condition, housed in a blue velvet case. It was not included in the 1991 Prestige Set, as was the Mount Rushmore issue.

1992
Olympic Games

Reason for issue: To support the training of American athletes participating in the 1992 Olympic Games.

Authorized per act of Act of October 3, 1990: 6,000,000 half dollars; 4,000,000 dollars; 500,000 gold $5

Official sale price:

Uncirculated Denver clad half dollar: $6, later $7.50

Proof San Francisco clad half dollar: $8.50, later $9.50

Uncirculated Denver dollar, $24, later $29

Proof San Francisco dollar: $28, later $32

Uncirculated West Point gold $5: $185, later $215

Proof West Point gold $5: $195, later $230

Production figures

Date	Business Strikes	Assay Coins	Proofs	Melted	Net Mintage
1992-D 50¢	?	?	-	?	Pending*
1992-S 50¢	-	?	?	?	Pending*
1992-D $1	?	?	-	?	Pending*
1992-S $1	-	?	?	?	Pending*
1991-W $5	?	?	-	?	Pending*
1991-W $5 Proof	-	?	?	?	Pending*

* Minting and melting figures not released by the Mint. Program was still active at the close of writing.

Current market values

	MS-60	MS-63	MS-64	MS-65	PF-65
1992-P 50¢	9.00	9.25	9.50	10.00	*
1992-S 50¢	*	*	*	*	12.00
1992-D $1	35.00	36.00	36.25	37.50	*
1992-S $1	*	*	*	*	40.00
1992-W $5	260.	265.	270.	285.	290.

Half Dollar Designs

Obverse by William Charles Cousins

Female gymnast in motion, against a background of a partial American flag. In the upper bar of the flag is IN GOD WE TRUST. Date 1992 and USA above the interlocking Olympic rings are under the gymnast's outstretched leg. Below that in large letters is the inscription LIBERTY.

Reverse by Steven Bieda

The Olympic torch, crossed by an olive branch, along with inscribed Olympic motto CITIUS ALTIUS FORTIUS meaning "Faster, Higher, Stronger." UNITED STATES OF AMERICA arcs above; HALF DOLLAR below. Motto E PLURIBUS UNUM is in the right field.

Dollar Designs

The Uncirculated 1992 Olympic dollar has a combination reeded-lettered edge design. In addition to the reeding, which is about 50 percent finer than normal, are the words XXV OLYMPIAD four times, two of which are inverted. This is a first for commemorative coinage. (The last regular issue coin to have a lettered edge was the 1933 $20 Saint-Gaudens gold piece.)

1992 Olympic dollar with edge lettering

Obverse by John R. Deecken, modeled by Chester Y. Martin

Depicted is a baseball player, firing the ball to home plate. Many coin and baseball card collectors claim it resembles Texas Ranger's star pitcher Nolan Ryan, seen on the 1991 Fleer's baseball card #302! The manufacturer claims it's pure coincidence. LIBERTY is widely spaced around the upper border. USA and the Olympic rings are in the left field, while IN GOD WE TRUST is in the right. Designers' initials JRD-CYM are below and to the left of the pitcher's mound.

Reverse by Marcel Jovine

Portrayed is the Union shield with Olympic logo above and one vertical olive branch on each side of the shield. UNITED STATES OF AMERICA and denomination form the outer border. Motto E PLURIBUS UNUM is incused on the banner below the shield.

Gold $5 Designs

Obverse by Jim Sharpe

Depicted is a male sprinter reminiscent of Olympic track legend Jesse Owens in a burst of speed with American flag (resembling a track) in background. LIBERTY is at the top border, USA and rings at left, date and IN GOD WE TRUST at right.

Reverse by Jim Peed

Portrayed is a modernistic American eagle with Olympic logo above. UNITED STATES OF AMERICA arcs above; denomination FIVE DOLLARS below.

Origins of the 1992 Olympic Coins

The coins were offered individually, or in two-piece (50¢ and $1) Uncirculated or Proof sets and in three-piece Unc. and Proof sets, all housed in burgundy cases or in the six-piece complete set housed in a cherry wood box.

Issue's 50¢ and $1 creation is also combined with the standard 1992 five coin (1 cent through half dollar) Proof set to form the Prestige Set.

The 1992 Olympic Coins Today

At this point in time, I suggest acquiring just for the pride of ownership.

1992
White House Bicentennial

Reason for issue: To commemorate the 200th anniversary of the laying of the cornerstone of the White House on Oct. 13, 1792, which was supervised by Irish architect James Hoban.

Authorized per Act of May 13, 1992: 500,000

Official sale price: Uncirculated Denver: $23, later $28
  Proof West Point: $28, later $32

Production figures

Date	Business Strikes	Assay Coins	Proofs	Melted	Net Mintage
1992-D	?	?	-	?	123,572*
1992-W	-	?	?	?	375,093*

*Minting and melting figures not released by the Mint. Net mintage figures shown are not final, but represent the quantity distributed by the Mint as of March 19, 1993.

Current market values

	MS-60	MS-63	MS-64	MS-65	PF-65
1992-D	75.00	78.00	79.00	80.00	*
1992-W	*	*	*	*	65.00

Designs·

Obverse by Edgar Z. Steever

Depicted is the north portico of the White House with 1792-1992 inscribed above and IN GOD WE TRUST below. THE WHITE HOUSE is inscribed around the top border; LIBERTY is located at the bottom center. The designer's initials EZS appear in the field below the left corner of the building as you view the coin.

Originally, John Mercanti worked on this issue's design. It depicted behind and above the White House the prayer recited by John Adams, the first president to live in the White House: "May none but honest and wise men ever rule under this roof…" The design was pulled, according to some, by an influential female government employee who found the male reference offensive.

Reverse by Chester Young Martin

Depicted is the bust of James Hoban, the original architect of the White House, and the main entrance he designed. JAMES HOBAN is inscribed beneath the bust, with UNITED STATES OF AMERICA located along the top border and ONE DOLLAR at the bottom center. E PLURIBUS UNUM appears at right. The designer's initials CYM are located on an obtuse angle on Hoban's sleeve.

Origins of the White House Dollar

Public Law 102-281, which was signed by President Bush May 13, 1992, authorized this creation. Included in the price of each coin was a $10 surcharge, paid to the White House Endowment Fund. The fund will serve as a permanent source of support of the White House collection of fine art and historic furnishings, as well as for the maintenance of the historic public rooms.

This famous building became the official presidential residence Nov. 1, 1800. Although it was unfinished, John Adams, the second president, moved in. At the time, it was called the President's House and later, Executive Mansion. It was not until 1901 that the name "White House" appeared — on Theodore Roosevelt's stationery. Thomas Jefferson opened it to the public in 1801. When burnt almost to the ground by the British in 1814, all that remained were the scorched sandstone walls. It was rebuilt in 1815 and 1817 using part of the original walls. Today, the brass plate detailing the cornerstone laying remains buried within its stone walls! In 1902, the West Wing offices were constructed. They were enlarged in 1909, when the first Oval Office was built for William Howard taft. Since the original interior walls and wooden beams revealed significant deterioration, Harry Truman ordered, in 1948, a complete renovation and construction of the building's interior, which continued into 1952. Today, the rooms reflect the cultural heritage of this country.

The White House Dollar Today

The 500,000 maximum authorization is somewhat small for a modern commemorative silver issue, offering just one design and denomination. It therefore sold out before the order cut-off date. Unaudited sales figures reveal that about three-fourths of the mintage is the Proof, while the remainder are Uncirculated. The Proof, housed in a blue presentation case, rose to approximately three times the pre-issue price, while the Uncirculated version, housed in a blue gift box, rose to four times its pre-issue price.

Besides collectors, a large number of dealers and speculators purchased the coins. Several European dealers also needed 1,750 pieces for their clients. They were having some difficulty filling their orders. Thus, prices were forced upwards. In addition to dealer hype of the issue's "rarity," a large percentage of dealers who have the coins in their possession are selling only limited numbers, reinforcing the hype. As values begin to fall, watch the supply become more available. I highly recommend an immediate sell. Take profit now! You can replace your coins at lower price levels several years down the road. If desired, keep one or two pieces of the Uncirculated creation for the joy of collecting. That's what our hobby is all about. However, when the marketplace again gets hot, expect the issue — especially Uncirculated — to get pushed upward.

1992
Columbus Quincentenary

Reason for issue: To commemorate the 500th anniversary of the first
   voyage by Christopher Columbus to the New World.

Authorized per Act of May 13, 1992: 6,000,000 half dollars; 4,000,000
   silver dollars; 500,000 gold $5

Official sale price:

   Uncirculated Denver clad half dollar: $6.50; later, $7.50

   Proof San Francisco clad half dollar: $8.50; later, $9.50

   Uncirculated Denver dollar: $23; later, $28

   Proof Philadelphia dollar: $27; later, $31

   Uncirculated West Point gold $5: $180; later, $210

   Proof West Point gold $5: $190; later, $225

The coins were also offered as:

   2-coin Proof set (50¢, $1): $34; later, $38

   2-coin Unc. set (50¢, $1): $27; later, $32

   3-coin Proof set (50¢, $1, $5): $220; later, $250

   3-coin Unc. set (50¢, $1, $5): $205; later, $230

6-coin set (Proof & Unc.): $445; later, $495

All Proof coinage was housed in green presentation cases, while Unc. coin were placed in green gift boxes. Six-piece set packaged in wooden case.

Production figures

Date	Business Strikes	Assay Coins	Proofs	Melted	Net Mintage
1992-D 50¢	?	?	-	?	Pending*
1992-S 50¢	-	?	?	?	Pending*
1992-D $1	?	?	-	?	Pending*
1992-P $1	-	?	?	?	Pending*
1992-W $5	?	?	-	?	Pending*
1992-W $5	-	?	?	?	Pending*

Minting and melting figures not released by the Mint. Program active at close of writing.

Current market values

	MS-60	MS-63	MS-64	MS-65	PF-65
1992-D clad 50¢	7.00	8.00	9.00	10.00	*
1992-S clad 50¢	*	*	*	*	10.00
1992-D $1	20.00	22.00	23.00	25.00	*
1992-P $1	*	*	*	*	28.00
1992-W $5	185.	190.	190.	200.	190.

Half Dollar Designs by T. James Ferrell

Obverse

Depicted is a full-length portrait of Christopher Columbus at landfall, with his arms outstretched. Behind is his disembarking crew with their small boat, as well as the *Santa Maria*. LIBERTY is seen partially encircling the explorer. The anniversary dates 1492-1992 appear in the lower foreground. To their right is the motto IN GOD WE TRUST. The designer's initials TJF are located at the right rim, just below the tufts of beach grass. Mint mark is placed below Y of LIBERTY.

Reverse

Portrayed are Columbus' three ships under sail, within an inner circle. The inscription 500TH ANNIVERSARY OF COLUMBUS DISCOVERY circles above; E PLURIBUS UNUM floats on the waves below. UNITED STATES OF AMERICA arcs around the upper border; HALF DOLLAR below.

Dollar Designs

Obverse by John Mercanti

Depicted is a full-length portrait of Christopher Columbus holding a banner in his right hand and scroll in his left, standing next to a globe atop a pedestal. Below the pedestal are Mercanti's initials, JM. To the right of the globe is the motto IN GOD WE TRUST with the date 1992 below. Mint mark is located below the date. Around the bottom border is the inscription COLUMBUS QUINCENTENARY. Liberty appears at Columbus' elbow. At the top in the background are three vessels at sea.

Reverse by Thomas D. Rogers Sr.

Portrayed is a split image of the *Santa Maria* and the space shuttle *Discovery* with the earth and a star or sun to the shuttle's upper right. Designer's initials TDR appear below the wing, to the right of the engines. UNITED STATES OF AMERICA arcs above; ONE DOLLAR is in the right field, E PLURIBUS UNUM just below it. Anniversary dates 1492-1992 are at the bottom border.

Gold $5 Designs

Obverse by T. James Ferrell

Depicted is a profile of Christopher Columbus looking left at a map of the New World. His name is located at the bottom center within a circular border. Near his shoulder are located the designer's initials, TJF. LIBERTY is at the upper border; IN GOD WE TRUST at the lower. Anniversary dates 1492 and 1992 are at the 9 o'clock and 3 o'clock positions, respectivley.

Reverse by Thomas D. Rogers Sr.

Featured is the crest of the Admiral of Oceans. Such was an honor given to the famous explorer. In the lower left field are the designer's initials, TDR. The crest overlaps a map of the western Old World with the date 1492. E PLURIBUS UNUM is located above the crest and map. UNITED STATES OF AMERICA arcs above, FIVE DOLLARS below. Mint mark is near the last A of AMERICA.

Origins of the Columbus Quincentenary Coins

Public law 102-281 authorized the Mint to produce a gold half eagle, silver dollar and clad half dollar to mark the 500th anniversary of Columbus' first voyage of discovery. Surcharges of $35, $7 and $1, respectively, are to be paid to establish and endow the Christopher Columbus Fellowship Fund.

The Columbus Quincentenary Coins Today

By all rights, this commemorative program should have been a monster. Not only was the 500th anniversary of the major turning point in the prior millenium to be noted, but it also brings the United States commemorative program full circle — it has been 100 years since the first U.S. commemorative marking the World's Columbian Exposition in 1892! The program seems to have been widely ignored by the general populace, however. A dilution of the commemorative market by too many coins authorized by Congress recently may have had some effect. (In 1992 alone we had three coins for the Columbus anniversary, three more for the Olympics, and the White House dollar.) Also, Columbus suffered a wave of politically correct thinking. Demoted from hero to villanous conqueror by some, many of the tie-in events around the country throughout the year fell victim to demonstrations for one cause or another. Then, too, the United States failed to get on board a worldwide Age of Discovery coin marketing program that has seen phenomenal success in Europe and elsewhere.

In any case, at this point I recommend purchase only for the joy of collecting. Any future potential resides in the Uncirculated gold $5 coin, due to its low sales. Based on past performace of modern commemorative issues (1982-1991), values may well head south. Purchase in the secondary market, several years from now.

1993
Bill of Rights-Madison

Reason for issue: To commemorate the Bill of Rights and the role James Madison played in its adoption.

Authorized per Act of May 13, 1992: 1,000 silver half dollars; 900,000 dollars; 300,000 gold $5

Official sale price:
   Uncirculated West Point silver 50¢: $9.75; later, $11.50*
   Proof San Francisco silver 50¢: $12.50; later, $13.50
   Uncirculated Denver dollar: $22; later, $27
   Proof San Francisco dollar: $25; later, $29
   Uncirculated West Point gold $5: $175; later, $205
   Proof West Point gold $5: $185; later, $220

* The Unc. silver half dollar was available individually from the Mint in the Young Collector's Edition, a cartoon-colored holder designed to appeal to youngsters. The Young Collector's Edition sold out its 50,000 allotment within three weeks of the Jan. 22, 1993, launch.

Production figures

Date	Business Strikes	Assay Coins	Proofs	Melted	Net Mintage
1993-W 50¢	?	?	-	?	Pending*
1993-S 50¢	-	?	?	?	Pending*
1993-D $1	?	?	-	?	Pending*
1993-S $1	-	?	?	?	Pending*
1993-W $5	?	?	-	?	Pending*
1993-W $5 Proof	-	?	?	?	Pending*

Minting and melting figures not released by the Mint. Program active at close of writing.

Current market values*

* This program was very early in its sales period at the close of writing this book. Therefore, no accurate secondary market values can be given at this time.

Half Dollar Designs

Obverse by T. James Ferrell

Portrayed is James Madison penning the Bill of Rights. Below his elbow are the designer's initials, TJF. Madison's home Montpelier is seen in the right center field with the inscription JAMES MADISON FATHER OF THE BILL OF RIGHTS above and IN GOD WE TRUST below. The Mint mark appears in the lower right field. The word LIBERTY is located in the upper border; the issue date 1993 at the bottom.

Reverse by Dean E. McMullen

Depicted is a hand holding the torch of freedom. On its writst are the designer's initials. THE BILL OF RIGHTS is inscribed in the left field; OUR BASIC FREDOMS in the right field. UNITED STATES OF AMERICA and E PLURIBUS UNUM arc above, HALF DOLLAR below.

Dollar Designs

Obverse by William J. Krawczewicz (modeled by Thomas D. Rogers Sr.)

Portrayed is James Madison facing three-quarters right. In the otherwise stark field are the words LIBERTY and JAMES MADISON and the Mint mark. At the bottom border is IN GOD WE TRUST with the date, 1993. Designer's initials WJK and TDR appear on Madison's collar.

Reverse by Dean E. McMullen (modeled by Thomas D. Rogers Sr.)

Depicted is Montpelier, the Virginia home of James and Dolley Madison. Placed above is the motto E PLURIBUS UNUM; below is MONTPELIER. UNITED STATES OF AMERICA arcs above, ONE DOLLAR below. McMullen's initials are under the left wing as you view the coin; Rogers' under the right.

Gold $5 Designs

Obverse by Scott R. Blazek (modeled by William C. Cousins)

Depicted is Madison studying the Bill of Rights. His name and 1993 are inscribed below. IN GOD WE TRUST is at the lower left border; LIBERTY seems to emanate from Madison's forehead. The border at right is formed of 13 5-pointed stars. Mint mark is near the last star, at about the 4 o'clock position. Designers' initials are on Madison's sleeve.

Reverse by Joseph D. Pena (modeled by Edgar Z. Steever IV)

The central design features an eagle holding a parchment in its talons at the top. Below is the title BILL OF RIGHTS, followed by the inscription EQUAL LAWS PROTECTING EQUAL RIGHTS ARE THE BEST GUARANTEE OF LOYALTY AND LOVE OF COUNTRY. The words are Madison's. At the left border is a torch; at the right, a laurel branch. Designers' initials are on either side of the laurel stem. UNITED STATES OF AMERICA arcs above; E PLURIBUS UNUM and FIVE DOLLARS below.

Origins of the Bill of Rights-Madison Coins

The designs for these coins were chosen from 815 entries received by the Mint in an open competition. Public Law 102-281 provides for a surcharge of $30 on each gold coin, $6 for each dollar and $3 on each half dollar. According to a Treasury Department press release, all surcharges received from sale of the coins will be paid to the James Madison Memorial Fellowship Trust Fund to encourage teaching and graduate study of the Constitution of the United States.

With the Madison program, the Mint has experimented with some unusual packaging options. The most popular was the aforementioned Young Collector's Edition, which quickly sold out its 50,000 allotment. Another popular option was the Madison Coin and Medal Set, which included an Uncirculated silver half dollar accompanied by a bronze James Madison Presidential Medal (a replica of the original issued during his administration). The Coin and Medal sets were also limited to 50,000, and also quickly sold out. The pre-issue price was $13.50; later to be raised to $14.50.

The Uncirculated half dollar was not available by itself from the Mint. Other than the sets, it could be purchased in bulk lots of $5,000 or more.

Proof coins were issued individually in blue presentation cases. The Uncirculated coins were packaged in blue gift boxes as 2-coin (50¢, $1) or 3-coin (50¢, $1, $5) sets. The issue was also offered as a 6-piece set (three Proofs, three Uncs.) in a wooden box for $445, later raised to $495.

The Bill of Rights-Madison Coins Today

The Madison silver half dollar possesses the lowest authorized mintage for its denomination since 1940. It also breaks the string of copper-nickel clad commemorative half dollars issued since the 1986 Statue of Liberty program. It is also the first half dollar to bear the W Mint mark of West Point. It was offered with the Madison dollar in the 1993 Prestige Proof set, making the 1993 Prestige Proof set the first to offer two silver commems in addition to the usual Proof coinage.

The silver dollar and gold $5 authorizations are also low, by today's standards. However, at this point I would recommend acquiring these productions only for the joy of collecting.

1925
Norse American Medals

The 1925 Norse American medal by James Earle Fraser is a medal authorized by Congress. It was very popular among the "older generation" of U.S. commemorative coin collectors, and is therefore included here.

On the obverse is a Viking ship and its chieftain in full fighting regalia. A Viking ship with crew at sea can be seen on the reverse.

Records indicate that 39,850 silver pieces in total were struck at the Philadelphia Mint — like ordinary business strikings, then counted and bagged — and shipped to the Fourth Street National Bank of Philadelphia for the Committee.

Delivered in total were the following:

A) "Thick" (1/16") octagonal silver planchet (1¼" diameter); 33,750 struck, delivered at $0.45, sold at $1.25. Produced May 29, June 1-6, 8-13, 1925. Value depending on condition: $50-$90.

B) "Thin" (1/20") octagonal silver planchet (1¼" diameter): 6,000 struck, delivered at $.30, sold at $1.75. Produced May 21 (2000 pieces), May 22 (3000), May 23 (1000). Value depending on condition: $80-$150.

C) 100 Matte Proof pieces struck twice on a 1" diameter, 1/16" thick .900 fine octagonal gold planchet, delivered at $10.14, sold at $20. Produced June 3-4, 1925. Current value $6,500. Cleaned or abused pieces are worth less. Beware of Matte Proof pieces which have been polished and acid treated. These are worth between $1,000 and $2,000. I would peg its extant coinage at 47. Committee still owed the Mint money for total Norse production. To lessen the debt, 53 pieces were returned for melting. Add to the 47 count a trial piece kept by John R. Sinnock, Chief Mint Engraver, which now resides in the John J. Pittman Collection.

D) 75 pieces struck about seven months later on a 25/8" wide, ¼" thick silver-plated copper-bronze planchet. Produced after November 27, 1925. Some collectors estimate that only 50 or 60 of these medals were struck. Current value depending on condition: $2,500-$3,500.

Demand for the thin and especially the thick Norse medals is not as strong as it once was. Average future potential for the Norse thin. Just fair possibilities for the thick planchet! Very good to excellent potential for the Matte Proof gold creation. Average to good potential for the 25/8" wide copper-bronze, silver-plated medal.

An Investor's Guide To Commemorative Coinage

This section deals with all issues, and each coin produced within a particular issue, encompassing its past and current status for each grade and how it will affect its future performance. For example: There were some commemorative half dollars which sold for $1,700 in May 1989. Today, they can be acquired for between $340 and $400! Others have lost up to 60 percent of their past value!

Revealed will be those issues which will prove to be exceptional buys — when the market begins its upturn — as well as those specimens which will become simply promotional vehicles — making money mostly for the promoter.

Please be aware that the coin market can and does change very quickly. Certain coins are "hot" for a time, then fall out of favor as promotion ebbs. The author has attempted to provide a realistic assessment of the commemorative coin market. However, any statements regarding current or future value of any coin or other collectible item in this book must be considered the sole opinion of the author, and in any case is not a promise or guarantee of future value. Readers are advised to seek independent and individualized advice before purchasing or selling any coin for the purpose of financial gain.

World's Columbian Exposition Half Dollar

	Population Figures (NGC and PCGS combined)			
DATE	MS-63	MS-64	MS-65	MS-66
1892	1653	1516	546	59
1893	1491	1289	341	40
DATE	PF-63	PF-64	PF-65	PF-66
1892	10	5	0	4
1893*	1	2	1	0
DATE	** PL 63	PL 64	PL 65	PL 66
1892	39	50	26	6
1893	17	25	10	1

*I have yet to see an 1893 Columbian that I would classify as Proof. Too controversial.
**Only NGC uses the Prooflike (PL) designation.
To date, four 1892 pieces and one 1893 have been graded MS-67.

Aside from the common date Booker T. Washington and Carver-Washington issues, the 1892 and 1893 Columbians are the second most abundant commemorative half dollars in circulated condition. Average worn specimen is worth between $8-$10. Dealers will pay between $14-$18 for attractive EF-AU pieces. This is the kind of coin used in a decorative frame or sold in a holder and advertised between $35 and $75. Buy for the fun of ownership, or as a "numismatic seed" for some youngster or future collector. Appealing AU coinage, acquired in the $20-$30 range can be offered to the uneducated for various Uncirculated grades. There exists a respectable price spread between MS-60 and MS-64. However, all are fully priced at this time. Acquire for the joy of ownership.

Past radio, TV and telemarketing campaigns promoted the stuffing especially out of the latter rating. In fact, I know of some people who were sold MS-63 and MS-64 slabbed — and raw — coinage for $4,000 per coin! Bid values were $375 and $1200 respectively. They are burned forever. Required would be another similar promotion to increase values to past levels. Should such happen, sell; then, in time, buy back at cheaper prices. Census figures can be reduced between 25% and 30% for the latter category.

During our last market high (May 1989), the 1893 issue was bid at almost $6,000, while the 1892 striking was bid about a $1,000 less in MS-65 condition. At current levels, the higher mintage 1893 Columbian, which is rarer — because it received more abuse or less angelic protection — is the most desirable and undervalued coin. Possesses more future potential than the 1892 coin. I would deduct population count between 20% and 25% for each date. Pass on the unattractive or questionable offering. Never buy an unslabbed coin, if you truly cannot grade. I recommend NGC, PCGS or ANACS. When the market heat arrives, both dates will be pushed to much higher levels. Determine your exit point. You can repurchase at lower levels during a market slowdown. While I like both strikings of this popular issue, I prefer the 1893.

Columbians strictly graded MS-66 offer excellent future potential. I would lower census tabulation between 10% and 15%. They are truly rare coins in MS-66 and especially MS-67 states of preservation. Proof 1892 coinage is great to own in all categories. This special coinage has sold for the following prices: PF-62 $4,500; PF-64 $8,500; PF-64 $16,000+; PF-65 $35,000+. Values for this material has lost little when compared to the rest of the market. Excellent long term potential, especially in the higher grades.

Your 1893 Proof Columbian is too controversial! Pass on these pieces! They can possess deep mirror like fields — which are deeper than the 1892 creation — but lack total Proof striking characteristic requirements! After examining for the second time, in 1983, the very first 1893 piece struck, I declared it a first strike coin and not a Proof!

For those who can't afford Columbian Proof commemorative half dollars, attempt to acquire the next best thing. That's your prooflike coin, struck with a highly polished or even Proof die — but given one blow from the press. Prefer the coin in MS-64 condition ($2,000 appx.) or higher because lesser grades flaunt a bit too many scratches and other surface negatives which are magnified by the prooflike fields. There is nothing wrong with owning lower graded pieces.

Great future potential in attractive pieces of either date, grading MS-63+ and better. Beware of the buffed or polished raw coin offered as a Proof or prooflike specimen.

Isabella Quarter Dollar

Population Figures (NGC and PCGS combined)			
DATE	MS-63	MS-64	MS-65	MS-66
1893	820	772	303	105
DATE	PF 63	PF 64	PF 65	PF 66
1893	1	2	2	1
DATE*	PL 63	PL 64	PL 65	PL 66
	6	9	1	1

To date, 23 of these special quarters have been graded MS-67, while 5 have been granted the lofty MS-68 rating.

*Only NGC uses the Prooflike (PL) designation.

Isabellas grading EF-AU through MS-63 are fairly priced at current levels. When the next market heat arrives, prices will rise. Very popular issue grading MS-64 is somewhat underrated. Value should be based on the coin in question. Focus on the eye appealing MS-64+ specimen. Good future potential. Spread between the latter and MS-65 coinage during the May 1989 high was $3,700. I would delete between 20% and 25% from census. Expect values to rise.

In MS-65 condition, the Isabella quarter is undervalued. Pass on the dull and unattractive specimen. During the last market high, there existed a $5,000 spread between grades MS-65 and MS-66! Naturally that's past tense. I would delete 25% to 30% from census. Excellent future potential for this popular issue. In the loftier grades, she is a great coin to have in one's collection, should funds permit. Wonderful future lies ahead for our only commem quarter dollar.

For those who can afford a genuine Isabella Proof, suggest buying the creation, if available. Only a few have been slabbed.

They are down about 55% from their past high. Why? Dealers needed to free funds and pay bills, to exist in a slow marketplace. Other dealers kept lowering the bid on the coin, knowing money and clients were in short supply. Thus, an eventual sale transpired at lower levels to free the green. Great future potential.

For those who cannot afford the aforementioned, NGC prooflike (PL) encapsulations should be considered. Its worth — which can be double the rate for the listed grade — is dependent upon the coin's allure. A very popular item with an excellent future.

Lafayette Dollar

Population Figures (NGC and PCGS combined)				
DATE	MS-62	MS-63	MS-64	MS-65
1900	315	382	347	132

To date, 21 dollars have been encapsulated MS-66 and 5 graded MS-67.

The 1900 Lafayette dollar which was struck in 1899 is the only commemorative cartwheel produced until the 1983 Olympic dollar. On the surface, this issue appears to be fairly priced, in grades EF-AU through MS-65. Actually, this extremely popular collector coin is undervalued. (The keywords are "extremely popular"!) It's amazing to hear from collectors about their future acquisition plans, since present levels look very attractive. I would also note that 99½% couldn't care less about buying a specific variety which usually sells for little to no premium. That's not to say a collector wouldn't pay more when completion of the five-piece variety set is desired. Past high spread between grades MS-63 and MS-64 was $5,000. It was $9,500 between the MS-64 and MS-65 rating, and $13,000 between the latter and MS-66 condition! Howbeit, it's hard to say in what manner history will repeat itself, since our census was much lower. I would lower the census between 25% and 30% in MS-63 and MS-64 condition, as well as 30% to 35% in the MS-65 category. I know of one beautiful MS-64 Lafayette which was submitted 14 times with no upgrade! Out of disgust, the grading labels were trashed every time. (The coin truthfully was a MS-64+ Lafayette. The owner didn't think so.) Ditto five different MS-65 specimens that made four journeys each, in hopes of a higher grade. From what I heard, there were no scores.

Good future potential in MS-63 condition. Excellent possibilities reside in MS-64 and your loftier ratings for this very popular coin. Pass on the dull, dark, unattractive and arguable offering — even if it declares itself a MS-66! Certainly do not buy raw or unslabbed specimens, if you do not know how to grade! Beware the bargain! Seldom do they exist. Do not expect to receive a $3,000 coin for $300 or $900 or $1,500! Seek the advice of a recognized expert in the field, when assistance is needed!

Jefferson and McKinley Louisiana Purchase Gold Dollars

Population Figures (NGC and PCGS combined)

DATE	MS-63	MS-64	MS-65	MS-66
1903 JEF.	376	603	385	85
1903 McK.	375	471	279	72
DATE	**PF-63**	**PF-63**	**PF-65**	**PF-66**
1903 JEF.	8	5	4	6
1903 McK.	6	12	6	2

To date, seven Jefferson and four McKinley Louisiana Purchase gold dollars have been slabbed MS-67. One Proof McKinley has been graded PF-67. Three McKinleys have been rated PF-60 and two PF-62.

In grades EF-AU through MS-63, both issues appear fairly priced or a tad underrated. Ditto the Jefferson in MS-64 condition. Undervalued is the rarer McKinley in this grade. It's the best value! Very good future potential for MS-64+ specimens of each design. May 1989 market high spread between MS-64+ and MS-65 coinage was about $1,600. I would reduce census between 25% and 30%. Expect both popular issues to move upwards, when buyers become more active

In MS-65 condition, our rarer McKinley Louisiana Purchase gold dollar possesses much more future potential than the Jefferson striking. If not attempting to collect the 11-piece gold set, choose the McKinley. Howbeit, when our market heats up, both popular creations will rise in value. Last high differential between this grade and MS-66 was approximately $7,500. MS-65 census which was much lower then, can be reduced between 25% and 30%.

In MS-66 condition, both designs are too cheap at present levels. I would pass on the questionable offering. Wonderful future potential here and for the loftier grade. Watch prices go up, up and away when the green infusion starts warming up the numismatic scene.

For those who can afford the rare Proof coinage, I suggest acquisition. Also down from past market highs. Price is dependent upon A) the attractiveness of the Proof gold coin; B) whether the coin was purchased at today's levels, and C) how much of a loss or profit the owner desires. Sell prices can range from $10,000 to $45,000 for a PF-65 striking. If purchasing an unslabbed coin in the original frame, be certain the enclosed Proof is not a replaced prooflike issue! I know of several such frames!

Lewis and Clark Exposition Gold Dollars

Population Figures (NGC and PCGS combined)

DATE	MS-63	MS-64	MS-65	MS-66
1904	268	296	130	42

| 1905 | 239 | 183 | 49 | 5 |

To date, only 1 Lewis and Clark dollar has been graded higher than MS-66 (1904 NGC MS-67).

Most circulated offerings of our only two-headed coin are found abused in some fashion. Pass on the damaged or once soldered piece — which is worth much less than the undoctored gold disk. That's unless the price is very right. Popular issue is equally as rare, up to your MS-63 rating: Beyond, the 1905 striking is much rarer, especially in MS-65 and higher condition. At present, the Lewis and Clark gold dollars are quite undervalued and highly recommended in grades EF-AU and higher. Key is to procure a nice looking undoctored circulated piece which is free of deep cuts, or digs or scratches. Ditto pieces grading up to MS-62. MS-63+ offerings should also have present most if not all of its original luster. When funds permit, zero in on the MS-63+ offering. Tremendous future for these two dates grading strict MS-64 and loftier — especially the 1905 production. During our last May 1989 high, the price spread between the 1904 and 1905 creations in grades MS-63 and MS-64 respectively, was $2,500 and $5,500; in MS-64 and MS-65 condition, $14,000 and $22,000; and between MS-65 and MS-66 status: $20,000 and $43,000! While it appears that history will not repeat itself, and duplicate the noted vicinities, pleasant surprises do occur during a hot market. I would delete 25% to 30% from our MS-63 census and 35% to 40% from the MS-64 count. Ditto 25% to 30% from the MS-65 figures, as well as 14% to 20% just from the 1904, MS-66 population. I strongly suggest being part of Lewis and Clark's team before they move forward, on their next lucrative journey!

Proof pieces were struck for this issue. To date, none have been slabbed. I would pass on raw offerings. All that I have examined were early struck, prooflike pieces — some of which were accompanied by a letter of authenticity. Beware! Consult the true experts in the field.

Panama-Pacific International Exposition Half Dollar

Population Figures (NGC and PCGS combined)

DATE	MS-63	MS-64	MS-65	MS-66
1915-S	556	665	312	94

To date, 21 Pan-Pacs have been encapsulated MS-67.

Many circulated offerings of this very popular issue will exhibit some form of cleaning, polishing or whizzing. Pass, unless the price is very right or your objective is to only acquire a representative example of the issue. At current levels, pieces grading MS-62 and higher are undervalued. Lesser ratings should be acquired only for the joy of collecting. Attractive halves categorized as MS-63 and MS-64 offer very good future potential. Reject the dull, dark or questionable offering. There's a bright tomorrow for the alluring Pan Pac: rated MS-64+. During the last market high, our price spread between your MS-63 and MS-64 specimen was over $1,100, while the MS-64-MS-65 variance was $4,000. It appears history will not repeat itself in such a robust fashion for the aforementioned and loftier grades. Howbeit, one never should say never! I would reduce census between 20% and 25% for the MS-63 and MS-64 categories.

Strictly graded MS-65 Pan Pacs are certainly undervalued at current prices. It's a wonderful creation to possess. Pass on the dull, dark or questionable specimen. The May 1989 price zenith between our MS-65 and MS-66 rating was

$7,500! Census can be reduced between 25% and 30% for this rating. Excellent future potential! For the underrated, loftier MS-66 ranking, we can expect a very bright tomorrow. Should one be able to afford this rarer level, do so. Ditto the MS-67 grade. Tremendous possibilities for its owner.

Beware of the so-called specimen strikings. In my opinion, they as well as the so-called Satin Finish Proofs are nothing more than pieces struck from a new die — giving them somewhat of a different satiny appearance — but with some extra striking pressure. They do look beautiful. I have seen a few pieces graded MS-65 and MS-66. Don't go too overboard with the legal tender.

Panama-Pacific International Exposition Gold Dollar

	Population Figures (NGC and PCGS combined)			
DATE	MS-63	MS-64	MS-65	MS-66
1915-S	805	821	422	54

To date, one Pan-Pac gold dollar has been graded MS-67 (PCGS).

At current levels, all grades of this popular gold issue are undervalued. Best potential lies in pieces grading MS-63 and higher — especially the MS-64+ specimen. During the last high, spread between your MS-63 and MS-64 creation was over $1,400, while the MS-64-MS-65 variance was a walloping $4,500! Do not believe this potted history will be as impressive during the next arrival of the bull. I would reduce population figures between 25% and 30%. Good to very good potential for the above mentioned grades.

While population figures appear high, point to remember is that this gold commemorative series is very vox populi or desired by many collectors.

In strict MS-65 condition, this issue is underpriced. Very good to excellent future potential for eye-appealing strikings. Pass on that questionable offering. The May 1989 summit between our MS-65 and MS-66 rating was an enormous $19,000! Such will be very hard to duplicate. However, never say never! I would reduce census between 25% and 30%.

Tomorrow will be extremely bright, offering fantastic possibilities to the fortunate possessors of the lofty MS-66 and higher graded encapsulations. If funds are available make the plunge!

Panama-Pacific International Exposition $2½ Dollar Gold

	Population Figures (NGC and PCGS combined)			
DATE	MS-63	MS-64	MS-65	MS-66
1915-S	287	524	350	48

To date, 5 quarter eagles have been encapsulated MS-67.

At present levels, all grades of this extremely popular and highly desired creation are definitely undervalued! Pieces rated up to MS-64, offer very good to excellent future potential. Its May 1989, dollar pinnacle between the MS-63 and MS-64 levels was $2,400. The MS-64 to MS-65 difference was approximately 4,500! Census count for those grades can be reduced between 20% and 25%. It may not be easy for history to repeat itself, but it certainly will make the attempt.

In strict MS-65 condition, these $2½ commemorative gold strikings are quite undervalued. Just a wonderful addition to one's collection, should funds be available. Last market high between this and our MS-66 rating was a gargantuan

$16,000! A repeat performance will be difficult. From collector, dealer and personal experience, the $2¹/₂ design sustained definite shuttle service between the sender and grading services. Numerous attempts — after the crack outs — were made with the hopes of the upgrade which rarely occurred. Many grading labels were destroyed — without worry about future population accuracy — in the rush to resubmit the coins. Dealers were cracking out coins on the bourse floor, or in convention lavatories or in hotel rooms at 1 a.m. (above or next to my room), etc. I would reduce population count between 30% and 35%. Excellent future potential for the Pan-Pac quarter eagle in this grade. Tremendous possibilities also exist for this creation in MS-66 condition, should one be blessed to have the available funds.

Panama-Pacific International Exposition $50 Gold

	Population Figures (NGC and PCGS combined)			
DATE	MS-62	MS-63	MS-64	MS-65
1915-S ROUND	35	57	44	7
1915-S OCT.	76	78	31	7

To date, 2 Pan-Pac Rounds have been encapsulated MS-66. No Octagonals have been graded higher than MS-65 (NGC)!

Both well distributed issues are extremely popular, fully enjoyed and treasured by most who own them. I compare them to the rare fancy diamonds naturally colored pink, red, blue or green. They are the truffles and Beluga caviar of commemorative coinage, and outstanding celebrities in our coin world.

Based on past price history, the polished, whizzed or over-cleaned $50 slug will offer its owner little upside potential. At present price levels, all grades of each striking are quite undervalued. In the EF-AU through MS-63 categories, the Round $50 Pan-Pac is rarer than the Octagonal production. I would reduce their census count between 15% and 20%. Pieces rated higher are equally as rare. Population count indicates otherwise. Howbeit, I know of one MS-64 Round that was submitted eight times (in total), via three different dealers. Its collector-investor owner threw away seven of their insert grading labels — which can never officially be deleted from the census and population reports!

The following are bid prices for the $50 Round, in grades MS-60 through MS-67, during the May 1989 market peak: $39,000, $48,000, $64,000, $88,000, $140,000, $275,000 and $375,000! For the $50 Octagonal: $30,000, $38,000, $48,000, $89,000, $135,000, $260,000 and $360,000.

These strikings are rare in MS-64 and extremely rare in better condition. Blessed are they who can afford and procure during this lifetime! Future potential is just tremendous. History can easily repeat itself for this issue!

McKinley Memorial Gold Dollars

	Population Figures (NGC and PCGS combined)			
DATE	MS-63	MS-64	MS-65	MS-66
1916	616	675	272	70
1917	398	443	172	31

To date, only 2 McKinley gold dollars dated 1917 have been graded MS-67!

The 1917 production is the rarer of the two dates, which appear fairly priced at present in grades EF-AU through MS-64. While census figures are not exactly low, point to remember is that both strikings are popular collector items! One would be surprised as to how many of collectors want to complete the 11-piece gold commemorative set (1903-1926). When the market warms up, values will begin to rise. If buying only for the joy of ownership, procure what you can afford. Attempt to locate an attractive, undoctored, original surfaced gold disk that does not display a large or deep scratch across the portrait or flaunts fine hairline scratches across the coin. Should good future potential be your concern, zero in — should funds permit — on an attractive, fully original MS-64+ specimen. Favor the 1917 issue. Past high price spread between MS-64 and our MS-65 rating for the 1916 and 1917 creations were $5,600 and $5,000 respectively! That appears to be past history. I would lower census by 30% to 35% for each coin.

In MS-65 condition both issues are undervalued, at present. Attempt to procure attractive slabbed specimens. Favor the 1917 date. That doesn't mean one should reject the 1916 McKinley dollar. Pass on the unattractive and questionable. That May 1989 market high between grades MS-65 and MS-66 was a whopping $9,500 (1916) and $16,000 (1917)! I do not believe we will see such a price spread again. Fewer coins were encapsulated during this period, plus demand was high. I would reduce census between 25% and 30%. Very good future potential in this grade. In MS-66 condition, the undervalued McKinley gold dollars offer a bright tomorrow for their owners — especially the gold disks, dated 1917. That doesn't mean I would not love owning the previous production! Just pass on the unattractive or questionable coin. Population numbers can be reduced by 20% to 25%. Excellent future potential.

Lincoln or Illinois Centennial Half Dollar

	Population Figures (NGC and PCGS combined)			
DATE	MS-63	MS-64	MS-65	MS-66
1918	1094	1542	683	149

To date, 18 Lincolns have been graded MS-67. None have been rated higher!

This beautiful souvenir piece is not difficult to obtain in circulated condition. No significant price spread exists between the latter and MS-64 condition. Howbeit, this Lincoln creation — which is a collector favorite — is undervalued at current bid levels in grades MS-62 through MS-67! Real future potential begins in the flashy MS-64+ coinage. Past price difference between material rated MS-64 and MS-65 during the May 1989 market high was $2,000! I do not see history repeating itself to this degree. I would reduce population figures by 30% to 35% for the latter grade. Pass on the unattractive offering. Good future potential for pieces grading MS-62 through MS-64.

As noted, this favored design is undervalued in MS-65 condition. I advise passing on the dull, dark and questionable specimen. Dollar difference between our MS-65 and MS-66 classifications was $1,700. Estimate census can be deleted between 25% and 30%. Very good future potential. You can bet this issue will be pushed during the next market heat!

In MS-66 condition, this commemorative is quite underrated, at present levels. There's a bright tomorrow ahead in this grade and coinage granted MS-67 status. Great coin to have in one's collection.

Maine Centennial Half Dollar

Population Figures (NGC and PCGS combined)

DATE	MS-63	MS-64	MS-65	MS-66
1920	601	1043	569	93

To date, 6 of these 1920 commemorative half dollars have been graded MS-67, with none rated higher.

Issue is available in circulated condition, since many coins were used as pocket pieces. No large price spread exists between MS-60 and MS-63 coinage. Fairly priced at present, in grades EF-AU through MS-64. Acquire eye appealing coinage, only for the joy of ownership. Future potential exists in attractive pieces rated MS-64+. May 1989 dollar variation between the latter and MS-65 condition was $2,200! Don't expect a repeat. I would lower census between 25% and 30%.

Eye appealing MS-65 specimens are undervalued at current levels. Decline the dull, dark and unattractive offering. Past dollar high between grades MS-65 and MS-66 was $4,200! Don't count upon a similar performance. Future promoters will have the unaware believing it will happen! Census can be reduced between 20% and 25%.

There existed nearly a full original bag of this issue. Its owners said — some 13 years ago — that the coins would be sold only on an individual basis. Population count over the last two years rose in the MS-65 and MS-66 category. Were coins from this original bag sold individually and slabbed over this period of time responsible? If this not be the case, then figures will rise in the future. I would presently label tomorrow's potential as very good. This popular issue is currently undervalued in MS-66 condition and offers excellent future potential. I would reduce census between 20% and 25%. It's a rare coin in MS-67 condition. Wish I owned one of the six encapsulated pieces.

Pilgrim Tercentenary Half Dollars

Population Figures (NGC and PCGS combined)

DATE	MS-63	MS-64	MS-65	MS-66
1920	1132	1519	635	76
1921	395	831	388	42

To date, four Pilgrims struck in 1920 have been encapsulated MS-67 (PCGS), while only 2 dated 1921 have been granted such lofty status.

In circulated condition, the 1920 Pilgrim is not difficult to locate. Little price spread exists between grades EF-AU and MS-63 condition. Think MS-63+. Strong chance of average future gain does exist. Acquire for the joy of collecting. Ditto MS-64 coinage. Pass on the dull, dark and questionable offering. Past dollar variation between MS-64 and MS-65 coinage during the May 1989 peak was a huge $1800! It will be difficult for such happenings to be repeated. Census can be deleted by 25% to 30%. Good possibilities exist for pieces grading MS-64+.

In strict MS-65 condition, this issue is undervalued at current levels. Pass on the un-eye appealing silver disk. Price spread between the MS-65 and MS-66 ratings during the last high was an enormous $4,000! History will repeat itself, but not as strongly. I would reduce population figures between 20% and 25%. Good to very good future potential now exists.

Our 1920 Pilgrim, strictly graded MS-66, should be an addition to one's collection. Pass on the unattractive offering. Excellent future potential.

The 1921 Pilgrim which introduced me to U.S. commemorative coinage is undervalued in EF-AU condition, as well as in the MS-60 through MS-67 ratings. Future potential ranges from average in grades EF-AU through MS-62 and to very good in grades MS-63 and MS-64.

Suggest passing on the dull, dark and debatable offering. Dollar variation between MS-64 and MS-65 coinage was a big $2,100! History will repeat, but in a milder way. I would lower census by 25% and 30%. Excellent possibilities for the MS-64+ half dollar.

In strict MS-65 condition, this 1921 creation is definitely undervalued at current levels. Reject the unattractive silver disk. Past spread between MS-65 and MS-66 ratings during the last peak was a massive $4,300. History will repeat itself, but not as strongly. I would lower population count by 20% to 25%.

Very good to excellent future potential for the grade. Die-clashed 1921 Pilgrims displaying the blob in front of Bradford's nose are seldom seen in MS-65 or better condition! Future sleeper. Have sold for 50% more than regular issue.

This creation, grading MS-66 is a fantastic way to enhance one's collection. Definitely undervalued. Pass on the dull, dark and questionable coin. Excellent future potential. As noted, both creations are quite rare in the loftier MS-67 rating and are highly recommended.

Missouri Centennial Half Dollars

	Population Figures (NGC and PCGS combined)			
DATE	MS-63	MS-64	MS-65	MS-66
1921 2*4	407	637	76	2
1921 Plain	441	501	79	6

To date, no Missouri half dollars have been graded higher than MS-66.

That excessively rare Matte Proof was submitted to NGC (PF-65), as well as PCGS (PF-66). The NGC grading label was not returned, at present, for census deletion. There actually exists only one encapsulated coin!

Many of the circulated offerings will display some form of cleaning, whizzing or polishing. Pass on these pieces, unless the price is very right or you simply couldn't care less, since all that is wanted is a representative example of the Missouri issue. What is always desired are those flashy, undoctored AU-55 and AU-58 pieces. In grades EF-AU through MS-62, both coins are fairly priced and should be purchased only for the joy of ownership. Ditto the just made it or unattractive MS-63 specimen. For those interested in future potential, it begins with pieces rated strict MS-63+. Both undervalued issues grading MS-64 also offer good possibilities. Pass on the dull, dark or questionable coin. Alluring MS-64+ examples of each striking are worth much more than current levels. These are the coins that just look all MS-65, but possess some detriment. They usually sell fast when offered at coin shows, unless the asking price is unjustly high.

Sometimes a seller believes he or she possesses more of a coin than they really own! I know of both strikings which have been submitted over 15 times each, in hopes of an upgrade! The labels were cast away. Past high spread between this MS-64 and MS-65 No Star and Star rating was $10,000 and $12,000 respectively! I would reduce both population figures between 25% and 30%. Very good future potential.

Any strictly graded MS-65 Missouri is a rare, undervalued and wonderful commemorative to have as part of your collection, should you be blessed with the extra legal tender. Pass on the dull, dark and questionable offering. The May 1989 price zenith between grades MS-65 and MS-66 was approximately $9,500 for each striking! Census can be reduced between 25% and 30% for each creation. Excellent future potential. In the loftier underrated MS-66 category, the issue is very rare, especially the Missouri 2*4. If you can afford the rating, buy it. Tremendous possibilities for its owner.

Alabama Centennial Half Dollars

	Population Figures (NGC and PCGS combined)			
DATE	MS-63	MS-64	MS-65	MS-66
1922 PLAIN	454	624	136	4
1922 2x2	401	521	145	10

To date, only one 2X2 specimen was graded MS-67.

Circulated coinage should only be acquired for the joy of ownership. While the 2X2 is several times more difficult to locate than the available no 2X2 specimen, it is fully priced and offers little future advancement. Current price spreads between the MS-60 and MS-63 grades are somewhat undervalued. However, real growth for this issue lies in the specimen properly graded strict MS-63+ and loftier. Consider the latter "sleepers," or future winners.

I would estimate that at least 40% of the above MS-64 population figures can be safely deleted, due to crack outs and resubmissions. Grading labels were thrown away — in many cases — without concern for the importance of population deletion, for future accuracy. The hope of receiving a higher grade was all that mattered! During the last bull market, there existed a $3,500 spread between MS-63 and MS-64 encapsulated coinage! How many times would you resubmit your coin, if you though it had a chance of making the next highest grade? I know of several individuals who sent in the same five Alabama plains 43 times! (One coin was granted higher status.) Strictly graded, eye appealing MS-64 coinage for this issue is quite undervalued, at this time. Expect a future surge in its worth. Highly recommended for your collection or numismatic trove.

Specimens grading MS-65 for this issue offer exceptional future potential. The plain or no 2X2 striking holds the slight rarity edge. Just be happy to own either coin! I would cut the given population figures for each issue by more than 45%. Ditto here, resubmission and the thoughtless casting of grading insert labels. I would stay away from dull or dark coinage, or material that causes one to exclaim, "How in the world can this unattractive coin be slabbed MS-65?"

In MS-66 condition, your Alabama Plain is the rarer creation. Howbeit, with census figures as low as presented, be thrilled to own either coin! Tremendous future potential for the grade. To date, only one coin was graded MS-67 for this issue. (PCGS MS-67 Alabama 2X2). Wish I owned it!

Grant Memorial Half Dollar

	Population Figures (NGC and PCGS combined)			
DATE	MS-63	MS-64	MS-65	MS-66
1922 No Star	942	1102	476	71

| 1922 Star | 303 | 251 | 77 | 8 |

To date, 9 Grant No Star half dollars have been graded MS-67. None have been rated MS-68. No Grant With Star halves have been rated higher than MS-66.

In circulated condition, the Grant without star is available. Pieces exhibiting a small dot between the 22 of the date 1922 bring no premiums, at present. Our rarer Star issue is usually encountered whizzed or cleaned. These coins are worth less than the undoctored coin's bid level. Your higher mintage Grant Plain or no star, is fairly valued in grades MS-60 through MS-64. During the May 1989 market high, there existed an approximate $1,500 difference between the latter grade and our MS-65 coinage. Expect the item to be promoted during the next upturn. Acquire the aforesaid for the pride of ownership. I would reduce population figure between 20% to 25%. Real future potential begins with attractive flashy MS-64+ no star pieces. Certainly worth 25% to 50% over bid levels.

A strictly graded MS-65 Grant Plain is presently undervalued. Reject the dark, dull and debatable coin — which is not undervalued! Past price spread between this category and your MS-66 rating was $3,500! I would lower population figures by 15% to 20%. Excellent future potential here, as well as in the rarer MS-66 grade and MS-67 grades! Simply remember to pass if such a Grant without star should cross your path flaunting these lofty numbers, but doesn't salute you or address your fancy.

Our silver Grant with Star commemoratives, grading MS-60 through MS-62 have actually risen in value from the noted market high! Currently, they are fairly priced. Good future potential really begins with those pieces grading MS-63 and higher. Prefer an attractive original undipped MS-63+ coin. Ditto MS-64 coinage. Your non-clash mark variety can — but does not always — bring more money. Howbeit, all is dependent upon the coin. I would lower census between 25% and 30%. Past price spread between the latter grade and MS-65 was a whopping $14,000! Why? So few have been encapsulated at the higher level. Expect it to be heavily promoted in the next market heat.

Great coin to possess in MS-65 condition. Pass on the questionable. You want to see original surfaces should your coin be lightly toned. I would lower census between 15% and 20%. Excellent future potential for the rarest silver commemorative struck since 1892, in grades MS-62 and higher. In MS-66 condition we are talking about a very rare item. I would reduce its population by 45%! What a great coin to have in one's collection.

Grant Memorial Gold Dollars

Population Figures (NGC and PCGS combined)

DATE	MS-63	MS-64	MS-65	MS-66
1922 No Star	264	402	252	92
1922 Star	218	506	413	144

To date, 7 Grant No Star gold dollars and 16 Grant With Star gold pieces have been encapsulated MS-67. None have been graded MS-68!

When examining the entire commemorative production from 1892 through 1954, the single most expensive coin available in circulated condition is the Grant with Star gold dollar ($1100), followed by the No Star variety ($850). (There are circulated silver issues, such as the Hawaiian ($650 and Spanish Trail ($600) which are worth more than most lightly worn gold issues with the 11-

piece set.) At current levels, both strikings appear fairly priced in grades EF-AU through MS-64. Acquire for the joy of collecting. The rarer No Star variety in MS-63+ or MS-64+ condition, offers a better chance at future gains. Reject the unattractive and questionable pieces. During the noted marketplace high, price spread between MS-64 and MS-65 Grant gold dollars was approximately $3,300. I would lower population figures between 25% and 30%. Expect prices to rise during the next promotional market heat. Use that period to sell, then repurchase when values return to lower levels, if desired.

Grant plains grading MS-65 are undervalued at present levels. Eye appealing pieces offer very good future potential. Consider this variety over the star which is a tad underpriced. Reject the questionable offerings. Difference in value between this and your MS-66 striking was approximately $6,100 during the last high! Populations were much lower.

Excellent future for both creations lies in the undervalued MS-66 category. Together, they would have cost you $32,000+, several years ago! I wouldn't mind owning one of those lofty MS-67 pieces. Wonderful coin.

Monroe Doctrine Centennial Half Dollar

Population Figures (NGC and PCGS combined)

DATE	MS-63	MS-64	MS-65	MS-66
1923-S	1043	853	167	30

To date, only four Monroes have been graded MS-67.

This is one of the most common commems in circulated condition. In grades EF-AU through MS-64, it is fairly priced at present. Acquire — this not so popular design — only for the joy of collecting! Future potential lies in the flashy, underrated MS-64+ Monroe. Past high between the latter and your MS-65 category was a tremendous $7,000! I would lower population figures by 35% and 40%

In strict MS-65 condition, this creation is a rare and undervalued coin. Pass on the dull, dark and questionable offering. May 1989 high between grades MS-65 and MS-66 was $4,500. Census can be lowered between 20% and 25%. Excellent future potential. Ditto the very rare and undervalued MS-66 Monroe. Great coin to possess, should the "legal green" be available.

Huguenot-Walloon Tercentenary Half Dollar

Population Figures (NGC and PCGS combined)

DATE	MS-64	MS-65	MS-66	MS-67
1924	1317	579	113	5

To date, no Huguenots have been graded MS-68.

Little price spread exists between coins grading EF-AU and MS-63. Coinage graded from MS-60 through MS-64 are fairly valued. Acquire only for the joy of collecting. Future potential exists in attractive pieces rated MS-64+. During the past market high of May 1989, there existed a $2,600 spread between grades MS-64 and MS-65. I would reduce population figures between 25% and 30%. At current levels, MS-65 eye appealing "Huguenots" are undervalued. Very good future potential. Reject the unattractive and the questionable. Past value spread between this grade and our MS-66 rating was $5,200. There is certainly some "past history" in this figure. I would lower census between 25% and 30%. Creation will be promoted during the next market upturn.

In MS-66 and MS-67 condition, this issue is definitely undervalued. Excellent future potential for those who can afford the striking.

Lexington-Concord Sesquicentennial Half Dollar

Population Figures (NGC and PCGS combined)

DATE	MS-63	MS-64	MS-65	MS-66
1925	1054	1225	393	38

To date, no Lexingtons have been graded higher than MS-66.

This creation is not difficult to locate in circulated condition. Try to buy an undoctored, attractive nice looking coin with original surfaces. Small price difference exists between grades EF-AU and MS-63 condition. Ditto MS-63 and MS-64 rated material. Should funds be available, think at least MS-64. Acquire the aforementioned grades for the joy of collecting. Future lies in this issue grading an attractive MS-64+. Pass on the dull, dark and just made it MS-64 pieces, should a future profit be part of your objective.

Price variation between the latter state and MS-65, during the May 1989 high was $1,900! That very flashy coin with the half inch long hairline scratch in the field just would not be graded MS-65. Many of this type were constantly resubmitted. I would lower population figures between 30% and 35%.

Strictly graded, eye-appealing MS-65 Lexingtons are quite undervalued at current levels. It's that small quantity of unattractive and questionable material which drives the issue's value downward and the nicer pieces into hiding at this time. Dollar difference between the MS-65 and MS-66 rating was a whopping $4,500 during the market high. I would reduce census by 30% to 35%. Excellent future potential for properly graded MS-65 coinage. Popular commemorative half dollar is a rare coin in MS-66 condition. I would lower census between 15% and 20%. Wonderful future potential for this undervalued issue. None to date have been granted loftier status.

Stone Mountain Half Dollar

Population Figures (NGC and PCGS combined)

DATE	MS-64	MS-65	MS-66	MS-67
1925	2901	1414	328	62

To date, 2 Stone Mountain have been granted the lofty MS-68 status by PCGS.

This popular, high mintage issue is the fifth least expensive commemorative design available in circulated condition ($28). Your lowest priced is the Carver-Washington type coin ($8.50), followed by the BTW type coin ($8.50), and the respective 1893 then 1892 Columbian issues ($17 and $14). Pieces grading EF-AU through MS-64 should be acquired only for the joy of collecting. They are fairly priced in these grades, based on current supply and demand. As the market heats up, this half dollar should be promoted. It will return to current levels, unless demand becomes so intense or the creation is widely distributed among new collectors. Never say never. However such chances appear remote. Previous high dollar spread between MS-64 and MS-65 Stone Mountains was approximately $600. Past tense! I would lower census between 25% and 30% for the MS-64 category. Average future possibilities for the aforementioned ratings. Strictly graded flashy MS-65 and MS-66 pieces are somewhat undervalued at current levels. Former top price variance between the just noted categories was $1,050. History will repeat during a promotional period, but to a lesser degree. I would lower census by 20% to 25% for each grade. Good to very good future potential. However, it's hard to determine what percentage of Stone Mountains residing in roll form (20 pieces) in Southern vaults will enter the marketplace in the near future. I know of several individuals who own 60 of these original rolls in total! That's 1,200 half dollars! Pieces grading MS-67 ($1,725) presently offer very good to excellent future potential.

California Diamond Jubilee Half Dollars

Population Figures (NGC and PCGS combined)

DATE	MS-63	MS-64	MS-65	MS-66
1925-S	908	1039	601	225

To date, 36 pieces have been slabbed MS-67 while only one piece has been encapsulated MS-68 by NGC.

This popular issue exhibits a small price spread between the EF-AU and MS-62 ratings. Just think higher Uncirculated grade — for the joy of collecting. Ditto MS-63 material. When possible, zero in on your MS-63+ coinage. At current levels, only your flashy eye appealing MS-64+ pieces are undervalued. Recommended for purchase. Otherwise, acquire the just MS-64 specimen because you desire it. During a hot market values will rise for a short time, then return to previous levels. Pass on the dull, dark, unattractive or questionable offering. During our past market high, the price spread between MS-64 and MS-65 coinage was almost $2,000! I would deduct approximately 20% from the census figures. Your strictly graded MS-65 specimen is definitely undervalued at today levels. Highly recommended for purchase. What drives prices down in a rather illiquid marketplace are those limited quantities of unattractive and sometimes questionable MS-65 offerings! These are usually offered to the uneducated, bargain hunters and almost brain dead. Excellent future potential, when miner and bear have that stunning look — and do not emerge "grisly."

During the last high (late May 1989), there was almost a $3,000 spread between the MS-65 and MS-66 categories! I would lower population figures here by 25%. Pieces grading MS-66 are without question undervalued in today's coin world. Highly recommended. Again pass on the dull and dark offering. If iridescent toning is present, that rainbowlike play of colors should look alive. It should not appear as if they are trapped within a smoky surface. I would lower census figures for the grade between 20% and 25%. California Jubilees grading MS-67 and MS-68 offer tremendous potential. They are most highly recommended.

Beware of the Satin Finish Proof offering — even if accompanied by a letter of authentication! In my judgment, they do not exist! What we have here is a coin which was produced from an obverse-reverse die combination that was just placed into production. Extra striking pressure was employed. (Two blows were not applied!) Due to this, and new die surface-planchet encounter, we have a coin that will look somewhat different. Now if fortunate to receive angelic protection against bag marks, etc., it will certainly appear a bit dissimilar, as well as captivating, to the astute. Accordingly, it's labeled what it never was meant to be. Consult the real experts, if uncertain.

Fort Vancouver Centennial Half Dollar

Population Figures (NGC and PCGS combined)

DATE	MS-63	MS-64	MS-65	MS-66
1925-S	526	837	493	116

To date, 16 Vancouvers have been encapsulated MS-67, while 1 piece has been granted lofty MS-68 status (PCGS).

Most circulated offerings of this issue (which was struck at our San Francisco Mint with the S mint mark omitted) are usually seen whizzed, polished or abused. Procure the undoctored and attractive piece, when desired. At current levels popular issue is undervalued in all mint state grades and offers very good to excellent future potential.

During the 1989 market high, price variation in grades MS-63 and MS-64 was $400. Between our MS-64 and MS-65 ratings, it was a whopping $3,300! That now seems like past tense. Between the MS-65 and MS-66 categories, it was a lesser $2,800. In this case, history has a chance of repeating! I would lower census figures by 25% to 30% for our MS-64 and MS-65 grades and by 15% to 20% for the MS-66 class. Pass on the dull dark and questionable offering. An excellent issue to have in one's collection.

Sesquicentennial of American Independence Half Dollar

Population Figures (NGC and PCGS combined)

DATE	MS-63	MS-64	MS-65	MS-66
1926	1261	844	95	4

To date, no Sesqui has been graded higher than MS-66. None of the extremely rare Matte Proofs have been encapsulated to date.

This half dollar is located with no difficulty in ratings EF-AU through MS-62. There also exists little price spread. It's a tad underpriced in MS-63+ condition. Suggest acquiring the noted grades simply for the joy of ownership. Creation is undervalued in MS-64 condition, when it is very eye-appealing or flashy looking. Remember, all MS-64 encapsulations are not as just noted! Real future for issue begins with your very attractive MS-64+ half dollar or almost made it MS-65 striking. One raw coin was recently offered to me at $4,400. Bid was $5,900. It possessed the most flash and blast that I have ever seen for the issue. Upon inspection, a hairline scratch — which was not exactly the lightest — was seen across the heads of both presidents. On their foreheads and in the field above were some light hairlines. Bid for an attractive MS-64 specimen was $425. I would have paid $800+ for the piece. No doubt it was submitted for slabbing, then returned an MS-64 and thus cracked out of the holder. It's a high price, overgraded "lure coin" aimed at catching the "uneducated fish!"

These are the kind of coins which were and are constantly resubmitted in the hopes of an upgrade. During the May 1989 high, there existed a $1,700 price variance between MS-63 and MS-64 coinage. That's past history. Between your MS-64+ and rarer MS-65 specimen, a colossal $7,000 was the norm. History will repeat itself! We can reduce census figures by 25% for 30% for our MS-64 category. Pass on the dull, dark and unattractive coin. Excellent tomorrow exists for accurately graded and captivating MS-64+ coinage.

A strictly graded MS-65 Sesqui is a rare commemorative half dollar. Pass on the dull, dark or debatable offering. I have seen a limited number of pieces labeled MS-65 that I would not place in my collection, nor offer to clients! Population count can be reduced by 15% to 20%. Dollar spread during the last high between grades MS-65 and MS-66 was a gigantic $11,000! Great remembrance preserver to add to one's portfolio, should funds be available. Future potential is excellent.

In the MS-66 category, this creation is a very rare coin. Howbeit, past high was $20,000 in the grade. Current bid is $19,000. Little dollar decline over the past 3½ years. While anything is possible, I do not feel there is much upside potential in grade. I would rather possess three MS-65 Sesquis than one MS-66 encapsulation, although I wouldn't mind possessing a "six" coin.

Sesquicentennial of American Independence $2½ Gold

	Population Figures (NGC and PCGS combined)			
DATE	MS-62	MS-63	MS-64	MS-65
1926	1061	1406	836	94

To date, only one Sesqui $2½ gold piece was encapsulated MS-66 (PCGS).

There also exists one or possibly two excessively rare Matte Proof strikings. It's the only commemorative gold coinage with this surface! One such Proof, encapsulated by NGC, sold privately in June 1988, for $245,000. It was offered for sale, in June 1989, by a major New York City establishment for $325,000!

Had misfortune not transpired, their Texas client would have added this major rarity to his outstanding collection.

There were only two commemorative $2½ gold pieces produced from 1892 through 1993 that collectors can possess. One is the rarer and more expensive Panama Pacific striking. The other is the Sesquicentennial creation. While its population count is high for most categories, the issue is very popular and affordable. At current levels, in grades EF-AU through MS-66, it's undervalued. Pieces rated EF-AU and as high as MS-64, offer very good to excellent future possibilities. Those grading strict MS-64+ and higher afford their owners excellent future potential. Were we evaluating a similar issue with equal values and identical census figures — but which is not nearly as popular with collectors — would recommend its acquisition in grades EF-AU through MS-64 only for the joy of ownership. During the May 1989 high dollar spread among ratings were as follows: MS-62 and MS-63: $700; MS-63 and MS-64: $2,300 and MS-64 & MS-65: $20,000! History will repeat itself, but to a lesser magnitude.

I would reduce census in MS-64 condition by 25% to 30%; in MS-65 condition between 15% and 20%. Be aware of the fact that when the market heat begins to decrease, your higher population issues will become more abundant, as collectors, dealers and investors begin selling. Thus, values can rapidly decline.

Oregon Trail Memorial Half Dollars

	Population Figures (NGC and PCGS combined)			
DATE	MS-64	MS-65	MS-66	MS-67
1926	948	523	101	11
1926-S	1110	815	254	52
1928	445	485	148	22

1933-D	537	514	98	10
1934-D	882	551	81	4
1936	614	749	269	54
1936-S	267	460	328	68
1937-D	353	951	805	244
1938	416	600	211	30
1938-D	272	625	470	87
1938-S	381	652	308	52
1939	212	343	161	26
1939-D	174	325	222	51
1939-S	202	331	174	33

To date, the following issues have been granted MS-68 status: 1926-S (3), 1936-S (2), 1937-D (20), 1938-P (2), 1938-D (12), 1938-S (4), 1939-D (5) and 1939-S (2).

Most available circulated Oregons are dated 1926-P and 1926-S and to a lesser degree, 1937-D. Other issues are usually cleaned or abused Uncs.

No major price spreads exist for most of this issue between MS-60 and MS-64. The exceptions — although not sizable — are the 1928-P creation, plus the 1938 and 1939 sets. Therefore, we shall begin and concentrate on MS-64 coinage.

The best bets at present are the undervalued low mintage 1936-S striking, followed by the 1938-D issue, succeeded by the popular 1939 Oregon Trail D, S and P coinage. When looking for just a representative example of the series or type coin which possesses extra flash or luster and flaunts a strong strike, as well as good value, zero in on the 1937 Denver production. Acquire the 1926-P, 1926-S and 1934-D pieces only for the joy of collecting.

I would estimate that between 25% to 40% of this MS-64 population was resubmitted for upgrade in the past. Their insert grading labels were thoughtlessly discarded. Price spreads between the MS-64 and MS-65 category ranged from $270-$670 for your common issues and from $380 to $1,575 for the 1934-D creation! Is this not reason to try again and again to have your existing pumpkin turn into a Cinderella coach? Most affected were the 1934-D, 1933-D, 1928-P and the 1939 P,D,S set. Average future potential.

Acquisition best bets for this MS-65 category are as follows: 1939-S, 1939-D, 1939-P, 1936-S and 1928-P Oregons.

Certainly quite undervalued as individual issues — if strictly graded. Population figures for this classification should be lowered by 25% to 35%. Very good future potential. Many coins have been resubmitted in hopes of a higher grade. Price spreads were tremendous between our MS-65 and MS-66 categories. There once existed a $2,000 variance for the 1934-D issue! Definitely undervalued, as individual dates are the 1926-P, 1934-D, 1938-P and 1938-D strikings. Good future potential. The 1933-D issue is somewhat underpriced nowadays. Dates to consider only for the joy of collecting are the 1937-D, 1926-S and 1936-P Oregons — unless the depicted reverse Indian speaks to you!

The MS-66 issues which now offer the most potential and are extremely undervalued at current levels are the 1934-D, 1933-D and 1926-P strikings.

Other Oregons whose potential can be rated as excellent are the 1928-P, 1939-P, 1939-S and 1938-P creations. Dates offering very good future possibilities are as follows: 1939-D, 1926-S, 1936-P, 1938-S, 1936-S and 1938-D. Your 1937-D pieces should only be acquired for the joy of ownership — unless you see the

Conestoga wagon move. I would estimate that the population figures for this grade be lowered between 15% and 20% due to crack outs, based on higher grading expectations, and dumped insert grading labels.

In MS-67 condition, the first seven issues will be very difficult to locate — especially the 1934-D, 1933-D, 1926-P and 1928-P strikings. Exceptional future here. I would estimate that most population figures could be decreased by 15% to 25% for this grade. In the past, insert grading labels were too often unthinkingly discarded after the coin's crackout. The vision of the same coin being returned as an MS-68 specimen was too mesmerizing. Most were unsuccessful.

At present, these issues are extremely undervalued and offer excellent potential: 1926-P, 1926-S, 1928-P, 1936-P, 1936-S and the 1938 P and S coinage.

Acquisition at present levels should be considered a steal! Procurement will not be easy because these absurd levels usually keep virtually all such material from naturally entering the marketplace. Why that 1937-D creation is worth at least $1,500! All remaining dates are very underrated. Remember, a bargain can translate into being able to just own the issue — even when a premium has to be paid! Current asking price on the extremely rare 1926-P Matte Proof is $50,000+.

Vermont or Battle Of Bennington Half Dollar

	Population Figures (NGC and PCGS combined)			
DATE	MS-63	MS-64	MS-65	MS-66
1927	812	1087	556	104

To date, 5 Vermonts have been encapsulated MS-67.

At current levels, this very popular issue is somewhat undervalued in all ratings up to MS-64. Suggest procuring for the joy of ownership. Average to good possibilities for the just noted. Future is much brighter for the alluring MS-64+ Vermont. Past dollar high during the May 1989 market peak between grades MS-63 and MS-64 was a large $500. That's past tense. The difference in MS-64 and MS-65 ratings was $2,500, while the MS-65 and MS-66 was a massive $5,000! Needless to say, population figures were lower at the time. History will repeat for the aforesaid grades — but to a lesser degree. Reject the unattractive offerings.

Pieces strictly evaluated as MS-65 and MS-66 are underpriced at present levels. Pass on the dull, dark and questionable coin. I would reduce census count by 25% to 30% for the MS-65 category and by 20% to 25% for the loftier grade. Very good to excellent future potential in these ratings. MS-67 Vermonts are underrated. I would love to own the coin. Some collectors told me they would prefer having three MS-66 pieces in their portfolios, instead of one MS-67 coin. That's a good point. However that current $7,000 bid can jump to $8,000+ quickly, especially as the market warms.

Hawaii Sesquicentennial Half Dollar

	Population Figures (NGC and PCGS combined)			
DATE	MS-63	MS-64	MS-65	MS-66
1928	428	581	163	10
DATE	PF 63	PF 64	PF 65	PF 66
1928	2	11	3	0

To date, no Hawaiian commemorative half dollars have been graded MS-67.

Most circulated offerings are usually cleaned or whizzed and worth less than current levels. Undoctored EF-AU coinage is worth current bid-ask prices. Buy for the joy of ownership. Attractive AU material will usually bring MS-60 money or more, depending on the coin's makeup. This creation is the most expensive commemorative half dollar in circulated condition! In grades MS-60 through MS-63, the Hawaiian is fairly priced. Attempt to procure a nice MS-63+ specimen, if available. Again, obtain for the pride of ownership! In MS-64 condition, this very popular issue is somewhat undervalued. Real future potential exists in coinage which rates a MS-64+. Pass on the unattractive and questionable offering. Past price spread between the latter and your MS-65 grade was $2,300. I would lower between 25% and 30% from present population figures. When the market heats up, this issue will be promoted.

Pieces grading MS-65 are definitely undervalued at present — if strictly graded! There exist in the marketplace a small number of Hawaiians which leave much to be desired. They lack eye appeal and are liberally rated. It is this kind of material that drives values downward. Were they to be cracked out and resubmitted, a certain downgrading would take place. Pass on the dull, dark and smokily unattractive coinage, even if such possesses iridescent or colored toning. When the "right stuff" makes its appearance, it almost always brings much more than the aforesaid pieces. Excellent future potential here. Past price spread between this grade and our MS-66 rating was over $10,000! Population figures can be reduced between 20% and 25%. When the heat arrives, this issue will rise. You can bet it will be promoted. In MS-66 condition, we have a rare commemorative which is too cheap at current levels — if accurately graded. Excellent future potential. Pass on the unattractive offering.

A few Sandblast Proof Hawaiians have sold for about 55% of their value, since the last high in May 1989. Dealers needed funds to run their business in a soft market. This popular rarity, when available, offers exceptional future potential. I would lower the census by 40%, in Proof 64 condition. During the said high, an MS-64 Hawaiian sold for $50,000. The same coin brought near $20,000 in 1992.

Maryland Tercentenary Half Dollar

Population Figures (NGC and PCGS combined)

DATE	MS-63	MS-64	MS-65	MS-66
1934	678	1766	953	185

To date only 13 Marylands have been slabbed MS-67, with none graded higher.

While not exactly abundant in circulated condition, most offerings are of the abused variety. Issue is fairly priced in grades EF-AU through MS-64 condition. Little price spread exists between the just noted. Attempt to acquire an attractive MS-64+ specimen, when possible. May 1989 high dollar spread between MS-64 and our MS-65 grade was $1,100. Consider that past history. I would lower census between 20% and 25%. Howbeit, only buy into the aforementioned grades for the pride of ownership.

At current levels, your MS-65 specimen is also fairly priced. Only real future lies in attractive MS-65+ material. Expect promoters to push the Maryland, when our coin market gets hot. Sell into this puffery. Past high between MS-65 and MS-66 graded pieces was $2,800. That's history. I would lower population figures between 25% and 30%. Average future potential in this category.

This half dollar is undervalued in MS-66 condition — if eye appealing. Pass on the unattractive offering. I would lower census between 25% and 30%. Very good future potential. MS-67 Marylands are rare items. Those who are blessed to procure the item should do so. Your reward will arrive with the next market heat.

Texas Centennial Half Dollars

Population Figures (NGC and PCGS combined)

DATE	MS-64	MS-65	MS-66	MS-67
1934	1226	874	152	17
1935	351	759	495	82
1935-D	366	816	433	59
1935-S	434	707	233	20
1936	444	800	337	36
1936-D	321	801	597	86
1936-S	459	753	236	15
1937	370	563	182	25
1937-D	327	694	267	27
1937-S	319	619	248	15
1938	271	321	96	7
1938-D	202	412	139	20
1938-S	232	351	181	19

To date, the following issues have been granted MS-68 status: 1934-P (1), 1935-P (3), 1936-P (1), 1936-D (1), 1936-S (1) and 1938-S (3).

Also, NGC has designated 6 of the following 1937-S pieces prooflike (PL): 1 MS-63, 2 MS-64, 2 MS-65 and 1 MS-66.

Wow! This beautiful creation appears to have come out of the numismatic woodwork, since the last May 1989 market high! It now has entered the realm of the common — up to MS-66 condition — for the most part. Approximate current population totals for the given grades are as follows: MS-64: 5,322 pieces; MS-65: 8,470 pieces; MS-66: 3,596 pieces and MS-67: 428 pieces. That's a lot of coinage for these upper categories. Little price variance presently exists for such half dollars rated EF-AU, through MS-64. Acquire for the joy of collecting. Fair to average possibilities with the aforesaid. Type pieces and sets will be promoted during the next hot market. Values shall rise, but return to previous levels, should the scene begin to cool. Best bet in MS-64+ condition is the 1938-P and S issues, as well as the complete set. Average future potential. Ditto the MS-65 category. Too many pieces slabbed MS-65. Average potential here. Best bet again is the 1938 P, D and S strikings and the complete set. Just remember that this date's luster is almost always chromelike in appearance. Not too many pieces will display the appealing silver-white look. Past market highs are history.

In MS-66 condition, productions which are underrated and offer the best potentiality are as follows: the 1934-P, 1937-P and 1938 Texas coinage. We can expect very good to excellent future potential from the above mentioned — especially the 1938 Philadelphia issue. The remaining productions will offer average to good possibilities for tomorrow. For what its worth, census can be reduced by 25% and 30% for each date. Should demand within the numismatic world become so intense, prices will climb beyond expectations, until the proverbial bull begin to tire.

In MS-67 condition, most dates are undervalued. Type coin prices reflect your higher population 1935-P, 1935-D and 1936-D strikings. All other dates are undervalued as individual issues. A production with the same grade and census of 19 pieces should not be worth $45 more than one with 79 encapsulated coins. Problem is due to a combination of our present economic situation, limited and careful spending (at present) and a large population count for a date or dates within an issue. The latter especially helps dampen interest in the real sleeper pieces, as the masses see their values as very close to the higher census coins. It's the astute who attempt to locate an accurately graded specimen. They are placed in their collections, waiting to reap future mental and monetary rewards. What will help bring about the change? The key words will be awareness, desire to acquire and demand! More and more people are becoming aware of the value of semi-scarce and better low population issues. As the marketplace begins to heat up, and more money enters the numismatic scene, such will lead to a desire to acquire. These issues accurately graded are very difficult to obtain in a slow market! The new demand will cause values to justly rise, to deserving new highs, leaving behind the worth of the higher, now generic census pieces. (Apply the aforementioned to the entire U.S. commemorative series, as well as most U.S. coinage.) Excellent future potential for the aforementioned individual issues.

Daniel Boone Bicentennial Half Dollars

Population Figures (NGC and PCGS combined)

DATE	MS-64	MS-65	MS-66	MS-67
1934	333	467	109	8
1935	504	443	101	10
1935-D	343	205	46	3
1935-S	261	377	109	8
1935 W/'34	539	515	132	6
1935-D W/'34	150	164	74	11
1935-S W/'34	175	157	43	3
1936	599	610	156	20
1936-D	384	412	88	6
1936-S	306	400	142	18
1937	543	570	139	17
1937-D	206	214	62	12
1937-S	162	192	58	8
1938	201	183	34	4
1938-D	183	182	69	16
1938-S	162	152	49	16

Little value spread exists between grades EF-AU and MS-64, for the generic issues. There are just too many pieces of the now common, more available dates, such as both 1935-P issues and your 1936-P and D and 1937-P productions, than there is demand in these grades! Acquire only for joy of collecting. Type creations with good future potential are the 1935 D and S strikings with the added date 1934 on the reverse (referred from now on as, w/'34), the 1937-S and the 1938 coinage. All are undervalued. Attempt to procure attractive MS-64+ pieces. Pass on dull, dark or un-eye appealing coinage. I would estimate that your MS-64 population figures can be reduced by 30%.

Values appear inexpensive for MS-65 Boone commemorative half dollars. Unfortunately, too many pieces have been given this grade. Thus, the generic dated or high census silver disks are really fairly priced. Undervalued sleeper among the dates which are thought of as common is the 1935-D specimen. Other type dates highly recommended are the 1935 D and S w/sm '34, your 1937-S and the 1938 P,D,S pieces. Set wise, its the 1938 and 1935 w/sm '34 coinage. (Remember, the Philadelphia piece from the latter set is a common coin!) Very good future potential here. I would lower the MS-65 population figures by 35% for the generic dates and 25% for the lower census material. Again, only purchase eye appealing pieces. Never purchase without seeing the coin first!

Present MS-66 values are just too low — even if we combine the total higher census coinage. I would lower these latter figures by 25%. Excellent future potential for this grade, especially with the lower population strikings. I would decrease these numbers between 15% and 20%. Sleeper type dates are the 1938 P, D, S; 1935 D, S w/sm '34, the 1935-D and 1937 D creations. Set wise, it's your 1938 and 1935 w/sm '34 productions.

Excellent future potential in the undervalued lofty grade of MS-67.

To date, 10 Boones have been awarded the exceptional designation MS-68. From the 1935 w/sm '34 issue there now exist 1-P, 5-D and 2-S pieces. Add to the group one 1936-S and 1938-D striking. I would love to have one in my collection! Excellent future potential.

Some Boone pieces were produced from polished dies. These are classified as prooflike (P/L) by NGC. As of this writing, we can note that one 1936-S, three 1937-D, 17 1937-S, and three 1938-S pieces have been graded MS-64 PL. Three 1938-S pieces have been graded MS-63 PL; 16 1937-S graded MS-65 PL and two MS-66 PL. These are desired by collectors and command double to triple sheet prices. Beware of the raw polished, cleaned or doctored coin offered as a prooflike. They will not be slabbed by the major grading services. Always get a 30-day return agreement in writing should you purchase such a coin — which must be verified by an expert. Excellent future potential in all grades. The extremely rare Matte Proof 1938 set sold for $100,000 in April 1993! Consider this price a steal for the new owner!

Connecticut Tercentenary Half Dollar

Population Figures (NGC and PCGS combined)

DATE	MS-64	MS-65	MS-66	MS-67
1935	1274	897	179	11

Little price spread exists between pieces grading EF-AU and MS-63. Limited number of circulated offerings are usually cleaned or abused in some form. Think the higher grade, preferably an original flashy MS-63+ coin, should funds be available. Do the same for the MS-64 category. This is the area where any future potential begins — should that be your concern. Price spread between grades MS-64 and MS-65, during the May 1989 market high was $1,600! Appears to be past history. I would lower population count between 20% and 25%.

Attractive MS-65 strikings of this favored design are undervalued at current levels. Pass on the dark, dull and questionable offering. Spread between this and our next loftier rating was $2,000+, during the noted high. I would lower census count by 20%. Very good future potential.

Connecticuts grading MS-66 are too cheap at present levels. Pass on the dull, dark or questionable silver disk. I would deduct 20% from presented slabbed figures. Excellent future potential for this creation in MS-66 and MS-67 condition. The extremely rare Matte Proof was sold for $65,000 in April 1993!

Arkansas Centennial Half Dollar

	Population Figures (NGC and PCGS combined)			
DATE	MS-64	MS-65	MS-66	MS-67
1935	584	297	24	2
1935-D	409	300	52	5
1935-S	418	299	48	0
1936	438	157	18	2
1936-D	484	241	33	3
1936-S	454	235	15	3
1937	335	131	15	0
1937-D	367	195	24	2
1937-S	310	93	8	1
1938	224	100	9	0
1938-D	223	123	20	3
1938-S	209	95	7	0
1939	196	72	4	0
1939-D	184	104	20	0
1939-S	178	123	13	0

Not one Arkansas Centennial half dollar has been graded MS-68 to date!

Circulated type material usually encountered are those higher mintage strikings. Little price spread exists between such material graded EF-AU and MS-63. It is that abundant and offers little to average eye appeal. Thus, lack of strong interest. Same can be said for many of the 1935-1937 three piece sets grading MS-60 to MS-63, as well as unattractive MS-64 sets. Acquire for the joy of ownership.

Should one desire an MS-64 type coin of this issue, they total over 4,000 pieces graded — even if we lower the population figure by 20%! Focus only on the low census, attractive coinage, for any real future potential. Highly recommend the 1938 and 1939 P,D and S coinage — specially the 1939-S striking. As far as three-piece sets are concerned, attempt to locate at least MS-63+ material. If there exists a chance of any progress in the coming years, it resides here. Concentrate on the 1938 and 1939 sets — if funds permit. Otherwise just acquire for the pleasure of ownership.

In the 64 category, eye appealing 1938 and 1939 coinage must also be labeled underpriced. Unfortunately for the 1937 set, interest is lacking, although rarer than the earlier 1935 and 1936 sets. Real future lies in those alluring 1938 and 1939 sets when available. Add to this list any set which can be labeled MS-64+ "seductive," since the effect will be had by buyers 10 years from today. Such is highly recommended. Stay away from the dull, dark and unattractive coinage.

During the last market high (May 1989), the price for an Arkansas MS-65 type coin was $1,400! It has now fallen to $300. What happened? Let us begin by noting the now common date 1935 P, D and S strikings are too cheap. The scarcer 1936 D and S and 1937 D pieces are even more so, while all other Arkansas creations are extremely undervalued! It can be addressed that when combined, the population figure is high for the generic dates. Therefore, the value is realistic. Knowing how difficult accurately graded and appealing pieces are to come by, my response, based on 25 years of "battlefield experience" is that all is dependent upon the coin being examined. When it lacks drawing power and/or possesses surface negatives where they should not be or the grade is very questionable, I couldn't care less what the grading label insert indicates. To me, it's a MS-64.0 or MS-64.5 or MS-64.9 coin in a MS-65 holder. The real quality when offered will usually bring much more money. All is contingent on the buyer. However, most dealers will pay more for quality — especially in a hot market. Thus, the bad drives the good into hiding. It's a quantity of such lesser material in the marketplace which keeps prices from rising. I suggest never buying sight-unseen. See what you are acquiring. Predicated on the aforementioned and combined with grading label discarding, I would reduce population figures for the generic and semi-common dates by 45% or more. Census would be reduced by 35% or more for the rarer dates.

Highly recommend the following type dates in MS-65 condition for tremendous future potential: 1939-P, 1938-S, 1937-S, 1939-D, 1938-P, 1938-D, 1939-S and 1937-P creations. Set wise, focus on the 1937 through 1939 productions. All are extremely undervalued!

Same can be said for your MS-66 Arkansas commemorative half dollars. Even the higher 1935 D and S census dates are undervalued at these levels — if accurately graded. You can bet that few pieces rated at this level have been resubmitted in the past. Exceptional future here for all dates, especially the lower census issues.

MS-67 coinage is that rare. Only a few pieces have been granted such privileged status. Wish I owned a few! Tremendous potential in this grade.

Arkansas-Robinson Half Dollar

Population Figures (NGC and PCGS combined)

DATE	MS-63	MS-64	MS-65	MS-66
1936	769	1310	678	156

To date, 11 Robinsons have been encapsulated MS-67.

We have another issue which resides in the generic realm, up to grades MS-64+. Acquire only for the joy of collecting. Little price spread exists between pieces grading EF-AU through MS-63. Pieces rated MS-64 are fairly valued at present. Past dollar variation between the latter rating and MS-65 coinage was $1,500. History will repeat itself, but not as dramatically. Issue is also common in MS-64 condition, but not as easily located in the higher grades. I would reduce census between 25% and 30%. At this time, it's difficult to say whether President Clinton will become the catalyst for a future Arkansas and Robinson-Arkansas dealer promotion. Should this occur, expect prices to rise as more non-collectors acquire the coin.

Issue is undervalued and not as abundant, as its population figure indicates, in strict MS-65 condition. The key word is strict. I have seen a bit too many pieces which would not have been rated MS-65 during the last market high. These half dollars lack eye appeal or possess reverse facial negatives that would never have qualified them for the past high $1,800 bid. Pass on the dull, dark and questionable offering. Previous dollar spread between grades MS-65 and MS-66 was a huge $3,100. A historical replay will not be as strong. I would reduce census between 25% and 30%. Very good to excellent future potential for the strictly graded piece. Robinsons grading MS-66 are undervalued, at present levels. It's a great coin to own. Pass on the unattractive offering. I would lower census count by 20% to 25%. Excellent future potential. This issue is quite underrated and rare in the MS-67 category. Should funds be available, procure this creation.

Hudson, NY, Sesquicentennial Half Dollar

Population Figures (NGC and PCGS combined)

DATE	MS-63	MS-64	MS-65	MS-66
1935	614	856	370	44

To date, only 3 Hudsons have been graded MS-67.

Most circulated offerings will be of the cleaned and abused variety. They are worth much less than current bid levels. MS-60 coinage is usually not attractive, so think MS-63, should funds permit. Fairly priced at current levels in MS-60 through MS-64 condition. Acquire only for the joy of collecting. Potential gain — if that matters — begins with eye appealing pieces grading MS-64+. (Some people say they couldn't care less should the coin never gain value!) Past value spread between the latter and our MS-65 rating during the May 1989 high was $3,700. That appears to be history. I would lower census between 25% and 30%. Expect this issue to be promoted when the bull market arrives.

Real future for this issue resides in the eye appealing, strictly graded MS-65 specimen. Pass on the unattractive and questionable offering. Popular creation offers excellent possibilities and is recommended. Value spread between this grade and MS-66, during the said high was $5200. Population figures can be reduced between 20% and 25%. In the loftier grades, the Hudson is undervalued and offers excellent future potential, to those who can afford such a rating.

California-Pacific Exposition (San Diego) Half Dollars

Population Figures (NGC and PCGS combined)

DATE	MS-63	MS-64	MS-65	MS-66
1935-S	637	2646	4910	644
1936-D	307	1867	3198	265

To date, 31 1935-S half dollars have been encapsulated MS-67, while one piece was granted MS-68 status. Also 13 1936-D strikings have been rated MS-67.

With the highest population figures for MS-65 strikings, as individual and series coin totals, just procure EF-AU through MS-65 pieces only for the joy of owning a beautifully design coin. Buy it because you like it. Price spread between EF-AU and MS-64 rated pieces is almost nonexistent. Latter grade is slightly undervalued for both creations. Definitely a promotional candidate, when the numismatic scene heats up. Just remember that as the aforesaid runs its course, it's back to present value levels.

Each striking now has the honor of possessing the highest encapsulation figure in MS-65 condition. Part of a large hoard which entered the marketplace in the recent past is responsible. Several thousand pieces of each date from the said stockpile could still be submitted for slabbing! Both issues will then flaunt the true meaning of the word common. Their owners are rumored to be in at face value or close to it! During the past market peak, price variation between the MS-64 and MS-65 San Diego was $350 for the 1935-S production and $490 for the 1936-D creation. Between the MS-65 and MS-66 classification, spread was $1,870 and $2,500 for the respective dates. We should never say never, but I'll say that for this situation. Population figures can be reduced by 25% to 30% for MS-65 coinage. Who really cares, in this case?

In MS-66 condition, both popular issues are undervalued — especially the 1936 Denver coinage! Recommend the latter date. Very good future potential. Do not believe many of those hoard coins will inflate its census. Pass on the dull, dark and questionable offering. I would reduce population count by 20% to 25%, for each issue. Good future potential for the 1935-S commemorative, based on current values. However, think "36." Both strikings are also undervalued which rate MS-67 status. Very good to excellent future potential for each issue.

Old Spanish Trail Half Dollar

Population Figures (NGC and PCGS combined)

DATE	MS-63	MS-64	MS-65	MS-66
1935	218	787	889	223

To date, 16 Spanish Trails have been encapsulated MS-67.

This beautiful and very popular creation is currently the second most expensive circulated U.S. commemorative one-year design ($600) produced between 1892 and 1954. Your Hawaiian takes first place honors ($650), while the Antietam takes third ($380). The limited number which reside in this state are usually whizzed to some degree or abused, thus worth less. Little priced spread exists between grades EF-AU and MS-64. Think the latter rating if possible.

Average potential in your EF-AU-MS-63 classifications. Average to good potential in MS-64 condition. Pieces rated MS-65 offer good to very good possibilities. Pass on the dull dark and unattractive offerings. I would lower the census between 25% and 30% for the MS-65 and MS-66 categories.

Previous dollar variation between grades MS-64 and MS-65, during the last market peak was $1,600. Your MS-65 and MS-66, differential was a lesser $1500. That's past tense, unless the market becomes red hot. Excellent future potential exists in grades MS-66 and in the lofty MS-67 category. Definitely undervalued, at current levels ($3,300), in latter grade. Those who are blessed to have the means should make the acquisition.

Providence, RI, Tercentenary Half Dollar

Population Figures (NGC and PCGS combined)

DATE	MS-63	MS-64	MS-65	MS-66
1936	376	1114	805	128
1936-D	323	891	642	106
1936-S	359	785	416	49
1936 P/L	3	9	11	2

To date, two Philadelphia and San Francisco striking, as well as six Denver creations have been slabbed MS-67.

NGC has also encapsulated an MS-62 and MS-63 San Francisco half dollar with the PL or prooflike designation.

As for commemorative coin designs produced between 1892 and 1954, this issue's obverse does not rate too high among collectors. The depicted Roger Williams has the look of a robot from the old Flash Gordon serials. Remember Emperor Ming? Little dollar spread currently exists between grades EF-AU and MS-64. Thus, think the latter. Acquire up to a MS-63 or the just-made-it MS-64 specimen, only for the joy of ownership. Both branch mint productions are about equally as rare, in these grades. The Philadelphia striking is the most abundant. Somewhat undervalued in MS-64. Census figures reflect the true rarity for each facility. Should a type coin be desired, I recommend the branch mint strikings. Past peak dollar variance between grades MS-64 and MS-65 was approximately $600 for the type coin and $1,600 for the set. That's past history. I would lower population figures by 25% to 30%. Average future potential for this grade. Pass on the unattractive offering. Good to very good potentiality for the prooflike NGC encapsulations and the MS-64+ half dollar.

In strict MS-65 condition, our San Francisco creation is quite undervalued, as an individual issue. Bid level is almost equal to the higher census, other two Rhode Island productions. Excellent future potential for the west coast piece. Your Philadelphia and Denver issues are somewhat undervalued at current levels. Their combined population is not exactly small and the issue would not win a popularity contest. I would rate their future possibilities as good. Reject the dull, dark and questionable offering. Price spread between your MS-65 and MS-66 ratings was a large $1300 for the type coin and a whopping $11,000 for the 3-piece set. At the time, few S-Mint pieces had been encapsulated MS-66. History will repeat itself, but not to such extremes. I would reduce population numbers between 20% and 25%. Excellent potential for the NGC prooflike encapsulations.

In MS-66 condition, the issue is definitely undervalued, especially the San Francisco. It's the rarest of the 3-piece set and presently flaunts a bid $600 higher than the other strikings. There is always the chance that such can be procured at the type coin price, from the unalert seller. Pass on the unattractive offering. Excellent potential for the S Mint production. I would rate the other Mints possibilities as very good to excellent. To date, two Philadelphia prooflike pieces have been rated MS-66. Rhode Islands graded MS-67 are rare and great to own.

Cleveland Centennial-Great Lakes Exposition Half Dollar

Population Figures (NGC and PCGS combined)

DATE	MS-64	MS-65	MS-66	MS-67
1936	2365	1164	177	11

Little price range currently exists between grades EF-AU and MS-64! Consider acquiring only for the pride of ownership. Suggest MS-64+ specimens. During our last May 1989 market high, price spread between its MS-64 and MS-65 rating was almost $1,500. Will never come near past values again. Promotable item. Appears that the issue came out of the woodwork. I would reduce population figures between 25% and 30%. Still no real dent.

Only real hope of future potential lies in eye-appealing MS-65+ pieces. A $3200 spread existed during the last noted high between MS-65 and MS-66 material! That's past history, not to be duplicated. I would reduce census count by 30%. Undervalued in MS-66 and loftier condition. Excellent future potential here and in the loftier state of preservation.

Wisconsin Territorial Centennial Half Dollar

Population Figures (NGC and PCGS combined)

DATE	MS-64	MS-65	MS-66	MS-67
1936	1153	1979	845	106

To date, one Wisconsin has been encapsulated MS-68 (PCGS).

    With population figures like these, I suggest procurement only for the joy of collecting. Issue flaunts the fourth highest population figure in MS-65, as well as the third most abundant in MS-66, for an individual design. (The Iowa holds MS-66 first place honors!) No major price spread currently exists between EF-AU and MS-65 condition. During the last market peak, we had a price difference of $700 between MS-64 and MS-65 coinage and $1,100 between the MS-65 and MS-66 rating. Don't expect history to repeat itself! Fair to average long term potential. The Wisconsin was heavily promoted in the said grades during the last market heat. Pieces appear to have come out of the numismatic woodwork. Needless to say, as the next hot market arrives, expect the coin to be "pushed." The astute can profit from this situation — if not greedy! Don't hold too long! When the temperature begins to drop, so will this issue's value. I would reduce census count by 30% to 35%, in grades MS-64 through MS-66. Somewhat undervalued in the latter and MS-67 ratings, at present. Average future potential in grades MS-66 and MS-67 for the long term.

Cincinnati Music Center Half Dollars

Population Figures (NGC and PCGS combined)

DATE	MS-63	MS-64	MS-65	MS-66
1936	223	451	206	18
1936-D	181	528	432	108
1936-S	275	490	117	11

To date, only six pieces (4 PCGS; 2 NGC) all of which have been struck at the Denver Mint have been graded MS-67.

    Little price spread exists in grades EF-AU through MS-63. The limited number of coins which reside in your circulated category are usually cleaned or abused in some fashion. Focus sights on MS-63+ — as well as MS-64 coinage strictly for the joy of ownership! During a hot market, prices will rise for a short time, then retreat to previous levels. Attractive specimens not plagued by excessive bag marks and other surface negatives especially on the devices, are most recommended. The Philadelphia striking is the hardest coin to locate in the MS-64 classification. Denver coin appears to be the easiest based on population figures. The point to comprehend is that it is the nicest looking or flashiest of this issue. I would estimate that between 20% and 25% have been resubmitted in attempt to acquire a better grade. Figure about 15% crackout for the other branch mints (D & S) in this grade — with most of these grading labels cast into the garbage pail! There are a number of dealers who purposely destroy these inserts. Their objective is to inflate, in order to make an issue appear more available that it actually is. Type price spread between MS-64 and MS-65 during the May 1989 market high was about $2,000. In truth, much of the MS-64 Cincinnati material that I examined for higher grade possibilities never had a chance. Any hope for future potential lies in alluring MS-64+ and higher graded pieces.

There exists in this marketplace a limited number of MS-65 encapsulations which are not attractive and flaunt a questionable grade. Pass on these. Our Denver creation is the flashiest of the three coin production, as well as the easiest to obtain. I would deduct its census figures by 30% and reduce the others between 15% and 20%. Difference between MS-65 and MS-66 type coin value during the aforesaid market high was approximately $6,000! Excellent future potential for all three dates. A tremendous tomorrow will be in store for MS-66 coinage. It's quite difficult to locate — especially the rarer branch mint pieces. Owning an MS-67 rated jewel is analogous to placing the coin next to your ear and believing you are hearing the music of Stephen Foster.

Long Island Tercentenary Half Dollar

Population Figures (NGC and PCGS combined)

DATE	MS-63	MS-64	MS-65	MS-66
1936	1135	1658	748	130

To date, eight Long Islands have been graded MS-67.

Issue is not tough to obtain in less than Mint State condition. Procure a nice looking coin with undoctored, original surfaces. Not much of a price variance between pieces rated EF-AU and MS-63. It's a carbon copy of the said between our MS-63 and MS-64 classification. Should funds be available, procure the latter and lower rated Long Island commemorative half dollars, only for the pleasure of ownership. It's your MS-64+, alluring silver disk which is undervalued presently and offers a hopeful future. Pass on the dull, dark or unattractive piece. Price spread between this grade and your MS-65 rating during the May 1989 high was $2,000! That's past history. I would lower the census 20% to 25%. Accurately graded and flashy MS-65 specimens are undervalued at current levels. It is that small number of just made it MS-65 pieces and those not too attractive available encapsulations which keep price levels down. Were these cracked out and resubmitted, there's a strong chance most would be downgraded. Past price spread between MS-65 and MS-66 coinage was $3,100! Could be all past history. I would deduct between 25% and 30% from population count.

Eye appealing Long Islands, grading MS-66 are undervalued, at present levels. I would reduce census between 20% and 25%. Excellent future potential for our underrated creation in this grade and loftier.

York County, Maine, Tercentenary Half Dollar

Population Figures (NGC and PCGS combined)

DATE	MS-64	MS-65	MS-66	MS-67
1936	1011	1807	1034	279

To date, eight Yorks have been encapsulated MS-68.

With census figures as indicated, simply buy this issue because you like it and want to own it. Our York is now the fifth most encapsulated 1892-1954 commemorative half dollar, in MS-65 condition and second to the Iowa, when rated MS-66. No major price spread currently exists between the EF-AU and MS-65 classifications. During the last hot market of 1989, there was an approximate $800 difference between the MS-64-MS-65 and MS-65-MS-66 grades. No historical repetition here. I would lower census by 30%-35% for these levels. Unfortunately, our York coins came out in droves from the numismatic woodwork! Fair to average potential for this creation in all grades! Nonetheless, expect issue to again be promoted. Gains can be made by the astute, as long as they don't hold their hoard of Yorks too long or become greedy, awaiting the peak. Where will the buyers be for this very common issue, at these inflated levels, when the market begins to slip or starts losing some momentum? Ditto other similar productions, as the Iowa, San Diego, Wisconsin, etc.

Bridgeport, Conn., Centennial Half Dollar

Population Figures (NGC and PCGS combined)

DATE	MS-64	MS-65	MS-66	MS-67
1936	1678	1020	131	1

Little price spread between grades EF-AU and MS-64 condition. Very common coin up to MS-64 condition. Only acquire for the pure joy of ownership. When doing so, think flashy MS-64+! During the last market high, price spread between MS-64 and MS-65 was over $1,100! Past history. I would lower population figure between 30% and 35% for this grade. It's still no big deal. Ditto for the MS-65 category. At current levels, this coin is undervalued. Howbeit, too many Bridgeports graded MS-65 possess reverses which grade some degree of MS-64 or MS-64+, due to numismatic negatives and lack of metal fill marks. (Check out that modernistic eagle!) Coins possessing flash or real eye appeal and are on grade, will be the only MS-65 pieces which are recommended and have any future potential. Its design is not the most popular creation. Price spread between MS-65 and MS-66 during the last market high was over $4,200! How many times do you think one would resubmit a coin, if he or she believed it had a chance of making the next grade? When the market heats up, so will the accurately graded Bridgeport, although the population count may hold down the value of the issue.

Real future potential lies in the MS-66 grade, where it is certainly under priced and highly recommended! I would lower population figures between 10% and 15%. Focus on attractive pieces, staying away from any dark and unattractive specimens. To date, only one Bridgeport was graded MS-67. This informs one about the rareness of the issue in this grade.

Lynchburg, Va., Half Dollar

Population Figures (NGC and PCGS combined)

DATE	MS-63	MS-64	MS-65	MS-66
1936	448	1152	972	283

To date, 34 Lynchburgs have been graded MS-67, with none higher.

Of the limited number of pieces which reside in the circulated category, most are abused or doctored Uncs. Small price spread exists between EF-AU and MS-63 coinage. MS-64 material is fairly priced at present levels. Acquire for the joy of collecting. Should future potential be of concern, then think eye appealing MS-64+ specimens. Reject the unattractive offering. May 1989 market high spread between the latter and your MS-65 rating was $1,100! Don't expect a historical repeat. I would reduce population figures between 25% and 30%.

In MS-65 condition, the Lynchburg is somewhat underpriced at current levels. Pass on the dark, dull and unattractive offering. Should you possess the aforesaid, strongly recommend its sale when the issue is promoted in grades MS-64 and higher, during our next hot market. Attractive pieces offer good future potential. Past high price range between MS-65 and MS-66 rating was $2,500. Census can be reduced between 20% and 25%. History will not be repeated.

Real potential resides in alluring coinage rated MS-66. It can be flashy or possess beautiful natural colored toning. Very good future potential. I would lower population figures between 20% and 25%. It's an uncommon coin in MS-67 condition. However, I would rather acquire rarer and more popular issues at a lesser or similar price, such as the Lincoln or Illinois-Lincoln.

Albany Charter Half Dollar

Population Figures (NGC and PCGS combined)

DATE	MS-64	MS-65	MS-66	MS-67
1936	1435	1204	359	40

Issue is not abundant in circulated condition. Cleaned or whizzed (wire brushed) pieces which hide actual metal loss on reverse beaver's hip are usually offered. Little price difference between material graded EF-AU and MS-63. No real potential here. MS-64 coinage is slightly undervalued, while MS-65 specimens are fully priced at present. Latter is a promotional candidate. When promotion is over, it's a return to previous lower price levels. Only acquire the common Albany in the above mentioned grades for the joy of ownership or to possess as part of the 50-piece or 144-piece commemorative set. I would estimate that population figures for grades MS-64 and MS-65 can be lowered by as much as 30%, due to crack outs and the non-return of grading labels. That still leaves us with high population figures.

Future for this creation lies in your attractive MS-66 and loftier grades. I would consider a 20% census deduction from the given population figures. Certainly most recommended for acquisition at current undervalued levels. I know of 11 MS-67 Albanys that were cracked out from the slabs, in hopes of the wonder MS-68 grade. Wonder how many of the insert labels have been destroyed and not returned? Currently, not a single coin has been granted the grade!

Elgin, Ill., Centennial Half Dollar

Population Figures (NGC and PCGS combined)

DATE	MS-64	MS-65	MS-66	MS-67
1936	1709	1573	324	23

To date, no Elgins have been graded MS-68.

Not much of a dollar spread exists between this creation rated EF-AU and MS-64. Limited amount of circulated offering are abused Uncs. During the last May 1989 market high, the Elgin was bid at $1,550. Pieces were selling at $1,700+. Over the last couple of years, these coins seem to have come out of the wood-work, now placing it within the generic or common category. I would acquire an attractive specimen only for the joy of ownership. Based on its past value — which will never be attained again, unless massive inflation develops — it certainly is a great promotable item. Sell when values rise, during our next bull market. Future potential begins with strictly graded MS-66 material. Good future potential. Somewhat undervalued. In MS-67 condition, its a rare coin. Pass on the Satin Finish Proof Elgin. Too controversial. Nothing more than an early strike. Suggest ignoring accompanying documentation letter.

San Francisco-Oakland Bay Bridge Half Dollar

Population Figures (NGC and PCGS combined)

DATE	MS-64	MS-65	MS-66	MS-67
1936-S	1354	1155	347	52

To date, two specimens have been graded MS-68 by PCGS.

Little price difference exists between grades EF-AU and MS-63. Coins grading MS-64 are somewhat undervalued. However, issue can be obtained in all mentioned grades with little difficulty. Acquire for joy of collecting. For those who would like to see their silver bear rise moderately in value, suggest acquiring a flashy MS-64+ specimen. I would reduce this grade's census figures by 25%.

Today, this popular issue is also available in MS-65 condition. Large census figure could be reduced by 30%. Key is to acquire a bright, attractive specimen or one possessing the kind of toning which enhances the coin. Average future potential. Suggest procuring only because you like the creation. When the market gets hot, expect the Bay Bridge to be promoted. Suggest sale at that time. Can procure for less in the future.

Undervalued in the MS-66 category. Very good potential here. I would reduce population figures by 25%. Definitely recommend acquiring a captivating specimen, if he crosses your path.

Ditto the lofty MS-67 grade. Also very undervalued and highly recommended, should funds permit. I know of seven grading inserts which were cast to various garbage containers in the past, in unsuccessful hopes of the elusive MS-68 grade. Only two pieces graded as such to date.

Columbia, SC, Sesquicentennial Half Dollar

Population Figures (NGC and PCGS combined)

DATE	MS-64	MS-65	MS-66	MS-67
1936	536	705	265	21
1936-D	380	629	439	87
1936-S	426	645	424	32

To date, MS-68 status has been granted to six Denver and four San Francisco strikings!

Little price differential exists between grades EF to MS-63. Limited number of circ offerings are those Uncs which have been cleaned or abused in some fashion. Issue is fairly priced up to the MS-65 category. Slightly underrated. Procure for the pure joy of collecting. Great candidate for a future promotion, as is the MS-66 coin. During the May 1989 market high, there existed a $400 difference between MS-64 and MS-65 ratings. From MS-65 to MS-66, it was $1,000. Future potential exists in eye appealing pieces grading MS-65+. I would reduce census figures between 25% and 30% for the MS-64 and MS-65 categories.

In MS-66 condition, your Philadelphia creation is undervalued. Very good potential. Branch mints are moderately underrated. I would deduct population figures between 15% and 20%. MS-67 Columbians are somewhat underpriced at present levels. Best bets are the lower mintage Philadelphia and San Francisco productions, especially if they can be had at a type coin price. This reflects the most abundant offerings. I would eliminate 15% of their census figures. Excellent potential. Who would not want to own a slabbed MS-68 Columbia? During a hot market, their asking price has to skyrocket. Great coin to possess.

Delaware Tercentenary Half Dollar

Population Figures (NGC and PCGS combined)

DATE	MS-64	MS-65	MS-66	MS-67
1936	1332	939	238	12

To date, no Delawares have been graded MS-68.

Little price spread exists between EF-AU and MS-63 ratings. Limited supply of circulated offerings are usually abused Uncirculated pieces of this not too popular design. Fairly priced — if not fully priced — up to MS-64 condition. Only acquire for the joy of collecting. Future potential, should that be your concern, begins with attractive pieces rates MS-64+. Price difference between the latter grade and MS-65 was almost $1,400 during the May 1989 high. I would remove between 20% and 25% from current population figures.

A strictly graded MS-65, eye appealing Delaware is the type of coin which can only be declared undervalued. Howbeit, continued population growth can have a future negative effect on the issue and its value. Only time will tell. Pass on the dull, or dark, or unattractive offering. Do likewise for the rainbow toned or flashy coin — exhibiting just too many surface negatives in the primary focal areas, as discussed within the Delaware chapter. They just seem to cross my path. These were not the $2,000 kind of coin offered during our two market highs in 1988 and 1989. Spread between the latter and MS-64 ratings was $1,400. I would lower census figures by 30%. Strictly grades MS-66 Delawares are too cheap at current levels. Again, pass on the dull, dark and questionable. Exceptional future potential here, as well as in the rarer MS-67 category.

Battle of Gettysburg Half Dollar

Population Figures (NGC and PCGS combined)

DATE	MS-64	MS-65	MS-66	MS-67
1936	1478	942	175	18

To date, one Gettysburg has been graded MS-68, by PCGS.

At present, not much of a price spread exists between EF-AU and MS-64. When available, circulated offerings are cleaned or souvenir abused Unc.

Acquire for the joy of acquisition. Limited future potential begins with attractive pieces grading MS-64+. During the last market high, a $1,500 difference existed between the later and our MS-65 rating. That's past tense. I would lower census count between 10% and 15%. At current levels, the eye appealing MS-65 specimen is undervalued. Popular design offers very good future potential. Pass on the dark, dull and disputable offering. During the aforesaid high, a spread of $4000 existed between your MS-65 and MS-66 categories! More past history.

Undervalued in MS-66 condition, especially if a captivating specimen. Remember those reverse shields can exhibit only a few minute marks — unless the coin glows in the dark. I would lower population figures between 15% and 20%. Excellent future potential at this level and for Gettysburgs rated MS-67.

Norfolk, Va., Bicentennial Half Dollar

Population Figures (NGC and PCGS combined)

DATE	MS-64	MS-65	MS-66	MS-67
1936	495	1196	1279	345

To date, 42 Norfolks have been graded MS-68! That's the most of any individual commemorative half dollar struck between 1892 and 1954! (Your Iowa striking owns the largest total in MS-66 condition).

Small quantity of existing circulated material usually turns out to be that of the cleaned or abused variety. Not much of a dollar spread currently exists between EF-AU and MS-65 condition. These are fairly priced. Acquire all grades up to MS-66 only for the pure joy of collecting. Creation came out of the numismatic woodwork! Fair future potential. I would reduce population figures in grades MS-64 through MS-66 by 30% to 35%. Procure the attractive offering. Only real tomorrow for the Norfolk appears to lie in the MS-67 category. Great promotional candidate, as will be the MS-65 and MS-66 coinage. Good future potential for the "Lofty 67."

Roanoke Island, NC, Half Dollar

Population Figures (NGC and PCGS combined)

DATE	MS-64	MS-65	MS-66	MS-67
1937	1441	1867	601	130
PL	5	13	1	0

To date, four Roanokes have been graded MS-68; one rated MS-63 PL (NGC).

This creation resides in the realm of the common. Not much of a price spread currently exists between grades EF-AU and MS-65. Think a minimum of MS-64. Acquire up to grade MS-65 — only for the pride of ownership! Latter rating is slightly undervalued. Past dollar variance between your MS-64 and MS-65 ratings was $550! Between the just noted and our MS-66 classification, there once existed a $1,400 difference. That's now past tense. This issue like the Elgin, Iowa and San Diego appears to have emerged from the numismatic woodwork in droves. I would reduce census figures in grades MS-64 through MS-66 between 20% and 30%. Fair to average potential.

In MS-66 condition, our Roanoke population figures are high for the grade. Nonetheless, you have only a one year production. It's a grade that is desired by many who could not afford or chose not to spend the required $2,300 during the May 1989 high. Thus, promotion and demand should offer this design good to very good future potential. Ditto your lofty MS-67 specimen with its high count for the grade. During the last market heat, bid was at $5,000. Census was much lower. Historical repetition doesn't appear likely — although you can bet issue will be promoted.

Battle Of Antietam Half Dollar

Population Figures (NGC and PCGS combined)

DATE	MS-64	MS-65	MS-66	MS-67
1937	970	1285	436	69

Five pieces have been graded MS-68 (NGC 1; PCGS 4).

Few Antietams saw actual circulation. Those offered in this grade are usually cleaned or possess whizzed surfaces. Little price spread between EF-AU and MS-64 condition. Too many specimens are now slabbed MS-65, as well as MS-66. Currently, fairly priced in these states. Even if an estimated 30% population deduction in grades MS-64 and MS-65, as well as 20% in MS-66 — due to resubmissions and grading label throw aways — were right on the money, the issue must be classified as common in these grades. Slabbing census now makes this quite apparent. Acquire the above noted grades only for the joy of collecting. Howbeit, continuous demand for the MS-66 coin will make values rise.

At present, the MS-67 specimen is the only noted rating which offers the most future potential. (Who would not love to own one of those MS-68 pieces?) Should one be able to afford this creation, it is highly recommended.

New Rochelle, NY, Half Dollar

Population Figures (NGC and PCGS combined)

DATE	MS-63	MS-64	MS-65	MS-66
1938	251	1125	1218	294
PL	4	32	23	21

To date, 30 New Rochelle commemorative half dollars have been graded MS-67, as well as six prooflike pieces.

If there were only 50 presentation pieces struck for the Westchester County Coin Club, why have 86 pieces been granted prooflike (PL) status by NGC? Not all prooflikes were presentation pieces! Those coins possessing lesser deep mirrored field, are the prooflike coins — struck after the special production. Their count is combined with the deeper mirrored presentation New Rochelles — which for a short period were labeled SPECIMENS by NGC. Also add to this total the crackout labels which were discarded and not deleted!

Limited number of circulated offerings are abused or doctored Uncs. Not much of a price spread between pieces rated EF-AU and MS-65. Issue appears fairly priced at present, in grades MS-60 through MS-65. Recommend acquiring the eye appealing New Rochelle — hopefully in MS-65 condition — only for the joy of collecting! Pass on the dull, dark and unattractive offering — unless the price is very right and only a representative example is needed. Apply same logic throughout the series.

Creation whose MS-64 and MS-65 census can be lowered between 25% and 30%, should increase in value if promoted during the next hot market. Fair future potential. Seems as if this creation came out of the woodwork in grades MS-64 through MS-65. In strict MS-66 condition, issue is somewhat undervalued. Any real future resides in this rating. Pass on the un-eye appealing coin. I would reduce population figures by 20% and 25%. Good future potential. Underrated in the celebrated MS-67 category. Very good future potential.

Iowa Statehood Centennial Half Dollar

Population Figures (NGC and PCGS combined)

DATE	MS-64	MS-65	MS-66	MS-67
1946	1738	3150	1572	232

To date, eight pieces have been graded MS-68.

The Iowa Centennial half dollar — be it raw or slabbed — should be acquired only for the joy of collecting. Little price spread exists between your EF-AU and MS-64 category. Future potential does not look promising for this lovely creation. The exception will be your MS-67 and MS-68 grade (Pop. 9) for those who can afford this lofty level.

Should you buy one of the 500 commemorative half dollars offered by the State of Iowa — which were set aside in 1946 for scheduled sale in 1996 — but now offered at $510? At this asking price only purchase especially created, sealed plastic case containing issue for the joy of owning a piece of U.S. commemorative history! It's just too expensive and appears to offer little if any future potential. In all fairness, this $510 tab was set when bid levels fluctuated in the $500-$510 range for MS-65 coinage and $900 for pieces grading MS-66. Since that period, values have plummeted to $100 in MS-65 condition and $225 in your MS-66 grade. Moreover, each of the historical coins (as well as the extra 500 pieces set aside for sale in the year 2046) are coated with Egyptian lacquer, which can hide surface negatives such as hairline scratches, small nicks or hits, etc. According to a numismatic staff member of the Smithsonian Institution, even boiling the coin in hot water — as per removal instruction of the person who coated these 1,000 coins in 1946 — will not eliminate 100% of this glossy surface coating. Others who have experimented or used this substance claim your coin can turn dark! Aforesaid appears to be the reason why the major slabbing services would not encapsulate these coins. Howbeit, they were never sent nor was the said ever considered. If the asking price were lowered to $200-$250 instead of $510, thereby adjusting to current market and economic conditions, chances of a sellout would seem more likely.

Booker T. Washington Half Dollars

DATE	Population Figures (NGC and PCGS combined)			
	MS-64	MS-65	MS-66	MS-67
1946	935	861	177	10
1946-D	561	515	114	7
1946-S	911	726	176	16
1947	289	214	9	0
1947-D	203	149	5	0
1947-S	224	330	16	0
1948	312	355	12	0
1948-D	299	355	26	0
1948-S	242	464	42	1
1949	295	386	27	1
1949-D	327	372	18	0
1949-S	205	506	57	0
1950	244	297	14	0
1950-D	264	258	11	0
1950-S	325	646	73	2
1951	538	291	28	2
1951-D	233	311	18	1
1951-S	123	462	64	1

To date, no B.T.W. coinage has been encapsulated MS-68.

All of this creation should be acquired only for the joy of collecting, up to grades MS-64. Interest in the series is lacking. Were this to change, prices would rise. Pass on the dull, dark and unattractive individual coin or set.

Most people who own BTW MS-64 coinage usually observe enough surface negatives to not even consider slabbing. They believe it isn't worthwhile, with the cost of slabbing, and price levels so low. Census would be much higher if they submitted! Should MS-64 coinage be desired, consider the 1951-S, 1949-S, 1947-D, 1947-S, 1950-P and 1950-D strikings! Average potential in this rating.

At current levels, all sets are quite underrated. Problem stems from lack of heavy interest in the series. Howbeit, when the market heat arrives, prices will rise! I would rate the 1947-D, 1947-P and 1950-D as the rarest issues in MS-65 condition. Specimens dated 1951-P, 1950-P and 1951-D are about equal in rarity. Pieces dated 1947-S, 1948-D, 1948-P, 1949-D and 1949-P follow suit but are somewhat more available than the aforesaid dates. Still more abundant, but equal in difficulty to obtain are the 1948-S, 1951-S, 1946-D and 1949-S creations. The 1950-S is not hard to locate, while the 1946-P and S strikings are the most abundant and easiest to obtain.

Unless one desires the complete set in MS-65 condition, I would only recommend the 1947-D, 1950-D, 1951-P and 1947-P for type acquisition. Pieces should be attractive.

Issues offering very good to excellent future potential are the 1947-D, 1947-P and 1950-D BTW. Except for the most common issues which possess little potential, the less abundant dates such as the 1951-P, 1947-D, 1950-P, 1951-D and 1947-S offer good to very good future potential. I would reduce population figures for each date between 10% and 20%.

As you may have gathered, the real value for the rarer individual type coins and some sets are unjustly held down by the more abundant MS-64 and MS-65 1946-1951 BTW coinage within the series. Population figures in total certainly reflect large availability, should a type coin be needed. What should matter is the attractiveness of the silver disk. Too many coins that I've encountered which graded MS-65, didn't give a flicker! When contemplating acquisition, it should not be of the common variety.

At current levels, all recommended issues are certainly undervalued. The individual striking and three-piece sets are too cheap. However, it's a get in-get out quick situation for the grade.

I would rate the 1947-D the rarest issue in MS-66 condition along with the 1947-P, 1948-P, 1950-D and 1950-P. Specimens dated 1947-S, 1949-D, 1950-P and 1951-D won't be much easier to locate. Your 1948-D, 1949-P, 1951-P and 1948-S strikings also won't be too readily available. Equal in rarity. BTWs dated 1949-S, 1951-S and 1950-S will be somewhat more procurable than the previous dates. They certainly won't be seen in abundance, as most reside in collections. One's chance of possessing a MS-66 BTW type coin or set lies in the 1946-S, 1946-P and 1946-D commemorative production.

In MS-66 condition, I strongly suggest the 1947 P-D-S and 1948 P-D-S.

1950 P-D-S, 1949-P, 1949-D, 1951-P AND 1951-D for type acquisition. Needless to say, I don't know of too many people who would not find a complete eye-appealing BTW MS-66 set desirable!

In MS-67 condition, the 1946 issues make up the most of your population. A delight to add to your collection. One beautiful slabbed NGC rainbow toned

1946-S specimen just sold for $1,500! Bid price for the set is $2,000! What does bid mean in this instance? Excellent future potential for this lofty grade!

NGC Prooflike BTW Census

DATE	MS-64	MS-65	MS-66
1946	0	0	0
1946-D	0	0	0
1946-S	4	2	0
1947	0	0	0
1947-D	0	0	0
1947-S	9	13	2
1948	0	1	0
1948-D	0	0	0
1948-S	3	6	0
1949	1	1	0
1949-D	0	0	0
1949-S	0	0	0
1950	0	0	0
1950-D	0	0	0
1950-S	3	14	3
1951	0	0	0
1951-D	0	1	0
1951-S	0	6	3

No PL coins have been graded MS-67 to date. Two 1947-S pieces have been slabbed MS-63.

Should one possess prooflike MS-63 pieces, it will pay to submit if it is not cleaned or whizzed. Coin will certainly bring much more money than if kept unslabbed! PL surface must be present on both side of the coin! These creations produced from repolished dies are not abundant as one can observe. I know of collectors who will pay many times over bid for the issue. They resemble near brilliant Proofs. Excellent future potential in all grades.

Be aware of the unscrupulous offering raw or unslabbed PL specimens offered for sale. Many which were evaluated in coin collections or have crossed my path at coin shows had been polished or dipped in liquid mercury on a few occasions, to dupe the uninformed. Other legitimate pieces were whizzed on BTW's portrait to improve the coin's appearance and grade or were cleaned and not slabbable, while others were PL on only one side.

George Washington Carver-Booker T. Washington Half Dollars

	Population Figures (NGC and PCGS combined)			
DATE	MS-64	MS-65	MS-66	MS-67
1951	305	86	13	1
1951-D	363	146	6	0
1951-S	289	439	33	1
1952	1358	656	71	0
1952-D	344	95	1	0
1952-S	357	305	18	1
1953	340	113	6	0
1953-D	357	76	1	0

1953-S	514	344	30	1
1954	459	142	14	0
1954-D	425	96	4	0
1954-S	556	333	25	0

The larger 1952-P, 1954-S, 1953-S and 1951-P strikings will be located with little effort, in grades EF-AU through MS-64 condition. Price spread is almost non-existent, so think MS-64. In fact, the entire 1951-1954 coinage can be located easily in grades MS-60 through MS-64. Current values are rather low — but few seem to care. When promoted, the sets rise in worth to some degree. However when the promotion is over, prices return to past levels. Set rarity order in MS-64 condition: 1951, 1953, 1952 and 1954. Average future potential.

The issues most difficult to locate in strict MS-65 condition are the 1953-D, 1951-P, 1952-D and 1954-D followed by the 1953-P, 1954-P and 1951-D. As you know there are some very questionable slabbed MS-65 specimens and there exists solid MS-65 coinage. The first four noted dates are highly recommended. Remainder of strikings are available — especially the 1952 Philadelphia issue.

I would reduce population figures for each date between 10% and 20%. Excellent future potential for the above mentioned rarer issues.

Good to very good potential in the remaining dates. Average potential for the very common 1952-P and 1951-S productions.

In MS-66 condition, we are talking about a rare coin, if accurately graded! The only dates that one might have a chance of acquiring slabbed by the three major services (ANACS, NGC, PCGS) are the 1952 Philadelphia, plus 1951 and 1953 San Francisco strikings. I know of seven 1954-S and eight 1952-S specimens graded MS-66 which were resubmitted in the hopes of a higher grade. Labels were not returned for population deletion! All MS-66 C-W coinage is highly recommended! Excellent future potential in lofty grade for the issue. Needless to say, MS-67 "Carvers" are rare pieces.

Modern Commemorative Coinage 1892-1993

Most of the issues produced to date should only be acquired for the joy of collecting. Buy them because you desire to own the coins, or to support a special cause, and do not care about making a profit down the road. Buy them because you want your grandchildren to enjoy them in the future. Currently, the future of most modern commems does not appear very upbeat. Too many coins have been produced. All who wanted these productions acquired them. No real sustaining secondary market developed because collector-dealer demand was absent. Many of these modern designs have fallen below their issue price. The exceptions are the 1992 White House and 1991 USO silver dollars. The White House values increased three times or more from their issue price. Also, due to dealer promotion, the USO creation doubled and tripled in value. When promotions cease, watch values return to lower levels.

There are a few creations which will prove to be winners in the next go around. As the sun begins to heat up our numismatic marketplace, there are several issues which are quite undervalued at current levels. They have the best chance of increasing in value. (Were the price of gold to increase significantly, those modern gold commemoratives — which are now worth bullion value or slightly above — will increase proportionally.) I personally like the Uncirculated

1984 Denver Olympic silver dollar which was well distributed and reached a past high of $165. Ditto the 1984 Philadelphia and Denver Proof $10 Olympic gold pieces. Both popular strikings sold for $900 and $750 respectively during the last peak. The final selection from all the modern commem coinage struck to date is the 1986 West Point Statue of Liberty Unc. $5 gold piece. It's a very popular, undervalued and well distributed striking which once sold for $700. All other productions to date currently lack demand or are fully priced for their respective issues, offering little upside potential. Again, buy the coin because you like it and want to own it.

Commemorative Population Summary

From 1892 through 1954, there were 48 different silver half dollar designs produced. When the 1893 Isabella quarter and 1900 Lafayette dollar are included, the group is called the 50-piece type set. Should one desire every silver coin struck of the same design, (including the said quarter and dollar) but at the diff rent Mints during this period, the complete set totals 144 pieces. Gold comm moratives have been also intermittently produced between 1903 and 1926 They were comprised of six $1 designs (plus three issues bearing the same comp sition) and two $2½ coins constituting the 11-piece set, plus two $50 coins. Thi equals 13 coins. Thus, we have 60 type or individual designs and a 157 total c in production.

Since 1982, counting up to the 1993 Bill of Rights-James Madison coinage, the Mints have produced the following:
  A) Two Uncirculated and two Proof silver half dollars, plus five Uncirculated and five Proof copper-nickel clad halves, totaling seven different designs or 14 total varieties.
  B) Fifteen silver dollar designs totaling 31 varieties.
  C) Eight $5 gold designs totaling 16 varieties, and,
  D) One $10 gold design creating five varieties.

Remember one design can be produced at more than one Mint. The 1984 $10 Olympic gold coin was struck at West Point in Unc. and Proof condition. Shortly thereafter, Philadelphia, Denver and San Francisco were striking Proofs of the same design.

A complete 1892-1993 half dollar type set would now consist of 55 coins, while the complete half dollar set would require 156 coins.

The complete 1892-1993 type set housing every type commemorative half dollar and type silver dollar struck would total 70 pieces (55 + 15). One can add to this the Isabella 25¢. Your complete commemorative set, consisting of every Unc. and Proof half dollar and dollar will total 187 coins. With the Isabella 25¢ it is 188. Virtually all collectors assemble the $1 and $2½ gold coinage in the 11-piece format. Thus, one can add all the 1984-1993 modern gold type $5 (8 pieces) and one $10 striking to form a set of the 21-coin production. We now have 90 silver and clad and gold type or individual designs. To assemble a complete 1892-1993 silver and gold commemorative set, 222 coins are needed!

Of course, as this book is being written, the Mint is putting two more authorized issues into production, and many more proposals are before Congress, so this total looks to continue rising for some time!

Appendix
Specifications of
commemorative coins

In general, the commemorative coins of the United States follow the same specifications as their circulating counterparts. There have been exceptions, however, as in modern coinage where silver and gold commemoratives are produced when no precious metal coins are produced for circulation. All commemorative coins of the United States are fully legal tender.

Specifications by denomination are as follows:

Denom	Years of Issue	Composition	Total Weight (grams)	Precious Metal (troy oz.)	Diameter (inch)	Edge
25¢	1893	90% silver, 10% copper	6.25	0.18	0.96	Reeded
50¢	1892-1982, 1993*	90% silver, 10% copper	12.5	0.36	1.21	Reeded
	1986-1992	75% copper, 25% nickel bonded to a pure copper core (92% copper, 8% nickel by weight)	11.34	None	1.21	Reeded
$1	1900, 1983-1993	90% silver, 10% copper	26.73	0.77	1.5	Reeded**
	1903-05, 1915-17	90% gold, 10% copper	1.67	0.04	0.59	Reeded
$2.50	1915, 1926	90% gold, 10% copper	4.18	0.12	0.70	Reeded
$5	1986-1993	90% gold, 10% copper	8.36	0.24	0.85	Reeded
$10	1984	90% gold, 10% copper	16.71	0.48	1.07	Reeded
$50	1915	90% gold, 10% copper	83.55	2.40	1.74	Reeded

* 1993 Bill of Rights-James Madison.
** The 1992 Olympics Uncirculated $1 also has edge lettering in addition to reeds.

Index

Symbols

2★4 45
2X2 48
49er 68

A

Acheson, Dean 194
Adams, John 242
Adams, John Quincy 56
Age of Discovery 246
Aitken, Robert I. 123
Alabama Centennial 48–51, *261*
Alamo 97
Albany Charter *282*
Albany, NY, Charter 250th Anniversary 155–157
Allen, Ira 87
American Historical Revue and Motion Picture ... 57
American Legion Texas Centennial Committee 97
American Numismatic Society 18
S.S. Ancon 30
Andrews, Theresa 224
Andros, Sir Edmund 107
Annunzio, Frank 206, 215
Anthony, Susan B. 14
Antietam, Battle Of 179–181, *285–286*
Archimedes 123
Arkansas Centennial 110–115, *274–275*
Arkansas-Robinson 116–119, *275–276*
Atlanta Journal 67
Austin, Stephen F. 97
Ayres, Louis 69

B

badger 137
Balboa 28
Baltimore 93
Baltimore and Ohio Railroad 64
Bank of Hawaii 91
Barber, Charles E.
    9, 13, 16, 21, 27, 28, 34
Barnum, Phineas Taylor 150

Bartlett, Paul Wayland 17
baseball player 28, 241
Bates, Emily 111, 116
Battle of Bennington 87
Bay Bridge. *See* San Francisco-Oakland Bay Bridge
Beach, Chester 56, 90, 120
bear 68
beaver 155
Bebee, Aubrey 19
Bebee's of Omaha 190
Beck, Ralph 56
Beckerman, Thelma Marcus 214
Bell, Enid 116
Bell, Sydney 72
Benson, John H. 130
Bibb, William Wyatt 48
Bieda, Steven 240
Big Turtle 103
Bill of Rights 247–249
Black Fish 102
Blazek, Scott R. 249
Board of Lady Managers 14
Boone, Daniel 45, 101
Boone, Daniel, Bicentennial 101–106, *272–273*
Borglum, Gutzon 63, 232
Bowers & Merena Galleries 91
Bradford, William 41
Brady, Matthew 53
branch Mint
    first to strike commem half dollar 30
Breuckelin 144
Bridgeport, Conn., Centennial 150–152, *281*
Brown, J. Carter 216
Brownell, Charles De Wolf 107
Brown's Garrison 147
Buchanan, Angela "Bay" 208
bullion coin 216
Burnside Bridge 179
Burr, Edward Everett 111, 116

C

Cabeza de Vaca 127
Calgary Olympics. *See* Olympic Games, 1988
California Diamond Jubilee 68–71, *265*

California Tower 124
California-Pacific Exposition 123–126, *276–277*
Calvert, Cecil 93
Calvin, John 59
Carcabla, Hubert W. 121
Carey, Arthur G. 130
Carver, George Washington 193–196, *289–290*
catamount 88
Catamount Tavern 88
Century of Progress Exposition 83
S.S. Champagne 18
Chapel of Saint Francisco 124
Charter Oak 107
Chicago Historical Society 11
Cincinnati Music Center 139–143, *279–280*
Cincinnati Musical Center Commemorative Coin Assoc 140
Clapp, George H. 18
Clark, William 24
clashed dies Pilgrim 43
Cleaveland, Moses 133
Cleveland Centennial 133–136
Cleveland Centennial-Great Lakes Exposition *278*
Coca-Cola Bottling Company 64
coconut tree 91
de Coligny, Gaspard 58
Collins' History of Kentucky 102
Columbia, S.C., Sesquicentennial 164–168, *283–284*
Columbus, Christopher 9, 244
Columbus Quincentenary 244–246
commem boom 38
commemorative bubble 113
Commission of Fine Arts 40, 102, 162, 190
Communism 194
compass 134
compass needle 90
Conestoga wagon 81
Congress Bicentennial 225–228
Connecticut Land Co. 133
Connecticut Tercentenary 107–109, *273–274*
Constitution Bicentennial 219–221
Cook, James 90
Coolidge, Calvin 75
Coppini, Pompeo 97
counterstamp Cleveland 135
counterstamped Stone Mountain coins 64
Cousins, William C. 249
Cousins, William Charles 233, 237, 240
cow 127

Cranston, Alan 206
Crawford, Thomas 226
cross of St. Andrew 49

D

D.M. Averill and Company 25
D'Amato, Al 215
Dare, Eleanor 177
Dare, Virginia 176
Davison, Abraham Wolfe 164
Day, Charles 175
Declaration of Independence 75
Deecken, John R. 241
Delaware Tercentenary 169–171, *284*
Desert Storm Victory Parade 238
Diamond Head 91
diamonds 111
Dick and Jane 207
Discovery 246
Discus Thrower 204
Dodge, Henry 138
Douglas, Col. William Boone 102
Dunn, Frank 106
Dutch West India Company 58, 59
DuVall, Frank 18

E

E PLURIBUS UNUM, first on commem 28
Eggers, John H. 86
Eisenhower Centennial 229–230
Eisenhower, Dwight D. 229
El Paso 128
El Paso Museum Committee 128
Elgin Ill. Centennial 158–160
Elgin, Ill., Centennial *282–283*
Ellis Island 213
Ellsworth, Col. James 10
Elysee Palace 18
Embarcadero 162
Equitable Trust Company 171
eureka 123

F

Farouk, King 78
Farrell, T. James 232, 236, 248
fatt calfe 182
Fay's Tavern 88
Federal Council of Churches of Christ in America 59
Ferrell, T. James 245, 246
Fine Arts Commission 88, 215
Fisheries 93
fleur-de-lis 183
Flitter, John 166
Flynn, Errol 176

Ford's Theatre 233
Fort Boonesborough 102
Fort Hall, Fort Laramie and Jason 83
Fort Vancouver Centennial 72–74, *266*
Forward, Dewitt A. 145
Foster, Stephen 139
Fowler, Philip 214
Franklin Mint 206
Franklin Trust Company 79
Fraser, James Earle 49, 57, 58, 69, 81, 250
Fraser, Juliette May 90
Fraser, Laura Gardin 48, 53, 72, 81
Freedom, Statue of 226
French, Daniel Chester 61
frontiersman 45

G

Gasparo, Frank 233
Gettysburg, Battle of 172–173, *284*
Gibbs, J. Wilson Jr. 65
Glass, Carter 153
globe 76
gold $1.50 coin 77
gold miner 68
Graham, Robert 205
Grand Concord Man 61
Grant, Horace M. 131
Grant Memorial 52–55
    gold dollar *262–263*
    half dollar *261–262*
Grant, Ulysses S. 53
Grant With Star 54
Grant's Hobby Shop 131
Great Harvest Campaign 64
Great Lakes Exposition. *See* Cleveland Centennial
Green, E.H.R. 100
Green, Hetty 100
grizzly bear 68, 161
Gustaf V 170
Guttag, Julius 121

H

Half Moon 120
Hall of Fame 189
Hammer, Armand 206
Harding, Warren G. 50, 63
Hartford Connecticut Trust Company 109
Hartford National Bank and Trust Co 109
Hartford National Connecticut Trust Company 109
Hathaway, Isaac Scott 189, 194

Hawaii Sesquicentennial 90–92, *269–270*
Hawkins, Benjamin 137
headless figures 205
Henriques, Edgar 92
Hewitt, Lee F. 156
Higinbothan, H.N. 10
hippocampus 28
Hoban, James 243
Hoffecker, L.W. 127, 128
Hoffecker, M.L. 159
Holy Bible 130
Hope 131
Houdon, Jean Antoine 16
House of Representatives 226
Houston, Sam 97
Hudson Bay Company 72
Hudson, Hendrik (Henry) 120
Hudson, N.Y., Sesquicentennial 120–122, *276*
Huguenot 59, 182
Huguenot-Walloon Tercentenary 58–60, *263–264*
Humbert, August 31

I

Iacocca, Lee 214
Iaukea, Col. C.P. 92
Illinois Centennial 37–38, *258*
IN GOD WE TRUST
    first commems to have 27
Independence Hall 77
Indian 81
Iowa Statehood Centennial 185–187, *286–287*
Isabel, Queen of Castile 13
Isabella quarter dollar 13, *252–253*

J

Jackson, Gen. Thomas J. ("Stonewall") 63
James II 107
Jefferson, Thomas 21
Jester, Beauford H. 98
Joice Heth 151
Jones, Elizabeth 204, 214, 223
Jovine, Marcel 220, 223, 230, 232, 241
Justice 164

K

Keck, Charles 87, 153, 190
Kelly, Lt. Oakley G. 73
Kilby, Thomas E. 48
Klicka, Emil 125

Korean War Memorial 235–236
Kosoff, Abe 117
Krawczewicz, William J. 248
Kreiss, Henry G. 107, 116, 150
Krider, Peter L. 16

L

Labor 93
Lafayette Commission 17
Lafayette Dollar *253–254*
Lafayette Monument 16–20
Lamb, Robert 233, 237
Lathrop, Gertrude K. 155, 182
Lawrie, Lee 111
Lazard Freres 206
Lazarus, Emma 214
Lee, Gen. Robert E. 63, 179
Lee, Jason 83
legal tender 292
lettered edge, Olympic dollar 240
Lewis & Clark Exposition 24–25,
    254–255
Lewis, Jerry 216
Lewis, John Frederick 76
Lewis, Meriwether 24
Lexington Herald 102
Lexington-Concord Sesquicentennial
    61–62, *264*
Liberty Bell 76
Lincoln. *See* Illinois Centennial
Lincoln, Abraham 37
Lineberger, Rep. Walter F. 57
living person on coins 48, 117, 154
Lone Star 97
Long Island Tercentenary 144–
    146, *280*
Longman, Evelyn B. 30
Lord Baltimore 93
Los Angeles Olympics 203–211
Lost Colony 176
Louisiana Purchase Exposition
    21, 21–23, *254*
Lukeman, Augustus 63, 102
Lynch, John 154
Lynchburg, Va., Sesquicentennial
    153–154, *281–282*

M

Madison Coin and Medal Set 249
Madison, James 247–249
Maine Centennial 39, *259*
mania in the 1930s 141
Martin, Chester Young
    226, 230, 232, 241, 243
Maryland Tercentenary 93–95, *270–271*

Maryland Tercentenary Commission
    94
Matte Proofs 95, 106, 108
May Festival Association 140
Mayflower 42
McAdoo, William Gibbs 30
McClellan, George B. 179
McKinley Birthplace Memorial
    Association 35
McKinley Memorial 34–36, *257–258*
McKinley, William 21, 34
McLoughlin, John 72
McMullen, Dean E. 248
Medallic Art Company 134
Medusa 123
Meeker, Ezra 82
Mehl, B. Max 22, 35, 38, 112
Melish, Thomas G. 134, 141
Mercanti, John 205, 213, 227,
    229, 233, 235, 238, 245, 242
mermaid 121
Minerva 29, 123
Minuteman 61
Missouri Centennial 45–47, *260–261*
Modern Commemorative Coinage
    290–291
Monarch II 161
Monroe Doctrine Centennial 56–
    57, *263*
Monroe, James 56
Montgomery, James 46
Montpelier 248
Moore, Charles C. 31, 49, 107, 140
Mora, Joseph 68
Morgan, George T.
    10, 21, 27, 28, 34, 37, 58
Morgenthau, Henry 107
Morris, John H. Jr 50
motion picture industry 57
Mount Hood 72
Mount Rushmore 63
Mount Rushmore Golden Anniversary
    231–234
mountain lion 88
Myron 204

N

National Sesquicentennial Exhibition
    Commission 77
Neptune 121
New Colossus, The 214
New Haven Savings Bank 109
New Netherland 58
New Rochelle, NY, 250th Anniversary
    182–184, *286*
New York University 189
Nichols, George Ward 140

Nieuw Nederlandt 59
Norfolk, Va., Bicentennial 174–
175, *285*
Norse American medals 250
North Carolina. *See* Roanoke
Colonization 350th Anniversary

O

Occidental Petroleum 206
O'Connor, Andrew 37
octagonal 29
Old Spanish Trail 127–129, *277*
Olympic Games
1984 *See Los Angeles Olympics*
1988 222–224
1992 239–241
Olympic Gateway 205
Oregon Trail Memorial 80–86, *267–269*
Orphan Issue 113
Ortega, Katherine Davalos 214
Ortmayer, Constance 139
Owen, Mrs. Marie Bankhead 49
Owens, Jesse 241
owl 30
oxen 81

P

Palmer, Mrs. Potter 14
palmetto tree 165
Pan-American Exposition medal 56
Panama Canal 26
Panama-Pacific International
Exposition 26, 26–33
$50 gold *257*
gold dollar *256*
half dollar *255–256*
quarter eagle *256–257*
Paris Exposition of 1900 16
Parsons, David 137
Peale, Charles Wilson 24
Peed, James M. 205, 241
Pell, John 182
Peloso, Matthew 214
Pena, Joseph D. 249
Peters, Rep. John A. 40
Philbrick, Arthur L. 131
Pietz, Adam 185
Pilgrim Tercentenary 41, *259–260*
Pioneer gold 31
Pioneer Memorial 158
Pope, Donna 208
Population Summary *291*
Poseidon 28
Prestige Proof set 210
prospector 68

Providence, RI, Tercentenary 130–
132, *277–278*
Public Works Administration 108
puma 88
Putnam, Brenda 133

R

Rainey, Rep. Lilius 50
Raker, John 69
Raleigh, Sir Walter 176
Raymond, Wayte 118
Reich, John 21
Remington Standard Typewriter 10
Retail Credit Company 67
Rhode Island. *See* Providence, RI,
Tercentenary
Rich, Walter H. 147
Roanoke Colonization 350th
Anniversary 176–178, *285*
Roberts, Gilroy 194
Robinson, Joseph T. 116
Rogers, John W. 86
Rogers, Thomas D. Sr 246, 248
romance 91
Roosevelt, Franklin D. 103, 186
Ross, Nellie Tayloe 111, 140
Rossi, Angelo J. 69
Rovelstad, Trygve Andor 158
rub test 10
runners 205
Rushmore. *See* Mount Rushmore
Golden Anniversary
Ryan, Nolan 241

S

San Diego. *See* California-Pacific
Exposition
San Francisco-Oakland Bay Bridge
161–163, *283*
sandblast Proofs 91
Santa Maria 10, 245
Schmitz, Carl L. 169
Schnier, Jacques 161
Schuler, Hans 93
Schuyler, Peter 155
Scott Stamp & Coin Co. 14, 83
Sedalia Trust Company 46
Senate 227
Senn, Edmund J. 127
Seoul Olympics. *See* Olympic Games,
1988
Sesquicentennial of American
Independence 75–79
half dollar *266–267*
quarter eagle *267*
Shanahan, T.W.H. 31

Sharpe, Jim 241
silver bullion coin 216
Simpson, Marjorie Emory 174
Simpson, William Marks
    174, 176, 179
Sinnock, John Ray 37, 75, 106, 108,
    160, 184, 250
six flags 97
Smith, Jedediah 82
Somogyi, Marika H. 232
South Carolina. *See* Columbia, S.C.,
    Sesquicentennial
Southern Fireman's Fund Insurance
    Company 64
space shuttle 246
Spanish Trail. *See* Old Spanish Trail
specifications 292
spinner 13
Springfield Chamber of Commerce 38
Stack's 115, 117, 190
State Rock 130
Statue Of Liberty-Ellis Island
    Centennial 212–218
Statue of Liberty-Ellis Island
    Foundation 215
Stearns, Dr. Charles R. 64
Steever, Edgar Z. IV 213, 226, 242,
    249
stockade 73
Stone Mountain Memorial 63–67,
    264–265
Stoudt, Rev. John Bear 59
Swedish colonists 169
sweet potatoes 103
Swiatek, Anthony 18

T

Taft, Larado 112
Texas Independence Centennial 96–
    100, *271–272*
Thomas, Theodore 140
Torch of Freedom 76
trapper 72
triangles 90
Truman, Harry S. 186

U

United Daughters of the Confederacy
    65
United Service Organizations. *See*
    USO 50th Anniversary
United States Olympic Committee
    206, 223
Urquhart, John T. 72
USO 50th Anniversary 237–238

V

Vancouver 72
Verani, Patricia Lewis 220, 223, 226
Vermont-Bennington Sesquicentennial
    87–89, *269*
Vestal, Albert H. 69
Victory 97
Vittor, Frank 172

W

W Mint mark, first 208
Waikiki Beach 91
Walloon 59
Warner, Olin Levi 9
warrior chief 91
Washington, Booker T. 188–192, 193–
    196, *287–289, 289–290*
Washington County Historical Society
    180
Washington, George 16, 75
Weinman, A.A. 144
Weinman, Howard Kenneth 144
Wells Fargo & Co. 12
Westchester County Coin Club 183
Western Hemisphere 56
Western Reserve 133
Western Reserve Numismatic Club
    135
whale 121
White House Bicentennial 242–243
Whitman, Marcus 83
William the Silent 58
Williams, Roger 130
Winter, Sherl Joseph 213, 223
Wisconsin Territorial Centennial 137–
    138, *279*
Witch Of Wall Street 100
Wood, Howland 18
Woodward, William 226
World's Columbian Exposition 9–
    15, *251–252*
Wormser, Moritz 59
Wyckoff, Seamans and Benedict 10

Y

York County, Maine, Tercentenary
    147–149, *280–281*
Yorktown Centennial Medal 16
Young Collector's Edition 247
yucca tree 127

Z

Zerbe, Farran 22, 25, 31